LUTHERANISM

Legacy and Future

ESSAYS IN HONOR OF ERIC W. GRITSCH
ON THE 50TH ANNIVERSARY OF HIS ORDINATION

EDITED BY

HOLGER ROGGELIN/ SCOTT GUSTAFSON

ISBN 978-0-7414-7881-8
Library of Congress Control Number: 2012945774

Printed in the United States of America

Published September 2012

INFINITY PUBLISHING
1094 New DeHaven Street, Suite 100
West Conshohocken, PA 19428-2713
Toll-free (877) BUY BOOK
Local Phone (610) 941-9999
Fax (610) 941-9959
Info@buybooksontheweb.com
www.buybooksontheweb.com

TABLE OF CONTENTS

iii

iv

v

CONTRIBUTORS

DAVID P. DANIEL Professor at the Evangelical Theological Faculty. Jan Comenius University, Bratoslava.

MARTIN N. DREHER. Professor and Historian of Brazil at the Universidade do Vale Rio dos Sinos in Brazil.

MARIA E. ERLING. Professor of Modern Church History and Global Missions at the Lutheran Theological Seminary at Gettysburg.

TIBOR FABINY. Director of the Center of Hermeneutical Research. Budapest Hungary.

GÜNTHER GASSMANN. Former Directory of Commission on Faith and Order at the World Council of Churches, Geneva, Switzerland, and Distinguished Visiting Professor at the Lutheran Theological Seminary at Gettysburg.

DOUGLAS JOHN HALL. Emeritus Professor of Theology at McGill University. Montreal, Canada.

EERO HUOVINEN. Former Bishop of Helsinki in the Evangelical Lutheran Church in Finland. Retired professor from the Faculty of Theology. University of Helsinki

ROBERT W. JENSON. Retired Senior Scholar for Research at the Center for Theological Inquiry in Princeton, NJ.

ROBERT KOLB. Professor Emeritus.Concordia Seminary. St. Louis, MO.

WILLIAM H. LAZARETH. (deceased) Former Bishop of the Metropolitan New York Synod of the ELCA and Professor of Systematic Theology Lutheran Theological Seminary in Philadelphia.

WILSON B. NIWAGILA. Serving the Desk for Evangelism for the United Evangelical Mission with the World Council of Churches.

OTTO HERMANN PESCH. Professor Emeritus of Systematic Theology at the Protestant Faculty. Hamburg, Germany.

JOHN REUMANN. (deceased) Professor Emeritus of New Testament at the Lutheran Theological Seminary at Philadelphia.

MICHAEL ROOT. Professor of Ecumenical Theology. Catholic University.

RISTO SAARINEN. Professor of Ecumenical Theology at the University of Helsinki, Finland.

KIRSI STJERNA. Professor of Reformation Church History and Director of Institute for Luther Studies Lutheran Theological Seminary. Gettysburg, PA

JANE E. STROHL Professor of Reformation History at Pacific Lutheran Theological Seminary, Berkley, CA

YOSHIKAZU TOKUZEN. Rector of Japan's Lutheran Seminary and President of Japan's National Christian Council.

TIMOTHY WENGERT. Professor of Reformation History and Lutheran Confessions. Lutheran Theological Seminary. Philadelphia, PA.

MARKUS WRIEDT. Professor of Historical Theology/Church History at Goethe University, Frankfurt/Main and Visiting Professor of Theology at Marquette University.

INTRODUCTION

This project, which honors Eric W. Gritsch, has been in the planning stages for many years and at last has come to fruition. The collection of essays reflects the depth and scope of Dr. Gritsch's scholarly work as it crosses over time and space.

His commitment to ecumenism bridges denominational and international boundaries. This collection presents a world-wide view of Lutheranism. Over my ten year tenure at Zion Church of the City of Baltimore, ELCA, where Dr. Gritsch is a member, I have often heard him say that "Lutheranism is never isolated – it is constantly building bridges." This collection demonstrates such a reality.

The Rev. Dr. Holger Roggelin, Co-Editor
Pastor of Zion Church of the City of Baltimore, ELCA

Much more than most of us, Eric has been faithful to his vocation, and this is not without risk or controversy. Such faithfulness may have first been expressed by the 14-year old boy who defied death in his flight from both the Nazis and the Russians at the war's end. Less dramatically, Eric's faithfulness to his vocation is the reason for the debates and controversies in which he engaged. He has spoken for those who cannot speak. He has stood with the marginalized, and he has done so in a way that is consistent with the best of Martin Luther. In the seventies, he spoke on behalf of those who cannot speak in the controversy on infant communion. He stood up for those marginalized by their race in the sixties and those marginalized by their sexual orientation in more recent years. He continues to speak the unspeakable in his recent book on Luther's Anti-Semitism, a book long overdue in Lutheran circles.

Vocations are not our idea. They are God's idea. As such, they take us to places we neither dreamed nor planned. This is so with Eric. His vocation led him to international ecumenical discussion and theological debate. Through his vocation, he calls *us* to a more global understanding of Lutheranism and its history. Pastors and bishops receive guidance from him. When called upon, he has always supported the varied ministries of many congregations, and he is a faithful member of Zion Church in Baltimore. In the essays that follow, the reader can clearly see the influence of Dr. Eric W. Gritsch throughout the Church. God has blessed Eric with 50 years of ordained ministry, and Eric has blessed us all through his wise use of his many gifts.

I count it a privilege to work with Eric's pastor, Holger Roggelin to bring this project to fruition. Truth be told, however, we both received much inspiration from Eric's wife Bonnie Brobst. This would not have been completed without her loving dedication to both Eric and the project.

The Rev. Dr. Scott W. Gustafson, Co-Editor
Herndon, VA.

ENCOMIUM LETTER

The Reverend Mark S. Hanson,
Presiding Bishop, *Evangelical Lutheran Church in America*
President, *the Lutheran World Federation*

The scholarly legacy of the Reverend Eric W. Gritsch nourishes in wholesome ways the Lutheran communion throughout the world. More particularly, his writings also contribute profoundly to the life of the Evangelical Lutheran Church in America.

In his research, teaching, articles, and books, he has demonstrated insight into both the content and context of the documents and developments of the sixteenth century Lutheran Reformation. He has guarded against the temptation to which some succumb to read into the writings of Martin Luther and others controversies, concerns, and trends among contemporary Lutherans and other Christians. He has been mindful that the twentieth and twenty-first centuries cannot be superimposed as a lens for interpreting events of the sixteenth century. Rather, he has provided apt analysis of the ways in which the social, political, economic, and religious context of the sixteenth century both contributed to and helped shape aspects of the Lutheran movement of reform.

Dr. Gritsch has fostered a constructive identity for contemporary Lutherans. In so doing, he has widened Lutheran vision in regard the obligations and opportunities of being a movement of reform within the whole Church.

The bibliography of Dr. Gritsch at the end of this volume offers a vivid picture of the range of his contributions as a professor, researcher, scholar, participant in ecumenical endeavors, and pastor. His publications—including *A History of Lutheranism* (2002), *Introduction to Lutheranism* (1994), and *Lutheranism: The Theological Movement and Its Confessional*

Writings as co-author (1976)—shall serve well people throughout the Lutheran communion for many years to come.

It is particularly appropriate that this *Festschrift* honor and celebrate the work of Dr. Gritsch. It represents a vivid symbol of the high gratitude of so many for Dr. Gritsch's scholarship, creativity, and insights. The life of the whole Church is enriched through the fruits of his endeavors.

ENCOMIUM LETTER

Herman G. Stuempfle, Jr.
President – Emeritus, *Lutheran Theological Seminary at Gettysburg*

Eric Gritsch joined the faculty of the Lutheran Theological Seminary at Gettysburg in the fall of 1961. He had already been awarded the Ph. D. degree from Yale University where Roland Bainton and Robert Calhoun had been among his teachers. He had also taught for a year at Wellesley College. His earlier studies had been in the seminary of the Austrian

Evangelical Lutheran Church and in Basel and Zurich where such luminaries as Barth, Cullmann and Jaspers had been among his mentors. Thus he brought to his work at Gettysburg a background that represented the best in European and North American scholarship. Not to be overlooked is the influence of his experiences in the Lutheran church of Austria during its struggle with the occupying forces of Nazi Germany. These diverse academic and existential streams were important to and informed his subsequent career as an educator and scholar.

As a member of the Gettysburg faculty, his primary teaching responsibilities were in the areas of Reformation history and theology and Luther studies. He was a stimulating and challenging teacher who was able to engage his students in a vital way with the fundamental resources of the Lutheran tradition, always with a concern for how what they learned in the classroom would shape their ministries in the church. Students always found him accessible outside the classroom, often in gatherings in the intimacy of his campus home. Without question he had a lasting influence on several generations of Gettysburg graduates who could and do testify that what they learned from him was important to them as they struggled to relate Lutheran theology to parish practice. At least two of his students (represented in this

Festschrift) have gone on to graduate studies and seminary teaching in fields where he had been their mentor.

Teaching and scholarship can never be separated, and they were mutually enriching elements in Eric Gritsch's vocation. A steady stream of publications - books, articles and reviews, accompanied and enriched his career as a teacher, as well as contributing to the broader world of Reformation studies. Particular mention should be made of LUTHERANISM, co-authored with Robert W. Jenson, which has become a standard text for study of the Lutheran Confessions, not only at Gettysburg but at many other schools of theology.

Another major contribution to Luther scholarship which must be mentioned is Eric Gritsch's strong leadership of the Seminary's Institute for Luther Studies. The idea for this now widely recognized institute was generated during an informal luncheon discussion among faculty members in early 1970. In April of that year the Seminary Board of Directors voted to establish the Institute and named Professor Gritsch as its director, a position he held until his retirement in 1994. Under his guidance it became an important arm of the Seminary's outreach through the annual Martin Luther Colloquium, during which noted Luther scholars addressed topics relating Luther' thought to current issues in church and society. The subsequent publication of those lectures contributed significantly to the field of Luther studies in this country and abroad.

In summary, the contributions to theological education of Eric Gritsch, a colleague of nearly thirty years in the work of Gettysburg Seminary, have been manifold and enduring. Clearly his vocation as teacher and scholar has not yet ended but continues in other forms and in other places. This Festschrift will celebrate and help perpetuate his legacy.

ENCOMIUM LETTER

Avery Cardinal Dulles, S.J.
Fordham University, the Bronx

I am delighted to be asked to write an introductory word for this volume. Professor Eric Gritsch abundantly deserves the current *Festschrift* because of his long list of scholarly accomplishments. I felicitate him as one of my oldest (in the sense of "earliest") Lutheran colleagues, since I knew him in the 1960s, when I was teaching at Woodstock, Maryland, and he at the Lutheran Seminary in Gettysburg, Pennsylvania.

Eric and I joined the United States Lutheran-Catholic Dialogue about the same time, in 1972, and we continued to work on that dialogue until it was temporarily suspended twenty years later. He was our Lutheran specialist on Reformation theological history, and I was one of several Catholic systematicians. The twenty years of that dialogue were very fruitful, since they witnessed the production of statements on Papal Primacy (1974), Teaching Authority in the Church (1978), Justification by Faith (1985), The Mediation of Christ and the Intercession of the Saints (1990), and Scripture and Tradition (1992). Eric wrote numerous papers, some of which were published in the dialogue volumes. It so happened that he and I were often members of the Drafting Committee composing the joint statements.

I cannot begin to surmise all of the activities in which Eric was engaged. He was the founding director of the Institute for Luther Studies at Gettysburg. Beginning in those years, he composed a series of important books on Luther and Lutheranism, all of which were clear, interesting, informative, and challenging.

On the dialogue Eric exhibited rare objectivity. He never yielded to the common temptation to depict Luther or Melanchthon unrealistically either in pro-Catholic or in anti-Catholic colors. He was thorough and accurate to the extent that his views were rarely challenged and hardly ever (if ever) overturned by the group.

Eric was and is a pleasant friend and associate. He has a wonderfully rich biography, including the time when he used his "adoption" by gypsies to avoid being executed as a Hitler Youth by the Russian soldiers who had invaded Austria in 1945. He was a delightful host at Gettysburg, well equipped to give us a tour of the battlefield with full details of the tactics of both sides. Now that he has become a senior theological statesman in Baltimore, he and his wife Bonnie have the leisure to entertain, offering famous concoctions of Maryland crabs. In their own way, the crabs, relished in such beatific company, seem like a foretaste of the heavenly banquet.

PART I

Martin Luther: Life and Theology

Joseph and Jesus: *Luther's Lectures on Genesis*

Jane E. Strohl, *Pacific Lutheran Theological Seminary*

When I was a student at Gettysburg Seminary in the mid 1970's, Eric Gritsch taught the survey course in Reformation history. He gave an oral exam and required students to work in groups to prepare for and answer the questions posed. Eric concluded by asking each member of the panel to identify what part of Luther's legacy he or she thought was the least valuable for contemporary Christians. My group was surprised by the question; it was certainly not one that had occurred to us as we studied for the final. We scrambled. The general consensus was that Luther's writings on the Jews and the Peasants' Rebellion were about as bad as it could get and of no help to would-be pastors in the late twentieth century. Eric surprised us even more by his own response. He identified Luther's biblical commentaries as the least useful part of the corpus of his works, since they were hardly the kind of rigorous critical analysis one now expected of biblical studies.

As was often the case with Eric the teacher, he challenged us by this judgment to think further, to go beyond the negative statement. If Luther's writings on the scriptural books were not of much use as biblical scholarship, what were they good for? Eric did not say that they were good for nothing. Indeed, their purpose and power lie in what was always Luther's primary concern: the proclamation of the gospel, that is, the revelation of God's mysterious ways entwined with human history, circling always around the cross and resurrection of Christ, the font of free grace.

This essay will explore Luther's proclamation of the gospel according to the Book of Genesis. The narratives of the patriarchs and matriarchs are among the most engaging stories in the Bible, and Luther, being a robust story-teller, recounts them with delight in his *Lectures on Genesis*. He elaborates the basic plot, providing extensive character development and elaborate detail. He does let the stories stand for themselves and, of course, regards them as actual historical accounts. Luther then goes on to claim that these accounts point beyond themselves to divine realities of which the participants were only dimly, if at all, aware. However, Christians, who cannot read any part of scripture apart from what they know of the Lord Christ, are able to recognize in the history of the patriarchs and matriarchs a foretelling and confirmation of the gospel.

The focus of this essay will be on the Joseph narratives. Luther develops a threefold typology for Joseph. He presents him as an image of Christ, as an image of God, and as a model for discipleship. Ultimately, however, Joseph proves not to be the most apt embodiment of the believer, the *simul iustus et peccator* who sins boldly and lives by grace as he or she advances God's plan for salvation. As we shall see, the experience of believers is better revealed in the more morally ambiguous figures of Joseph's forebears.

I. Joseph as the Image of Christ

Luther comments at great length on Genesis 45:1-3, where Joseph reveals his identity to his brothers after deceiving them with his apparent hostility. Although he initially conceals his good will toward them, yet ultimately he shows himself to be their champion. Luther sees here an analogue with the hidden God, that is, the inscrutability of a merciful God encountered in a seemingly unfeeling savior.

> But you will say: 'I do not see that the Lord is so merciful and propitious.' Right indeed! But give ear to the fact that He is your Savior! Although He conceals and hides His mercy and salvation, and conducts Himself as though He were completely ignorant of you, nevertheless He sits at the right hand of the Father, governs you, cares for you, and is concerned about you.[1]

---

[1] LW 8:9 all citations are to the American edition of *Luther's Works*.

20

So Joseph, serving as the honored agent of the pharaoh, chastises his brothers so that they may be brought to repentance and receive his favor. Luther also compares Joseph's action to that of Christ recalling Peter after the latter's denial. As both Joseph and Christ make clear, it is hard work to restore a person, oppressed by grief and fear, to faith in his lord's mercy and kindly intent.

The climax of the story comes for Luther with Joseph's announcement to his brothers, "I am Joseph" (Genesis 45:3). In this revelation he sees a foreshadowing of Christ's self-revelation in the resurrection and at the end of time.

> Accordingly, I give this warning in order that we may not look at this manifestation of Joseph only in passing but may consider the great affection of the heart by which both Joseph and his brothers were benumbed. I would not know how I should have reacted when he said, 'I am Joseph.' Nor do they know. What will happen, then when our Lord and Savior JESUS Christ comes, who also disciplines us in various ways in this life and allows us to be troubled, scourged, killed, etc.? What great joy there will be after that sudden and unexpected change, since we previously felt that He was a very harsh tyrant who wanted to destroy everyone in a trice! Then He will say: 'I am Joseph; I am your Savior.'[2]

Indeed, Luther refers to Christ as "our completely friendly Joseph." The latter suffers at the hands of his cruel and vindictive brothers, just as Jesus was later to be despised and condemned by his own people. Moreover, Joseph lives out the theology of the cross in both ways in which Christ embodies it. He stands dumb before his persecutors and endures bitter suffering. Like Jesus, Joseph has no way of knowing for sure that he will be vindicated. Indeed, the appearances suggest that he has been abandoned by God, and he has only the promise that the God of Abraham, Isaac and Jacob will be his God as well to sustain him. "In this manner," Luther writes, "God allows Joseph to be crucified, hurled into prison, and to suffer reproach, which is simply to be destroyed, removed, wiped out. For all these things do not happen otherwise in the world. But before God that same thing is to send him for

---

[2] LW 8:15

salvation."[3] Joseph's "destruction" becomes the means by which his family is saved, for ultimately it leads to his high position in pharaoh's court and his ability to relieve his family's need in the time of famine. His suffering precipitated by his brothers' betrayal, his elevation to the right hand of pharaoh and his share in the imperial rule, his power and open-hearted willingness to effect reconciliation within his broken family, and finally the wonder of his return to life amongst those who had given him up for dead – in all these ways Joseph foreshadows the story of Jesus.[4]

Luther draws parallels between Joseph's treatment of his brothers and Jesus' response to his bewildered and deserting disciples. Both offer assurance of their true identity and make plain the meaning of what they have suffered; both offer compassion and forgiveness. Yet in this process one discerns the second aspect of the theology of the cross embodied in Christ. Like Jesus, Joseph not only bears the cross but also imposes it. He exercises the law in its second use. As Luther reminds his audience, although the brothers and disciples are overjoyed at the reunion and the kindness with which they are greeted, they nevertheless remain mindful of their sins against the one who now

---

[3] LW 8:29

[4] "Accordingly, Joseph is very careful to give this one instruction to his brothers that they should bring this word of consolation and liberation to their father and announce that his son has been appointed lord of all Egypt. But Joseph knew that his father, too, would find this difficult to believe. For he thought: 'My father has been mourning for me for 22 years now, and he is nearly consumed and exhausted by grief of heart; for he has long since despaired of my life and safety, since he could learn nothing certain or joyful about me. Therefore despair has gripped his heart to such an extent that he cannot hope for or believe in any safety, much less that I am living as ruler and lord of Egypt.' Accordingly, he carefully urges his brothers to relate everything accurately to their father.

"And it was an altogether difficult and incredible story -- a story like that of the angel at the tomb of Christ. 'Why do you seek the living among the dead?' the angel asked (Luke 24:5). And later, when the women make the same announcement to the apostles, they nevertheless do not believe; for those very great and incomprehensible works and counsels of God are not grasped suddenly. They are so lofty and noble that we cannot believe them at once. (LW 8:46)

receives them with mercy and are driven to a state of bitter repentance.

So far Joseph has aimed at humbling his brothers, in order that they might despair completely of their safety and of returning to their father and might have certain and perpetual slavery before their eyes. But when they have been disturbed and terrified, he pardons them with such great clemency and affability that he even weeps with them as they weep.[5]

Just as Jesus remains with his disciples for forty days so that he might strengthen them, so, according to Luther, Joseph strove for several days to heal the wound of his brothers with friendly discussions and intimate companionship. He charges them to forgive as they have been forgiven, letting his example of reconciliation, of forgoing all desire for vengeance, move them to live in peace with one another. Luther concludes in his commentary on Genesis 45:14-15 that "the example of Joseph is a true and clear picture of the resurrection of Christ."[6]

II. Joseph as the Image of God

In Luther's interpretation, Joseph serves as a figure of the divine hiddenness in the second person of the Trinity. Luther also presents Joseph as exemplifying the alien work of God the Father. He plays with his brothers, even deceives them by harshness, threats and false accusations. Yet Luther characterizes this as a salutary and helpful lying, for it brings the brothers to honest confession and repentance. So God deals with us, says Luther, and the story of Joseph and his brothers is told to console the saints when they are being "afflicted by God, or even cast off and neglected."[7] In general, Luther compares God's harsh discipline to that of a father who chastises the child with the rod and whips.

Yet this is a game of the Divine Majesty, likewise of godly parents and teachers, who undoubtedly do not want their children destroyed. For the affection implanted in their hearts

---

[5] LW 8:26

[6] LW 8:54

[7] LW 7:232

by God does not allow this. But paternal love and pity demand blows, whips, and stripes, in order that children may be improved, even though this cannot be done without pain and grief, just as Joseph pretends to be a complete stranger to his brothers and upbraids them harshly, threatening them with death and destruction. Nevertheless, his heart is completely gentle and kind. Nothing is farther from his mind than punishment and vengeance. Indeed, it is his purpose to exalt, glorify, and honor them in every way.[8]

He also portrays God in a maternal role, insisting that a mother does not put her baby into a cradle without first cleansing it from filth. This washing is an expression of her love for the child, and even though the infant wails, she perseveres. So God vigorously washes away the impurity of body and soul that disfigures us throughout our lives. Clearly Luther does not attribute greater gentleness to the female figure; a mothering God is just as relentless a disciplinarian. Joseph, like God, plays hardball with his brothers, disciplining them for their own good through a calculated game of threats and favors. This theology will not sound like good news to most people, one suspects, but it worked for Luther as a way of comprehending and mastering suffering and doubt. Behind the threats and the terror, Joseph is nonetheless constant in his love for his wayward brothers, just as is God for his children.

The beneficent fruit of Joseph's ferocity is revealed in the transformation of Judah. After Jacob's youngest son Benjamin is found in possession of the stolen cup that Joseph "in play" has had planted on him, Judah steps forward, implores Joseph's mercy for the boy and offers himself in Benjamin's place. Luther says that Judah reminds Joseph of his promise: "Therefore we have carefully carried out your words and commands, since we relied on your promises and instructions."[9] Luther makes Judah a model for his readers, for he exhorts them similarly to stand firmly on the ground of God's promises as they cry out to the Lord in their desperation and need:

---

[8] LW 7:232
[9] LW 7:373

Would that I could call upon God with the same ardor as often as I wished! For when I have prayed in this manner, it seemed clear that the following answer was given: 'Let what you are asking for be done. The answer shall be yes.' No man could despise a prayer of this kind – a prayer that proceeds from the depths of the heart. Much less can it be futile before God.[10]

Joseph's game has been successful; Judah, humbled and helpless, surrenders himself to Joseph's judgment and implores his mercy. Yet Judah too prevails. Taking upon himself the peril threatening his father and his youngest brother, he emerges "all on fire and without any fear."[11] Bold in his prayers, he obtains what he so desperately wants. Not only does he rescue Benjamin, he prompts Joseph to reveal his identity so that now the other lost son is recovered as well and Jacob's sorrow can cease. Judah here embodies what Luther considers the core of discipleship – courage and faithfulness that will not let go until they has attained what is desired. The fatherly game God plays with his children is a manifestation of divine power that masters and molds the child's willful nature. The child must suffer the blows of the rod and trust that there is love beneath this rough, painful discipline. Yet at the same time the child is emboldened to face up to the father and demand his portion, that is, that his lord will honor the promises he has made to the ones over whom he rules. Thus the humbled child becomes simultaneously the uninhibited petitioner, who calls God to account.

This part of the Joseph narratives reiterates a pattern already well-established in the *Lectures on Genesis*. For example, a similar dynamic is at work in Luther's interpretation of the wrestling match between Jacob and the angel, whom Luther understands to be the Lord Christ himself, at the ford of the river Jabbok.

For God in His boundless goodness dealt very familiarly with His chosen patriarch Jacob and disciplined him as though playing with him in a kindly manner. But this playing means

---

[10] LW 7:375

[11] LW 7:371

25

infinite grief and the greatest anguish of heart. In reality, however, it is a game, as the outcome shows when Jacob comes to Peniel. Then it will be manifest that they were pure signs of most familiar love. So God plays with him to discipline and strengthen his faith just as a godly parent takes from his son an apple with which the boy was delighted, not that he should flee from his father or turn away from him but that he should rather be incited to embrace his father all the more and beseech him, saying 'My father, give back what you have taken away!' Then the father is delighted with this test, and the son, when he recovers the apple, loves his father more ardently on seeing that such love and child's play gives pleasure to the father.[12]

Jacob will not let go until he is granted the blessing he seeks, and indeed he emerges from the encounter, lamed to be sure, but also blessed. Despite the doubts that inevitably assail him, Jacob lives by the Word alone and fights fiercely for what is rightly his: "God has given me orders, called me, and sent me to return to my fatherland; I shall not believe you nor agree with you. Even though God kills me, well, let Him kill me, but I shall still live."[13] His faith, says Luther, is very weak and likewise very strong.

This same remarkable understanding of discipleship appears in Luther's interpretation of the story of the Syro-Phoenician woman (Matthew 15), whom he explicitly compares to the wrestling Jacob.[14] She has only the word she has heard about Jesus to go on.

---

[12] LW 6:130

[13] LW 6:135

[14] "He Himself, our Lord Jesus Christ, tested Jacob not to destroy him but to confirm and strengthen him and that in this fight he might more correctly learn the might of the promise. Indeed, He added this strength and power to Jacob that he might conquer and joyfully praise the vision of the Lord.

"In the grips of tribulation and the struggle itself he did not speak thus, just as others under the cross are never in the habit of uttering such happy and joyful words. But those who are godly and spiritual must nevertheless maintain the struggle and reach the point where they see the face of God, as was said previously concerning the woman of Canaan. She had seen and heard Christ, and when He withdrew into a house to

On the basis of this report, she travels to him, trusting that he has both the power and the heart to heal her daughter. When she comes into his presence, his disciples want to drive her away. She remains, despite the hostile reception. Jesus is no kinder, telling her he was sent only to the lost sheep of the house of Israel and that it is not right to take the bread from the children and feed it to the dogs. To this she replies, "Yes, Lord, yet even the dogs eat the crumbs that fall from their master's table." Then, moved by her faith, Jesus hears her prayer and heals her daughter. Luther sees here the same hiddenness of God, appearing to be other than what we know him to be by his Word that Joseph embodies in his deception of his brothers. And Judah, like his father Jacob and the Syro-Phoenician woman, is ultimately not deterred, but approaches the one whose help he needs with that peculiar bold desperation that is central to Luther's understanding of the life of faith.

As extraordinary as Jacob's wrestling match is, the patriarch's experience nonetheless serves as instructive for ordinary believers. They won't take God on *mano a mano* physically, but they too will be pushed to the brink of despair. Like Jacob, Judah and the desperate mother, having been made empty by their lord's discipline, they must refuse to leave his presence empty-handed.[15]

---

conceal Himself, she followed Him there and pressed on until she succeeded in storming Christ's heart, which was too obstinate, it seemed, in repelling her. Having conquered in such a struggle, we can with the patriarch Jacob congratulate ourselves and boast that we have seen Peniel, that is, the face of the Lord. For in this way Jacob both attests the difficulty of the struggle which he had experienced and his joy; and he wants to say: 'Good God, in what great troubles and difficulties I have been involved, and in what great consternation! But thanks are to God, for I have now withstood the struggle and am safe! My soul has been freed and rescued from these troubles, and now I give thanks to the Lord my God.'" LW 6:144-45

[15] The sacraments, so foundational to Luther's theology and piety, are in their objective reality crucial weapons in the believer's struggle: "For if God sent an angel to say: 'Do not believe these promises!' I would reject him, saying: 'Depart from me, Satan, etc.' (cf. Matt. 16:23). Or, if God Himself appeared to me in His majesty and said: 'You are not worthy of My grace; I will change My plan and not keep My promise to you,' I

III. Joseph as Model of Discipleship

Similarly, Joseph also serves Luther as a model of such faithful discipleship, for in the years before he finds the pharaoh's favor, he is sorely tried and tempted. Yet through all this he perseveres and believes that God will deliver him:

> But Joseph is set before us not only as an example of all virtues, but a description of God is also placed before our eyes in a beautiful manner, in order that we may know what God is. . . . This, then, is the true knowledge of God: to know His nature and will, which He reveals in the Word, where He promises that He will be my Lord and God and orders me to take hold of this will in faith. For here a sure and firm foundation in which hearts find rest has been laid. But later the experience follows, when Joseph is disciplined by exile imprisonment, dangers, and false charges. Then he determines as follows: 'I see that this is the will of God, who is undoubtedly contemplating something greater and more sublime than I could now understand. I am certain that He will not forsake me or cast me off. His will is incomprehensible; but in spite of this it is very good, and I do not doubt that He is willing and able to redeem me from these misfortunes.'[16]

The vicissitudes of his experience reveal the nature of God, "who makes all things out of nothing, has death, hell, and all evils in His hand, and wants all things to work together for good for the elect."[17] In the eyes of God we are all Josephs, and with time God's love will work through our tribulation to bring honor and wholeness.

---

would not have to yield to Him, but it would be necessary to fight most vehemently against God Himself. It is as Job says: 'Though He slay me, yet will I hope in Him' (cf. Job 13:15). If He should cast me into the depths of hell and place me in the midst of devils, I would still believe that I would be saved because I have been baptized, I have been absolved, I have received the pledge of my salvation, the body and blood of the Lord in the Supper. Therefore I want to see and hear nothing else, but I shall live and die in this faith, whether God or an angel or the devil says the contrary." (:LWW 6:131)

[16] LW 8:18

[17] LW 8:37

IV. Wundermaenner and Wunderfrauen

In his discussion of the patriarchal and matriarchal narratives Luther uses the concept of the extraordinary hero or heroine (*Wundermann, Wunderfrau*) who dares to transgress the boundaries of commonly accepted morality. On the one hand, they serve as models of discipleship. Figures like Sarah and Rebekah are lauded because they faithfully pursue their ordinary callings as wives and mothers. Sarah, for example, is praised in Luther's portrayal, for her hospitality, modesty and obedience. Yet she is the one who holds most firmly to the promise of God that she and Abraham will have a son through whose descendants all the world will be blessed. When Hagar in her pride presumes to usurp that place with her son Ishmael, Sarah pressures her husband to cast them off. Her defiance and hardheartedness must be acknowledged as sinful; they are not in themselves models for daily discipleship. Yet, says Luther, these actions are in some sense exonerated by their role in advancing God's saving work. The promise was to pass through Isaac, and if Abraham was too soft-hearted to secure its succession, then Sarah had the mettle to step up to the plate. So with Rebekah, who does not hesitate to deck Jacob's arms with hairy skins so that he can deceive his aged father Isaac into thinking he is Esau. Abraham lies about Sarah's identity, passing her off as his sister. Jacob cheats his brother of his patrimony. Tamar poses as a prostitute to seduce Judah and thereby secure her marital rights. These are not the kinds of things Luther advises the average disciple to try at home, but at crucial moments these servants of God do not hesitate to stain their hands for the sake of God's promised redemption.

Joseph falls into this category of the salvifically amoral in the sense that he glibly lies to his brothers, withholding his true identity and threatening them with dire consequences that he has no intention of carrying out. However, for the most part Joseph comes across in Luther's commentary as practically perfect in every way. (A student in one of my seminars commented that he could understand why Joseph's brothers wanted to deep six him, coat of many colors and all). His Christ like patience and obedience are uncompromised. He "plays" with his brothers with regal abandon, but there are no mixed motives at work here. Despite his brothers' anxious suspicions, Joseph never succumbs to vengeance. When he first reveals his identity to them he assures them that they have been the instruments of God's will: "I am your brother, Joseph, whom you sold into Egypt. And now do not be distressed, or angry with yourselves, because you sold me here; for God sent me before you to preserve life" (Genesis 44:4-5). After Jacob's death the brothers fear that, without their father's restraining presence, Joseph may at last give sway to his hate and pay them back for the evil they have inflicted upon him. They send him a message imploring his forgiveness and assuring him that Jacob had commanded them to relay his wish that Joseph pardon them. Without hesitation Joseph begins to weep and assure them of his fraternal love and mercy: "Fear not, for am I in the place of God? As for you, you meant evil against me; but God meant it for good, to bring it about that many people should be kept alive, as they are today. So do not fear; I will provide for you and your little ones" (Genesis 50:19-21). It is striking how at the last Joseph does not identify himself with the divine role that Luther has artfully constructed from the patriarch's behavior in testing and tempting his brothers. Rather than acting as the enforcer of the second use of the law, Joseph eschews any claim to being in the place of God. He sees himself as the vulnerable, faithful one who has watched and waited upon the favor of the Lord and who has suffered while persevering in the midst of tribulation. "As for you, you meant evil against me" – and the evil was very real and life-threatening. "But God meant it for good" – for those who are kept alive by Joseph's agency and for Joseph himself, who is restored to life, reunited with his father and reconciled with his brothers. In the end Joseph identifies himself with the other sons of Jacob as first and foremost the recipient of God's healing grace. He is definitely more sinned against than sinning, but he too must submit, and trustingly does so, to the mysterious actions of a God both hidden and revealed.

Conclusion

Joseph's virtues make him a model of discipleship, yet in the end it is important to note that the genealogy of Jesus does not run through his line. The Christ like Joseph is not the forbear of the true Christ. The key figure in this genealogy is Judah, not either of

Jacob's favored sons Joseph and Benjamin, born of his beloved wife Rachel. Judah is a striking example of the complexity of the human beings through whom God works to accomplish God's purposes. When the brothers betray Joseph and contemplate killing him, first Reuben urges them to shed no blood, and then Judah advises them to spare the boy's life and thus their own consciences. "Then Judah said to his brothers, 'What profit is it if we slay our brother and conceal his blood? Come, let us sell him to the Ishmaelites, and let not our hand be upon him, for he is our brother, our own flesh.' And his brothers heeded him" (Genesis 37:26-27). As discussed above, when Benjamin is apprehended with the stolen cup Joseph has had concealed in his belongings, Judah urgently offers himself as prisoner in the boy's place.

> Now therefore, when I come to your servant my father, and the lad is not with us, then, as his life is bound up in the lad's life, when he sees that the lad is not with us, he will die and your servants will bring down the gray hairs of your servant our father with sorrow to Sheol. . . . Now therefore, let your servant, I pray you, remain instead of the lad as a slave to my lord; and let the lad go back with his brothers. For how can I go back to my father if the lad is not with me? I fear to see the evil that would come upon my father. (Gen. 44:29-33)

It is this act of generosity that precipitates Joseph's revelation of his true identity to his family.

Judah is a more complicated character than the virtuous Joseph, who so ardently resists the advances of Potiphar's wife. Mention has already been made of Tamar, one of the matriarchs whose own infamous act of courage is integral to the working out of the divine plan that culminates in the person and work of Jesus Christ. Tamar was wed to Judah's firstborn son, Er, who, according to the Genesis narrative, was wicked in the sight of the Lord and consequently slain, unfortunately before he and Tamar had any children. Judah then wed her to his second son Onan and charged him to raise up children for his brother with his brother's widow. Onan in turn was slain for his refusal to do so. Judah then tells Tamar to remain as a widow in her father's house until Judah's third son comes of age. However, he does not keep his word. Tamar sees that the youngest son has indeed grown up, but no offer is made to bring them lawfully together as man and wife. To recover what is rightfully hers, especially the gift of children; she disguises herself as a prostitute and seduces Judah. When later he is told that his daughter-in-law is pregnant, he demands that she be brought out and burned for her promiscuity. Having required certain tokens of him at the time of their illicit encounter, Tamar now presents him with these. Judah acknowledges that he has wronged her: "'She is more righteous than I, inasmuch as I did not give her to my son Shelah.' And he did not lie with her again" (Genesis 38:26). She then bears twins, Perez and Zerah, who, like their grandfather Jacob and his brother Esau, precipitate some confusion as to who is rightly to be called the firstborn.[18]

> When the time of her delivery came, there were twins in her womb. And when she was in labor, one put out a hand; and the midwife took and bound on his hand a scarlet thread, saying, 'This came out first.' But as he drew back his hand, behold, his brother came out; and she said, "What a breach you have made for yourself!" Therefore his name was called Perez. Afterward his brother came out with the scarlet thread upon his hand; and his name was called Zerah. (Gen. 38:27-30)

According to the genealogy in the first chapter of Matthew's gospel, Jesus Christ is descended from Jacob's line through Judah and Perez (Matthew 1:3). He is thus twice over the descendant of usurpers. Judah, in his relations to his daughter-in-law, is a cheat and deceiver like his father Jacob. And Tamar, though wronged and rightly protesting her treatment, nevertheless transgresses boundaries with lurid abandon in her search for justice. Joseph's ambiguous behavior Luther finds justified by its witness to the divine hiddenness. Not so with these forebears. They are simply sinners doing the best and the worst that they can. For the understanding of the Gospel by which, for Luther, the church stands and falls, it is of immense importance that these are the ancestors of the Savior. He comes of thoroughly blemished stock, and simultaneously he draws blood and bone from those who, with astonishing care, transgress the boundaries of propriety to harvest the fields of grace. "Sin boldly, only believe even more boldly . . ."

---

[18] Genesis 25:21-26, 29-34; Genesis 27

Luther notoriously advised a colleague. This is for him the witness made to us by the patriarchs and matriarchs. Though the particulars of their extreme discipleship are not to become the blueprint for our daily conduct of affairs of the faith, we will nonetheless have our own transgressions to risk and consequences to endure so that the grace of God in Christ Jesus our Lord might flow freely.

Eric Gritsch's evaluation of the inadequacy of Luther's commentaries as biblical scholarship, according to contemporary canons, still stands firm. Yet as proclamation of the evangelical Gospel, the promise of forgiveness and reconciliation to those who endure as simultaneously saint and sinner throughout their earthly lives, these works are peerless. Moreover, they challenge Christians openly and honestly to think about the relationship of the two testaments to one another. Too often we pay lip service to the authority of what is for Christians the "Old Testament" and then proceed to preach and teach as functional Marcionites. Luther, however, was unwavering in his certainty that the same God was at work in the same unfathomable way in all chapters of the history of God's people.

Martin Luther in the Judgment of Roman Catholicism: Between Demonization and Grateful Appropriation

Otto Hermann Pesch, *Munich*

I. Luther is "In" Again

Some time ago, the Roman Catholic and (Lutheran) Protestant teachers of religion in the public schools of southern Germany were invited to a routine, common continuing education event. The topic was to be problems of common interests regarding cooperation in the schools. The event had to be canceled; there was too little interest! In November of 2004, another such event was scheduled for the same teachers. This time, the theme was "Luther and the Reformation in Religious Instruction." The key question was, "Can historically grounded common judgments be worked out in such a way the Protestant and Roman Catholic school students are definitely protected from mutual traditional stereotypical judgments?" Twice the number that the organizers estimated registered. Luther was again "in." The reason, of course, was the Canadian Luther film which became a hit in Germany. The Lutheran Church of Germany not only promoted the film, but also made it part of the curriculum. This is the context for our topic, that is, the question: what is the modern Roman Catholic image of Luther, and how does this image relate to the contemporary ecumenical dialogue and the ecumenical relations between the Roman Catholic Church and the churches of the Reformation? We begin with a brief overview of the history of the Roman Catholic Luther image. It reminds us of the "Echternach Spring Procession" – an old custom in the small town Echternach in Luxemburg: two steps forward, one step backward. But if we go back to the sixteenth century, we must say, one step forward and two steps backward.

II. Roman Catholic Luther Research in the Twentieth Century: In Big Steps

1. The "Catholic" Contemporaries

In the late fall of 1517, the prior of the Franciscan monastery in Memmingen received a copy of Luther's *Ninety-Five Theses*, which, without Luther's intention, were being widely distributed throughout Germany. After reading them, the prior called his friars together and declared "He is here, the one who will do it." Luther's appearance unleashed the long-held hope that finally, after two centuries, the continuing call for "reform in head and members" might begin. Much of what Luther seemed to personify had been in the air since the beginning of the sixteenth century, last but not least, the use of the vernacular in the liturgy and the translation of the Bible into the native language. No wonder, then, that many of the leading intellectuals of the day aligned themselves with Luther, above all Humanists, including Philipp Melanchthon, Johann Brenz, and in the beginning even Johann Cochläus. Little wonder, too, that the broad masses of people acclaimed Luther as their hero. On his journey to Worms in 1521, they cheered Luther in every city in which he stopped, giving him a triumphal welcome. This was in direct contrast to Luther's own somber mood, for he knew exactly what awaited him at Worms--- at worst, burning at the stake. That was the "step forward." But, as is well known, things changed. Two quotations that speak for themselves. [1]

---

[1] 1. The text of the Edict of Worms, April 8, 1521, promulgated at the close of the

Diet on April 26, in *Deutsche Reichstagsakten, Jüngere Reihe,* vol. 2, 643-659. The quote is from the modernized German in Heiko A. Oberman (ed.), *Kirchen-und Theologiegeschichte in Quellen,* vol. 3: *Die Kirche im Zeitalter der Reformation* (Neukirchen-Vluyn 1981), 62-65: 64. It is well known that Duke Frederick the Wise „abducted" Luther in an attempt to protect him from the Edict of Worms which made him an enemy of the state and kept him in the secret seclusion at the Wartburg. For the biographical details surrounding this event, see Martin Brecht, *Martin Luther,* 3 vols. tr. J. L. Schaaf (Minneapolis, 1990-93), 1, 298-324. Brief summary in Eric W. Gritsch, *A History of Lutheranism,* 2nd ed. rev. (Minneapolis, MN, 2010), 29-33.

1. Luther teaches to live a free, selfish life, without any laws, like an animal. It would take too long to tell of all other innumerable evils. But this one, not a human being, but as the Evil One in human form in the figure of a man in a cowl, a heretic who collected the worst, condemned heresies in a stinking pool.

2. I will open the eyes of any honorable men, whether it is Christian or evangelical, that a lousy, run-away monk and knavish lover of nuns --- who has neither a home nor a family, an ignoble changeling, born of a bath-maid and devours the alms, an endowed monastery, with a run-away nun --- may slander a prince as a stable-boy.

2. Two Steps Forward; One Step Backward: From Heinrich Denifle to Joseph Lortz

The following quote characterizes the Catholic image of Luther at the beginning of the twentieth century:

Luther's gospel, viewed in its effect, manifested itself as a school, as a seminar of sins and vices. The "gospel," which caused people to speak of an "evangelical reformation" and "evangelical Christians," made the masses insolent and callous in sinning to which they were already accustomed.

This is the opinion of the famous scholar of the Middle Ages and infamous despiser of Luther, Heinrich Denifle, as articulated in his three-volume work on Luther and Lutheranism.[2] A few years later,

---

2. From the apology, written in 1533 by the Humanist John Cochläus in defense of Duke George of Saxony against Luther's reproaches. First a sympathizer of Luther, he was soon to become an embittered enemy. Later in 1548, he would write notorious "Luther Commentaries," an important source of Luther's life and events of the Reformation. It is part of a nearly unspeakable genre of polemics which was as rude as Luther's designation of Cochläus as a "snot-nosed brat" (*Rotzlöffell*). On Cochläus see the Index in Brecht. On his influence in Catholic research see Adolf Herte, *Das katholische Lutherbild im Bann der Luterkommentare des Cochläus,* 3 vols. (Munster, 1943).

[2] Heinrich Denifle, *Luther and Lutherdom,* tr. Cornell University Library (Cornell, 2009. Paperback).

after his death, Denifle's evaluation received the highest official endorsement from Pope Pius X who was eager to reform in liturgical matters, especially Eucharistic reception. Concerning the Reformation, he wrote in his 1910 Encyclical on St. Charles Borromeo: "In those days arrogant and rebellious people appeared, enemies of the cross of Christ....people with secular minds...whose god is the belly."

It is not exactly clear if it was an improvement or yet a new low point when, a few years later Hartmann Grisar did not call him a thoroughly corrupt villain (as Denifle did) but instead a psychopath.[3] Nevertheless, this image of Luther had a greater international influence as did the blistering polemics of Denifle.

But now the two steps forward! Already in 1904, another Catholic Church historian, Sebastian Merkle in Würzburg[4] wrote in a review of Denifle: "if dogmatic polemics and defamation of Luther could bring about an agreement, then Catholics and Protestants would have had embraced rather than be at logger-heads. Calm, objective presentation of facts can prepare, to be sure, not unity but at least an understanding between the confessions." [5] "I put my opinion against anxious minds that anyone who still has a trace of a sense for truth and justice, must also protect the opponent if he is unjustly attacked." [6] And twenty-five years later, the same Merkle wrote in an essay "Something Good About Luther and Something Bad About his Critics:" the illusion as if he is the best Catholic, who can most defame him, would be a mockery of the Christian faith and of Christian love. Whoever refuses to be led by these two stars, in the dispute about

---

[3] Hartmann Grisar, *Martin Luther*. His Life and Work, Tr. (Puerto Rico, 1930. German ed., Freiburg i.Br. 1911/12)

[4] The teacher of Hubert Jedin, the great explorer of the Council of Trent.

[5] Sebastian Merkle, "Referat über Heinrch Denifle *Luther und Luthertum in ihrer ersten Entwicklung'"* und „Luther in rationalistischer und christilcher Beleuchtung," *Deutsche Literaturzeitung* 25 (1904): 1226-40. Quotation 1239.

[6] Sebastian Merkle, *Reformationsgeschichtliche Streitfragen. Ein Wort zur Verständigung* (Munich, 1904).

Protestantism, throws a bad light on his own church and deepens the gulf between the Communions instead of bridging it" [7]

With such words, to which others could be added, the foundation was laid for the work of the man whose work would lead to a breakthrough in the Roman Catholic understanding of Luther, Joseph Lortz. He had been educated in Rome before the First World War and was a church historian in Münster before the Second World War and afterwards in Mainz. In 1939, ten years after Merkle, this native of Luxemburg published his *The Reformation in Germany*.[8] The then unheard- of essence of his Luther image, which almost caused measured against Lortz from Rome, was the assertion that Luther was a thoroughly devout man and as such is worthy of respect and even admiration. Luther had truly rediscovered great ecclesiastical and theological tradition from earlier centuries. He became a "heretic" only through his literal *hairesis*, his "choosing!" However, Luther himself was only half guilty and, that is, on account of his own disposition which Lortz called a "rooted subjectivity:" only that which passed through the filter of his "subjective" experience and convinced his innermost heart can be a binding truth of faith. Everything else is rejected. Naturally, this occurs not arbitrarily, as Denifle surmised, but with biblical and also theological justifications. Still, Luther's subjectivity prevented him to allow himself be seriously questioned by the great Catholic tradition, to be a "full hearer" of Holy Scripture. The other half of being guilty is the fault of the theology of Luther's time, especially in the most influential school of the late Middle Ages, the *via moderna*, in the wake of William of Occam and Gabriel Biel.[9] This "modern" theology of the late Middle Ages, according to Lortz, obstructed the view of its

---

[7] Sebastian Merkle, "Gutes an Luther und Übles an seinen Tadlern" in A. Von Martin (ed.), *Luther in ökumenischer Sicht* (Stuttgart, 1929), 9-19..

[8] 2 vols., tr..Ronald Walls (New York and London, 1968).

[9] Too little attention to this fact has been paid in Germany. There are, however, three worthwhile books in English: Denis R. Janz, *Luther and Late Medieval Thomism. A Study in Theological Anthropology*, Waterloo (Ontario/Canada) 1983; by the same author, Luther *on Thomas Aquinas. The Angelic Doctor in the Thought of the Reformer* (Stuttgart, 1989). John L. Farthing, *Thomas Aquinas in German Nominalism on the Eve of the Reformation* (Durham, London, 1988).

disciples of the truly great tradition of the theology and of the church, indeed, it was in essence not Catholic, and Luther was right when he fought against it at the beginning of his teaching. Thus, Lortz arrived at the following conclusion.

> Luther overcame within himself a Catholicism that was not Catholic...This must be finally realized by everyone: if there is present in Luther a misdirected understanding of revelation, then it was not through laziness nor a lack of depth, but besides his stubbornness, the result of an exaggerated earnestness, of a zeal, and magnitude...They are poor interpreters of history who believe that a superficial spirit without any religious depth would have been enough for the immense blow that tears apart the church. It would be a hard indictment of the church, if that were possible. No, only the exposure of its own innermost possession could create such a wound, and then only by a one-sided and thus objectively false presentation. [10]

3. One Step Backward. The Long Mistrust of Lortz

One sees that the distance between Lortz and his predecessors Denifle, Grisar and, if I may say so, to Pius X could not be greater. But Lortz and his new image of Luther were not at all greeted with enthusiastic applause. One still hears today the sigh of relief, as it were, when Lortz wrote in the Preface to the second edition of his book (in 1941) that the papal newspaper *Osservatore Romano* had acknowledged his strict Catholic stance. Nevertheless, after the Second World War, it was problematic attaining the church's permission to publish (*imprimatur*) new editions of *The Reformation in Germany*. [11] Moreover, it did not help when

---

[10] Translation from the unrevised German edition, *Die Reformation in Deutschland* 1,176;192.

[11] See the Epilogue of Peter Manns in the edition of 1982, 2,356-7.For the effect and reception of Lortz's work, there are many informative and insightful essays in Rolf Decot and Rainer Vinke (eds.), *Zum Gedenken an Joseph Lortz (1887-1975). Beiträge zur Reformationsgeschichte und Ökumene* (Stuttgart, 1989). From its inception to his death, Lortz was the Director of the Institute for European History in Mainz where there is no lack of ecumenical interest! See Winfried Schulze and Corine Defrance,

Cardinal Willebrands, then head of the Pontifical Council of Promoting Unity in Rome, lectured on the appreciation of Luther, exactly in the spirit of Lortz, before the Full Assembly of the Lutheran World Federation in 1970 in Evian, near Geneva. He was met with very critical voices within the Curia on his return. [12] It was not until 1983, in the ecumenical celebrations surrounding the 500th anniversary of Luther's birth, that one began to hear --- though not in official documents from the Curia, yet nevertheless from high-placed Roman officials --- the assessment of Luther as a religious personality, acknowledged by Lortz. But in the meantime, quite different "Luther sympathizers" had become targets. [13]

4. Two Steps Forward: "The Golden Age" of Catholic Luther Research

Since the 1950s, new orientations both in reference to Luther's person as well as to his theology became known. They have not only evoked frowns from the church hierarchy but also provoked concentrated opposition from Joseph Lortz and his students and friends, above all, Hubert Jedin, Erwin Iserloh, and Peter Manns. [14] Lutheran theology was understandably skeptical of the new appreciation of Luther as a result of Lortz, especially in regard to questions of substance. Never before had a Catholic theologian been so positive in his evaluation of Luther; but they assumed that

---

Die Gründung des Instituts für europäische Geschichte in Mainz (Mainz, 1992).

[12] Text of the speech in *Lutherische Rundschau* 20 (1970): 447-60.

[13] See Pesch, „Erträge des Luther-Jahres für die katholische systematische Theiologie" in Peter Manns (ed.), *Bilanz des Luther-Jahres* (Stuttgart, 1986), 81-154. The official. recognition can be found in, Lutero visto dai Cattolici ieri e oggi" in the Jesuit journal *La Civita Catholica* 134 (December 17, 1983): 521-38.

[14] See the reports on research, especially Manns, *Lutherforschung heut. Krise und Aufbruch* (Wiesbaden 1967) and my response in "Der 'katholische' Luther und der 'lutherische/' Luther. Eine späte Antwort an Peter Manns in *Gerechtfertigt aus Glauben. Luther's Frage n die Kirche*(Freiburg i.Br., 1982), 95-144

Lortz must surely be the limit of what one could expect in a positive Catholic appreciation. [15]

A new generation of Catholic Luther scholars raised two simple questions, based on Lortz's religious acknowledgment of Luther. 1) If Luther can be valued as a pious personality in relation to his appreciation of the Christian faith, then he was, despite all historical divisions, a partner in dialogue on questions regarding one and the same faith. If so, then it would not suffice to explain Luther's theology only in terms of his personal struggle or to consider only its historical origins. Rather, one must ask whether and where his theology was simply correct. 2) Is it really so certain that the heresy, the "one-sided choice" in which Luther went his own way, began exactly at the point where Luther goes beyond that which even in the "great tradition of the church" had been, or could not have been, stated this way? Or, to spin out Lortz's thesis even more challengingly: if it were indeed possible, according to Lortz, that a whole era of two centuries of church history and theology represented a "Catholicism" that was in fact "not Catholic," then could such a situation later, and even today, be simply dismissed? As an unavoidable consequence, could it even be that Luther would have to say and ask something about unfinished business also in the contemporary Catholic Church, not to mention the Lutheran one --- despite all ecumenical progress?

So began, in the words of the American Catholic scholar Franz Posset, the "golden age of Roman Catholic Luther Research." A small flock of young Catholic theologians (not exclusively from Germany) began to study Luther, simply and free of traditional bias, together with other great theologians of history, and to ask what he might have to say concerning the clarification of specific problems of the church and of Christianity.

Naturally, this turn of events did not unfold without controversy. Although the commonality of the new questions was not at all agreed upon, it was seen by the other side --- and that means all of the "Lortz school"--- frankly as a conspiracy. The climax of the

---

[15] See the summary of important reactions from Lutheran scholars (Heinrich Bonkamm, Rudolf Herrmann, Friedrich Wilhelm Kantzenbach, Leif GFrane, etc.) in Pesch, "Twenty Years of Catholic Luther Research," *Lutheran World* 13 (1966): 303-16.

controversy peaked, not accidentally, in 1967 --- the 450th anniversary of the posting of the *Ninety-Five Theses*! Hubert Jedin, the great church historian of the Council of Trent, issued an inquisitorial warning: "anyone who wishes to make the whole Luther a Catholic, will himself become a Lutheran." [16] He clearly had in mind a particular scholar, namely, the author of this essay! I was also the chief target in 1967 in the famous lecture of Peter Manns, the champion student of Joseph Lortz. [17]

These new orientations were also furthered not least by the Second Vatican Council. The concern to establish a new understanding, if not even a communion with the churches separated from Rome, gained strength at the Council and went beyond the original intention of Pope John Paul XXIII at the Council. [18] Although it did really start the work of ecumenical dialogue on the Catholic side, it encouraged the already numerous, but lonely voices in the wilderness by removing them finally from the suspicion of disloyalty to the church and thereby encouraged a young generation of theologians to do ecumenical theology. Whoever made the effort in the 1960s to work on ecumenical topics, and made an effort to learn through encounters with Luther's theology, could feel to be at the cutting edge of Catholic theology.

The details cannot be discussed here. Yet, one thing is clear: the "subjectivism" thesis now stopped to have an effect on history. The "young" Catholic Luther research now worked, directly and without any recourse to the biography and personality of Luther, with substantive topics: justification, sacraments, sin, faith,

---

[16] Hubert Jedin, "Zum Wandel des katholischen Lutherbildes" in Helmut Gehrig (ed.), *Martin Luther. Gestalt und Werk* (Karlsruhe, 1967), 46.

[17] Peter Manns, *Lutherforschung heute. Krise und Aufbruch* (Wiesbaden, 1967)

[18] Details in Pesch, *Das Zweie Vatikanische Konzil. Vorgeschichte-Verlauf-Ergebnisse-Nachgeschichte* (Würzburg, 2001. English translation forthcoming. By the same author "'Hierarchie der Wahrheiten'. Ein vergessenes Stichwort des Zweiten Vatikanischen Konzils und die Zukunft der Ökumene" in Uwe Rieske-Braun (ed.), *Konsensdruck ohne Perspektiven? Der ökumenische Weg nach "Dominus Jesus"*(Leipzig, 2001), 118-38.

assurance of salvation, ethical questions, church and office, Luther and the Jews. Here rules, as it were, a silent, but impetuous rejection of any attempt to derive specific theses of Luther from his biography and even psyche. The Lortz School also no longer defended the claim to be the only Catholic way of Luther research. Current research is more concerned with the historical context rather than with an answer to the question, "Where does the heresy begin?" At various conferences, questions arise, of course, about church-dividing differences as seen from the new perspective. [19]

The Lortz student Erwin Iserloh had the most lasting effect in the Protestant world. He asserted in 1962 (and again in a long engagement with his critics throughout 1968) that the famous *Ninety-Five Theses* were ready to be posted on October 31, but had not at all been nailed in dramatic fashion to the door of the Castle Church in Wittenberg. [20] After some initial, but unsuccessful attempts to refute this thesis, no serious Luther scholar today would attempt to speak of the nailing of the theses as a matter of fact.

The most beautiful fruit of the Lortz School probably is Peter Mann's illustrated biography of Luther for the jubilee year 1983. It not only reads like a novel but also mirrors, indirectly and imperceptibly, the transition from a biographical theology to a theological biography. It represents the culmination of scholarship begun by Lortz. [21]

5. From the Second Vatican Council to the "Joint Declaration on Justification."

Since 1966, Roman Catholic Luther scholars have been invited to The International Congress for Luther Research and

---

[19] See, for example, the much disputed view of Peter Manns who called Luther "Father of the Faith" in *Vater im Glauben. Studien zur Theologie Martin Luthers* (Stuttgart, 1988), 400-23.

[20] Erwin Iserloh, *The Theses Were not Posted: Luther Between Reform and Reformation*, tr. Jared Wicks (Boston, 1968). See the brief review of the controversy in Pesch, *Hinführung zu Luther* (Mainz, 1983), 307-09.

[21] Peter Manns and Nils H. Loose (pictures), *Martin Luther ---An Illustrated Biography*, tr. Michael Shaw (New York), 1982.

have been entrusted with leadership in principal lectures and seminars. What is taken as a matter of course today, was then a noteworthy event. It was not until the Third Congress that someone had thought to invite Roman Catholic scholars. Accordingly, the high point of the "golden age" was the Sixth Congress in Erfurt (1983). It becomes the starting point to the way into the contemporary situation. [22]

After Pope John Paul II first visited the Federal Republic of Germany in November of 1980, a Joint Ecumenical Commission of representatives from the Protestant Church in Germany (EKD) and the Roman Catholic German Bishops' Conference was established. It instructed Protestant and Catholic theologians to produce an opinion asking whether the condemnations of the sixteenth century were still church-dividing. The opinion was ready in 1985 and published the next year. [23] This document became the basis for work on the "Joint Declaration on the Doctrine of Justification" in connection with a similar project in the USA. This Declaration was signed by representatives from the Lutheran World Federation and the Pontifical Council for Promoting Christian Unity on October 31, 1999 in Augsburg. The very lively discussion, as well as the official ecclesiastical reactions to both these documents need not be discussed here. But it must be noted that, regarding the Catholic side, both documents would have been impossible without the work of Catholic Luther

---

[22] Proceedings of the Third Congress in Jävenpää (near Helsinki) are found in Ivar Asheim (ed.), *Kirche, Mzstik, Heiligung und das Natürliche bei Luther* (Göttingen, 1967).. Proceedings of the Sixth Congress in Erfurt in *Lutherjahrbuch* 52 (1985). For the reaction to these events, see Claus Jürgen Roepke (ed.), *Luther 83. Eine kritische Bilanz* (Munich, 1984); Otto Herman Pesch (ed.), *Lehren aus dem Luther-Jahr Sein Ertrag für doe Ökumene* (Munich and Zürich, 1984); Hans Süssmuth (ed.), *Das Luther-Erbe in Deutschland.. Vermitlung zwischen Wissenschaft und Öffentlichkeit* (Düsseldorf, 1985). Peter Manns (ed.), *Zur Bilanz des Lutherjahres* (Stuttgart, 1986).

[23] English translation in Karl Lehmann and Wolfhart Pannenberg (eds.), *The Condemnations of the Reformation Era. Do They Still Divide?*(Minneapolis, 1990). There are 4 vols of collections of evidence on 1) Justification, sacraments and ministry; 2) the theology of justification; 3) sacraments and ministry, and 4) reactions to official church positions.

scholars in the 1960s. It is not often that academic theology can have such a profound effect on the church's hierarchy and bureaucracy in such a relatively short time .Every Catholic theologian, who before October 31, 1999 was certain of the positive elements in Luther's thought and who hoped for an ecumenical rapprochement, risked the critical question: "and what does the doctrine of the church say?" If one had to answer truthfully, one would have to reply: "I present my own personal scholarly opinion on the matter, though I am not alone in my opinion, not everyone shares it with me." Yet after the events of 1999, the situation is reversed: whoever opposes the conviction that the traditional disagreements on the doctrine of justification are still church-dividing may say so, but must also know that it is a private opinion. But any speaker who sides with the Declaration can now say: "I present the opinion of both churches." Who would wish to underestimate the change in the situation, also in regard to the work in the parishes?

III. Luther's Way in the Church

1. A Theological Biography

How visible is Luther's way, based on the new Catholic Luther research, not in the church that names itself after him, against his will, but in the church in which he became a theologian? In which he, as one who was baptized, also remains excommunicated? One needs no recourse to mental stress. One can show from the social and theological presuppositions, how Luther developed his theological positions, known as "Reformation theology." He did it by becoming acquainted with a challenging history of theology and piety, by discovering forgotten traditions, and, last but not least, by hard academic work. Summarizing the inter-confessional work, we can say today much better than to some extent in 1983 how Luther became "Luther." Last, but least: how little Luther was the stubborn revolutionary, "arbitrarily raging" (Denifle), endangering the foundations of Western culture, as he was depicted positively and negatively for centuries.

2. The Piety of the Late Middle Ages

What do we know better? One must gather together some basic knowledge about the Christians of the late Middle Ages and of the sixteenth century in general, and about Luther in particular. Then everything is much clearer than through psycho-analytical long-distance diagnoses. The young Luther was a pious Christian of the late Middle Ages. And all pious Christians then were filled with many anxieties; anxieties over the many political and social uncertainties of the time, beginning with famines, by the terror of impoverished and thus violent knights, as well as by marauding mercenaries and real wars. They were fought not for higher principles, such as justice, but for pure power politics; bishops and popes were no exception. But the people of this time, earnest Christians, demonstrated a piety that was varied and extensive. We do not exactly know why Luther decided to join the Augustinian Friars and to study theology (much to the disappointment of his father) only shortly after beginning his study of law. [24] The final impetus may have been the thunderstorm in which Luther found himself terrified while traveling on foot near the town of Stotternheim on the way to Erfurt. A lightning bolt nearly struck him down and in a spontaneous expression of gratitude Luther made a solemn vow to enter the monastic life. Today, such a vow would not be binding because it was not freely made. Nevertheless, Luther felt bound by it. On July 17, 1505 after a bibulous farewell party with friends who were not entirely supportive, Luther entered the monastery of the Augustinian Hermits in Erfurt. [25] He did so without enthusiasm, as he later continually attested. He cited two reasons: to fulfill his vow, and to be sure to enter

---

[24] In our days, the old legend has been warmed up about a homicide of Luther as reason for his entry into the monastery. Information and a clear judgment in Pesch, "Warum wurde Martin Luther Mönch? Warnung vor einer neuen alten Luther-Legende und ihrem theologiepolitischem Missbrauch" in *Stimmen der Zeit* 1203 (1985): 592-604.

[25] The Augustinian Hermits are, in contrast to the Augustinian Canons, more flexible, governed by the Rule of St. Augustine, and not bound to their respective houses, related to the Dominicans in their organization and life-style. No wonder that the soon beginning quarrel about the Dominican propagation of indulgences was perceived as an expression of rivalry between the two orders.

heaven rather than hell. At that time, it was self-evident that the monastic life was the most certain and secure way to eternal salvation.

3. The Personal Problem – Fed From Four Sources

So Luther's personal problems intensified. Whoever takes note of this as a modern person will quickly be inclined to judge that Luther was exaggeratedly scrupulous, if not something worse. But he had the "most imaginable" reasons. He could evade them only if he had a less serious commitment to the Christian faith and especially to his monastic life, or accept milder compromises. But he was not such a man. We can identify at least four sources from which Luther drew the most imaginable objective grounds for his anxiety.

a) Monastic rules dictated that monks must read from the Bible every day. Luther did so with a passion that became decisive for his entire life. The New Testament states that one must love God "with all your heart, and with all your soul, and with all your mind, and with all your strength (Mark 12:30). Accordingly, the spiritual instruction of the young monks intensifies the obligation to a "perfect love of God." What is a conscientious and sensible young monk such as Luther to do when confronted with the irrefutable experience that perfect love of God is not attainable, that one can never be certain whether one has attained it as blamelessly as the divine commandment demands?

b) This experience of being unable to do justice to the divine commandment of perfect love is fundamental to the anxiety about the Last Judgment which characterizes all of the late Middle Ages. Luther himself, along with countless numbers of his contemporaries, was convinced that the end of the world and the return of Christ in Judgment were at hand already in his lifetime. This anxiety reveals itself in the many images of Christ as Judge. Every day of his life in Wittenberg, Luther was confronted with this image. In the graveyard of the Town Church stands a sandstone relief of Christ in Judgment, with a double-edged sword

proceeding from his mouth steadied by his hands, pro-
nouncing judgment. [26]

c) Luther prayed the Psalms daily with his fellow monks.
Many times these psalms speak of God's "righteousness"
and "judgment" Should this have helped to alleviate the
anxiety over the judge who comes again?

d) But is there anywhere the joyous pronouncement of grace,
of the forgiving love of God as a counter-balance for sinners? Objectively speaking, the answer is yes! But even
clever theologians manage to bend even this message into
a theme of judgment. In 1507, as preparation for his ordination, and as was customary, Luther read the commentary on the Mass by the afore-mentioned late-scholastic
Tübingen theologian Gabriel Biel (1410-95), today the
first of the solemn prayers in the Catholic liturgy. This
prayer, on the right side of the page across from an image
of the cross that takes up the entire left, begins with the
words: *"te ergo clementissime Pater* ("Therefore, Most
Merciful Father, we beseech you ...")*. But the Commentary declares, contrary to the text and the image, that the
priest stands before the Father and Judge. It is well-known
that this notion threw Luther into an anxiety-psychosis at
the celebration of his first Mass!

In the context of these objective reasons for anxiety, the basic
question is formed in Luther which he later cast into the often
cited words, "How do I find a gracious God?" [27] The Sacrament of
Penance, which Luther received occasionally every day, did not
answer this question. He overcame it finally when he detected that
is was incorrectly framed. We do not have to find a gracious God,
we may believe that we have such a God.

---

[26] A copy of this stone is displayed in the Luther House in Wittenberg.

[27] The phrase is used in a sermon on baptism, February 1, 1534. *D.
Martin Luthers Werke* Kritische Gesamtausgabe [Schriften]
(Weimar1883-) Cited as WA. WA 37, 661:20-30.

4. The Theological Problem

But Luther had not yet come this far. After his ordination (1507), his monastic superior obliged him – as was customary –to pursue theological studies and finally, after some intermediary stations, graduated as a Doctor of Holy Scripture in October 1512 and became Professor of Holy Scripture, or as we would say today, Professor of Biblical Exegesis . He could now work on his personal problem of piety scientifically and theologically. Two impressions prompted his thinking. While studying theology in Erfurt, where the "modern way" (*via moderna*) dominated in the wake of the theology of William of Occam and the afore-mentioned Gabriel Biel, he learned that the absolution of the Father Confessor in the Sacrament of Penance is valid only under the condition that the penitent stirs up "perfect repentance," that is, remorse about sins not based on fear of punishment but on love of God ---the kind of love Luther was unable to experience for himself. But should it be true that the sacrament of forgiving sin becomes a new source of sin because forgiveness remains in abeyance? Now he knew why the Sacrament of Penance did not help him in his anxieties. Moreover, he became acquainted with the tradition of "German mysticism", which received little attention at the university. There he read, surprised and half liberated, that in order to be "righteous" before God we do not have to rely on our good works, God be praised, but only on what Jesus Christ has done for us.

5. The Exegetical Problem

A further insight becomes crucial. In the fall of 1514, Luther prepared a series of lectures on the apostle Paul's Letter to the Romans. He studied the relevant works of Augustine, the "father" of his order, available in a new edition in Basel though Erasmus of Rotterdam, above all the treatise "On the Spirit and the Letter" (*de spiritu et littera*). There he read that the church father (and after him the entire exegetical tradition) understood the famous passage of Rom. 1:17 ("For in it [the gospel] the righteousness of God is revealed through faith for faith"), not as the rewarding and punishing righteousness used against humanity but as a gift given by God through the promises of the gospel, without our works.

49

6. The Ecclesiastical Problem

On the basis of these theological and exegetical solutions, Luther began already in some sermons in 1516 with a massive critique of the use of indulgences. They were offered as a possibility to be released from the punishment of sins, for oneself or even for those who had died, be it in this life or in the "Purgatory," by doing something, indeed, seize the arm of God in order to oblige God to be merciful. First, Luther criticized the absurd notion to use money for avoiding the duty to repent and the suffering of just punishment. Above all, he emphasized, with the support of Paul and Augustine, that the grace and mercy of God are not based on any conditions, also not on ecclesiastical authority, or on anything else, in order to gain an indulgence. The decisive thesis of the ninety-five is No. 58: "Nor are they [the indulgences] the merits of Christ and the saints, for, even without the pope, the latter always work grace for the inner man." [28]

So the personal, theological, and exegetical reflections became the ecclesiastical problem for Luther. For his opponents, who were not at all personal beneficiaries of the indulgence traffic – certainly not Cardinal Cajetan who interrogated him after careful preparation in Augsburg in October 1518---rightly heard in the quoted thesis a dormant reservation against certain claims of papal power. This is quite correct as far as indulgences are concerned. But Luther was still far from viewing the papacy as anti-Christian. For the time being, the theses on indulgences were running like wild-fires all over Germany, against his will, and also initiated the Roman legal proceedings and the afore-mentioned interrogation by the papal legate. In the conflict which, on the one hand. involved a decisive ecclesiastical issue and, on the other hand, theological school opinions and financial interests, Luther saw himself surrounded, to his most painful surprise, not only by theological opponents. Suddenly, the whole church in all its official representatives was against him and wanted to force him to recant that God alone, and not an ecclesiastical authority, decides to who will receive God's grace and love.

---

[28] "The Ninety-Five Theses," 1517. *Luther's Works*, 55 vols ed. Jaroslav Peilikan and Helmut Lehmann (Philadelphia, St. Louis, 1955-1986), 31, 30.

7. The New Personal Problem

The ecclesiastical problem became a new personal problem. Luther had to ask himself: on what do I have to rely? On cooperation, without questions about everything that happens in the church, or on the gospel that promises me God's unconditional love and forgiveness, and confronts me, in case of conflict, only in Holy Scripture, not in various traditions of interpretation and in church practices?. So it also became clear that the late medieval thesis he had learned was false, namely, that the absolution of the father confessor is valid only under certain conditions. For Christ says, "Whatever you loose on earth will be loosed in heaven (Matt. 16:19b). This applies directly to the absolution of the father confessor. Whoever doubts the validity of the absolution makes Christ a liar!

In the subsequent years Luther brought up this topic again and again. It is the decisive reason and, at the same time, the decisive content of Luther's thesis about the certainty of salvation. When Cajetan rejected this argument in the Augsburg interrogation, Luther had to perceive it as a demand for apostasy. That is why he wrote to his Wittenberg colleague, Andreas Bodenstein of Karlstadt – then still a friend and partisan --- the sentences that have no dissonance and bundle together the whole "typically Lutheran" topic of "the certainty of salvation:" "I know that I would be most accepted and loved if I would speak this one word, '*revoco*,' that is, 'I recant'. But I do not want to become a heretic by recanting the opinion that made me a Christian. I'd rather die, be burnt, exiled, and slandered." [29]

8. The Ignored and the Heeded Call to the Gospel

The rest is well known. For political considerations regarding Luther's territorial ruler, Elector Frederick the Wise, Cajetan had been instructed not to arrest Luther if he refused to recant. So he was left in relative peace for two years, a time when "Reformation theology" ("the "principal writings") could spread. As soon as Charles V had become German emperor, contrary to Rome's

---

[29] *Briefwechsel* [correspondence] (Weimar, 1936-48). Cited WA.BR. 1, 217:59.

expectations, the legal proceedings were revived: the Bull to threaten excommunication, final attempts of mediation, no recantation, the burning of books at the Elster Gate in Wittenberg, excommunication in January 1521, imperial ban in April 1521.

The theological situation did not change in Rome. Luther's well-founded call for the cause of the gospel as the means of salvation against the abuses in the church was not heeded, but was perceived as undermining the foundations of the church. Luther, of course, had become more specific and, based on elaborated foundations, dealt with more topics, above all, the question of sacraments. Would he have to retract his letter to Karlstadt? Is it surprising, that positions hardened on both sides, getting stuck in consequences ending in exaggerations – avoidable if one had been used to listen better to one another instead of immediately setting boundaries?

IV. Luther: Our Teacher? A Brief List of Topics

1. One Step Backward?

We, the "young wild ones" of the past and "wise heads" today, are in the process of passing on the baton of Catholic Luther research to a younger generation. But it does not help to be pretentious. There is again one step backward. In the last three decades, the former Leipzig pastor and honorary doctor at the Theological Faculty in Regensburg, Theobald Beer, has been established as a counter pole against people of the "golden age of Catholic Luther research." On the sleeve of the second, strongly revised edition of his book of 1980, he is called "the most profound and exact Luther specialist among Catholics and Protestants." [30] Beer considers Luther a heretic because he did not stay with the tradition that Lortz considered "un-Catholic in its roots," namely, Occam and his school, and he demonstrates this, above all, in Christology and in the dogma of the Trinity. The resulting judgments suffer from a hardly tenable bias about the

---

[30] Theobald Beer, *Der fröhliche Wechsel und Streit. Grunsdzüge der Theolgie Martzin Luthers* 2d ed. rev. (Einsiedeln, Switzerland, 1980).

definition of obligatory church doctrine. According to Beer, Luther was no longer Catholic in his earliest beginnings.

In the 1983 edition of the journal *Theologisches*, an old sixteenth-century legend was warmed up in an "investigation," eager for hypotheses, by a theologically incompetent economist lawyer, namely, that Luther killed a fellow-student in a duel prohibited by the rules of the university and entered the monastery to escape from punishment under the law of asylum. This also explains his anxious quest for a gracious God. Theobald Beer and Remigius Bämer, whose aversion to Luther is even older than that of Beer, had given advice to the editorial staff and had no objections to the dissemination of this legend. [31]

In 1966, a book took Luther sharply to task, written by the Indologist and convert Paul Hacker, *The Ego in Faith: Martin Luther and the Origin of Anthropocentric Religion*. [32] It was well documented, but, like Beer's book, founded on a questionable judgment. The basic thesis: Luther related the truth of faith again and again to the ego, to individual responsibility, and that is a perversion of the faith that is, according to its nature, selfless surrender to God. This perversion, however, is the essence of Luther's *Reformation* understanding of faith. Thus Hacker's bewailing summary judgment: if Luther would have stayed with his early theology, he would have become one of the greatest theologians of church history! But everything was ruined and spoiled by "reflexive faith, "as he called it, and ended in a "confused Spirituality." Joseph Ratzinger had written a cautious Preface, calling for a discussion of substantive matters, without offering his own view of Hacker, claiming incompetence in the field. Hacker, of course, became a favorite speaker and popular author in ecumenical circles. The book has been published again in 2002 posthumously with the explanation that it had been silenced because it did not fit into the euphoric mood after the Second Vatican Council. But it could now become the cultic book for those who had already always claimed to know that Luther was, of course, the ancestor of the "theology of experience" that judges the truth of church doctrine according to what can pass

---

[31] See below, n. 25.

[32] Chicago, 1970. German in Vienna, Graz, and Cologne, 1966).

through the filter of subjective experience --- an intensified return to the "subjectivism' thesis of Lortz which was thought to have been overcome for a long time.

Finally, in his most recent book of collected essays, *Ecumenism. The Steep Path of the Truth,* [33] Leo Cardinal Scheffczyk offered a massive critique of the existing ecumenical efforts and also launched frontal attacks against me. He was afraid of "Protestantization of the Catholic Church" Many of his judgments could be criticized, but can easily be dismissed with the motto, "proofs are no help against facts."

So it is true: there is the danger of a step backward, if the indicated forces should succeed to prevail officially in the church. How, then, can we make again two steps forward? Through nothing else than patient work with texts, with historical connections, and with questions of substance as they are assigned to us today. Could not Luther here be our common teacher? To that end, some chosen pointers.

2. Two Steps Forward: Catchwords and Themes

How fascinating can Luther be to a Catholic, assuming he has been correctly understood? Just a few pointers. [34]

a) *The so-called "common priesthood", or better: the "common priesthood of all the baptized".* This does not mean, as is often misunderstood, that all Christians are "office-bearers", and that the ecclesiastical office is only a question of organization. The real meaning is that all the baptized have communion with Christ and thus stand directly before God, without any intermediaries. This is and has been part of the best Catholic tradition. But in practice and, at times, also guided by unnecessary theories of special interests, other notions proliferated in the church, and

---

[33] *Ökumene. Der steile Weg der Wahrhei* (Cologne, 2004).

[34] Extensive expositions in my *Hinführung zu Luther*, as well as in „Was hat Luther den Katholiken (noch) zu sagen? Eine Art Nachruf" in Udo Hahn and Marlies Mügge (eds.), *Martin Luther --- Vorbild im Glauben. Die Bedeutng des Reformators für das ökumenische Gespräch* (Neukirchen/Vlyn, 1996), 122-44.

Luther's teaching was perceived as a denial of the office endowed by Christ. In the second chapter of the Constitution on the Church of the Second Vatican Council the doctrine of the common priesthood of the whole people of God was solemnly put in writing, for the first time in the church after the Reformation and without any contact anxieties --- and displayed as a Catholic tradition.

b) *"Faith Alone."* Luther's opponents viewed it as an impossible formulation because they had a notion of "faith" in their heads that meant only an agreement of the mind with the truth of the Word of God. The *alone* is also accomplished by demons and grave sinners, according to Luther *and* the Catholic tradition. This act of understanding becomes an essential event of our relationship with God when it is imbedded as one part of a moment in the *whole* human surrender to God. The Catholic tradition calls it: "formed" by love of God; Luther said that one should not remain stuck in a "historical faith" but take to heart that everything faith confesses happens "for me, "for us," that is, related in complete trust to one's own existence. Both love and trust are, according to the explicit doctrinal declarations of the Council of Trent, not the result of one's own impetus but are gifts of God's grace. Both "theories" are closer to each other than one thinks. In any case, good works are not a *condition* for the saving power of faith but *follow* it. One can reject Luther's famous formulation only if one misunderstands his holistic idea of faith. But that has been common property among alert Christians for a long time. Whoever asks for faith asks, "On what can I rely in life and death?" If someone then can answer with faith in God, what "additions" and "supplements" could still be requested? What other reliance is there except reliance on God?

c) *The "Concealment of God in Opposites."* Luther had a totally modern experience expressed in medieval language, the "absence of God." He put it this way: If one looks at the world, as it is, one could become convinced that not God but the Devil is in charge. But since the reality of God is established by faith one must conclude that

God *wants* to hide behind the seemingly contradictory reality. Concealment of God is not only "invisibility" but concealment under the opposite of everything reason and even faith expect of God. This view is the consequence of his theology of the cross where God hid his power under powerlessness, his wisdom under foolishness, his love under scandal (1 Cor. 1: 18-25). This has a hard and simultaneously a soft consequence for faith. The *Anfechtung*, or uncertainty in modern terms, indeed doubt, belong to faith and are not something evil that must be overcome as soon as possible. They are normal – because God does not want our faith on the basis of triumphant proofs but in the endurance of the tension between confidence and confusion.

d) *"Real Ethics."* Truly a trump-card of Lutheran theology! Because good works – our ethical effort and struggle --- are no longer a condition of our salvation for God but the consequence of the granted salvation, we are completely free for service. The only standard is whatever *really* helps the neighbor who needs our help. There is nothing more absurd than the reproach that Lutheran theology favors moral easy-going. It is historically and substantially false --- and it is, by the way, also contradicted by the highly problematic moral social control in Protestant territories. It is, of course, true that "faith alone" as the foundation of our salvation offers the greatest freedom to seek the best solution for ethical problems, ranging from helping with the neighbor's fence to genetic engineering. Disputed, and even wrong decisions (discovered usually later as such) may be ventured in the certainty of God's forgiveness if we have done everything to make decisions according to the norms of the gospel.

e) *The Unity of Word and Sacrament.* Luther understood, as is well known---far away from the misjudgment that he had "abolished" the sacraments ---the sacrament as instituted by Christ himself as the form of the word in action: in the administration of the sacraments the word of salvation and of communion with God is pledged to the face, as it were. This is also the best ecclesiastical tradition, as could be demonstrated in Thomas Aquinas. The oppressing history how the sacrament became a competition to word and faith --- indeed was understood since Duns Scotus as the "safer" way opposite "mere faith in the Word – cannot be repeated here. In any case, the Council of Trent rejected proposals to establish the prominence of the sacrament opposite the proclamation of the word. Nevertheless, since then it is typically Catholic to understand the sacrament as the proper mediation of salvation and the proclamation of the word as mere preparation of it. The Second Vatican Council broke with this anti-Reformation contraction in the Constitution on Liturgy and in liturgical reforms. Whoever attends the liturgy can really experience –assuming the use of proper rubrics --- how now the proclamation of God's promises and the administration of the sacrament constitute a unity. They also are now confirmed by every single recipient with the "Amen." Here, Luther indeed "found his Council" as the Catholic Luther scholar Albert Brandenburg put it.

Conclusion

What is left to do? The "Joint Declaration" itself attaches themes: the understanding of the church, the office of ministry, and sacraments. It should be noticed that the problems in all three topics are *also* not only related to Luther but even more so to later Lutheran developments --- the Catholic corresponding counter-development. It is not easy for both sides to detect this. But in any case I see land on the level of substantive theological discussion. I would really like to know what new argumentation, be it for or against more harmony in understanding and in subsequent practice, could be introduced that has not been introduced in the discussion of the last thirty years. These sensitive topics generate sometimes the suspicion that laziness of mind and heart become immune to clear argumentations and deprive our parishes of more community in faith and witness than would certainly be possible.

So I conclude with a somewhat impudently formulated summary judgment that I have often used in such a context.

We cannot condemn Martin Luther when he said and thought about something what today also Catholic theology and church say. And we cannot condemn Luther when he already rejected what is no longer maintained by Catholic theology and the church.

Regarding positive learning from Luther, I take the liberty to repeat the final sentence of my dissertation about "Theology of Justification in Martin Luther and Thomas Aquinas." It was written forty years ago, on June17, 1964 at 49 minutes after midnight: "This gift [of the theology of Luther] is so precious that we --- modifying a statement of Ulrich Kühn about the relation of Protestant theology to Thomas --- dare to express the opinion that Catholic theology will have to ask itself whether it is good for Catholic theology to let Luther be with Lutheran theology without a fight."

Philip Melanchthon and Martin Luther As Partners in Evangelical Conversation[1]

Timothy Wengert, *Lutheran Theological Seminary at Philadelphia*

There are several different ways to approach the question of the relation between Martin Luther (1483-1546) and Philip Melanchthon (1497-1560). Already in 1527 during the prelude to the antinomian disputes, John Agricola (1492-1566) pointed out the differences between the two men's interpretations of Galatians.[2] In later years, after Luther's death, similar charges of deviating from the older man's biblical interpretation, especially in texts germane to the Lord's Supper controversy, would dog Melanchthon. A second, related way to compare the two is by contrasting their theology. During the Cordatus controversy in 1536 over the necessity of works, not only Conrad Cordatus (1475-1546) but also Nicholas von Amsdorff (1483-1565) accused

---

[1] Abbreviations: *CR*: *Corpus Reformatorum: Philippi Melanthonis opera quae supersunt omnia*, ed. Karl Bretschneider and Heinrich Bindseil, 28 vols. (Halle: A. Schwetschke & Sons, 1834-1860); *Manlius*: Johannes Manlius, *Locorum communium collectanea ... per multos annos pleraque tum ex Lectionibus D. Philippi Melanchthonis, tum ex aliorum doctissimorum uirorum relationibus excerpta, et nuper in ordinam ab eodem redacta*, 4 vols. (Basel: J. Oporinus, 1563); *MBW*: *Melanchthons Briefwechsel: Kritische und kommentierte Gesamtausgabe: Regesten*, ed. Heinz Scheible, 13+ vols. (Stuttgart-Bad Cannstatt: Frommann-Holzboog, 1977-); *WA*: *Luthers Werke: Kritische Gesamtausgabe* [*Schriften*], 65+ vols. (Weimar: H. Böhlau, 1883-); *WA Br*: *Luthers Werke: Kritische Gesamtausgabe: Briefwechsel*, 18 vols. (Weimar: H. Böhlau, 1930-1985); *WA TR*: *Luthers Werke: Kritische Gesamtausgabe: Tischreden*, 6 vols. (Weimar: H. Böhlau, 1912-21).

[2] See Timothy J. Wengert, *Law and Gospel: Philip Melanchthon's Debate with John Agricola of Eisleben over* Poenitentia (Grand Rapids: Baker, 1997), 121.

Melanchthon of betraying Luther's reformational insights.[3] Of course, after Luther's death, this charge became the drumbeat of criticism leveled against Germany's preceptor by his gnesio-Lutheran opponents. A third approach, fostered by the protagonists themselves, involved the construction of personae, concocted chiefly for the public and based only slightly on reality, that contrasted the rough woodsman, Luther, to the happy farmer, Melanchthon.[4] As the comments translated below indicate, Melanchthon comments (in this case about Moritz of Saxony [1521-1553]) could be very caustic.[5]

In the twentieth century, Gustav Mix tried to demonstrate their relation by assembling an exhaustive catena of comments by Luther and Melanchthon.[6] Building on his work, others later used the psychological category of "friendship" to explain how the two men worked together in Wittenberg. Despite the fact that Heinz Scheible has demonstrated just how unhelpful and untenable such a presupposition is, this "psychogram," as he calls it, has refused to die.[7] The problem with such an approach is not so much the use of the term "friendship," which can have very broad connotations,

---

[3] Timothy J. Wengert, "Caspar Cruciger (1504-1548): The Case of the Disappearing Reformer," *The Sixteenth Century Journal* 20 (1989): 417-441.

[4] See *WA* 30²: 68, 12 – 69, 1 and Timothy J. Wengert, "Melanchthon and Luther/Luther and Melanchthon," *Luther-Jahrbuch* 66 (1999): 57-62.

[5] Part of the cause for the widespread acceptance of this view of Melanchthon can be laid at the doorstep of his first biographer (and closest friend) Joachim Camerarius (1500-1574). See Timothy J. Wengert, "'With Friends Like This . . .': The Biography of Philip Melanchthon by Joachim Camerarius," in: *The Rhetorics of Life-Writing in Early Modern Europe: Forms of Biography from Cassandra Fedele to Louis XIV*, ed. Thomas F. Mayer and D. R. Woolf (Ann Arbor: University of Michigan, 1995), 115-31.

[6] Gustav Mix, "Luther und Melanchthon in ihrer gegenseitigen Beurteilung," *Theologische Studien und Kritiken* (1901): 458-521.

[7] Heinz Scheible, "Luther and Melanchthon, *Lutheran Quarterly* 4 (1990): 317-339. See also Wengert, "Melanchthon and Luther/Luther and Melanchthon," 84-88. For the most recent revival, see Jonathan Zophy, "Philip Melanchthon as a Family Man and Friend," *Lutheran Quarterly* 12 (1998): 430-44.

but with the way particular presuppositions about this particular relationship can distort the historical record. Once historians posit a friendship between the two—even when the word friendship is taken more narrowly than present-day American usage—then they seem forced to explain the "rifts" and "crises" in that relationship, including Melanchthon's imagined failure during Luther's time at the Wartburg in 1521-22, the exchange of letters between Coburg and Augsburg in 1530, and other later disputes (especially the one involving Luther's objections to the Cologne *Reformatio* and the "blabbermouth" Martin Bucer's [1495-1551] understanding of Christ's presence in the Eucharist).

Despite his insistence on such a friendship, Jonathan Zophy actually has brought the debate a step closer to resolution by focusing on Melanchthon's definition of the term "friendship" in his lectures on Aristotle. Using classical sources, Melanchthon insisted: "Properly speaking, friendship is a kind of *iustitia* [justice or righteousness] in which mutual kindness is returned for kindness, and by which some particular and open exchange of respectful actions is established."[8] He then proceeded to define friendship by its efficient, material, formal and final causes, as well as its effect. But it is in describing friendship's formal cause that Melanchthon expressed the depth of the relationship: Friendship "is a union [*copulatio*] and conjunction of souls by which one friend embraces another as his very self. Thus, the sayings have arisen, 'a friend is a second I [*alter ego*]' and 'friendship is equality.'"[9] Although Luther and Melanchthon could be thought of as "friends" according to the first part of the definition, even a cursory look at the relation between Melanchthon and Luther proves that such an equality or conjunction did not exist. Luther was hardly Melanchthon's alter ego (and certainly not *vice versa*), and they were not equal in age, experience or reputation.

---

[8] *CR* 16: 157.

[9] *CR* 16: 160-61. Melanchthon is quoting Plato, *Symposium* II.i.6 and Aristotle in his *Nicomachean Ethics*, bk. 9. Aristotle goes on in book nine to discuss "unequal friendships," which we would characterize as business, political or familial relations not friendships in the strict sense of the term.

Moreover, perhaps the most telling bit of evidence against characterizing their relationship as a friendship is that Melanchthon never uses the term in addressing letters to Luther. Unlike his correspondence with Joachim Camerarius, Veit Dietrich (1506-1549), Martin Bucer and a host of other figures, where Melanchthon addresses letters "amico suo" (to his [Melanchthon's] friend) or "amico meo" (to my friend), the younger man *never* uses this term for Luther.[10] Luther, too, in his famous 1545 preface to his Latin works refers to Melanchthon as his working partner in theology (*socius laboris in Theologia*).[11]

The difference in age, personality, authority, and experience militated against a deep friendship. However, they were also never enemies, and (despite the lively imaginations of some twentieth-century historians) their relationship remained strong throughout their lifetimes. As Scheible rightly proposes, these two giants in Wittenberg were *colleagues*, who tolerated differences far better than their later students, who truly respected and admired each other, and who worked side-by-side as teachers and theologians in the developing evangelical church and its school in Wittenberg. The remarkable thing in their collegial relationship was that it lasted, without serious break, from August 1518, when the younger man arrived in Wittenberg and gave a smashing oration on the necessity of humanist studies, until February 1546, when Luther departed this life. Their relationship did not depend upon friendship ties so much as upon mutual goals and respect, as they worked together in the joint causes of humanist reform and evangelical proclamation in university and church.

---

[10] A perusal of *Luthers Werke im WWW* shows only one place, in 1519, where Luther refers to Melanchthon as "amicus noster." See *WA Br* 1: 439, 4 (no. 191: Luther to Spalatin, dated ca. 10 August 1519). In his article, Scheible admits that in the initial counter there was a kind of initial excitement which could perhaps be characterized (at least from Luther's side) as a kind of friendship.

[11] WA 54: 182, 4-8. ""Eodem anno [1518] iam M. Philippus Melanthon a Principe Friderico vocatus huc fuerat ad docendas literas graecas, haud dubie, ut haberem socium laboris in Theologia. Nam quid operatus sit Dominus per hoc organum, non in literis tantum, sed in Theologia, satis testantur eius opera, etiamsi irascatur Satan et omnes squamae eius."

This broader, more flexible characterization of their relationship allows historians and theologians of today a fresh approach for measuring their contributions to the Reformation. Hypersensitivity to theological differences (as, for example, in the wording and intent of the Augsburg Confession)[12] actually arises out of a tacit misconstruing of their interaction. Even differences over the Lord's Supper or human freedom did not finally wreck the relationship, which was based upon mutuality and a common conviction that evangelical theology did not arise by fiat but through mutual conversation and consolation.[13] Later Lutherans sometimes operate out of a series of caricatures from the Reformation and are more likely to shout, "Here I stand!" in defense of deeply held personal opinions, rather than "Do I hear where you stand?" to colleagues with whom they disagree. This sensitivity, specifically embraced by Luther in at least one dispute where he and his colleague disagreed, might well be one of Luther and Melanchthon's most lasting gifts to the Lutheran churches.[14]

Of all the sources available to measure the strength and complexity of the relation between these two, one of the most remarkable falls under the rubric of "table talk." Unlike other sources of this genre that were handed down with only sporadic references to place and time and that focused only on Luther's words, the material translated below comes directly from the period and was probably recorded by one of the most accurate scribes in Wittenberg, Caspar Cruciger, Sr (1504-1548).[15] I have

---

[12] See the convoluted work of Wilhelm Maurer, *Historical Commentary on the Augsburg Confession*, trans. H. George Anderson (Philadelphia: Fortress, 1986). Maurer seems to think that only by proving total agreement between the two thinkers can the text of the Augustana be rightly understood. In fact, the work of both thinkers and the rhetorical genius of Melanchthon provide the more appropriate backdrop upon which to understand the text and its development.

[13] Cf. Martin Luther, Smalcald Articles, III.iv.

[14] See Timothy J. Wengert, "Luther and Melanchthon on Consecrated Communion Wine (Eisleben 1542-43)," *Lutheran Quarterly* 15 (2001): 24-42.

[15] This exchange, like many other references in *WA TR*, was first published by a formidable opponent of Melanchthon, Johannes Aurifaber, the court preacher in Weimar in the 1550s and beyond, in his

argued the details of their collegial relationship elsewhere. However, I know of no better source to demonstrate its intricacies than this one table talk, recorded on a single night in 1542. Its translation here provides an especially fitting tribute to Professor Eric Gritsch, whose translations in *Luther's Works* (to say nothing of his fine translation of the Augsburg Confession) are among the best and whose biography of Luther broke new ground by profoundly merging Luther's life with his thought.[16] By employing the kind of historical imagination that Professor Gritsch used so well throughout his career, we can elucidate the relation between these two equally talented colleagues and provide for the English reader more insight into their daily interactions than has hitherto been possible.

A Conversation of Dr. Martin Luther with Mr. Philip Melanchthon in the House of Dr. Caspar Cruciger: 11 April 1542[17]

Johannes Mathesius (1504-1565), who later became Luther's first serious biographer, had just completed his course of theological studies.[18] (He would receive his ordination papers two

---

Tischreden oder Colloquia Mart. Luthers so er in vielen Jaren, gegen gelarten Leuten, auch frembden Gesten und seinen Tischgesellen gefüret (Eisleben: Gaubisch, 1566).

[16] The title of that work, *Martin Luther, God's Court Jester*, was a further tribute to Prof. Gritsch's skill at expressing the central points in Luther's thought using remarkable language of his own.

[17] A translation of *WA TR* 5: 133-42, no. 5428. Two manuscript copies of the original, neither in Cruciger's hand, have come down to us (Bav. 1, 886 and Clm. 937), and other later collections contain portions of the material. Parallel material in *WA TR* 5: 142-46, no. 5428a, comes in part from a copy of a letter from Jerome Besold to Veit Dietrich (dated the middle of April 1542) and contains similar and in some cases more detailed discussion about the impending battle over Wurzen. *WA TR* dates this material to 12 and 13 April 1542. Unlike 5428, 5428a concentrates much more on Luther's own comments not Melanchthon's.

[18] For the most recent work on Mathesius in English, see Christopher B. Brown, *Singing the Gospel: Lutheran Hymns and the Success of the Reformation* (Cambridge: Harvard University Press, 2005).

days later on 13 April.) As was customary, he hosted a farewell meal marking his departure for Joachimstal, where he had received a position, held at the house of Caspar Cruciger, Sr., a professor of theology. In the course of the festivities, Cruciger, a noted stenographer,[19] probably was the one who took detailed notes and produced one of the fullest account of conversation among Wittenberg's professors ever recorded.

First, they discussed the current news. In 1542, the Smalcald League had laid siege to Wolfenbüttel in an attempt to bring its prince, Duke Henry of Braunschweig (1489-1568), to heel. The operation was successful, but it revealed deep rifts within the evangelical camp, especially between the two lines of the Saxon house: John Frederick (1503-1554), elector of Saxony (from 1532-1546) and his cousin, Duke Moritz (elector from 1548). In April 1542 a new controversy erupted between the two over the town of Wurzen. Under agreements worked out in the fifteenth century when the House of Wettin split into its Ernestine and Albertine branches, the bishopric of Meissen was under the joint jurisdiction of both branches.[20] In March 1542, to prevent all the proceeds of the "Turkish tax" from going to the opponents of the evangelical side, John Frederick occupied the territory around Wurzen, collected the tax, and introduced the Reformation. When the bishop of Meissen, Johann VIII von Maltitz (in office from 1534-1549), called upon Moritz for help against this aggression, the young prince was only too happy to oblige and began mustering an army—this despite the fact that he, too, was on the evangelical side. The Wittenbergers first received word of this impending conflict in early April and made various appeals for peace.[21]

---

[19] For Melanchthon's opinion, see *Manlius*, 3: 93f., "Doctor Casparus Crucigerus poterat quorunque pennis optime pingere."

[20] For details, see Martin Brecht, *Martin Luther: The Preservation of the Church 1532-1546*, trans. James Schaaf (Minneapolis: Fortress, 1993), 287-95.

[21] Besides the sources listed in Brecht, Melanchthon's correspondence was filled with reports. See, between 4 and 15 April 1542, *MBW* 2927 (to Nicholas von Amsdorf, evangelical bishop of Naumburg-Zeitz), 2928 (to Veit Dietrich), 2930, 2931, 2934-2940 (to or from Landgrave Philip of Hesse, who served to mediate the dispute), 2932, 2933, 2941 and 2942

[133] Philip said, "Ey, Herr Doctor, it is terrible weather now and a filthy wind."

Luther responded, "Ja, it is now on the brink between winter and summer."

Philip: "It won't be good weather for the poor soldiers who are now encamped [in and around Wurzen]."

Doctor Luther: "What can be done about it? Why did our princes start such a game?

Philip: "It is said that Duke Moritz has assembled a large army."

Luther: "It doesn't depend on the size of the army or the cost of the weaponry. It depends on who has a good cause and on a good attack when the forces engage."

Veit [Ortel of] Winsheim[22]: "That's true, Herr Doctor. In the Lüneburger Heath, [the duke of] Braunschweig had three men for scarcely one of his opponents', and still he was beaten."

Doctor Luther: "Precisely! He certainly was thoroughly throttled. Ach, there's a devilish thing about the natural disposition of the Meisseners [ducal Saxony]—with the exception of Dr. Cruciger [born in Leipzig, a part of ducal Saxony]. It instigated this plan so long ago."[23]

[134] Philip: "Our elector knows well what the situation is. [The ducal Saxons] want to oppress [our] prince and elevate theirs against the other parties, so that they may completely annihilate us. That's what they intend."[24]

(to Melanchthon's friends: Joachim Camerarius [in Leipzig], Simon Leupold [in Schwerin], Nicholas Medler [in Naumburg], Jerome Weller [in Freiberg], respectively).

[22] Veit Ortel (1501-1570), often called by his birthplace, Winsheim, came to Wittenberg in 1523, where in 1528 he received his Master of Arts degree. He taught rhetoric and Greek in the Arts faculty and, after receiving his M.D. in 1550, medicine.

[23] For Luther's bias against ducal Saxons, see Brecht, *Martin Luther*, 65-74.

[24] A marginal note in the manuscript copy reads: "In 1547 the wretches finally and completely rejected [us]."

Doctor Luther: "'The prayer of the pious avails much.' [James 5:16] What does David say [in the Psalms]? 'But I prayed to the Lord.' [Psalm 109:4, Vulg.] Let us pray. That faction cannot be defeated by arms or council of war but only by prayer."

Philip: "Herr Doctor, they will have plenty on their hands when they are set against each other. I've heard some terrible things! Dr. Jerome [Weller][25] told me how [Christopher] von Carlowitz[26] and [Simon] Pistorius[27] are so pugnacious and lovers of arguments, like no others."

Doctor Luther: "Look, let's leave those clever and eloquent speakers to their own devices. They will probably bring the matter to a head. [After all], they started it without us. Dr. [Gregory] Brück[28] has often said, 'Those on Duke [Moritz's] side are no good to our people at all. One has to be on guard all the time, because at some point they're going start something.'"

Philip, "It certainly is a tremendous scandal that they have started."

Doctor Luther: "That's true. What can a person do to them? You can't change things now."

Philip, "[I'm sure] they already know about this in Rome. The pope will write the emperor and congratulate him. The king of England will find out about it. And in Paris at the French king's court they will say that the house of Saxony is caving in upon itself and will rot of its own accord."[29]

Doctor Luther: "That's true. Do you think the devil ever sleeps? He will have brought the news to Rome long ago. The pope will laugh up his sleeve."

Philip: "That's for sure, Herr Doctor. They will say, 'That's the Evangelicals for you. That's the fruit of their teaching.'"

---

[25] Jerome Weller (1499-1572), theologian.

[26] Christoph von Carlowitz (1507-1574), counselor to Duke Moritz.

[27] Simon Pistorius (1489-1562), ducal chancellor to Duke Moritz.

[28] Brück (1483? – 1557) was electoral Saxony's chancellor until 1548.

[29] That is, respectively, Pope Paul III (1468-1549), Emperor Charles V (1500-1558), Henry VIII (1491-1547), and Francis I (1494-1547).

Doctor Luther: "Right. They will talk about it in Rome and say, [135] 'They are going to fight among themselves and root out their teaching by themselves.' That's what we're going to hear! May God prevent it! If you only pray diligently, God will do it. Philip, you must pray, and the rest of you, too. I prayed Duke George[30] to death. We could probably pray Carlowitz and Pistorius to death inside a year. May God grant that it goes for the instigators of this game the way it went for Judas [Matthew 27:5] and Achitophel [2 Samuel 17:23]."

Philip: "Duke Moritz is a young man, scarcely twenty-one years old! To think that we expended such great effort in the [ducal Saxon] church to restore [good] teaching against the pope and the whole world, so that no one could refute us.[31] And then, along comes this young squirt and starts a game among ourselves, so that we have no clue how to find our way out. No one can trust anyone else in life. Distrust and resentment remain in the heart."

Doctor Luther: "That's true. Even if they established a treaty, one would still shun the other, because their hearts are divided."

Philip: "All of this will not happen without great disturbance in the church.

Doctor Luther: "There will be disturbance and shaking in the church. But God will doubtless preserve the church. Duke Moritz is a young man and does not understand the matter yet. He imagines that his advisors are trustworthy and want only what is

---

[30] Duke George of Saxony (1471-1539), Luther's intractable enemy since the Leipzig debates of 1519.

[31] Upon the death of Duke Georg of Saxony (17 April 1539), one of the bitterest opponents of the Wittenbergers, his son Heinrich, who had already introduced the Reformation into his own lands the previous year based upon a new publication of the Saxon Visitation Articles (*Unterricht der Visitatoren*; *WA* 26: 175-194), became duke and invited the reformers to Leipzig to assist with the Reformation. They entered Leipzig triumphantly, where Luther preached on 24 May 1539 (*WA* 47: xxii-.xxiii; 772-79). On their way to Leipzig, according to a note recorded by Mathesius, the reformers (including Caspar Cruciger, Sr., whose family haled from there) sang songs in the carriage, "secundum alphabetum" (*WA TR* 4: 403 [no. 4615]). Heinrich's sudden death put Moritz in charge of ducal Saxony.

best for him. But he will most likely come to understand to his great harm. Then he will not trust them."

Philip: "Duke Moritz is like a flute. Whatever his advisors blow into him, that's what he whistles."

When the laughter died down, there was a pause in the conversation.[32] Melanchthon then brought up another interesting bit of news. Some Hungarian pastors had come to Breslau for ordination and had been sent on to Wittenberg.[33] This happened quite often after this time, as another reference in the Table Talk indicates.[34] The Reformation was an international movement, and Wittenberg its most important center.

Afterwards, Philip said: "A group has come from Hungary (the part controlled by Ferdinand[35]), whom the Breslauers [*today: Wrocław, Poland*] were supposed to ordain, but they sent them instead to us."

Doctor Luther: "Why didn't they ordain them in Breslau?"

Philip: "Ferdinand forbade them."[36]

Doctor Luther: "Do they consider ordination to be a great thing in Hungary?

Philip: "Yes, Herr Doctor. They consider it to be a great, glorious thing—even greater than baptism."

---

[32] Or perhaps in the recorder's notes.

[33] See *MBW* 2943 (*CR* 4:805), Melanchthon's letter to the pastors in Breslau (Ambrose Moibanus [1494-1554], Johannes Hess [1490-1547], and Andreas Winkler [1498-1575]) on 17 April 1542, which mentioned one such candidate.

[34] *WA TR* 5: 434, no. 6007.

[35] Ferdinand I (1503-1564) was brother of Charles V, King of Hungary and later Holy Roman Emperor. Hungary was divided into three parts, one part under the direct control of the Turkish Empire, one part a satellite of the Turks and Upper Hungary (Slovakia), which Ferdinand still controlled.

[36] The Habsburgs also controlled that city after it introduced the Reformation in 1523.

[136] Doctor Luther: "That is true. Under the papacy, no one was allowed to touch the Sacrament [of the Altar] unless he was ordained. But ordination is not so big a deal. Baptism is much greater than ordination. Baptism justifies and forgives sins; ordination does not justify or forgive sins. I have baptized, administered the Sacrament [of the Altar], and preached the forgiveness of sins. Those are the glorious offices of the church. O, baptism is a glorious, great thing!"

At this point, the discussion of ordination under the papacy triggered Luther to reminisce about life under the old regime. Melanchthon, too, matched him story for story. In some ways, these stories must have sounded like ancient history to their younger listeners. (For example, Cruciger and Mathesius were both born in 1504 and had received much of their training in Protestant schools.)

Then Doctor Luther said: "They likewise hold the canonical hours in high esteem. O, if they miss even one [of the seven times for daily prayer], they imagine that they have committed a terrible sin."

At this point, Philip told a story.[37] "Herr Doctor, I have an acquaintance named Peter, with whom I stayed for several days in

---

[37] This story is also recounted in *Manlius*, 1: 114f., where we discover more detail. "At the diet of Speyer [13 March to 25 April 1529], we had rooms with a priest, who knew my parents and kinfolk. Because I arose early in the morning, as I was accustomed, he also arose to recite the canonical hours. I sat beside him while he badly crucified his Psalter. Then I said, 'Sir Peter [that was his name], you have three passions. First, you crucify your God; second, David; third, yourself.' 'I know,' he said. 'You ought not reproach me about that, for it is necessary that I read those prayers.' I said to him, 'You are already old; you should not get up so early but should sleep a little longer. For morning sleep especially benefits the old. Afterwards, when you get up, recite the Lord's Prayer, and the Creed, and a chapter from your Bible, or Psalm 51 or 130. And, while I am here, I will read to you the letter of Paul to Timothy.' He obeyed me and slept longer. When he arose, after his prayers, I explained to him the difference between Mohammedan [sic! probably monastic] and the Christian religion. When I taught him, he was almost like a child. 'Ah, dear God,' he said. 'I never believed such good things were in Paul,

Heidelberg.[38] He always prayed his canonical hours each day but didn't understand a thing. He also couldn't really read [Latin]. So I said to him, 'Dear Herr Peter, if you only knew as well as I do how much you annoy our Lord God with your prayers, you would completely abstain from praying. David [the Psalmist] can hardly thank you either, given the way you torture his book.' Then he said, 'Ja, I have to pray; it is my duty.' To this I responded, 'But you don't understand it!' Then he confessed that he couldn't read [Latin], let alone comprehend it. I said to him, 'The canonical hours were established not to be prayed by someone who did not understand them but to be sung in church.'"

Dr. Luther [*interrupted the story and*] said [in Latin], "Their *oratio* was merely *murmuratio*.[39] All the words meant the same thing."

But Philip continued his story. "So he said to me, 'Is that really true?' I said, 'Certainly. You are sixty; you shouldn't plague yourself so with these prayers!' But he replied, 'Maybe, but if I omit them, I'll probably be committing a sin!' Then I said, 'No. I'll take that sin on myself.' I added, 'Do what I say. Get a full night's sleep. Afterwards, when you awake, look over a chapter of Paul. For example, take up the [first] epistle of Paul to Timothy, and I will tell you what it means.' So I convinced him to take my advice and, while I was with him, I explained the epistle for him. Then he said, 'I had no idea that there were so many good things in Paul.' That's the way I weaned him from the canonical hours. What he did after I left, I do not know."

[137] Then the Doctor said, "I worked so hard to keep the canonical hours."

At that, Philip [*acting as if he knew what story was coming*] replied, "Herr Doctor, your responsibilities prevented you from reciting the canonical hours."

---

which plainly I had not understood. Therefore I am pleased with you.' So after that he followed my advice."

[38] Cf. *Manlius*, 1: 114f. It was doubtless Speyer, during the imperial diet of 1529 and not Heidelberg.

[39] "Their prayer was merely mumbling."

The Doctor responded: "That's right. When I was busy, I would manage to collect two week's or even a month's worth of canonical hours. They'd pile up to the ceiling. Then I would take off an entire week, or a day, or several days, lock myself in my cell without food or drink, and pray away the entire pile. But it wasn't so long before I'd heaped up another set, until I had to pray so long that I'd make myself sick. In the end, I had stored up a quarter-year's worth. That was just too many, so I had to let them go."

Then Philip said, "Doctor Kirchberg was a famous man.[40] When he was dying, he allotted thirty florins to a Master [of Arts in Heidelberg], who prayed the canonical hours at his bedside while he was sick, so that he might complete the times that he had missed because of his illness."[41]

The Doctor replied, "You know what a professor in Erfurt from my cloister did? He was gone for three months. When he returned, the backlog of canonical hours had grown to such an extent that he couldn't catch up. So he took two other friars aside and gave them some money to help him pray so that he could catch up more quickly."

Then Philip responded: "That would be a costly strategy for our lazy bishops! If they were to collect their [canonical] hours, they could take one person—or twenty—, organize them, and let them pray up the hours. That way they'd get rid of them more quickly."

To that the Doctor added, "My prior[42] even did the following. Immediately after having sung the hours in the choir, he would

---

[40] The reference is to Master Laurentius Cleinclauß von Kirchberg, who presided when Melanchthon received his Bachelor of Arts in Heidelberg in 1511.

[41] Melanchthon told this story more than once. Cf. *Manlius*, 1: 112f., and Georg Loesche, ed., *Analecta Lutherana et Melanthoniana: Tischreden Luthers und Aussprüche Melanthons, hauptsächlich nach Aufzeichnungen des Johannes Mathesius* (Gotha: Perthes, 1892), 151 (no. 185), where Melanchthon indicated that the prayers were recited after the man's death. Only in the table talk do we discover the man's name.

[42] Possibly Eberhard Brisger, the last prior of the Wittenberg Augustinian Cloister.

imagine that he had perhaps left something out. Then, when he returned to his cell, he would begin to pray the hours all over again. Thus, it was a most aggravating labor, a real prison and purgatory, in which we were tortured. You all know nothing about this. In the end, I learned a special method that I imagined was a better way, so that when I recited my hours, I would designate a particular part of my fingers for every word. For example, 'law' was the middle joint of the first finger, then 'thy' was the next joint, etc. That way, when I had an entire psalm in one hand, with the other hand, I would count the words, which using this method had in the fingers their *loci communes*. That was torture!"

The reference to loci communes *must have brought a smile to Melanchthon's lips. Luther often complimented Melanchthon for his work in dialectics [what we call logic], in which* loci communes *[topical commonplaces] were a major constituent.*[43]

Philip replied, "Herr Doctor, while I was in Heidelberg, I lived with a professor[44] who [138] always prayed his canonical hours, too. He would often pray the *Gloria patri* for an entire hour, repeating it over and over. Finally he would say, 'Philip, where am I?' When I knew, I would say, 'Herr Doctor, you are in this or that psalm.' However, at times I didn't know either where he was with his prayers."

Thereupon the Herr Doctor said, "They had a 'triple intention': the material, the formal, and the spiritual. If a person had the formal, so that he could mumble his prayers, that was enough. Moreover, there's a canon in the *Decretals*[45] that states when a person wants to consecrate something 'with his first intention' and begins to recite the words, then, if something else occurs to him so that he

---

[43] See *WA TR* 1: 470, no. 935 (= 2: 82, no. 1389 and 3: 169, no. 3092); 4: 392, no. 4591; and 4: 647, no. 5082a (= 4: 647, 5082b).

[44] Probably Pallas Spangel (d. 1512), a professor of theology in whose house Melanchthon lived. For other versions of the story, see *Manlius*, 1: 112f. and Otto Waltz, "Dicta Melanthonis," *Zeitschrift für Kirchenge-schichte* 4 (1880-81): 330f. (no. 22).

[45] The *Decretalia* was the standard text and commentary on canon law, assembled in the Middle Ages by Gratian (d. before 1159).

forgets the first, nonetheless it remains consecrated by virtues of his first intention."

There was another lull in the conversation. It gave another, younger participant at table the chance to share the latest news— probably about troop movements and the ducal Saxons. Luther tried to make light of the situation. For Melanchthon, it cast a pall over the entire evening.

Thereafter Master [Sebastian] Fröschel[46] shared the latest news. To this the Doctor said, "You always know the latest news! You are a regular news wagon."[47]

But Philip became very serious and said, "This commotion with Duke Moritz will hardly die down without the shedding of blood. And I venture that I will be caught up in the fray, as God wills. I will be hacked to pieces or stabbed to death. I must commend myself to God."

To this, the Doctor replied, "Ey, my Philip, it will not come to that. Only pray!"

However, Philip responded, "No one will convince me otherwise! I will die soon!"

The Doctor said angrily, "Ey, be quiet, Philip! You are in a bad mood."

Philip said, "Greater people than I have died. Wasn't Judas Maccabeus a great man who did much for Israel? But in the end he met a terrible death.[48] In the same way, Josiah died.[49] What do you think? Was there ever a more wonderful person than he? And yet he died in a terrible, shameful way."

---

[46] Fröschel (1497-1570), who had received his Master of Arts at Leipzig where he became a priest until driven out for his evangelical beliefs, obtained the post of third deacon at Wittenberg's St. Mary's Church in 1529 at the latest. In 1542, he signed an ordination certificate as "vice-pastor" in Bugenhagen's absence.

[47] Literally: "vehiculum novitatis."

[48] 1 Maccabees 9. Judas decided it was better to die in battle than to retreat.

[49] 2 Kings 23:29. Josiah died in an attack on Egypt.

Doctor Martin: "Ja, those are not public cases but private, very foolish cases."

Philip: "Herr Doctor, it *is* true. O, how often I have thought about this!"

Doctor: "Ey, we have to get used to such things. Great people owe our Lord God foolishness, which they have to pay honestly. No great man commits a small foolishness. Instead, he has to play the fool so that he shows clearly what wisdom and prudence are. What did David do? He had plenty of wives! And still he took the wife of another and became both an adulterer and a murderer.[50] That's playing the fool."

Philip: "Ja, Herr Doctor, he had to pay a right dear penance, so that scarcely ten years later he was a widow[er]."

Again the conversation trailed off. Melanchthon's talk of death led the others to consider their age. In a world without middle age, people were either young or old. For Melanchthon to talk of death at age 45 put him squarely on the cusp between the two.

After that the gentlemen talked about how old they were. The Doctor said, "I am now sixty years old."

Philip interjected: "Herr Doctor, you are only [139] fifty-eight years old. Your mother told me so."

But the Doctor said, "You must not make me too young! I am certainly sixty years old."

But Philip refused to give in. [*And well he shouldn't have. He was right!*]

[Veit Ortel of] Winsheim said, "I was born in 1501 according to my mother. I even had Master Erasmus [Reinhold][51] cast my horoscope."

---

[50] 2 Samuel 11:27.

[51] Professor of Mathematics [a field closely associated with astrology in the sixteenth century] who died in 1552. See Karin Reich, "Melanchthon und die Mathematik seiner Zeit," in: *Melanchthon und die Naturwissenschaften seiner Zeit*, ed. Günther Frank and Stefan Rhein (Sigmaringen: J. Thorbecke, 1998), 105-121, esp. 114.

Whether it crossed Luther or Melanchthon's mind to hold one of their famous debates over the scientific nature of astrology at this point is uncertain.[52] Instead, Melanchthon brought up a new question, very likely connected to the military action in Wurzen and to the knowledge of their younger companion, Veit Ortel.

Philip then asked who had built the Monastery of Döberlein [*today: Dobrilug*].[53]

[Veit Ortel of] Winsheim answered, "Herr Praeceptor, the princes of Meissen were the first founders. They gave the villages and towns to it. Afterwards, Ferdinand also gave something to it. Recently, he stripped away ten villages. There are still eighteen there. Moreover, it was built in the year that St. Bernard (1090-1153) died."

Doctor Martin: "Let's see. St. Bernard lived under the emperors Henry IV and Henry V and [Lothar] I."[54]

Philip: "Ja, he even lived under Lothar."

Doctor Martinus: "During his lifetime he built a hundred monasteries, and, despite that, he was a godly monk."

[Veit Ortel of] Winsheim then said, "Herr Doctor, I think Döberlein may be a star-crossed place.[55] Every year someone is killed there. Even I barely escaped a calamity. My students—one time when I was a dinner guest with my young lord, Duke Otto Ernest von Lüneburg[56]—they wanted to beat up on each other. Afterwards, a nobleman wanted to hack my superior to pieces. In the cloister I saw no less than six ghosts. It was a beautiful monastery, though. In the choir alone there were more than 100

---

[52] See Wengert, "Melanchthon and Luther/Luther and Melanchthon," 75-76 and the references cited there.

[53] Dobrilug was less than thirty miles west northwest of the castle Torgau. It lay on the border between Saxony and Oberlausitz, which was controlled by the Bohemian crown and, hence, Ferdinand.

[54] They ruled, respectively from 1056 to 1106, 1106 to 1125, and 1125 to 1137. Bernard was born in 1090 and died in 1153.

[55] Text: *locus fatalis*, haunted region or deadly place.

[56] Ernest von Lüneburg (1497-1546).

stalls, which were constructed in such a way that a person could lean back in them almost as if he were lying down."

Philip said, "I always figured that if the plague came here, we could always move the university there."

The Doctor said, "For goodness' sakes, no, Philip! Brother Rausch[57] is the abbot there. They would like to destroy themselves and everyone else!"

Philip: "We recently sent them and Liebwerda[58] each a preacher at the direction of my gracious lord [John Frederick]. But you have to figure these places are not worthy of them."[59]

The guests fell quiet again. Perhaps other things were said, but Cruciger has left us no clue. Suddenly Luther broke the silence with an entirely different theme—one that was also very much in the news: the Turks.

After this, the Doctor began to talk about the Koran, saying how many great lies were found there.[60] He said, "They have a book, written by Mohammed (ca. 570-632), that is called "Twelve Thousand Words." When the Saracens ask whether everything written in there is true, they answer, 'No, a third of what's in there is not true; but another quarter is true.' Now that is a strange thing,

---

[57] "Brother Rausch" was a German household spirit responsible for getting people drunk. In 1488 a satire appeared in the Low German dialect (1508 in High German), in which the devil appeared as "Brother Rush," the cook in a monastery, who made fun of its inhabitants and supported their unchaste lives. (Cf. http://de.wikipedia.org/wiki/Bruder_Rausch.)

[58] Now: Bad Liebenwerda, just south of Dobrilug.

[59] Cf. *MBW* 2826 (CR 4: 877), dated 12 October 1541. Gregor Hirburg [alias: Hirleß, 1512-1558] from Sayda near Freiberg was ordained 12 October 1541 in Wittenberg to serve in Doberlug. Cf. also *MBW* 2814 (dated 30 September 1541), where Melanchthon and Bugenhagen tried to prevent the elector from sending the deacon in Liebenwerda, Thomas [NN] to Doberlug, and *MBW* 2823 (dated 4 October 1541), where the Elector responded favorably to their suggestion.

[60] See J. Paul Rajashekar and Timothy J. Wengert, "Martin Luther, Philip Melanchthon and the Publication of the Qur'an," *Lutheran Quarterly* 16 (2002): 221-28, and the literature cited there.

that the people believe lies. They wantonly condemn themselves. [140] Mohammed and the devil are excused before God and humanity, for they say, 'A fourth of it is certainly true; and another part is deception.' That would be like someone saying, 'A quarter of my sermon is true; a third is lies. But I wish to be in charge and would want to devour the whole thing.' Don't I condemn myself out-of-hand? It's the same way here. The people are at fault, not Mohammed or the devil. They're excused. Were someone to put a glass of wine on the table and say, 'A quarter of the wine is Madeira and a third is poison.' I'd love to see you drink from it! But the world is blind and wants to be damned and deceived."

Philip: "The world is also very ungrateful." At which point he cited the Greek verse: "'Quickly courtesy [*gratia*] decays, and the world becomes ungrateful.'[61] We have born the burden and torture, the execution of consciences."

With that, Mathesius had received a proper sendoff. Of course, he himself had written copious notes at Luther's table during his stay in Wittenberg. One time (7 November 1540 to be exact), Mathesius penned these words of "my dearest praeceptor" [Philip Melanchthon] at the very end of his notebook. They must have been still ringing in his ears as he departed for Joachimstal— another learned pastor trained in Wittenberg for Saxony's pulpits.

Give thanks to Christ, and do not forget patience. Furthermore, do not forget the saying, "Courage makes one cocky." But God has done, does, and will do all things well. This is most certainly true.[62]

This snapshot of a single evening conversation between Luther and Melanchthon accurately demonstrates how they related to one another. They were both evangelical (Lutheran) theologians in their own right, judging their situation using their own experience: in the late-medieval church, in the Holy Roman Empire, and in terms of their own theological methods and convictions. They were deeply concerned for the religious and

---

[61] The citation is from Homer, *Odysseus*, 4, 695. The other manuscript copy of this table talk (Clm. 937) has the Greek: "οὐκ [modern versions: οὐδε τις] εστι χαρις μετοπισθεν ευεργεων."

[62] *WA TR* 5:64 (no. 5341).

political situation of their day, and so, without always agreeing, their conversation moved easily from politics and the state of the church to prayer, ordination and death. Melanchthon's sensitivity about the last topic evoked in Luther a pastoral response. Without burdening their relationship with the psychologically laden term, "friendship," one must certainly admit to a deep and lively, collegial affection between the two men. Their inequality in age and the formality of their times shows through, with Luther using Melanchthon's Christian name but Melanchthon always calling his colleague "Herr Doctor."

In the final analysis, this brief encounter may reveal more about how theology was done in Wittenberg than many other, more formal sources. Luther has sometimes been used (and abused) by his followers, who have been only too glad to cite him above any other authority (scriptural or confessional). Similarly, Melanchthon has often been depicted as a weaker companion, dependent upon the stronger personality of Luther and only too ready to betray the entire Reformation at the drop of a hat (or, more frequently, upon the death of Luther). Instead, here we catch a glimpse of two equals, united in faith, varied in experience and theological expression, living *"mitten im Leben"* ("in the midst of life" to quote one of Luther's own favorite hymns) by faith alone in Christ.

The Case of Women: New Perspectives, New Interests in Luther and Reformation Studies

Kirsi Stjerna, *Lutheran Theological Seminary at Gettysburg*

I. Introduction

Eric Gritsch taught at the Lutheran Theological Seminary at Gettysburg for thirty-some years. He started, with his colleague Gerald Christianson, the Institute for Luther Studies which organizes an annual Luther Colloquy and gathers American and international scholars to Gettysburg every year. For this volume, I am contributing a modified part of a paper presented at the 2003 Luther Colloquy titled "Luther, Gender and Genesis" as an example of what kinds of interests gender studies and feminist perspectives may bring into Luther and Reformation scholarship.[1] In the following essay, I will explore what Luther concludes about gender and gender relations from examining the Genesis narrative of the Fall. Luther's explanation of the sin of Eve and its compensation in the glory of her motherhood, allows for some intriguing conclusions.

---

[1] In 2003, the Luther Colloquy offered lectures on Luther, Gender and Genesis. Doctors Jane Strohl, Kris Kvam and I presented on topics we had worked on the previous fall in Copenhagen at the International Congress of Luther Research. Lectures were published in the seminary publication Seminary Ridge Review, edited by Dr Brooks Schramm, professor of Old Testament, who also offered a response to the papers. See Kvam, Kristen,"Equality in Eden? Gender Dynamics and Luther's Lectures on the Creation of Adam and Eve," in *Seminary Ridge Review* (Spring 2004, 5-18); Stjerna, Kirsi, "Grief, Grace, and Glory: Luther's Insights on Eve and Tamar in Genesis 3 and 38," in *Seminary Ridge Review* (Spring 2004, 19-35); Strohl, Jane, "The Matriarchs in Luther's Genesis Commentary: Mother Knows Best," in *Seminary Ridge Review* (Spring 2004, 36-44).

But first, a brief description of some of the challenges and contributions gender awareness brings. One of the most important recent developments in both Luther and Reformation studies is the gradual inclusion of gender as a relevant perspective. Acknowledging that no study, theological or historical, is ever gender neutral and that gender and related assumptions and ideals have always been part of history writing and theological scholarship, is a good beginning for writing new chapters in the Reformation histories and Reformation theology studies. Three decades ago, Joan Kelly posed a provocative question, "Did women have a Renaissance?," igniting historians and theologians to rethink how women have experienced or participated in the significant eras of history, such as the Renaissance and the Reformation.[2] The findings of creative digging suggested that even amidst foundational cultural movements and changes in the Western world, women's lives have not necessarily improved. At least on the surface, it appears that much of the progress and many of the changes touched first and most directly the lives of men, and only indirectly or later had an effect on the lives of women. Also, in regards to the written historical record, women were at least theoretically marginalized from the places where their world was structured, and they were stripped from the essential means of naming their world from their experiences. The subsequent research has been significant. First, it illuminated women's actual roles, choices, and contributions. Second, it revealed the fallibility of the criteria and categories that had been used in interpreting past events, issues, participants and matters of "importance." It became clear that we cannot look at the history of men and women with the same presumptions. The starting points of men and women in regards to any development, including religious reforms, have been different (as a result, for instance, of limited access to education and power). Thus, the conclusions cannot be

---

[2] Kelly-Gadol, Joan, "Did Women Have Renaissance?" in *Becoming Visible: Women in European History*, ed. Bridenthal, R., C. Koonz and S. Stuard (Boston: Houghton Mifflin, 1977) 175-201. Kelly's approach has since been challenged and some of her findings refuted.

identical either; neither can the whole picture afford to be one-dimensional.[3]

We cannot conclude that, until recently, women have been insignificant, passive bystanders in Christian history.[4] Women have been actively involved, even if often without "permission" and through creative means. This activity has recently generated much interest. The challenge has become how to gather information and interpret that history apart from and in relation to the history of men that can no longer be considered the standard mirror for all participants in the Reformation(s). The entire premise of writing history and thinking about theology, the criteria and sources have had to change with the inclusion of both genders' experiences and perspectives. Methods, questions, sources and criteria of "importance" used in historical and theological study have had to expand. Part of this transformation has been the bringing of women into the conversation, naming women as subjects of history – their history – and finding their voices in a variety of sources. This is the other side to the (far from being completed task) of analyzing male reformers' thoughts about and for women.

Especially in the area of social studies, significant findings have been made that contribute to a more holistic understanding of life in the past; whereas in the areas of theology and church history movement has been slower. The "meaning" and "truth" questions are still waiting to be reevaluated with the insights arising from conversations between different conversation partners. That said, historians Merry Wiesner-Hanks, Sherry Marshall, Susan Karant-Nunn, Natalie Z. Davis, and Miriam Chrisman, to name a few,

---

[3] Lerner, Gerda, *The Creation of Feminist Consciousness* (Oxford: Oxford University Press, 1993). See Wiesner, Merry E. *Women and Gender in Early Modern Europe. New Approaches to Modern European History* (Cambridge: Cambridge University Press, 1993; Repr. 1994, 1995. 2nd ed. 2000). Also, Scott, Joan, "Gender: A Useful Category of Historical Analysis," *American Historical Review* 91 (1986) 1053-75.

[4] Sommerville, Margaret R., *Sex and Subjection: Attitudes to Women in Early-Modern Society* (London: Arnold, 1995) 8-39, 40-78.

have provided stimulus for further study.[5] As a step further towards a possibility of "in-depth" study of Reformation era women's thoughts, an increasing number of scholars, such as Elsie McKee, Peter Matheson, Mary McKinley, Nancy Roelker, and Holt Parker, have brought to daylight sources from and about individual women of the period, in the footsteps of Roland Bainton.[6] Charmarie Jenkins Blaisdell, Jane Dempsey Douglass,

---

[5] Davis, Natalie Z., "Women's History' in Transition: the European Case," *Feminist Studies* 3 (1976/1976) 83-103; idem, "City Women and Religious Change," in *Society and Culture in Early Modern France* (Stanford: Stanford University Press, 1975); Karant-Nunn, Susan, "Continuity and Change: Some Effects of the Reformation on the Women of Zwickau." *Sixteenth Century Journal* 12 (1982) 17-42; Chrisman, Miriam, "Women and the Reformation in Strasbourg, 1490-1530," *Archiv für Reformationsgeschichte* 63 (1972) 143-68; Marshall, Sherrin, *Women in Reformation and Counter-Reformation Europe: Public and Private Worlds* (Bloomington and Indianapolis: Indiana University Press, 1989); Monter, William, "Protestant Wives, Catholic Saints, and the Devil's Handmaid: Women in the Age of Reformations," in *Becoming Visible. Women in European History,* ed. Renate Bridenthal, Claudia Koonz, and Susan Stuard (Boston: Houghton Mifflin Company, 1987, 2nd ed) 203-219; Wiesner, Merry, "Women's Response to the Reformation," in *The German People and the Reformation,* ed. Po-chia Hsia, R. (Ithaca: Cornell University Press, 1988) 148-171; Wiesner, Merry E., *Women and Gender in Early Modern Europe. New Approaches to Modern European History* (Cambridge: Cambridge University Press, 1993. Repr. 1994, 1995. 2nd ed. 2000). Also Clark, Elizabeth and Herbert Richardson, "Luther and the Protestant Reformation: From Nun to Parson's Wife," in *Women and Religion,* ed. by E. Clark and H. Richardson (New York: Harper and Row, 1977), 131-148.

[6] Matheson, Peter ed., *Argula von Grumbach, A Woman's Voice in the Reformation* (Edinburgh: T&T Clark, 1995); McKee, Elsie, *Katharina Schütz Zell* (Leiden: Brill Academic Publishers, 1998); McKinley, Mary B., *Epistle to Marguerite de Navarre; and, Preface to a Sermon by John Calvin,* by Marie Dentiere, ed. and trans. Mary B. McKinley (Chicago, London: University of Chicago Press, 2004); Morata, *Olympia Fulvia, The Complete Writings of an Italian Heretic,* ed. Holt N. Parker (Chicago: University of Chicago Press, 2003); Roelker, Nancy, *Queen of Navarre: Jeanne d'Albret* (Cambridge: Harvard University Press, 1968); Bainton, Roland, *Women of the Reformation in Germany and Italy* (Minneapolis: Augsburg Publishing House, 1971/2001 Academic

and John Lee Thompson are pioneers in the still tender area of discussing theologically the reformers' theologies from women's perspectives. Issues of importance in the ongoing study are: what the Reformation teachings meant for women, what in the theology is redeemable for women, what continues to be problematic and in need of re-construction from feminist perspectives?[7] Examples of such feminist re-reading of the reformers' theologies have recently offered Deanna Thompson, Mary Solberg and Kristen Kvam and Jane Strohl.[8] The ever-expanding field of questions shows the

---

Renewal Press); idem, *Women of the Reformation in England and France* (Minneapolis: Augsburg Publishing House, 1974/2001 Academic Renewal Press); idem, *Women of the Reformation from Spain to Scandinavia* (Minneapolis: Augsburg Publishing House, 1977/2001 Academic Renewal Press). N.B. Mostly literature in English is referred to here, with the recognition that much important scholarship is taking place in various languages.

[7] Blaisdell, Charmarie Jenkins, "The Matrix of Reform: Women in the Lutheran and Calvinist Movements," in *Triumph Over Silence: Women in Protestant History*, ed. Richard Greaves (Westport, Connecticut: Greenwood Press, 1985) 13-44; Douglass, Jane Dempsey, "Women and the Continental Reformation," in *Religion and Sexism: Images of Woman in the Jewish and Christian Traditions,* ed. Rosemary Radford Ruether (New York: Simon and Schuster, 1974) 292-31; idem, *Women, Freedom and Calvin* (Philadelphia: The Westminster Press, 1985); Stjerna. Kirsi, "Naisnäkökulmaa reformaation spiritualiteettiin ja teologiaan" ["Gender Perspectives on the Spirituality and Theology of the Reformation"] in *Näen Jumalan toisin. Kristinuskon feministisiä tulkintoja [I See God Other Ways. Feminst Interpretations of the Christian Faith],* ed. Pauliina Kainulainen ja Aulikki Mäkeläinen (Helsinki: Kirjapaja, 2006).

[8] Thompson, Deanna A., *Crossing the Divide. Luther, Feminism, and the Cross* (Minneapolis: Fortess Press, 2004); Solberg, Mary, *Compelling Knowledge: A Feminist Proposal for an Epistemology of the Cross* (New York: SUNY, 1997); Kvam, Kristen, *Eve and Adam: Jewish, Christian, and Muslim readings on Genesis and Gender,* co ed. with Linda S. Shearing and Valaria H. Ziegler (Bloomington, IN: Indiana University Press, 1999); also Kvam, Kristen, "The Significance of Luther's Ideas for the Churches of the 21st Century: a Feminist Perspective," in *LutherJahrbuch: Organ der internationalen Lutherforschung* (forthcoming). See also Kvam, Kristen, "Equality in Eden? Gender Dynamics and Luther's Lectures on the Creation of Adam and Eve,*" Seminary Ridge Review* (Spring 2004, 5-18):, Stjerna, Kirsi, "Grief,

widespread ramifications of the "simple" question: how about women?

Feminist and gender studies have underscored the importance of experience and context: One cannot do theology apart from particular histories, contexts or human experiences, which, naturally, influence one's hermeneutics. Human experiences are gendered, and rooted in particular contexts. Naturally, then, theology is also contextual. Gender cannot be excluded. Regarding the theological roots of the Reformation, to acknowledge the reality that most of it was formulated by men with comparable backgrounds and experiences compels the ongoing reconstructive work to include more participants, such as the women who were affected by the Reformation theologies. Recovering the "lost" or hidden history of women in the church and examination of their experiences and contributions brings new information into the theological discussion about the "truth" and "meaning" questions of contemporary theology. As one of those important steps in the process of making peace with one's fallible tradition and rediscovering its promise, the study of women should not be "ghettoized" as a secondary tier apart from the "serious" theological discussion around recognized sources. While Luther, Calvin and others continue to deserve a solid place in the ongoing discussion on the Reformation legacy, they and we will benefit from being placed in the company of Katharine Schütz Zell, Marie Dentiere, Argula von Grumbach and Olympia Morata, to name just a few powerful writing Reformation era women – the Rosemary Ruethers and Sally McFagues and Elisabeth Schüssler Fiorenzas of the time. They reckoned with the importance of their gender, while lacking the modern framework of articulating gender issues. Luther himself, on some level, was aware of the importance of gender and tried, in his own limited way, to address it theologically.

Grace, and Glory: Luther's Insights on Eve and Tamar in Genesis 3 and 38," in *Seminary Ridge Review* (Spring 2004, 19-35); Strohl, Jane, "The Matriarchs in Luther's Genesis Commentary: Mother Knows Best," in *Seminary Ridge Review* (Spring 2004, 36-44).

II. The Case in Point: "All about Eve"

Had Luther been a woman and given birth, we would have never heard the end of it, so fascinated was he with the miracle of birth. In his late lectures on the Genesis, he returned to the theme of motherhood again and again when interpreting the stories of Eve and the matriarchs of the Old Testament. Especially when interpreting the women's sins, the solution or the "bigger picture" for Luther was, generally speaking, the glorious state of motherhood. Luther offered an empathetic reading of Eve and the Old Testament matriarchs, keeping his eyes focused on their redeeming motherhood and highlighting women's central role in the salvation history – probably unaware of the radical seed imbedded in his arguments. The story of Eve in Luther's Genesis interpretation reveals how Luther, blind to his own gender biases, dealt with the gender issue.[9]

Eve's poena laeta – Eve's unbearable but bearable punishment

According to Genesis 3:16, God said to the woman: "I will greatly multiply your sorrow when you are pregnant. In pain you will bear children and you will be under your husband's power; and he will rule over you."[10] According to Luther, Eve, the mother of all the living, the *mater omnis vivi* (3:19), brought about both the punishment and the blessing from God. First of all, through Eve, all women bear in their bodies the punishment of the sin of unbelief in the form of painful pregnancy and the other pains of motherhood. Women bear these afflictions impatiently and with murmuring, which Luther deemed ultimately bearable (anybody having gone through childbirth might have a bone to pick with

---

[9] Mickey Leland Mattox's, *Defender of the Most Holy Matriarchs: Martin Luther's Interpretation of the Women of Genesis in the Enarrationes in Genesis, 1535-45* (Leiden, Boston: Brill, 2003) is an extremely valuable source.

[10] "Ad mulierem vero dixit: Valde multiplicabo dolorem tuum, cum eris gravida. In dolore paries Filios, et sub Viri potestate eris, et ipse dominabitur tui" (Gen. 3:16; WA 42:147, 148; LW 1:198).

Luther here). Nonetheless, Luther considered these pains bearable because of the hope attached to them.[11]

The other part of the affliction is also bearable, argues Luther, but equally difficult: In the Fall, women lost their freedom and became subjected to men, "Now there is also added to those sorrows of gestation and birth that Eve has been placed under the power of her husband, she who previously was very free and, as the sharer of all the gifts of God, was in no respect inferior to her husband."[12] Luther's other, somewhat contradictory statements on Eve should be examined in light of this statement that Eve "was in no respect inferior to her husband" (*nulla in parte Viro inferior erat*).[13]

Luther saw the loss of freedom and the loss of equality for Eve as an affliction all women have to bear, even if unwillingly; he also reckoned women's resistance to this punishment. We may assume that Luther here spoke from experience. Katie enjoyed "modified" subjection to her husband since he recognized her superiority and autonomy in "appropriate" domestic arenas. Luther's basic view of post-lapsarian relations and tensions between men and women can be gathered from the following quote:

---

[11] "et tollerabile est, quicquid hac spe manente ac firma homini imponitur....Imponit poenam mulieri et tamen relinquit spem resurrectionis et vitae aeternae" (Gen. 3:16; WA 42:147, 148).

[12] "Nunc ad illas gestationis et enixionis Dolores accedit etiam, quod Heua potestati Viri subiecta est, quae antea liberrima et nulla in parte Viro inferior erat, social omnium donorum Dei" (Gen. 3:16, WA 42:151; LW 1: 202).

[13] "But God imposed Eve's subjugation to Adam as punishment after he discovered her sin. In addition all women must bear children in pain and carry the burden of raising children and running the household. But, according to Luther, Eve is not to be despised. She was neither abandoned by God nor separated from companionship with Adam for his sin. While she might have to bear children in pain, she recognized that the glory of motherhood belonged to her and regarded the pain as a joyful punishment. Woman's purpose in life is procreation, companionship to man, management of the household, and, because of her sin in the Garden, to be an antidote to lust." (Blaisdell, "The Matrix of Reform," 16; see LW 1:198, 293; Gen 3:16.)

If Eve had persisted in the truth, she not only would not have been subjected to the rule of her husband, but she herself would also have been a partner in the rule which is now entirely the concern of males. Women are generally disinclined to put up with this burden and they naturally seek to gain what they have lost through sin. If they are unable to do more, they at least indicate their impatience by grumbling. However, they cannot perform the functions of men, teach, rule, etc. In procreation and in feeding and nurturing their offspring they are masters. In this way Eve is punished; but, as I said in the beginning, it is a gladsome punishment if you consider the hope of eternal life and the honor of motherhood which have been left her.[14]

Interestingly, this punishment of subjection happens in relation to men, who for their punishment need to assume the role of a ruler, in order for women's punishment to take place. Much more flexibility is possible here compared to the punishments of the pains of childbirth and mothering, all of which is not optional but implemented in the physical nature of things. The pains of mothering are conditioned by biological fact; whereas the subjection to the other sex requires negotiating, reckoning and accepting. Also, Luther here affirmed the basic relation of the two sexes after the Fall: one is subjected to the other, and the two sexes execute different mastering in different domains. Luther takes the opportunity to argue theologically, from original sin, why women cannot be preachers or teachers but should happily pursue their God-given ordinance and calling: that of motherhood. While explaining the afflictions of the Fall and the difficulty of bearing painful childbirth and subjection to men, Luther has a major point of comfort to offer: the glory of motherhood is so great and

---

[14] "At si Heua in veritate stetisset, non solum non subiecta imperio masculorum est. Sunt autem foeminae fere huius oneris impatientes et naturaliter affectant, quod per peccatum amiserunt. At sum plus non possunt, saltem impatientiam murmure ostendunt. Hoc tamen non possunt, ut administrant virilia official, ut doceant, ut regant etc. Procreandae, aleandae et fovendae sobolis magistrae sunt. Ad hunc modum Heua punitur, Sed, ut initio dixi, est poena laeta, si respicias ad spem aeternae vitae et gloria maternitatis relictam." (Gen. 3:16; WA 42:151,152; LW 1:203.)

important that it should make it all worth it! He offered this pep talk more than once.

The glory and the hope attached to motherhood, with the divine promise of eternal life to the woman who sinned, was Luther's focus in explaining Eve's grave sin for which she was gravely punished – more than Adam (*peccatum graviter punitus est*). He found many positive things to say about Eve and the daughters of Eve because of his insights into God's grace on the one hand, and his fascination with the physical and spiritual aspects of motherhood on the other. Consistent with his theology of incarnation and redemption, he recognized divine glory in the act of human life beginning in a woman's womb – an emphasis not without significance.

Eve's created and lost equality

It is not surprising that Luther stressed the value of childbirth when explaining the effects of the Fall. This merely follows logically from his explanation of the creation of woman. Luther talks about God's definite plan to create a woman[15] as a partner in procreation.[16] After the sin, the loveliest and attractive Eve[17] received an added role to be the antidote against the sin of fornication.[18] One way or the other, Luther seemed to explain women's existence, at least to a degree, from sex/sexuality and procreation, which is not exactly uplifting for women who would like to see other reasons for their existence.

The Fall changed many things. Without sin, the divinely ordered marriage of Eve and Adam would have continued in the state of original blessedness, exemplified in the innocence and

---

[15] Gen 2:19; WA 42:90.

[16] Gen 2:20; WA 42:91.

[17] Gen 1:26, WA 42:50.

[18] "Magnum autem beneficium est, quod Deus nobis quasi invitis et nolentibus servavit mulierem tum ad generationem tum etiam ad medicinam contra peccatum fornicationis" (Gen 2:18; WA 42:89.) See also Blaisdell, "The Matrix of Reform: Women in the Lutheran and Calvinist Movements," 16-17; LW 1:198, 293. Sermon on Marriage LW 44:8-10.

glory of nakedness[19] but this was changed by the Fall. Deforma-tion, hideous lust and shameful sex replaced original innocence.[20] The *praestantissima parte corporis nostris* became tainted, the *genitalium Gloria* was turned into *summam ignominiam.*[21] Here Luther shared Augustine's tragic embarrassment with human sexuality and its unfortunate association with sin. What remained the same, however, was the glory of motherhood, even if tainted with sin and pain and affliction in its "execution."[22] Eve remained the mother of all the living.[23]

It is interesting that when pointing out Eve's sin, Luther did not make much of Eve disobeying her husband and his authority.[24] Rather, he reminded readers of the fact that in the original blessedness there was no subjection but that Adam and Eve were equal, while different. But how equal and how different exactly? Here Luther left room for ambiguity. On the one hand, in Genesis 1 and 3 Luther gathered evidence for how Adam and Eve were created in the image and similitude of God, with good will and sound reason,[25] and equality in righteousness.[26] On the other hand, already in that perfect nature Eve was already different from Adam. Eve was similar in respect to the *imago Dei* but was never

---

[19] WA 42:106,107; LW 1:142.

[20] Hendrix, Scott Luther. "On Marriage." *Lutheran Quarterly,* 14 (2000) 335-50; Karant-Nunn, Susan and Merry Wiesner-Hanks, *Luther on Women* (Cambridge: Cambridge University Press, 2003) Also Luther, Sermon on Marriage, LW 44:7-10; Ozment, Steven, *When Fathers Ruled: Family Life in Reformation Europe* (Cambridge, Mass.: Harvard University Press, 1983) 1-50. Also LW 36:2, 92-96; LW 45:13-15; LW 1:138; 2:23-24.

[21] WA 42:126; LW 1:168. "Post peccatum lepra libidinis hanc corposis partem invasit."

[22] Gen. 3:16; WA 42:149, 150; LW 1:200.

[23] Gen 3:19,20; WA 42:163,164; LW 1:219.

[24] LW 1:144.

[25] Gen 3:1; LW 1:141.

[26] "Ac quamvis Heua fuerit praetantissima creture, similes Adae, quod ad imaginem Dei attinet, hoc est, ad iusticiam, sapientiam et salutem, tamen fuit mulier" (Gen 3:1; WA 42:113, 114; LW 1:151).

fully equal in prestige to the male.[27] Luther speaks of Eve being weaker in nature, *mulieribus tanquam infirmiori vasi suum*,[28] and created with different members. Satan attacked Eve as the weaker creature. Luther compared Adam and Eve to the sun and the moon, with the sun being more excellent and Adam being stronger in nature, while both being equally righteous.[29]

Luther left much room for ambiguity in his explanation of the equality of the two sexes, but if there is consistency, it is as follows: The man and the woman were created equal in God's eyes; yet, one stronger and one weaker in nature. The weaker in nature sinned first; both were punished, though in different measure. The promise of mercy rested on the promise made to the weaker party, Eve. Luther's primary concerns here were not gender-relations or gender issues, but how to demonstrate God's mercy through the events of the first sin, to highlight the power of God's promise, and to highlight in the actions of Adam and Eve what sin is ultimately about – and, on the side, to argue for the glory of motherhood and procreation

The punishment: The struggle of the two sexes

This is how Luther explained the relationship between men and women after the Fall: "The woman bears hers on her own body when she suffers distress in her function as child-bearer, although the penalty is bearable, and the husband bears his penalty in the management of the household, when with difficulty and hard work he exercises authority in the home and supports his family."[30] Adam, because he listened to Eve, was also punished. Part of Eve's punishment, through marriage, would be transferred to her husband who is obviously not immune to the pain he sees.[31]

---

[27] Gen 1:27; WA 42:51,52; LW 1:69.

[28] Gen 3:16; WA 42:150.

[29] Gen 1:27; WA 42:51,52. Gen 3:1; WA 42:113, 114, 115.

[30] "Sicut igitur Mulier peccati poenam, sed profecto tolerabilem in corpore suo fert, dum affligitur in officio pariendi, Ita Maritus fert poenam in Oeconomia, dum cum difficultate et molesto labore gubernat domum et alit familiam." (Gen 3:17,18,19; WA 42:153,205; LW 1:205.)

[31] Gen 3:16; WA 42:149,150; LW 1:200.

Also, Adam would feel the punishment when the earth became cursed and by the sweat of his brow he would eat his bread. Moreover, and more specifically, as a result of the sin, man would struggle with lust and the burdens that come with being the ruler:

> The husband has a raging lust kindled by the poison of Satan in his body, without pain. But his position is burdened with a definite punishment, since it is the husband's duty to support his family, to rule, to direct, and to instruct; and these things cannot be done without extraordinary trouble and very great effort. On the woman obedience to her husband was imposed, but how difficult it is to bring this very condition about![32]

Very difficult indeed, if the other partner resents it, as Luther assumed was the case.

Adam's punishment, Luther explained, had two dimensions also: Adam would be burdened by two things: raging lust on the one hand, and labor and difficulty in ruling the world, (including his family), on the other. As with Eve, Adam's punishments are felt and acted out in relation to the other sex. Luther seemed to be aware of the ways sin(s) are manifest in human relations. Therefore, every human person can relate, even if we do not necessarily agree with his exact conclusions.

Luther acknowledged the difficulty for both men and women in maintaining the imposed affliction of female subjection to the male sex. There is a certain negativity in the relationship, with similarities to the enmity (*inimicia*) between the snake and Eve.[33] Adam and Eve are both set into conflict with the enemy, the snake, to which God is an enemy. The seed to overcome this enmity will be born from a woman, the seed that will crush the serpent.[34]

---

[32] "Itaque in marito est furens libido accensa veneno Satanae in corpore sine dolore. Sed officium certa poena gravatur, quod, cum Viri sit alere familiam, regere, gubernare, docere, illa sine singulari molestia et maximis laboribus non potest perficere. Mulieri impositum est, ut pareat Marito, sed quam difficulter hoc impsum obtineri potest?" (Gen. 3:16,17,18; WA 42:151,152; LW1:203.)

[33] Gen. 3:15; WA 42:139; LW 1:186-187.

[34] Here Luther points out a mistake in the Vulgate, arguing that the original text does not talk about the Virgin Mary as the "she" who

Luther explained that the enmity between the woman and the serpent was an encouragement about the hope of restoration.[35] The first couple was comforted in the knowledge that God does not curse Adam and Eve as God curses the serpent, and that the seed will be born to crush the serpent, and guilt will be forgiven.[36] But there is no promise that the enmity between a man and a woman will be resolved, is there? To Luther, this war of sexes originated from sin and is not what God intended. This said, if the fruits of original sin which plagues human life are to be conquered in this life with the means provided by the saving act of Christ, could one expect that gender relations should stand at the very heart of that restoration?

Eve and the Word of God – transgression and promise

In his Genesis commentary, Luther did not blame women for excessive disorderly lust, not even when explaining the fall of Eve, which he explains rather as an intentional turning away from the right teacher and right law – as unbelief. Eve sinned when she turned away from the Word;[37] Eve committed idolatry,[38] "The pitiable woman"[39] allowed herself to be persuaded, after resisting the temptation at first.[40]

Not seeing any trace of disorderly lust in the first woman and her disobedience sets Luther apart from the legions of Church Fathers who have seen Eve as the epitome of lust and, thus, the seducer of the first man, a curse carried by all women to come.[41]

---

crushes the head, as Lyra et al propose, but "you" refers to "woman" in general.

[35] WA 42:143, 144; LW 1:192.

[36] Gen 3:15; WA 42:142; LW 1:190.

[37] Gen. 3:4, 5; LW 1:159.

[38] Gen 3:1; LW 1:149.

[39] Gen 3:5; WA 42:116,117; LW 1:155.

[40] WA 42:106,107; LW 1:150,154,147.

[41] There is an interesting connection here to Luther's explanation of Tamar's sin, where he downplays the role of lust and desire and looks for reasons for the woman's fall from her will and calculated reasoning to seek motherhood at all cost – a desire that pardons her sin – and he sees

Luther thought that arguments explaining Eve's sin as a sin of lust are absurd. He ridicules those who would make Eve the lower part of reason, even if she was inferior to her husband.[42] Here again, Luther stands apart from a long tradition of teachers who deemed females as lusty creatures inferior to higher, rational men. He is not, necessarily, repeating the sexist dichotomous misogynist theories about dangerous female sexuality and women's thirsty wombs seeking to drain the males (as was speculated by theologians puzzled by sexuality alone, not to mention women). He at least made an effort to separate sin and sex and argues for the irrelevance of gender in terms of what constitutes a sin – while explaining how sin takes place in gendered relations.[43]

It is important to notice that Luther did not want to see Eve take all the guilt for the Fall: the guilt is shared. Adam was not only deceived by a woman but – first and foremost – was deceived by himself.[44] Also significant is that Eve's very capability for sinning – not with her lust but with her reason – implied that she has equal gifts and capacities for reasoning and choosing.

Luther recognized Eve's sin as grave, but he does not dwell upon it. Rather, he took an opportunity to illustrate through Eve what sin ultimately is: unbelief.[45] Sin is turning from faith to unbelief.[46] With Eve, Luther pointed out the wonders of God's

---

Judah rather as a slave to lust; Judah's lust originates from the punishment of the original sin, the raging lust placed in man's body. See Gen 38 and WA 44:312-332; LW 7:14-30. See Stjerna, Kirsi, "Grief, Glory and Grace: Insights on Eve and Tamar in Luther's Genesis Commentary," *Seminary Ridge Review* 6/2 (Spring 2004) 19-35.

[42] Gen 3:14; WA 42:137,138,139; LW 1:184,185.

[43] "Deinde in eo quoque absurditas est, quod Heuam interpretatur inferiorem partem rationis, cum constet, Heuam in nulla parte, hoc est, neque corpore neque anima inferiorem fuisse martio Adamo." (Gen. 3:14; LW 42:138,139; LW 1:185.)

[44] Gen 3:13; WA 42:136; LW 1:182.

[45] Gen 3:6; WA 42:121,122; LW 1:162.

[46] Gen 3:3,4,5; WA 42:116,117; LW 1:155. "Vere enim fons omnis peccati est incredulitas et dubitate, cum a verbo discreditur...discamus initium peccati originali fuisse hanc tentationem Diaboli, cum a verbo Dei abduxit Heuam ad Idolatrum." (WA 42:112.)

grace to sinners, emphasizing God's promise to Eve, the promise that from her seed would come the one to crush the serpent. The fact that God still speaks to Eve and Adam after the sin, testifies of the measure of God's grace.[47] In Luther's conclusion the promise that the first sinner would become the mother of all the living and the receiver of the promise of forgiveness for all humankind also speaks of God's grace. Luther's perspective on human life as *simul iustus et peccator* also shaped his view of the ambiguities of Eve's life: she is the bearer of punishments for the first sin as well as the bearer of the promise of redemption. Eve's story becomes the story of God's grace – Luther's favorite topic – and might we say, of a person justified with her inevitable sin. Also, Eve's story demonstrates the power and effectiveness of God's word and promise[48] – which is central to Luther's theology and spirituality – the Word makes all the difference, even with the woman who sins against God.

With Eve, Luther argued for the holiness of motherhood and the divine promises attached to that, something that continues even after the Fall, albeit with added afflictions. While explaining the punishment aspects of childbirth and mothering, Luther preaches the continuing glory of motherhood.[49] Eve, the first sinner, becomes for Luther the epitome of God's grace as the mother of all the living,[50] and her name becomes the joyous omen: *nomen Heuae laetum omen est vitae.*[51] Eve and her daughters embody concrete aspects of God's gracious acts in human life, through motherhood.[52]

It is interesting that it is in her motherhood, as the bearer of the promise in her body, that Eve can act even as a teacher – in the

---

[47] Gen 3:13; WA 42:135; LW 1:181.

[48] Gen 3:23, 24; WA 42:179,171; LW 1:229. Gen 3:15; WA 42:143,144; LW 1:192. Similar emphasis can be seen in Luther's interpretation on Tamar's sin and seeking for motherhood at all means.

[49] Gen 3:16; WA 42:148.

[50] Gen 3:19,20; WA 42:163,164; LW 1:219.

[51] Gen 3:21; WA 42:165; LW 1:221.

[52] "Christum nascendum in hunc mundum de Foemina et liberaturum humanum genus." (Gen 3:15; WA 42:145.)

role forbidden to women. She acts in that role when she roses to comfort her husband after the great Fall.[53] After the Fall, sad but with a heart full of hope, Eve comforted Adam: "I have sinned. But see what a merciful God we have. How many privileges, both temporal and spiritual, He is leaving for us sinners! Therefore, we women should bear the hardship and wretchedness of conceiving, of giving birth, and of obeying you husbands."[54] If only it were that simple.

III. Motherhood and the Domestication of Protestant Women

A few words about the Protestant glorification of motherhood are in order before concluding Luther's words on Eve. Clearly, Luther esteemed motherhood highly as one of the holiest of vocations. His observations on his wife fulfilling her call as a spouse and mother of six biological children (along with several adopted children) helped him to appreciate the demands of the domestic call; so much so that he granted a "doctorate" to his wife, "Doctorissa" Katie Luther. She excelled in her pioneering role as one of the first Protestant clergy wives and parsonage matrons. Luther appreciated her gifts and leadership in the domestic arena but nevertheless did not see it appropriate for her, or other women, to embrace duties of teaching and ministering or other such public roles; the honorable realm for women would be that of the home. With her marriage to Luther in 1525, Katie, an ex-nun, embraced the newly sanctified call as a mother and a spouse. She never pursued another public role, such as that of a teacher or a preacher.

---

[53] "Heua sine dubio in re tristissima, ut apparet, tamen gaudio pleumim pectus habuit ac fortasse Adamum suum consolata..." (Gen. 3:16; WA 42:148.)

[54] "Peccavi. Sed vide, quam misericordem habemus Deum? Quanta commoda tum temporalia tum spiritualia nobis peccatoribus reliquit? Quare nos Mulieres feramus laborem et miseriam istam concipiendi, pariendi et vobis Maritis parendi." (Gen 3:16; WA 42:148.)

In many ways, she was a typical sixteenth-century Lutheran mother with either no other interests or no other real options.[55]

Recent Reformation studies have paid attention to this theological justification for the "domestication" of women, something Katie so utterly exemplified. With its re-sacralization of marriage and domestic calls – seeing them equally important to other calls, which in itself is a very positive change of view – the Reformation, with its theologically argued domestication of women and exclusion from leadership roles beyond the home, actually did not improve women's lot any more than it caused regression. Some studies focus on the positive results of this and caution against projecting unfair and unreasonable expectations on the Reformers in terms of gender equality.[56] Safely one can conclude that whereas the Reformation sanctified one role for women, that of motherhood, it took away other important religious options, such as the roles of a nun, mystic, prophet, teacher, preacher, depriving women of a particular voice within the churchly hierarchy where male superiority and authority were both argued theoretically and applied in practice. No glorification of motherhood could compensate for this. At the same time, the stunning lack of protest from most women's part may speak of a satisfaction and expectations that do not necessarily resonate with those of women today.[57] "New" theology and spiritual models offered for most

---

[55] Stjerna, Kirsi, "Katie Luther: A Mirror of the Promises and Failures of the Reformation," in *Caritas et Reformatio: Essays on Church and Society in Honor of Carter Lindberg,* ed. David M. Whitford (St. Louis: Concordia Press, 2002) 27-39.

[56] Ozment, Steven, *Ancestors, The Loving Family in Old Europe* (Cambridge, Mass.: Harvard University Press, 2001); Roper, Lyndal, *Holy Household, Women and Morals in Reformation Augsburg* (Oxford: Clarendon Press, 1989).

[57] See Conrad, Anne and C. Gritschke, "In Christo ist weder man noch weyb," in *Frauen in der Zeit der Reformation und der katholischen Reform* (Münster: Aschendorff, 1999); Blaisdell, Charmarie Jenkins, "The Matrix of Reform, 13-44; Marshall, Sherrin, ed., *Women in Reformation and Counter-Reformation Europe: Public and Private Worlds* (Indiana: Indiana University Press, 1989); Ranft, Patricia, *Women and Spiritual Equality in Christian Tradition.* (New York: St. Martin's Press, 1988); Wiesner-Hanks, Merry, *Convents Confronting Reforma-*

women something positive that was worth giving a try, it seems. Issues of equality were not really even on the radar screen among women as a group, while individual women have expressed visions for that or assumed that as a given – of the latter, Marie Dentiere, Argula von Grumbach, Jeanne d'Albret and Katherine Schütz Zell stand out as exceptionally articulate and forthcoming women with no inferiority complex and with serious expectations of equality. Luther, even if unaware of the ramifications of his gender teachings, contributed to the growing concern for equality.

Charmarie Jenkins Blaisdell summarizes the very well concerning Luther's view on women's and men's equality:

> Scholars generally agree that Luther as well as Calvin was traditional in his views on women. He views women as creatures inferior to men, subject to impulse, governed by emotion, incapable of profound thought, vain, gossipy, and unsuited for responsibility beyond the home. His attitudes toward women were influenced by his own marriage and family life and later, after he became a public figure, by his acquaintance with women from a wide variety of backgrounds. While he treated women with respect, he never overcame his conviction that women had limited abilities and should be subject to man. Because of Eve's sin men and women are not totally equal.[58]

Even with the affirmation of justification by faith and the priesthood of all believers, Luther "believed women were not to teach or preach in church." At the same time, "Luther acknowledged women's spiritual equality with men – an equality which the Roman Church never denied but, on the other hand, never emphasized because of Eve."[59]

---

tion: Catholic and Protestant Nuns in Germany (Marquette: Marquette University Press, 1999).

[58] Blaisdell, "The Matrix of Reform,"15, 14.

[59] Ibid., 15. See LW 31:333-377, 345, 351; LW 36:192-196; LW 44:123-217; also LW 40:388-90 "This equality was a logical outcome of justification by faith and what came to be referred to as the 'priesthood of all believers.' This latter idea was not so much a belief in the individual's ability to intercede directly with God as it was acceptance of the

Does this mean that Luther was a misogynist? No. As Blaisdell says, "Luther liked women and acknowledged that men were extremely dependent on them in many spheres of life."[60] If he recognized any rights for women, it was their right to bear children. He failed to see the beauty and blessedness and right of not having children (that was beyond his understanding of the design of creation). Women's other rights were not his primary, or even secondary concern, which is of interest because "it is clear that Luther based his views as much on practical experience in his marriage with Katherine von Bora as on Scriptural exegesis."[61] We can understand how his exegetical work was influenced by the "social, economic, political, and religious assumptions and prejudices" of his time.[62] But what is more puzzling is the Katie influence in this matter. It may well be that Luther's statements about what women could and should do tell us as much about Katie's ambitions or lack of them as Luther's own thought. Certain issues of ours may not have been issues for Katie, who was not shy in expressing her own expectations.

Luther clearly had a major role to play in women's domestication and exclusion from public ministry in the Reformation. At the same time, however, as his interpretation of Eve shows, his theology holds a seed for gender emancipation that did not come to its fruition in Luther time. In all, Luther's at times progressive and at times blatantly patriarchal sexist statements regarding

---

importance of members of the church community teaching and supporting each other in the ways of the Christian life. Women were included in this task; although following St. Paul, Luther believed they were not to teach or preach in church." Blaisdell 15.

[60] Blaisdell, "The Matrix of Reform," 19. It needs to be noted that not all the utterances of Luther, such as the ones recorded in the "Tabletalks" are to be taken with equal value and meaning. See Wiesner and Karant-Nun for a colorful collection of excerpts from Luther's writings about women, *Luther on Women*, ed. Susan Karant-Nunn and Merry Wiesner-Hanks (Cambridge; Cambridge University Press, 2003).

[61] Blaisdell, "The Matrix of Reform," 19, footnote 28. Tabletalk LW 54:7-8 no. 49; 54:222-23 no. 3528; 54:444 no. 5524; 54:160-61, no. 1658.

[62] Blaisdell, "The Matrix of Reform," 14.

women demonstrate the ambiguity of the issue Reformation and gender.[63]

Conclusion

Looking at what Luther said about Eve and other women in the Old Testament, we could say that Luther's notion of gender relations is simple yet complex, with some remaining ambiguities. He is quite consistently a "medieval man" in explaining the division of duties between the two sexes, while he emerges as a "modern man" when asserting women's roles and duties as equal in value to those of men. He is most "fresh" when writing about the sacredness of motherhood and its theological (especially Christological) implications. His notion of motherhood and its crucial role in the history of salvation is inherently linked with his notions of the Incarnation, vocation, and holiness of life. In these areas, he is quite inclusive and visionary. Again, his experiences as a father and a spouse most certainly have shaped his insights here. From his encounters and correspondence with other women, Luther must have known that, regardless of the apparent lack of protest from the majority of his contemporary women, quite a few women had high hopes of spiritual equality and inclusion in church and theology as a result of the new reading of the gospel. Some assumed certain authority and liberties in their own places. Did Luther perhaps want to close his eyes to issues with which he did not want to be bothered or for which might be held culpable?

It is worth noticing that when discussing Eve in Genesis, Luther is interested in theology and right preaching of the gospel, not in the social implications of his theology. He failed to see the realm of theology and gospel broadly enough to include some of the basic human concerns; his interests and priorities are limited in that regard. He is interested in explaining issues he saw as theologically important, such as: creation, sin, redemption. He was

---

[63] See Sermon on the Estate of Marriage LW 44:7-14; The Estate of Marriage LW 45:17-49; Babylonian Captivity LW 36:92-106; Lectures on Genesis LW 1; and Table Talk LW 54. See Roper, Lyndal, *The Holy Household: Women and Moral in Reformation Augsburg* (Oxford: Oxford University Press, 1989;1991).

not interested in gender analysis or arguing for women's liberation and transformed gender relations. At the same time, he is trying to make sense of gender relations theologically (perhaps unaware of what he is actually doing), as he studied at Genesis for directives for daily life and order. With his assumption of the "equality yet difference" of the two sexes, Luther argued for the importance of ordered male-female relations and for the value and equality of women's and men's worlds; what differences he saw, he did not understand as qualitative but as functional.

Regarding women's lives in the time of Reformation, some changes occurred – positive and negative – as a result of Luther's teachings. While we cannot hoist him as an endorser of "women's liberation," must also remember his passion for liberation of the conscience, of men and of women. Further, we cannot simply blame him for his role in the continued sexism and subjection of women in the Reformation church and society. Whether Luther attempted to do gender-neutral theology (not possible), or gender-oblivious theology (often a mask for exclusivist theology), while trying to make sense of gender in his own limited ways, he followed laudable instincts arising from his fresh reading of the gospel as well as personal experiences with women. Nevertheless, he was not ready for or interested in changing the times' notions around gender; he could not see the limits of the very framework that shaped his thinking. This became clear from his inability to interpret all the biblical passages about women with the same gospel-given liberties he took when interpreting many of the other obviously time-bound restrictions that in his view clashed with the liberating spirit of the gospel. His own time-bound anthropology and limitations in the face of the complexity of the gender issue prevented him from bringing to fruition the emancipatory potential of the gospel, a potential dormant in his central theological insights and principles of biblical interpretation.

There is certain undermining logic in Luther's reflection that overrides inconsistencies. In offering a theological interpretation of the roots for gender and gender relations he read in the Bible and he witnessed in his real life, his ultimate concern and explanation turned out to be about one thing that has little if anything to do with human-made gender constructions: what God has done and is doing for humankind, things beyond our comprehension, through outrageous and incredible acts through many human lives, including sins of many kind, women's sins even – and the mystery of motherhood. We are challenged enough by Luther's searching to continue his work of trying to understand what it means to be a man and a woman, to pay more attention to the theological promise coming from both genders and the theological value of motherhood and womanhood, and to see God's presence in the physicality and humanness and the opposite of our expectations. Drawing into the conversation voices of the daughters of Eve who have experienced and encountered the divine in their own bodies and experiences is an enterprise, I believe, Luther would find ever so fascinating. Especially if it shed yet new light into the mystery of motherhood; a topic for which he had a soft spot in his heart.

God's Court Jester on the Masks of God: A Theatrical Metaphor in Luther's Exegesis

Tibor Fabiny, *Budapest*

1. Luther's Significance in Exegesis and Hermeneutics

Recent Luther scholarship has demonstrated that Luther became a reformer through his exegesis and hermeneutics. Though his great historical achievement was the Reformation, he was, nevertheless, primarily a doctor, a professor of theology at the University of Wittenberg. Far from being a systematic theologian, he was a biblical exegete. It has been suggested that if Luther had belonged to a modern theological faculty today, he would have been the professor of Old Testament exegesis.[1]

One of the key-issues in hermeneutics is the question of the literal sense. In his early career Luther practiced the medieval *Quadriga* (the idea that canonical Scripture can be read with four "senses:" the literal, the allegorical, the moral/tropological, and the anagogical/eschatological). Though he never entirely abandoned allegory for homiletical purposes the literal meaning was basically the only meaning for Luther. Even here, however, a further distinction is to be made: Luther's interest was not exclusively in the *sensus litteralis* (as in the case of Nycolas of Lyra and the rabbinic exegesis), but in the *sensus litteralis propheticus*. Therefore, his interpretation of the Psalms (and other texts of the Hebrew scriptures) was throughout christological. James Samuel Preus suggested that Luther's hermeneutical divide was no longer between the Old Testament as "letter and law" on the other hand,

---

[1] The suggestion of Heinrich Bornkamm in *Luther, und das Alte Testament* (Tubingen, 1948) quoted by Jaroslav Pelikan, *Luther the Expositor, Luther's Works,* Companion Volume. (Saint Louis: Concordia Publishing House, 1959) p. 46.

and the New Testament as "Spirit and Gospel" on the other hand. Instead, he found this divide was already within the Old Testament itself: the Old Testament, he recognized, contained both promises and laws from the very beginning. In this sense, could he speak about the Old Testament as a great "testimony" to Christ. The believer, therefore, had to read the Old Testament with Christ in his mind, *was Christum treibet*. This evangelical *hilaritas* leads us to appreciate the dramatic nature of his exegesis and theology.

2. The Dramatic Nature of Luther's Exegesis and Theology

I would argue that there was a dramatic aspect in Luther's exegesis. Eric W. Gritsch has shown us that Luther's self-image in his address *To the Nobility of the German Nation* was that of a court-jester" *(Hofnarr)* [2] and that Luther appears:

> to have worn his heart on his sleeve, tipping his cap to the troubled consciences of common folk, ringing his bells to warn the mighty in both church and world of God's unyielding power, and tapping his feet to the tune of the gospel's cheering and chilling news of Christ's lordship in a world nearing its end. [3]

Indeed, Luther seems to have radically appropriated and even enacted St. Paul's paradox concerning wisdom and foolishness especially in his *theologia crucis,* to which we shall return.

As Gritsch pointed out, Luther's originality lies also in his use of humor as a tool for interpreting Scripture. He frequently used dramatic terms in his theology, such as: "game," "laughter," "theater," "disguise," and "hiding." In 1532, Luther lectured on the "laughter of God" in Psalm 2, suggesting that God's laughter was a way of hiding his wrath from the stupidities of humanity. This should teach us to laugh at our enemies in times of suffering and anxiety: "Then it will come about that we shall laugh at the fury of the Turk, the popes, tyrants, sects, heretics, and all the

---

[2] Eric W. Gritsch, *Martin – God's Court Jester. Luther in Retrospect,* Ramsey, NJ, Sigler Press, 1991 p.33

[3] ibid p.viii

adversaries of Christ's kingdom, as a comical spectacle."[4] In Luther's non-dogmatic dramatic theology, "comedy and tragedy," "laughter and weeping," "concealment and revelation," and "hiddenness and recognition" are in a complementary relationship with each other. Gritsch quotes Niebuhr who said that: "Humor is, in fact, a prelude to faith; and laughter is the beginning of prayer."[5]

3. The Various Masks of God

Luther never failed to emphasize the difference between the revealed and the hidden God (*deus revelatus* and *deus absconditus*). The real God (*deus per se*) or the naked God (*deus nudus*) is never identical with what we experience of him either in his revelation or his hiddenness. Luther frequently mentions (following St. Paul, 1Cor 4:9) that Christians have become a "spectacle" for the world (*theatron to kosmo*). In this *theatrum mundi*, where Satan and his angels disguise themselves as angels of light (2Cor 11:14) and the Pope and the hypocrite clergy pose as representatives of God, it is necessary for God also to hide himself under various masks.

Luther says: "When God reveals Himself to us, it is necessary for Him to do so through some such veil or wrapper and to say: 'Look! Under this wrapper you will be sure to take hold of Me.'" (LW,15) One of his favorite quote is from Isaiah 45:15: "Truly, thou art a God who hidest thyself," and concerning this passage he says "For under the curse a blessing lies hidden; under the consciousness of sin, righteousness; under death, life; and under affliction, comfort." (LW 4,7) The following reflects the various masks of God Luther believed God employed.

---

[4] Quoted by Eric W. Gritsch, „Luther's Humor as a Tool for Interpreting Scripture" in, Mark S. Burrows and Paul Rorem (eds.) *Biblical Hermeneutics in Historical Perspective Studies in Honor of Karl fried Froehlich on His Sixtieth Birthday* Grand Rapids, William B. Eerdmans, 1991, p.188

[5] Quoted by Gritsch, „Luther's Humor as a Tool for Interpreting Scripture", p.187

a. The Mask of Creation

Luther also spoke about creation and history as the face or mask of God (*larva dei*): "Now the whole creation is a face or mask of God. But here we need the wisdom that distinguishes God from His mask. The world does not have this wisdom. Therefore it cannot distinguish God from His mask." (LW 26, 94)

b. The Mask of Secular Rulers

For Luther, God governs this world by secular rulers and authorities: "those masks of judges, magistrates, teachers, doctors, and lawyers are necessary … it is God's will that under these masks you should serve His ordinance and man's need ….Without these masks peace and discipline could not be preserved." The whole world is a *Mummenschanz,* a masquerade, and while a "masked God may frighten others, Christians know that behind every divine mask there is a gracious God."[6]

c. The Mask of Human Achievements

God hides himself not only beneath human, worldly powers (LW 9,41) but also beneath human achievement of which humans are never meant to boast: "He should regard all such preparation and equipment as being the work of our Lord God under a mask, as it were, beneath which he himself alone effects and accomplishes what we desire." (LW 45,331), and again "He uses our effort as a mask under which He blesses us" (LW 9,96)

d. The Mask of His Word

God hides himself also in his very word. With his promises as masks he protects humans being from the absolute, naked God. Concerning Psalm 51, Luther warned the reader not to interpret them as the words of the absolute (i.e., naked) God. David is "speaking with God as He is dressed and clothed in His Word and promises, so that from the name 'God' we cannot exclude Christ …We must take hold of this God, not naked but clothed and revealed in His Word; otherwise certain despair will crush us. This

---

[6] Gritsch, *Court Jester,* p.191 and p.258, cf. LW 26,95

God, clothed in such ... in such a pleasant mask... this God we can grasp and look at with joy and trust.... Satan is busy day and night, making us run to the naked God so that we forget His promises ..." (LW 12,312)

e. The Strange Mask of Joseph as the Strange Mask of God

One of Luther's favorite biblical heroes was Joseph. Joseph was sold by his bothers and, through much sufferings and afflictions, he rose to the court of the Pharaoh, "God allows Joseph to be crucified, hurled in prison" (LW 8, 30). Still, Joseph trusted in God, "For he saw God's back and waited until God should reveal and show forth His salvation" (LW 7,103). This Joseph, who had been tortured both by his brothers and his God, concealed his identity from his brothers when they come to Egypt. Instead of vengeance he, as Luther remarks, played a "very pleasant delightful game" by hiding a cup in his younger brother Benjamin's sack (LW 7, 237). The brothers are afflicted just as he was tortured and tried by God, "At the end of the trial, however, they see the greatest goodwill and love. 'Ah, how friendly our brother Joseph meant to be to us!'" (LW 7, 237). For Luther, Joseph thus becomes a God-figure: "After our liberation we have the same feeling about God, who allows us to be tried and afflicted in order that we may prove what His good and pleasing will is (Rom. 12:2)." (LW 7, 237) Joseph acted in a strange ways with his brothers, just as God also acts in a strange ways with afflicted humanity, "He afflicts us with evils and misfortunes of every kind." (LW 7,237) Job in his sufferings also accuses God with lying. It is not God, however, but we who are the liars, says Luther: "For we hide our sins; we do not want to be guilty of the sins we have perpetrated ....God plays with us and says: 'Because you are well pleased with your hypocrisy, flatter yourself, and dream that you are cleansed of every sin, I will disclose to you and show you what kind of person you are in My sight and will remove from you that mask of smugness and hypocrisy.'" (LW 7, 237)

Thus, Joseph played the *deus absconditus* with his brothers; he tortured them to make them repent. His brothers are frightened; they think they are confronted with the devil. But at the end in the recognition scene he reveals that "I am your brother Joseph" just as God reveals his true self and true work (*opus proprium*) after his "strange acts" (*opus alienum*). Joseph, just as God, revealed his mercy and love for his brothers in an indirect way.

f. God Wearing the Mask of Satan

If the world is a huge masquerade where both God and Satan wear masks to hide themselves, then the greatest problem for the believer is to discern God under the mask. Commenting on Isaiah 45:9, Luther remarked:

> The children of God have all the afflictions. The ungodly children of Satan enjoy the highest state of well-being. Everything seems the opposite of what it should be. The godly are maltreated, the ungodly receive gifts. In this vein the flesh blasphemes the work of God. So today we see our word and God's Word to be futile, everything seems exactly the opposite of what it should be, and then we see God's work to be unjust. So God and Satan weary us with masks and external spirits so that we are led to believe that what is of God is Satan and what is Satan is of God, and then we say in our heart, 'I wish I had never been born.' (LW 17,127)

Likewise, commenting on Galatians 5:11 Luther again remarks:

> Thus God wears the mask of the devil, and the devil wears the mask of God; God wants to be recognized under the mask of the devil, and He wants the devil to be condemned under the mask of God. (LW 27,43)

God hides himself in the mask of his opposite. The culmination of God's hiddenness, according to Luther, is on the cross where the glory and the beauty of God is hidden in ugliness.

g. Christ Wearing the Mask of a Worm

The Son of Man becomes a worm on the cross, as Christ makes reference to Psalm 22. This worm, says Luther in his commentary on Psalm 8:4 "is mocked, spit upon, scourged, crowned, and crucified .... His appearance was so marred, beyond human semblance, and His form beyond that of the sons of men. He had no form or comeliness that we should look at Him, and no beauty that we should desire Him. He was despised and rejected by men." (LW 12, 123) In his exegesis of John 3(vs. 15), Luther identified this worm with the brazen serpent of Moses:

This signifies that Jesus Christ, God's Son, born of a virgin, became like us condemned people and hung on the cross like a poisonous, evil, and harmful worm. Yes, He resembles the serpent which got us into trouble in Paradise, that is, the devil. He was so despised, condemned, and rejected by the world that He was finally sentenced to an ignominious death and hanged as an arch villain among the murderers . . . . He was not regarded as a godly person but as a venomous worm unworthy of having the sun shine onto Him, as a menace to the entire world. Such was the low esteem in which the world held Him, and His Christians today share this with Him. (LW 22. 340)

As a result, then, true Christians are also seen as disgusting, venomous worms by the world: "Paul declared that we are looked upon as the most obnoxious and venomous worms, which mislead and pollute the whole world, as καθάρματα and περιψήματα, the most damnable and the most infectious people, the world's curse and purgatory." (LW 22,340)

Reflecting on Luther's words here, Kenneth Hagen says "The meaning of Christ as worm on the cross carried the connotations of Christ being abject, the object of contempt, forsaken, nauseating, abominable, rotten stench, scandal, offensive or, simply, rotting worm."[7] The most horrible mask of the God's Son is that of the worm.

We know, however, that this was not the end of the story. We can speak about the resurrection of the worm (i.e., Christ) and therefore, the hope of our own resurrection. Commenting on the Genesis story of Sarah's death Luther remarks: "it has pleased God to raise up from worms, from corruption, from the earth, which is totally putrid and full of stench, a body more beautiful than any flower, than balsam, than the sun itself and the stars." (LW 4,190) To the unbelievers of this world, Christ appearance is that of a worm. But to the believer, only this worm (which has

---

[7] Kenneth Hagen, „The Testament of a Worm: Luther on Testament and Covenant", *Consensus* 8 (1982) p.19

emerged from the cocoon of the grave a most beautiful butterfly) can save us from perdition and heal us from our terminal disease.

h. The Mask on the Cross (Luther on Galatians 3:13)

Luther also used the image of the Cross as a mask in his exegesis of Galatians 3:13 ("Christ redeemed us from the curse of the law, having become a curse for us – for it is written 'cursed be every one who hangs on a tree"). Jesus took upon himself the mask of the sinful men: "Christ was to become the greatest thief, murderer, adulterer, robber, desecrator, blasphemer, etc., there has ever been anywhere in the world. He is not acting in His own Person now. Now He is not the Son of God, born of the Virgin. But He is a sinner, who has and bears the sin of Paul, the former blasphemer, persecutor, and assaulter; of Peter, who denied Christ; of David, who was an adulterer and a murderer." (LW 26,277) However, says Luther, we should rejoice because Christ took upon himself the sins of all mankind and thus became the greatest sinner (*maximus peccator, peccator peccatorum*); this is "the joyous of all doctrine" and the source of most comfort:[8]

By this fortunate exchange with us He took upon Himself our sinful person and granted us His innocent and victorious Person. Clothed and dressed in this, we are freed from the curse of the Law, because Christ Himself voluntarily became a curse for us, saying: 'For My own Person of humanity and divinity I am blessed, and I am in need of nothing whatever. But I shall empty Myself (Phil. 2:7); I shall assume your clothing and mask; and in this I shall walk about and suffer death, in order to set you free from death.' Therefore when, inside our mask, He was carrying the sin of the whole world, He was captured, He suffered, He was crucified, He died; and for us He became a curse. But because He was a divine and eternal Person, it was impossible for death to hold Him. Therefore He arose from death on the third day, and now He lives eternally; nor can sin, death, and our mask be found

---

[8] This has also been suggested by Finnish Luther research. See: Tuomo Mannerma, *Christ Present in Faith. Luther's View of Justification*, Minneapolis, Fortress Press, 2005, p.15

in Him any longer; but there is sheer righteousness, life, and eternal blessing. (LW 26,287)

4. Luther's Theology of the Cross

The theatrical metaphor, the idea of the mask, and the notion of revelation by concealment are not accidental images for Luther. Rather, they form a coherent theology which scholars have come to call *theologia crucis*, the theology of the cross. What is then, the subject matter of the theology of the cross? Against many misunderstandings and misconceptions Gerhard O. Forde says that "It is a particular perception of the world and our destiny, what Luther came to call looking at all things through suffering and the cross."[9] He says that "it is so radical and deep for its time that it is still vital for our time,"[10] this is a story that "claims us"[11] and wants us to become theologians of the cross,[12] it teaches us "to say what the thing is," and "to call a spade a spade."[13]

Luther first formulated his theology of the cross during the Heidelberg Disputation (1518). He called his theses "theological paradoxes," which was the reformers' new way of forming arguments against the traditional syllogism of scholastic theologians. The central notion, the great divide between the way of glory and the way of the cross, is described in theses 19-21 of the *Heidelberg Disputation*:

19) The man who looks upon the invisible things of God as they are perceived in created things does not deserve to be theologian (*Non ille dignus theologus dicitur, qui invisibilia Dei per ea, quae facta sunt, intellecta conscipit*).

---

[9] Gerhard O. Forde, *On Being a Theologian of the Cross. Reflections on Luther's Heidelberg Disputation, 1518,* Grand Rapids, William B. Eerdmans, 1997, p. xii

[10] ibid

[11] ibid p.9

[12] ibid p.4

[13] ibid.p.13

20) The man who perceives the visible rearward parts of God as seen is suffering and the cross does, however, deserve to be called a theologian (*Sed qui visibilia et posteriora Dei per passiones et crucem conspecta intelligit*).

21) The theologian of glory calls evil good and good evil. The theologian of the cross says what a thing is.[14]

The theology of glory wishes, with human achievement and free will, "to see through" the cross in order to find, by speculation, a "transcendent meaning" (virtue, wisdom, goodness etc.) and contemplate the invisible greatness of God. Luther asserted, however, that "peering into 'invisible things of God' only 'puffs up, blinds and hardens.'"[15] The cross, however, teaches us to see differently: the cross is not transparent, we cannot look behind it; it is a mirror and we are forced to gaze upon it. We cannot explain the cross; nevertheless we must preach the cross. The theology of the cross reveals that things are not what they seem; it makes us recognize that there is a crucial discrepancy between appearance and reality. According to the theology of the cross, it is the cross that reverses our way of seeing. Only by faith is it revealed that God concealed himself in the form of its opposite: in the shame of the cross. The cross cuts down the wisdom of the wise, the vision of the theologian of the glory. It is only through suffering and the cross that we can come to know God. Only through this suffering can we learn what things really are, that the spade is a spade.

The idea is that "God's revelation can take place in the form of opposites, *sub contrario*. God does his alien and wrathful work before he does his proper and loving work; he makes alive by killing, brings to heaven by going through hell, brings forth mercy out of wrath."[16] The alien work is the *opus alienum* and the loving

---

[14] The English translation of theses 19-20 is given on the basis of McGrath, *Luther's Theology of the Cross,* Oxford, Basil Blackwell, 1985, p.148.and the thesis 21 on the basis of Forde's *On Being a Theologian of the Cross,* p.71. The translation of „posteriora" has caused the same conflict in the English translation as in the Hungarian one (Magyar Luther Füzetek 8. p.28)

[15] Forde, *On Being a Theologian of the Cross,* p.77

[16] ibid.p.31

work is the *opus proprium*. In Isaiah 28:21 it is called "the strange work" and "the strange act" of God. It is God who assaults and inflicts us; he causes the terrors of temptation, the *Anfechtungen*. In Forde's words: "Knowledge of God comes when God happens to us."[17] Luther even goes so far as to suggest that God, in his alien work, becomes a devil for us before becoming God for us: "God cannot be God unless He first becomes a devil. All that God speaks and does the devil has to speak and do first."[18]

Alister MacGrath mentions five marks[19] of the theology of the cross: 1) *theologia crucis* is a theology of revelation rather than a theology of speculation 2) This revelation must be regarded as indirect and concealed 3) This revelation is to be recognized in the sufferings of the cross of Christ 4) This knowledge of God who is hidden in his revelation is a matter of faith 5) God is particularly known through sufferings, he makes himself known through sufferings. God is the source of *Anfechtung,* he assaults man in order to break him down and thus to save him. It is significant that God is hidden and the *Deus absconditus* hides his mercy under his wrath.

Conclusion

Luther's *theologia crucis* is a frequently discussed *topos* in Luther studies. Eric W. Gritsch has even extended this term to Luther's ecclesiology when he spoke of "A Cruciform Church" in the tenth chapter of his *Court Jester*. Gritsch's always creative, witty, and even dramaturgically-sensitive approach has inspired the author of the present article to identify the mask as a crucial theatrical metaphor in Luther's exegesis. Martin Luther and Eric W. Gritsch have taught us that imagination, metaphor and humor give rise to theology.

---

[17] Forde, *On Being a Theologian of the Cross*, p.90

[18] ibid p.90 cf. LW 14,31

[19] Alister McGrath, *Luther's Theology of the Cross*, Oxford, Basil Blackwell, 1985. p.149-151

PART II

Martin Luther: Teacher of Faith Today

The Role and Image of Martin Luther in the Formation of the Lutheran Church

Robert Kolb, *Concordia Seminary (St. Louis)*

"Court jester," Martin Luther's playful designation for himself that Eric Gritsch has used to illuminate the reformer's career and thought with great insight,[1] is but one of a host of designations visited upon the bold but humble monk turned professor from Wittenberg. In his career of less than thirty years as public spokesman for the reform of Christendom, Luther significantly changed the Western church and the cultures of Europe. He was not only dubbed "court jester" but also much more, and his name was graced with both accolades and abuse.

As a professor at a recently-founded university, which had not yet earned a reputation of any kind, Luther had an impact unique in the annals of Christendom. In polls taken in several countries in the year 2000 he was ranked among the "ten most influential" figures of the second Christian millennium. Germans voted him the second most important person in their history in a contest sponsored by a television network in 2004. On a much more significant level, his writings have been deemed important enough to win recent translations into Spanish[2] and Portuguese[3] in Latin

---

[1] Luther used the term describing himself in his "To the Christian Nobility of the German Nation," 1520, *D. Martin Luthers Werke* (Weimar: Böhlau, 1883- 1993 [henceforth WA]), 6:404,24-25, *Luther's Works* (Saint Louis/Philadelphia: Concordia/Fortress, 1958-1986 [henceforth LW]), 44:123. See Eric Gritsch, *Martin – God's Court Jester. Luther in Retrospect* (1983; Ramsey, NJ: Sigler, 1990).

[2] *Obras de Martino Luthero*, ed Carlos Wittos et al. (Buenos Aires: Editorial Paidós, 1967-1985), ten volumes.

[3] *Martino Luthero, obras Selecionadas* (São Leopoldo: Editoria Sinodal, and Proto Alegre: Concordia Editora, 1987-2000), seven volumes.

America, into Japanese,[4] Korean,[5] and Chinese[6] in Asia. Even if some churches in historical Lutheran lands in Europe are retreating from the label "Lutheran," others, especially across the southern hemisphere, are confidently assuming ecclesiastical and theological leadership under the banner of his name.

Lutheran churches may be classified in four categories: established churches in the historic homelands of the Lutheran confession in Europe; minority churches in Europe, especially those oft-persecuted churches which suffered at the hands of the eastern European early modern Counter-Reformation and the twentieth century dictatorships of National and International Socialism; the immigrant churches of the Americas, South Africa, and Australia; and the mission churches of the two-thirds world. All of these churches are posing questions regarding their identity as heirs of the Wittenberg Reformation and wrestling with elements of their specific ecumenical tasks as Evangelical Lutheran witnesses to the gospel of Jesus Christ in the twenty-first century. Therefore, the question of the role of Luther in the formation and continuing life of the Lutheran church burns anew. As has been the case throughout Lutheran history,[7] the role of Luther and the reading of Luther will be different in different Lutheran churches of the twenty-first century, to be sure. Nonetheless, the question assigned for this essay is for all of them a practical question but one with deep historical roots.

---

[4] (Tokyo: Seibun-Sha, 1963ff.), ten volumes.

[5] Edited by Won Yong Ji (Seoul: Concordia, 1981-1989), twelve volumes.

[6] Edited by Peter Li and Lei Yutian (Sanlian Publishing Company, 2003ff.), two volumes of a projected fifteen have already appeared.

[7] Cf. the study of Carl Axel Aurelius, "Luther in Sweden," *Word & World* 18 (1998): 299-306, which demonstrates much less conscious use of Luther's image in Sweden in the early modern and modern period than was the case in Germany and elsewhere, as shown in studies listed in note 20 below.

Defining the Church through Confessing the Faith

In the sixteenth century members of Luther's Wittenberg circle decided to define their own project, and their own nature as the church of Jesus Christ, through public confession of the faith. At Augsburg in 1530 Philip Melanchthon, Luther's colleague and companion in reform, decided that the term and the activity "confession" offered the appropriate vehicle for exercising the most important purpose of Christ's people, the proclamation of the Word of God, which delivers salvation to sinners by creating faith in Jesus Christ.[8] If the reform movements of the sixteenth century were indeed re-forming Western churches and cultures by "Christianizing" or "Rechristianizing" them, as Scott Hendrix argues,[9] the Church in Luther's and Melanchthon's understanding had to be drawn away from its medieval ritualistic foundations and formed anew around God's Word in its oral, written, and sacramental forms.

Because of this, in the final official expression of Lutheran identity of the sixteenth century, the Formula of Concord of 1577, the focus fell on the Word of God rather than on the person whom its authors regarded as a prophetic proclaimer of that Word, their mentor and instructor, Martin Luther. The Formula was first published in the Book of Concord of 1580, along with the other documents of confession which the Lutheran churches accepted as their secondary authority for public teaching. It served as their "body of doctrine," a term that the Wittenberg theologians had come to use as a designation for the *analogia fidei* and then for the collection of documents in which this rule of faith, a summary of biblical teaching, might be found.[10] The preface of the Book of Concord did call attention to the fact that its content represented the message of "that highly enlightened and pious man, Dr. Martin

---

[8] Robert Kolb, *Confessing the Faith, Reformers Define the Church, 1530-1580* (Saint Louis: Concordia, 1991), esp. 13-62.

[9] Scott H. Hendrix, *Recultivating the Vineyard, The Reformation Agendas of Christianization* (Louisville: Westminster, John Knox, 2004), especially 148-174.

[10] See the study of the term in Irene Dingel, "Melanchthon und die Normierung des Bekenntnisses," in *Der Theologe Melanchthon*, Günter Frank, ed. (Stuttgart: Thorbecke, 2000), 195-211.

Luther." It made it clear that those who defined their church in terms of what was contained in the Formula of Concord and the Book of Concord wished "nothing more than that our churches and schools might have been kept in the teaching of God's Word and in loving Christian unity and, under the guidance of God's Word, might have been established and transmitted in a wholesome, Christian manner – just as during the lifetime of Dr. Luther . . . ."[11] The authors of the Formula acknowledged that they were confessing the faith which had been "purified and elucidated anew on the basis of God's Word by Dr. Luther."[12] Indeed, they believed that the written symbols that they claimed as summaries of the Biblical message were "a summary and model of the teaching that Dr. Luther of blessed memory had thoroughly set forth in his writings, on the basis of God's Word"[13] even though, apart from the ancient creeds, only three, the catechisms and the Smalcald Articles, came from Luther's pen. (Three came from Melanchthon's hand [the Augsburg Confession, the Apology, and the Treatise on the Power and Primacy of the Pope], and one was composed by their students or disciples [the Formula of Concord]). Nonetheless, when Lutheran churches defined themselves through this book, not Luther as a person or the whole corpus of his writings exercised adjudicatory authority over their teaching. The specific documents mentioned were chosen to do so. The earlier documents – the ancient creeds, and those written by Luther and Melanchthon – were being joined to their Formula of Concord as the public delineation of what it meant to be Lutheran. Luther's role and function in the definition of the Lutheran church, in the eyes of the Concordists, stood behind or at the basis of their characterization of who they were. One could say Luther provided the frame for their definition. But so great as his informal influence may have been, he and his writings in general did not

---

[11] Book of Concord, Preface, §4 and 6, *Die Bekenntnisschriften der evangelisch-lutherischen Kirche* (11. ed.; Göttingen: Vandenhoeck & Ruprecht, 1992 [henceforth BSLK]), 3-4, *The Book of Concord*, ed. Robert Kolb and Timothy J. Wengert (Minneapolis: Fortress, 2000), 5-6.

[12] Solid Declaration, Definitive Repetition, §1, BSLK, 829-830, *The Book of Concord*, 524.

[13] Solid Declaration, Concerning the Binding Summary, §9, BSLK, 836-837, *The Book of Concord*, 528.

bear formal authoritative weight for the Lutheran churches even though his witness occupied a special role in their lives.

Luther's Authority

Not all the contemporaries of these authors of the Formula of Concord had agreed. The earliest positive appraisals of Luther had pictured him, according to Robert Scribner, "as monk, as doctor [university instructor], as man of the Bible."[14] Other contemporaries dubbed him a "German Hercules." In the words of his later foe, Ulrich Zwingli, and others, Luther was fulfilling late medieval popular expectations that a "prophet" would come to reform the world.[15] In the following generation many of his own students had regarded him as a national hero of Herculean proportions. Even more regarded him as a teacher of the church, indeed a prophet of God, to whose authority as "our dear master and preceptor, a true instrument of God," the ministerium of Mansfeld county could appeal as a secondary norm or standard for public teaching in disputes over the proper interpretation of the primary authority of Holy Scripture.[16] Upon his death his colleagues in Wittenberg,

---

[14] Robert W. Scribner, *For the Sake of Simple Folk: Popular Propaganda for the German Reformation* (Cambridge: Cambridge University Press, 1981), 15.

[15] Robert Kolb, *Martin Luther as Prophet, Teacher, and Hero. Images of the Reformer, 1520-1620* (Grand Rapids: Baker Books, 1999), 17-33.

[16] *Bedencken das diese Proposition oder Lere nicht nu[e]tz/not/noch war sey/vnnd one ergernis in der Kirchen nicht mo[e]ge geleret werden. Das gute werck zur seligkeit no[e]tig sind. Vnd vnmu[e]glich sey, one gute werck selig werden* (Magdeburg: Lotther, 1553), [Aiiij]^v, [Diiij]^r. On the development of Luther as a citable authority in this era, see Kolb, *Martin Luther as Prophet*, 39-65, and Irene Dingel, "Strukturen der Lutherrezeption am Beispiel einer Lutherzitatensammlung von Joachim Westphal," in: *Kommunikationsstrukturen im europäischen Luthertum der Frühen Neuzeit*, ed. Wolfgang Sommer (Gütersloh: Gütersloher Verlagshaus, 2005), 32-50, idem, "Ablehnung und Aneignung, Die Bewertung der Autorität Martin Luthers in den Auseinandersetzungen um die Konkordienformel," *Zeitschrift für Kirchengeschichte* 105 (1994):35-57, and idem, *Concordia controversa, Die öffentlichen Diskussionen um das lutherische Konkordienwerk am Ende des 16. Jahrhunderts* (Gütersloh: Gütersloher Verlagshaus, 1996), 607-619.

Philip Melanchthon, Justus Jonas, and Johannes Bugenhagen heralded him as the third Elijah, a greater teacher, prophet, apostle, who had restored the gospel to the church.[17] Not long thereafter Anton Otto, pastor in Nordhausen and a former student of the reformer, pleaded with Jonas in dramatic tones to record the life of "our saintly father Luther," a task Jonas in fact did not take upon himself. Otto mentioned that he himself was gathering "table talk" from the reformer's lips so that the world and the church could have more of what had thought and confessed.[18]

But Luther's writings as a whole did not remain a viable option for such a secondary authority within the church. They proved to be too long and thus too cumbersome; too historically conditioned and thus sometimes contradictory; and too much bound to one person and therefore not salutary for the Church's authority structure, based on the ultimate sole authority of Scripture. Official adherence to his complete oeuvre proved to be impractical.[19] Nonetheless, even among the minority within the larger Wittenberg circle who did not accept the Book of Concord, there remained agreement with the judgment of the Concordists that Luther had purified and elucidated the Christian faith anew on the basis of God's Word and that his writings, his teaching, continued to serve as a useful tool in formulating public teaching of the gospel of Christ. All his students and followers in the second-half of the sixteenth century regarded him as a faithful teacher and a model confessor of the biblical message.

Over the following four centuries Luther was anachronistically heralded as a German national hero, as a valiant defender of individual freedom and a forerunner of Enlightened thinking, or as

---

[17] See the summary of the sermons, orations, and hymns written to commemorate Luther's life at the time of his death in Kolb, *Martin Luther*, 34-37.

[18] The letter from Otto to Jonas is dated by Gustav Kawerau 1550; it contains no dating in its own text but must come from this period, see *Der Briefwechsel des Justus Jonas*, ed. Gustav Kawerau, 2 (1885; Hildesheim: Olms, 1964), 300.

[19] Kolb, *Martin Luther as Prophet*, 65-74.

a principal source of modern racial anti-Semitism.[20] None of these views of Luther provide much serviceable or useful help for thinking through the question of how twenty-first century Lutherans can or should turn to the figure whose name they bear or whose confession of the faith they wish to continue.

Luther as Confessor

Nor do all of the positive images of Luther as one who proclaimed the Word of God continue to be serviceable in the early twenty-first century. Some of them reflect the apocalyptic mood of late medieval western Europe, with its longing for the direct intervention of God through a new prophet that would change everything from earth to heaven. As Luther first issued his call for reform, a crisis of pastoral care gripped the Church. Western European society was in turmoil as lands plagued by the Black Death a century and a half earlier were finally rising again to their full stature, able to stand on their own legs once more. Central political authorities were striving to aggrandize their own power and littler people from knights to peasants and artisans were

---

[20] Studies of Luther images beyond the sixteenth century include Horst Stephan, *Luther in den Wandlungen seiner Kirche* (Giessen: Töpelmann, 1907), Heinrich Bornkamm, *Luther im Spiegel der deutschen Geistesgeschichte* (Heidelberg: Quelle & Meyer, 1955), Ernst Walter Zeeden, *Martin Luther und die Reformation im Urteil des deutschen Luthertums, Studien zum Selbstverständnis des lutherischen Protestantismus von Luthers Tode bis zum Beginn der Goethezeit, I. Band: Darstellung, II. Band: Dokumente* (Freiburg/B: Herder, 1952), *Interpreters of Luther, Essays in Honor of Wilhelm Pauck*, ed. Jaroslav Pelikan (Philadelphia: Fortress, 1968); *Luther in der Neuzeit, Wissenschaftliches Symposion des Vereins für Reformationsgeschichte*, ed. Bernd Moeller (Gütersloh: Gerd Mohn, 1983), Ulrich Michael Kremer, "Martin Luther in the Perspective of Historiography," in *Seven-Headed Luther, Essays in Commemoration of a Quincentenary, 1483-1983*, ed. Peter Newman Brooks (Oxford: Clarendon, 1983), 207-229, and Walter Mostert, "Luther, Martin. III. Wirkungsgeschichte," *Theologische Realencyclopädie* 21 (Berlin: de Gruyter, 1991) 567-594. See also the critique of the myth of Luther as a source of modern anti-Semitism by Uwe Siemon-Netto, *The Fabricated Luther, The Rise and Fall of the Shirer Myth* (Saint Louis: Concordia, 1995).

feeling the squeeze. The public mood mixed anxiety and fear with a sense of expectation.[21] In this kind of atmosphere it was inevitable that Luther would be embraced in popular thought as an eschatological figure. Indeed, it should not surprise that many recognized him as the fulfillment of the prophecy of an angel who would come to proclaim the eternal gospel to the peoples of this earth (Rev. 14:6). This association with angel of the Apocalypse began early in his career; in the 1520s his disciple, pastor and mathematician Michael Stiefel, composed a hymn of fifty-two stanzas presenting the reformer as this angel, prophesied in Revelation, and defining his message explicitly as that of the proper distinction of law and gospel.[22]

To be sure, even among Luther's most ardent followers were some who did not interpret the angel of the Apocalypse strictly as a reference to Luther alone but rather put it in the larger context of God's guiding the proclamation of his Word. Matthias Flacius Illyricus (1520-1575), professor in Jena and private scholar (organizer of the great historical project, the *Magdeburg Centuries*, and pioneer in hermeneutics with his *Clavis Scripturae Sacrae*) altered the more prevalent interpretation of Revelation and defined the second angel, described in Revelation 14:8, as those who had perceived the Antichrist (the papacy) for what it was. This included "Luther and others after [John] Huss and [John] Wiclef." They had preached the gospel between the first angel, representing the apostles and their successors (Rev. 14:6), and Flacius's own contemporaries, Luther's heirs (of whom the third

---

[21] While much work has been done on early modern apocalypticism, the study of Will-Erich Peuckert, *Die Grosse Wende,(Band I) das apokalyptische Saeculum und Luther* and *(Band II) Geistesgeschichte und Volkskunde* (Hamburg, 1948), remains a good place to begin, supplemented for later Lutheran history by Robin B. Barnes, *Prophecy and Gnosis, Apocalypticism in the Wake of the Lutheran Reformation.* (Stanford: Stanford University Press, 1988), and Volker Leppin, *Antichrist und Jüngster Tag. Das Profil apokalyptischer Flugschriftenpublizistik im deutschen Luthertum 1548-1618* (Gütersloh: Gütersloher Verlagshaus, 1999).

[22] *Das deutsche Kirchenlied von der ältesten Zeit bis zu Anfang des XVII. Jahrhunderts*, ed. Philipp Wackernagel 3 (Leipzig: Teubner, 1870), 74-79.

angel was a type, Rev. 14:9), who were continuing to teach the truth of Christ.[23] One of those contemporaries, David Chytraeus (1531-1600), professor in Rostock and member of the committee that composed the Formula of Concord, explicated the figures of all three angels as "types of the preachers or pastors of the church." They included "in our era, John Huss, Martin Luther, Philip Melanchthon, and others in other regions, who preach the eternal gospel, or the Word of God which remains forever . . . ."[24] In part, this broadening of the eschatological figure of the angel reflected the experience of these students, who had absorbed much from Melanchthon, Bugenhagen, Jonas, and other teachers, both on the Wittenberg faculty and in other places (Johann Brenz and Urbanus Rhegius were the most prominent among the theologians who influenced the thought of the Wittenberg students). But even more, the broader interpretation of this prophetic figure indicates that the focus of their understanding of the Reformation of the church lay in the proclamation of the gospel of Christ.

Even though not all his own students restricted the application of the angel of the Apocalypse to Luther, this way of depicting Luther did not vanish. A generation after Flacius and Chytraeus the Saxon court preacher of early Lutheran Orthodoxy Matthias Hoe von Hoenneg (1580-1645) preached five sermons in Dresden in 1604 in which he explicated Luther's contributions to Christendom on the basis of the angel of the Apocalypse in that passage, albeit with a host of other characterizations as well, such as "God's chosen, precious instrument," "the genuine apostle of Christian Germany," and "the prophet of God."[25] The theme of

---

[23] Flacius, ˜*Novvm testamentvm Iesv Christi filii Dei . . . Glossa compendaria* (Basil: Peter Perna and Theobald Dietrich, 1570), 1367. On Flacius' use and interpretation of Luther, see Irene Dingel, "Flacius als Schüler Luthers und Melanchthons," in *Vestigia pietatis, Studien zur Geschichte der Frömmigkeit in Thüringen und Sachsen. Festschrift für Ernst Koch*, ed. Gerhard Graf, Hans-Peter Hasse et al. (Herbergen der Christenheit: Sonderband 4; Leipzig, 2000), 77-93.

[24] Chytraeus, *Explicatio Apocalypsis Ioannis perspicva et brevis* (Wittenberg: Johannes Crato, 1564), 285.

[25] Hoe, *Christliches Geburt vnd Lobgeda[e]chtnis/ Des Hocherleuchten/ Thewren/ Werthen Mannes Gottes/ Herren D. Martini Lvtheri seeliger/ der Christenheit getrewen Apostels vnd Euangelisten. . . . In fu[e]nff*

Luther as prophet and apostle for the German nation, the teacher and confessor of the faith as the end of the world approached, permeated Hoe's appraisal of the Wittenberg professor's work and calling.[26] Hoe amplified his identification of Luther as the angel of the Apocalypse in his commentary on Revelation, first published in 1610.[27] He believed that God had made Luther a key figure in his plan for the spread and realization of his kingdom in the world.

Hoe inherited this view of Luther from many in the previous generation, those who had still experienced him as instructor and preacher. Andreas Musculus (1514-1581), professor in Frankfurt an der Oder and an author of the Formula of Concord, composed a *Compendium of Christian Doctrine Collected from Holy Scripture, the Holy Fathers of the Church, and the Holy Luther*. In this work he emphasized that "our German prophet Luther" cleansed the Church and in the clearest possible way proclaimed the distinctions between works and faith, law and gospel, Moses and Christ, the righteousness of the flesh and that which comes from God . . . ."[28] Musculus compared his teacher in Wittenberg to Elijah, certain that, although Elijah did not return in Luther's flesh, Luther did assume the same function and he did fulfill the same prophetic calling or office as Elijah and John the Baptist. "For since the time of the apostles no greater man has lived or come to

---

Predigten gehalten . . .(Leipzig: Henning Groß, 1604), esp. 1a, 23b; cf. Hoe's defense of Luther against alleged misrepresentation in the work of the Bremen Calvinist Johannes Lampadius: *Pro beato Lvthero, Avgvstana Confessione, et veritate historica Adversus Iohannis Lampadii . . . Apologia maximé necessaria* (Leipzig: Abraham Lamberg, 1611).

[26] E.g., see also Hoe's *Orthodoxa natalitia domini Ac Salvatoris nostri Iesu Christi. Item. Memoriam Anniversariam Beatissimi viri D. D. Martini Lvtheri Reformatoris Germaniae Contra Sacramentarios / Papistas* . . . (Wittenberg: Zacharias Lehmann, 1605), esp. 1, 28-38, but passim.

[27] I have used the edition, *Commentariorum in Beati Apostoli et Evangelistae Discipuli Christi encolpaei, Johannis Apocalypsin* . . . . (Leipzig and Frankfurt/M: The heirs of the Schürer brothers and Johannes Fritzsch, 1571), 503, 520-529, 537-542.

[28] Musculus, *Compendivm doctrinae Christianae collectvm. S. Scriptura, Ex S. Ecclesiae Patribus, S. Luthero* (Frankfurt/Oder: Johannes Eichorn, 1573), A2b.

earth, who has been granted so many great and unsurpassed gifts from God as Luther."[29] Musculus rehearsed a series of points of comparison which demonstrated how his own teacher had functioned as a prophetic successor of Elijah.[30]

Another of Luther's own students, Cyriakus Spangenberg, long-time pastor in Mansfeld county, son of one of Luther's earliest disciples, Johann Spangenberg, shared this widely-held Wittenberg perception that Luther had followed in Elijah's train. The younger Spangenberg preached a series of sermons on Luther, two per year, over nearly a decade, the 1560s, on Luther's birthday and deathday, analyzing and praising Luther's roles as confessor and proclaimer of the Word of God. In a study of these sermons Wolfgang Hermann expressed his regret that these sermons do not "present any of his personal impressions of Luther." Instead, Hermann rather superficially read the sermons as mere hagiography, in which the reformer is presented as an artificial figure of such mythical proportions that he appears as no more than a stereotypical part of a chain of warriors, "who finally is distinct from everything human."[31]

In fact, however, Spangenberg did offer hearers and readers his real impressions, gained from conversations at the reformer's table and from lecture hall and worship service. Preaching on "the great prophet of God, Dr. Martin Luther, that he was a true Elijah," on February 18, 1564, Spangenberg recalled, "Everyone who heard him knows what kind of man Luther was when he preached or when he lectured at the university. Shortly before his death he lectured on and interpreted Genesis. What sheer genius, life, and power he had! What he could only say! That brings me to consider that all my days I have experienced nothing more inspiring. For when I heard his lectures, it was as if I were hearing an angel of the Lord . . . . Luther

---

[29] Musculus, *Von des Teufels Tyranney/ Macht vnd Gewalt/ Sonderlich in diesen letzten tagen/ vnterrichtung* (Erfurt: Georg Baumann, 1561), A2b-A5a, republished in *Teufelbücher in Auswahl*, ed. Ria Stambaugh, 4 (Berlin: De Gruyter, 1978), 191-194.

[30] *Von des Teufels Tyranney*, A4a-A8r, *Teufelbücher in Auswahl* 4:192-195.

[31] Wolfgang Herrmann, "Die Lutherpredigten des Cyriacus Spangenberg," *Mansfelder Blätter* 39 (1934/1935): 59.

had a great command of Scripture and sensed its proper meaning at every point. Dear God, there was a huge gift of being able to properly interpret the Scripture in that man."[32] As exaggerated as such an estimation sounds in twenty-first century ears, it conveys a genuine impression, one gained during the five years he studied in Wittenberg while his mentor still lived. Spangenberg continued, "I do not disdain the fine gifts of God in other teachers, but I must say that Luther was above them all, an extraordinary man sent by God. He knew how to bring out the meaning of passages that others passed over and left uninterpreted, and he knew how to speak of matters in a way that people could understand. . . . No one ever treated and unfolded the distinction of law and gospel so clearly and plainly as Doctor Luther."[33]

Precisely the reformer's teaching on law and gospel and his hermeneutical principle of the distinction of these two forms of God's Word headed the list of contributions made by Luther which Spangenberg offered readers in the preface to the entire series of his sermons published in 1589. Luther had given the church a clear exposition of the proper significance of the law and of its functioning, and therefore of what sin really is. Luther had taught the gospel with the proper interpretation of God's grace and a genuine understanding of Christ and the righteousness he gives. Thirdly, he demonstrated how to practice the distinction of these two forms of God's Word, law and gospel. As Spangenberg expanded the list of the gifts God had given his church in the person of Martin Luther, the Mansfeld preacher focused largely on matters pertaining to the Word of God and its application to the daily life of the believer. Luther had taught the proper understanding and use of the sacramental forms of God's Word. He had shown people how to live the life of good works properly. His affirmation of God's callings in

---

[32] Spangenberg, *Theander Lutherus. Von des werthen Gottes Manne Doctor Martin Luthers Geistlicher Haushaltung vnd Ritterschafft: Auch seinem Propheten: Apostel: vnd Euangelisten Ampt. Wie Er der Dritte Helias: Andere Paulus: vnd rechter Johannes: Der fu[e]rtrefflichste Theologus: Der Engel Apocal:14. Ein bestendiger Zeuge: Weisslicher Pilgram: Vnd trewer Priester: Auch ein nu[e]tzlicher Arbeiter/ auff vnsers HERRN Gottes Geistlichem Berge gewesen. Alles in Ein vnd Zwantzig Predigten verfasset* (Ursel: Nicolaus Heinrich, 1589), 70a-b.

[33] Ibid., 70b.

secular government and in family and economic life and his encouragement of education for the general population helped Christian society return to a God-pleasing way of life. His exposition of all the articles of faith was flawless. He had fostered good instruction for children and adults through his catechism and had brought the church to song through his hymns. He had restored proper worship in his reform of the liturgy and proper life of the church through his visitation of the church and the establishment of responsible agencies to govern its life. He had translated the Bible into the German language with a clarity not found in other translations. His life of public witness provided a model for opposing false teachers, and he had brought freedom from papal oppression. His prayer life was also exemplary.[34] Furthermore, Spangenberg treated the pastoral side of Luther's person and ministry in some detail, sketching for hearers and readers his role as *Seelsorger* or curate of souls.[35] According to Ernst Walter Zeeden, this pastoral aspect of the reformer's life provided the focus for the biographical sermons preached at approximately the same time as Spangenberg began his series by Johannes Mathesius (1504-1565), pastor in Joachimsthal, who had also lived in Luther's home and heard his lectures.[36]

Two other passages from Spangenberg's sermons summarize the heart of his estimation of his mentor, focusing on what the professor himself regarded as the heart of his own life and the center of the biblical message, the person and work of Christ. "In all his writings

---

[34] Ibid., A3b-B4a.

[35] Ibid., e.g., 17b-18a.

[36] Zeeden, *Martin Luther*, 1:37. Cf. my comments on this judgment, Kolb, *Martin Luther*, 88-89, with arguments for the depiction as prophet as the central motif of Mathesius' sermons; whether my opinion is correct or not, Zeeden's observation does capture an important element of Mathesius' understanding of his mentor and of the understanding of Luther held by many contemporaries. See also Hans Volz, *Die Lutherpredigten des Johannes Mathesius: Kritische Untersuchung zur Geschichtsschreibung im Zeitalter der Reformation.* (Halle: Waisenhaus, 1929) and the treatment of Mathesius and the role of music in Joachimsthal by Christopher Boyd Brown, *Singing the Gospel. Lutheran Hymns and the Success of the Reformation* (Cambridge: Harvard University Press, 2005).

Luther stressed nothing more zealously and did not seek to do anything else than to preach the Lord Jesus Christ to troubled hearts and to bestow him, to offer his promises and to give assurance to those hearts regarding who he is, what he has done and suffered for us, and make that well known for us. He strove only to teach the true, one gospel, the joyous message of the forgiveness of sins in Christ Jesus."[37] As the angel of the Apocalypse Luther had confessed to the end of his life that "Christ Jesus alone is our way, ladder, bridge, and path, our light and lamp, our protector and guardian, our prince who accompanies us, our Lord and master, in whom we should see all and trust, follow him and hearken to him, honor, love, and fear him, and await from him protection, comfort, help, shelter, and liberation. He often said, 'I, Dr. Luther, want to know no other God than alone the one who has hung on the cross, Jesus Christ, Son of God and Son of the Virgin Mary.' He also said, 'Our only comfort, that we believe on Christ, lets us hold him fast alone. I want to remain by him and want him to bury me. I have been baptized in him. I can do anything else and know nothing else than what that Man has taught me. Apart from Christ no one can find comfort, counsel, or help, but in him is pure comfort and complete joy, in the setting of faith, in the Word, for the highest article of our Christian faith is Christ . . . ."[38] Luther wanted to see Jesus only; he wished only to confess him as Savior and Lord.

Seeing Jesus only led Spangenberg to define what it meant to be a disciple of the Wittenberg reformer. For both disciple and teacher theology was a practical matter. Spangenberg sketched Luther's expectations of preachers and teachers in the following words: they should "not only preach in a general way to the congregation but they should so bring what they are teaching and present it, and devote all their energy, to bringing each listener to be able to take from the sermon what will serve him best and be useful to him." For "Luther often emphasized when he reminded hears or readers of his writings and taught and admonished them how everyone of them should apply the teaching and examples in

---

[37] *Theander Lutherus*, 130a.

[38] *Theander Lutherus*, 168a-b.

Scripture to their own lives, make it their own, useful in their own walk of life."[39]

Neither Spangenberg nor Luther imagined that this kind of conveying of God's Word is an easy matter. Both understood the sinful world eschatologically. Believers are involved in a fight between God and Satan, between truth and deception, between faithfulness to God and betrayal of Creator and creation through sin. Nonetheless, the student, like his professor, was of good cheer in the face of evil's attack. In his sermon on the "spiritual knighthood of this faithful Servant of Jesus Christ,"[40] Spangenberg employed an image frequently used for stalwart believers in the Middle Ages, and set forth Luther's simple faith as a prescription for his followers. "A true Lutheran should know that everything belongs to God and all rests in his hands. We should strive and suffer, but stand alone on God and know that the weapons of our battle are powerful in God. Therefore we should stand firm and rest easy, and say, 'I will not give in' . . . . These matters are to be placed upon God alone."[41]

Martin Luther, a Man for this Season

Many of the reasons which Lutherans have found to celebrate the person and work of Martin Luther in earlier eras have vanished in the twenty-first century. He has no significance as a German cultural hero outside the German-speaking lands. Heralding him as a forerunner of the peculiar concepts of human freedom venerated in contemporary democratic capitalism was always a false reading of his history. If Luther remains important for Lutheran churches and the whole household of faith in the twenty-first century, it is

---

[39] Ibid., 311b.

[40] This image had shaped Spangenberg's father's concept of the Christian life, as he set it forth in his tract, *Vom Christlichen Ritter Mit was Feinden er kempffen mus/ Ein kurtzer vnterricht aus der heiligen Schrifft* (Wittenberg: Georg Rhau, 1541), edited and translated in *A Booklet of Comfort for the Sick, and On the Christian Knight By Johann Spangenberg*, ed. Robert Kolb (Milwaukee: Marquette University Press, scheduled for release 2006).

[41] Ibid., 32b.

as a teacher and confessor, a model for the content of proclamation and the method of practicing theology.

Luther and his colleagues in Wittenberg, as well as their students and disciples, practiced theology in a manner quite distinct from the scholastic method of their predecessors. This "via Wittebergensis" also differed significantly from the adaptation of this scholastic method prevalent among some of these students' contemporaries and certainly put to use by their successors. The Wittenberg method of theology presumed that the task of theology is to lay the groundwork for the proclamation of God's Word to call sinners to repentance and to console troubled hearts and comfort torn and tattered consciences.[42] It presumes that the task of the theologian is to provide the care of the Shepherd for his sheep. This method intends to search the Scriptures as the source of true human life and to convey its message to people caught in every form of evil, separation from God, and rebellion against him, and to give them life through the power that God has placed in his Word.[43] Practicing theology according to this method presumes the ability to distinguish God's Word that kills sinners, his law, from his Word that restores them to true life and genuine humanity through the work of Christ and the restoration of human trust in God, the gospel. Bringing God's Word in this manner to people not only gives them information. It changes their lives and the framework of reality within which they live.

This method can be put to use in cultures that do not share Luther's personal convictions regarding human guilt. It has the ability to engage and address of every form of evil which casts its entrapping web over human beings. It comes to those trapped in each form of alienation from the Creator of life and from genuine human life itself with a message from outside their ability to know. This is the message of God in Jesus Christ, the Creator reclaiming his chosen people through the work of his own

---

[42] In this regard, Gerhard O. Forde, though without reference to sixteenth century practice, captured much of this method in his *Theology is for Proclamation* (Minneapolis: Fortress, 1990).

[43] I have attempted to show how this method functioned in *Bound Will, Election, and Wittenberg Theological Method From Martin Luther to the Formula of Concord* (Grand Rapids: Eerdmans, 2005).

incarnation in Jesus and his death and resurrection as his Holy Spirit re-creates their relationship with their God, the relationship that stands at the heart of our humanity. The message of new life in Christ has always made its entry into new cultures as a foreign language, a communication from outside the domain of every culture, but it is at the same time a message which makes itself at home with God's children from every people and land.

The content of Luther's theology cannot be separated from its method. Its content must indeed be translated not only linguistically but also culturally, but this content serves as a most suitable agenda for the proclamation of the church of Jesus Christ around the world in the twenty-first century. The discussions that have been set in motion by the *Joint Declaration on the Doctrine of Justification* may prove ultimately to be more important than those that led to this agreement between the Lutheran World Federation and the Roman Catholic church.[44] Whatever the case at the level of inter-confessional ecumenical exchange, Lutherans will continue to search for the best ways to convey in their own cultures the message that God restores humanity at its heart, its trust in him, re-established by the Holy Spirit on the basis of the work of Christ, through his Word of restoration that forgives as it bestows life and salvation. However the dilemma of human life is expressed in any culture, this Word that cuts through the evils of life to restore the human relationship to God is a message for this time, and one that Lutherans are especially well prepared to formulate anew for new societal definitions of evil. This search for what Luther called human righteousness and we more likely dub our individual identity ought not take place without the benefit of the reformer's insight into human righteousness, that is, what makes a human being truly human. His distinction between active and passive righteousness, between the human performance that results from the gift of our identity as children of God and that gift itself, is a key to bringing his insights to the whole church in every part of the world. This anthropological foundation for Luther's treatment of human life also contains his concept of human

---

[44] See Richard J. Schenk, "The Unsettled German Discussions of Justification: Abiding Differences and Ecumenical Blessings," *Dialog* 44 (2005): 152-163.

freedom – it is significant that his first formal treatise on justification is entitled *The Freedom of a Christian* – and of the reality of human limitations and bondage. These insights assist those wresting with what it means to be human in every society.

Luther's anthropological presupposition for discussing the doctrine of justification must be set alongside Luther's fundamental definition of who God is. Both the full Trinitarian theology that permeates his works and the focus on Jesus only as Lord and Savior provide critical help in bringing peace and joy to the people of every land and culture at the beginning of the twenty-first century. Luther was at home in God's creation, and he believed that God was at home in his creation, too. That is why he treasured God's use of selected elements of his created order to be instruments of his carrying out his saving will. Probably because of his Ockhamist training, Luther saw the great divide in reality between the person of the Creator and all his creation, not between the spiritual and the material. Therefore, he believed that God does use human language and sacramental elements, as he came to humankind incarnate as the God-man Jesus the Messiah, as his means for bestowing his grace upon sinners. Lutherans are called to convey to others in the household of faith this particular insight – not unique but rarely put to use in Christian churches – as a part of the evangelistic confession, the ecumenical conversation, and the edificatory care of God's people in our time.

On the basis of his distinction of passive and active righteousness and the distinction of law and gospel, Luther was able to recognize that God has designed human life for living in two realms, two dimensions. His insights into the dynamics of the life of faith are often celebrated, but his dynamics into the way human beings are summoned by God to fulfill his commands and practice the uprightness he designed for human life within the structure of vocations or callings in home, occupation, society, and congregation provide every culture with a pattern for thinking about life and the ethics that informs our way of living. At least in Europe, Australia, and North America, the critical questions that give Christians entrée into the lives of others and the crucial dilemmas that fellow believers pose often revolve around the decisions of everyday life. Luther's understanding of its structure and its design at the hands of the Creator provide a firm basis and framework for beginning conversations with such people.

In opening his chapter on Luther's "Christocentric theology" in *Court Jester*, Gritsch commented on Luther's observation that "true theology is practical, and its foundation is Christ,"[45] Theology is practical when it is related to the reality of life – with its struggles, suffering, joys, and frustrations – for, realistically seen, life is overshadowed by one's continual desire to be in charge, to dominate, 'to be like God.' The way of the serpent always seems more attractive than the way of Christ; the sin of pride is stronger than love of neighbor . . . . Good biblical theology, Luther contended, will always have to insist on the centrality of 'Christ crucified.'[46]

Here Gritsch points the way to an understanding of Martin Luther that makes his insights practical because they are biblical and Christ-centered. The churches that bear his name are called to continue to give witness to the historic biblical faith through this kind of proclamation of the Word of God.

---

[45] WA Tischreden 1:72,16-19, #153, LW 54:22.
[46] Gritsch, *Court Jester*, 164-165, 168.

Doctor communis? The ecumenical significance of Martin Luther's Theology

Eero Huovinen, *Bishop emeritus of Helsinki*

Introduction

Two modes of thinking converge in Professor Eric W. Gritsch, and this has made him a respected figure across national and denominational boundaries. On the one hand, Prof. Gritsch is an academic theologian in the highest and truest meaning of the word. Many students and teachers have been able to rely upon his most trustworthy and well-documented research, in the New as well as in the Old World. A good example of this is his rather new study on the history of Lutheranism.[1] On the other hand, he is a Lutheran theologian who has given strong support to the spirituality of the Lutheran churches. That is how I recall him on the Board of the Institute for Ecumenical Research, Strasbourg, where we sat together for six years. That is how he is appreciated in Finland as well.

The theology of Martin Luther has been the core of the re-search work of Prof. Gritsch. Therefore, I desire to honor Eric Gritsch by asking what the significance of Martin Luther and his theology is for our day. On the basis of Luther's *Small Catechism* and his doctrine of Holy Communion, I will attempt some answers as I proceed along this quest. Before doing that it is necessary, nonetheless, to briefly recall the history of Luther studies and to enquire what ecumenical significance has previously been afforded Luther.

---

[1] Eric W. Gritsch, *A History of Lutheranism*, Minneapolis 2002.

Martin Luther as ecumenical "problem"

In the Fifth Assembly of the Lutheran World Federation at Evian, France (1970), Cardinal Jan Willebrands applied the classic Roman Catholic title of *doctor communis* to Martin Luther. Cardinal Willebrands referred to the well-known principle of Luther that justification is the doctrine upon which the church stands or falls. In speaking of this matter, Luther can also be a "common teacher" for the Roman Catholic Church, because Luther desires that "God will remain our Lord and that our most important human response is unconditional trust and respect for God."[2]

The title Cardinal Willebrands used of Luther, *doctor communis*, is one of the honorifics of St. Thomas Aquinas. According to Cardinal Willebrands, St Thomas and Luther, the Middle Ages and the Reformation, belong together. Luther represented and continued a common tradition. Nevertheless, *doctor communis* is not simply a historical title, pointing us to the past. With this title, the Cardinal wished to show us that Luther had something to say jointly to the Roman Catholic and Lutheran churches of our day.

To these thoughts of Cardinal Willebrands, the Roman Catholic Bishop of Mainz, Cardinal Karl Lehmann, joins when he writes of the ecumenical significance of Luther's *Small Catechism*. Cardinal Lehmann states that the *Small and Large Catechisms* – in contrast to certain other writings of Luther – are an excellent example of the linkage of the Reformer with earlier tradition. Within the history of the church Luther's *Catechisms* are neither new nor the random contrivance of a single theologian. Rather, they are closely related, both as to their structure and their content, to the classical theology of the early church and the medieval church. According to Cardinal Lehmann, Luther is a "teacher of the faith" (*Lehrer des Glaubens*).[3]

---

[2] J. Cardinal Willebrands, *Mandatum unitatis. Beiträge zur Ökumene*, Paderborn 1989, 124.

[3] Karl Lehmann, *Luther als Lehrer des Glaubens? Die ökumenische Bedeutung seiner Katechismen. – Lutherische Kirche in der Welt. Jahrbuch des Martin-Luther-Bundes.* Folge 45. 1998, 131–146.

Just as Luther's valuation as *doctor communis* has not been self-apparent to Roman Catholics, it has not been that clear to Protestants either. Although the churches' evaluations of Luther have differed greatly throughout history as to content and estimation, both sides have long held certain features to be common. Luther has been interpreted as an individual, a person who started something new – whether that was negative or positive. Luther created a new "protestant" Christian belief – or at least he presented an interpretation of the original belief which differed radically from the faith of earlier centuries.

According to Roman Catholics, Luther departed from the one, catholic tradition – that was his downfall. In the assessment of Protestants, Luther departed from tradition, and that was his accomplishment. Overstating the case only slightly, we can say that Luther was not *doctor communis* for either side. For Roman Catholics, Luther has been one of those deviating from the main tide, a heretic; while for the Protestants he has been a guiding light whose significance is emphasized against an otherwise dark firmament overshadowing the Church. And even when Luther has been studied in relation to his background of ecclesiastical and general history, his qualities, uniqueness and digression from the norm, that is to say, his significance as an individual has come to the fore. So it is rather understandable that there has not been enough motivation for scrutinizing Luther as *doctor communis*, as a representative of the one, classical Christendom.[4]

Luther: An Individualist destroying the Church?

Already during the Reformation, Roman Catholics depicted Luther as an arch-heretic and as a destroyer of the unity of the church. Even at the beginning of the twentieth century, Luther was seen in dark colors, not only to be avoided in doctrine but also to be studied under the typology of a personal pathology. For

---

[4] "Die Bedeutung des überkommenen Dogmas für Luther kann schwerlich überschätzt werden; sie ist in der Forschung weithin zu gering veranschlagt worden." Bernhard Lohse, Martin Luther. *Eine Einführung in sein Leben und sein Werk*. München 1981, 171. On the history of Luther-research, see pp. 207–246.

example, Heinrich Denifle claimed that Luther had created his doctrine of justification simply in order to be able to live a carefree, libertarian life himself. From these viewpoints, we can say that both Luther the person and Luther the theologian are viewed as a sum of individual flaws and biases.

On the eve of the Second World War, there was a new breakthrough both academically and ecumenically in the publication of Joseph Lortz's book: *Die Reformation in Deutschland.* Lortz critiqued the errors of the medieval church. He strove to understand Luther's own spiritual intentions. He appreciated Luther as a "religious personality." Nonetheless, he concluded that as a theologian Luther was a "subjectivist." In Lortz's view, Luther represents a catholicity without being catholic in an authentic sense. In a unique way Luther had stressed the significance of the Apostle Paul. Yet, Luther did not attend fully (*Vollhörer*) to the Holy Bible. The revolutionary Luther was entirely a prisoner of his own deliberations.[5]

The theory of Luther's subjectivism was soon re-evaluated by Roman Catholic scholars. Lortz's own students, in particular Erwin Iserloh and Peter Manns, held that the thesis of subjectivism was overly superficial and denigrating. Of Luther, Manns used the name "father in faith" (*Vater im Glauben*). Manns examined Luther with especial reference to the devotional life of the medieval and early churches, and the title "father in faith" arises from that spiritual tradition.

In his broad-ranging study of St. Thomas Aquinas and Martin Luther, Otto Hermann Pesch asserted that their understanding of the doctrine of justification was not mutually exclusive. Thus, Luther's theology is to be properly situated among the common traditions of Christendom, regardless of the denomination of the

---

[5] Joseph Lortz, *Die Reformation in Deutschland*, Bd. 1-2. Freiburg 1941. See also: Eero Huovinen, *Die ökumenische Bedeutung des Luther-Verständnisses von Joseph Lortz für die Lutherforschung in Finnland. - Zum Gedenken an Joseph Lortz. Beiträge zur Reformationsgeschichte und Ökumene.* Hrsg. von Rolf Decot & Rainer Vinke. Wiesbaden & Stuttgart, 1989, 262-292.

person doing the evaluation.[6] In official Roman Catholic evaluations after Vatican II, the position afforded Luther is also substantially different from those given at the beginning of the twentieth century. In addition to Cardinal Willebrands and other ecumenics, Pope John Paul II in several instances quoted Luther's spiritual texts, e.g. the *Commentary on Romans*. Furthermore, he spoke positively of Luther's significance for all of Christendom.

A precursor of individual freedom?

Mutatis mutandum, Protestant Luther research has followed the same channels as Roman Catholic scholarship. Protestant studies have either historically or systematically tended to support a view of Luther as "the Reformer." Indirectly, this research setting has quite possibly led to an emphasis on Luther's distinctiveness and exceptionality. In examining the history of Protestant Luther studies,[7] it is rather amazing how radically Luther is emphatically viewed as extraordinary and original. During the period of Lutheran Orthodoxy, Luther was held by many to be unique, even infallible, as a teacher of correct doctrine. Luther was considered to correspond to the angel in Revelation: "having an eternal gospel to preach to those who dwell on the earth and to every nation and tribe and tongue and people" (Rev. 14:6). Pietism regarded Luther's theology as an expression of individual piety, i.e., from the point of view of regenerated, living faith and sanctification. In such a view, the significance of the Christian faith lies in the internal and personal experience of belief.

During the Enlightenment, Luther was construed as the precursor of the freedom of reason and the conscience, the one who freed the Christian faith from the dark disbelief of the Middle Ages. The general anthropological mode of thought, characteristic

---

[6] Otto Herman Pesch, *Theologie der Rechtfertigung bei Martin Luther und Thomas von Aquin.* Mainz, 1967; Otto Herman Pesch, *Martin Luther, Thomas von Aquin und die reformatorische Kritik an der Scholastik. Zur Geschichte und Wirkungsgeschichte eines Missverständnisses mit weltgeschichtlichen Folgen.* Göttingen, 1994.

[7] See Lohse 1981, 213–240.

of the era, led to a delineation of Luther as a situation-bound thinker whose thoughts cannot claim normativity. Luther was esteemed as a great person and fighter, but he too was to be critically evaluated on the basis of reason and the ethical demands of the conscience. Gotthold Ephraim Lessing boasted of Luther that he set people free from the bondage of tradition. The task of the Enlightenment was only to carry this liberation to its fruition. Frederick the Great was not satisfied even with this, but rejoiced that Luther, the "poor, damn devil," freed the people from the yoke of the priests and thus increased the income of the state. Lutheranism began to change into Protestantism, which turned into enlightened subjectivism. Albert Ritschl strove to place Luther into his own historical framework. Nevertheless, Ritschl was of the opinion that Luther's worth lay more in the overturning of old speculative metaphysics and mysticism. At bottom, Luther proclaimed freedom and independence of the soul.

More recent Luther research has been deeply influenced by the same Protestant theological models. In popular church discussions Luther is often held to be a situation-bound dilettante, or an otherwise unrestrained exception in the history of theology, one to whom Christians following current trends should not be too committed. Such comments often reflect, in their background, the same setting of the question: Was Luther a private sage or *doctor communis?* Contrary to the previously used paradigm emphasizing the differences between the Catholic Middle Ages and Luther, we find that particularly in the United States, Robert Jenson and Carl Braaten's theological interpretation of the "Catholicity of the Reformation" has brought new points of view to the fore.[8] In Finland, similar new thoughts have also been introduced by Tuomo Mannermaa and his students.[9] Both of these parties have

---

[8] See Carl E. Braaten & Robert W. Jenson (ed.), *Catholicity of the Reformation*. Grand Rapids (USA) & Cambridge (UK) 1996.

[9] On Finnish Luther research, see for example *Luther und Theosis. Vergöttlichung als Thema der abendländischen Theologie* (Hrsg. von Simo Peura und Antti Raunio. Schriften der Luther-Agricola-Gesellschaft. A:25. 232 pp. Helsinki 1990) and *Luther und Ontologie. Das Sein Christi im Glauben als strukturierendes Prinzip der Theologie Luthers.* (Hrsg. von Anja Ghiselli, Kari Kopperi und Rainer Vinke. Schriften der Luther-Agricola-Gesellschaft, 31. 185 pp. Helsinki 1993).

delineated the philosophical, theological, and spiritual nature of the Middle Ages, thus attempting to understand the era preceding Luther. Furthermore, they have fastened their attention to how the modern image of Luther has been colored by various philosophical preconceptions and trends.

So, back to our fundamental question: Was Luther exceptional, unique, i.e. in some manner a *novum*, or was he rather one link, one witness on the chain of the shared classic Christian faith? Without a doubt, this question is, to the observant academic researcher, quite general. Nonetheless, answering it may be a justifiable attempt to understand heuristically what is at stake in Luther's theology and, shall we dare to say, the whole of Christian belief. Was Luther simply the father of Lutheranism or was he also, for all of Christendom, *"Vater im Glauben"*? *Doctor privatus* or *doctor communis*?

The ecumenical significance of Luther's Catechisms

In attempting an incipient answer to the question above, I want to adapt the interpretation of Karl Cardinal Lehmann. According to Lehmann's view, particularly the *Catechisms* of Luther can, for their part, shed light on both Luther's relationship to the tradition preceding him and on his significance for the church today. Cardinal Lehmann says he was astonished how little Luther's *Catechisms* have undergone ecumenical evaluation.[10] There appear to be at least six well-founded reasons for giving the *Catechisms* an ecumenical reading.

First, the *Small and Large Catechisms* are examples of Luther's deepest desire to be *doctor communis*. In the *Catechisms*, if anywhere, Luther was *doctor*, a teacher of the ordinary people and a guide of priests in need of theological knowledge and

---

[10] Lehmann 1998, 142. In 1999 the Finnish Evangelical Lutheran Church approved a new official *Catechism*. Its base text was written by Eero Huovinen. Due to its historical and ecumenical significance, the *Catechism* included the entire text of Luther's *Small Catechism*. This new *Catechism* has been translated, e.g., into English, Swedish, Latin, Arabic, Russian, Chinese, Hungarian, German, Spanish, Croatian, and French.

training. Among Luther's writings, the *Catechisms* emphasize most visibly what is common to the classic Christian faith. In accord with the basic idea of a catechism, Luther wanted to teach what is necessary in being and living as a Christian. As *doctor*, Luther, the catechete, was primarily a spiritual teacher. His goals of teaching and learning were not just to increase knowledge for its own sake, but to foster faith in God and to strengthen love for one's fellow human being.

Second, in his *Catechisms* Luther was *doctor communis* in the sense that he structured his catechetical teaching on the foundation of a long tradition. That is to say, Luther's *Small and Large Catechisms* were firmly, knowingly built on the framework of the tradition of the early church (the Decalogue, the Creed, the Lord's Prayer, and the Sacraments). Even in their own time, Luther's catechetical ideas were not original or a new plan. The Commandments, Creed, and Lord's Prayer were the didactic heritage of the Middle Ages. Although catechetic-type books of this form had not been written, the three primary points mentioned above were the main body of Christian upbringing. Peter Abelard prepared his famous *Commentary on the Apostles' Creed and the Lord's Prayer*, which all Christians were to study together and learn by heart. Erasmus of Rotterdam wrote a catechism soon after 1510. This is the structure Luther developed and deepened. The very framework of the catechism emphasizes continuity with the tradition of the faith. The Ten Commandments are the foundation of the Judeo-Christian way of life. The Apostles' Creed has its roots in the first Christian century. The Lord's Prayer is the model prayer taught by Jesus. The solutions of Luther's *Catechism* are more those of the Jews, the New Testament and Early Christianity than they are innovations of the Reformation.

Third, Luther's *Catechisms*, especially the explanation of the Third Article of the Creed, is constructed on two classic dogmas of Christianity, i.e. the doctrines of the trinity and the two natures of Christ. Although justification is not mentioned as a term in the catechisms, it is implicitly a central theme and is firmly based on Trinitarian doctrine and christology: Salvation is the work of the triune God, which is grounded in the person and work of Jesus Christ. Currently, the Roman Catholic Church, the World Council of Churches, the Lutheran World Federation, as well as the constitutions of many other ecumenical organizations are built upon these dogmata.

Fourth, Luther's *Catechisms* are witness to the common faith also in the sense that, in them, controversial theology aimed at either Rome or the radical Reformation remains only in a subordinate role. The *Small Catechism* does not include any direct polemic. The *Large Catechism*, intended for pastors, has some critical comments on the "church of the Pope" and on spiritualistic baptismal concepts; in comparison to Luther's other tomes, however, it does not have an anti-ecumenical, controversialist character.

Fifth, in line with Karl Lehmann's thoughts, in Luther's *Large Catechism* one can discern a spiritual self-critical ethos, which may also have ecumenical significance. The *Large Catechism* is a good example of what an honest and open-minded analysis of the church and Christendom could be. At the same time the *Catechism* boasts of the breakthrough of the Gospel, it appraises not only the problems of its theological opponents but also, in the same measure, the pitiful mediocrity of the Christian life of its own camp. In the Preface, we read that it is expressly its own "shepherds," i.e., the priests who had migrated to the Reformation camp, who were afforded an earful as "lazy bellies" (*faule Wänste, ignavos vetres*) and "presumptuous saints" (*vermessene Heiligen, praesumptuosos sanctos*). They are depicted as being more interested in the perquisites of their office than in the duties of the office, than in such matters as prayer, study and serving the parishioners: "These shameful gluttons and servants of their bellies are better suited to be swineherds or keepers of dogs than guardians of souls and pastors." Self-criticism in regard to one's own Church and one's own state of Christianity is a precondition for genuine ecumenical relations.

Sixth, in the explanations of the Sacraments at the end of the *Large Catechism*, Luther attempts to link up with the teaching of his predecessors. This too has positive ecumenical significance. Sacramental teaching is characterized by a strong theological realism and an understanding of the effectiveness of the word of God. Baptism, confession, and Holy Communion do not simply refer to matters outside of themselves, but they include and give

Christ and all his works. They are the effective signs of Christ's presence, God's grace and the communion of Christians.

The central place of the Sacraments

The Holy Sacraments have central standing in the *Catechisms* of Luther as well as in his other texts. Baptism joins one both to Christ and to his Church. In accord with the strong words of the *Catechism*, in baptism God donates to the believer "victory over death and the devil, forgiveness of sin, God's grace, the entire Christ and all his Works, and the Holy Spirit with his gifts."[11] Simultaneously, it is made clear that the one who is baptized each and every day needs teaching, prayer, exhortation, and the support of other Christians in order to prevail over troubles, to persevere in faith, and to be strengthened in love.

In addition to Baptism, there is a link established to theological realism in the explanation of Holy Communion in the *Catechism*. The Eucharist is the meal of Christ's presence, which joins us to other Christians and donates "the forgiveness of sins and everlasting life." Currently, the doctrine and praxis of Holy Communion remain a central ecumenical issue between Lutherans and Roman Catholics as well as other churches. Holy Communion includes nearly all theological *loci* from creation to redemption and eschatology. The bottleneck choking off the visible unity of the Churches is the theology of the office, which reaches its culmination in Holy Communion. Thus, it is interesting to ask what Martin Luther's concept of Holy Communion could bring to the rapprochement between the churches in our day. Could he be *doctor communis* also for the theology of the Eucharist?

The Sacrament of Christ's presence

To Martin Luther, the Eucharist was the sacrament of Christ's real presence. Thus it is not only a feast of remembrance where we recall Jesus' teachings and deeds. Neither is it a mere symbolic feast where the bread and the wine might remind us of Christ's

---

[11] *Large Catechism*, Baptism, 41-42.

body, absent and distant in heaven. Luther frequently repeated the words of institution, that is, "this is my body," *hoc est corpus meum*. These words are to be interpreted simply and realistically. The Host does not merely signify the body of the Lord, referring only to a Christ dwelling elsewhere. The words of institution include and effect what they promise.

The concept of the real presence, naturally enough, is not the sole content of Holy Communion in the Bible and tradition. Luther, too, links other motifs to Communion: grace and the forgiveness of sins, the communion of Christians, the remembrance of Christ, a meal of gratitude, and a confession of faith in God. It is at one and the same time the representation of the sacrifice given by Christ on Golgotha and the foretaste of the heavenly feast.

According to Luther the essence of the Eucharist is, however, the real presence of Christ's body and blood in the bread and the wine. To Luther this faith was no abstract theological theory or philosophical idea. He wanted to rely on the simple Word of God, on the New Testament instituted by Christ himself. Christ has given his own body "for us for the forgiveness of sins" (Matt 26:28). Faith in the real presence of Christ at the Eucharist has always united Lutherans and Catholics. We have always wanted to have confidence that Christ himself is present at the Holy Eucharist in the bread and the wine "truly and in substance," *vere et substantialiter*, giving the baptized believer the reality of all of salvation. As a community, the Church lives in the true meaning of the words *de eucharistia*, out of the mystery and gift of the Eucharist. In accordance with the Lutheran theology of the Eucharist, Christ's real presence is based on the doctrine of God, on Christology and on the doctrine of justification. To Luther, God is in his essence the Giver and the Donor.

According to the Creed, the Triune God is not a jealous judge or a merchant demanding compensation, but rather self-sacrificing Love, who loves us and wants good things for us. Luther summed up the message of the Creed by using the metaphor of giving gifts: "We see here in the Creed how God gives himself completely to us, with all his gifts and power... the Father gives us all creation,

Christ all his works and the Holy Spirit all his gifts."[12] God's love is the reason for Christ's incarnation and the basis for the Sacrament of the Eucharist. Out of love for us God became man in Christ, making peace with us. Out of love for us Christ instituted the Eucharist so that he might continue to be present among us and to bring the gifts of reconciliation to our lives.

Christ's real presence at the Eucharist is thus in inseparable union with the gift of the Sacrament, its efficacy. The Eucharist is the feast of Christ's death and resurrection, where we partake of the reconciliation on the cross, the forgiveness of sins, life eternal - all in all we partake of Christ himself. Trust in Christ's real presence in the Sacrament of the Eucharist is such a treasure of faith which could bring Lutherans ever closer to Roman Catholics, the Orthodox, and to other Christians who confess this faith in doctrine and practice.

It is this mystery of faith that Pope John Paul II wrote about in his encyclical *Ecclesia de Eucharistia*. Christ, the true man and the true God is present in the bread and the wine of the Eucharist really, wholly and entirely.[13] We Lutherans can also wholeheartedly join in the words of the encyclical concerning Christ's presence and the gift of the Eucharist. Christ's presence is true "in objective reality," *in ipsa rerum natura*, and "independently of our minds," *a nostro scilicet spiritu disiuncta*. The Sacrament of the Eucharist, apart from bringing Christ's person and work into the present, also donates them to us personally. "The Eucharist thus applies (*applicat*) to men and women today the reconciliation won once for all by Christ for mankind in every age."[14]

---

[12] Luther, *Large Catechism*, Kolb-Wengert, 440. "Here in the Creed you have the entire essence, will, and work of God exquisitely depicted in very brief but rich words... For in all three articles God himself has revealed and opened to us the most profound depths of his fatherly heart and his pure, unutterable love... We see here in the Creed how God gives himself completely to us, with all his gifts and power, to help us keep the Ten Commandments: the Father gives us all creation, Christ all his works and the Holy Spirit all his gifts." *Large Catechism*, II, 63-69.

[13] *Ecclesia de Eucharistia*, §15.

[14] *Ibid.* §12.

The Eucharist and Christ's sacrifice

As a feast of the presence of Christ crucified and resurrected, the Eucharist is also a feast of sacrifice. During the Lutheran Reformation a dispute arose as to how the Eucharist could be understood as a sacrifice in the genuine sense so that the sacrifice would not cancel out the gift. In describing Christ's sacrifice on the cross, the New Testament uses the Greek word *ephapax*, meaning something sufficient, perfect, unique, something not repeatable (Heb 10:10). What is the relation of this sacrifice given by Christ on the cross to the sacrifice of the Eucharist?

In ecumenical dialogues with the Roman Catholic Church, we Lutherans have been concerned about the sufficiency of Christ's cross, asking: If the Eucharist is understood as being an independent propitiatory sacrifice, does that not render the sacrifice on the cross insufficient, questioning Christ as the only mediator?[15] Roman Catholics, likewise, were concerned about the efficacy of the Eucharist. They asked: If the connection between the Eucharist and Christ's sacrifice were to be severed, would the benefit of the cross and its fruit be left in the past, in which case also the Eucharist might lose its significance?

In the light of ecumenical studies and discussions we can state that despite the differences in emphases we are of one accord in two vital issues. United we can say that: 1) Christ's sacrifice is unique and sufficient and 2) it is efficaciously present in the celebration of the Eucharist. The commission on the Lutheran-Catholic dialogues in 1980 stated: "Catholic and Lutheran Christians together recognize that in the Lord's Supper Jesus Christ 'is present as the Crucified who died for our sins and who rose again for our justification. As the once-for-all sacrifice for the sins of the world' (USA III, I.1a, 188). This sacrifice can neither be continued, nor repeated, nor replaced nor complemented; but rather, it can and should become effective ever anew in the midst of the congregation."[16]

---

[15] *The Eucharist*, §59, Lutheran / Roman Catholic Joint Commission, LWF 1980.

[16] *The Eucharist*, §56, Lutheran / Roman Catholic Joint Commission, LWF 1980.

For us Lutherans it is important that Christ's sacrifice need not be repeated or complemented. Without the perfect and sufficient propitiatory work performed by Christ we lack the strength to live. Our faith and sacrifice arise out of joy and gratitude that our reconciliation is perfect and that we can talk about it in the past tense: Sin *is* reconcil*ed*, victory acquir*ed* and final peace achiev*ed*. Is this not actually the entire core and content of the Gospel?

Nevertheless, in a great many meanings we can, together with Luther, call the Eucharist a sacrifice. First, at the beginning of the liturgy of the Eucharist, we carry bread and wine to the altar as an offering and as a symbol of thanksgiving for creation.[17] Second, in Holy Communion Christ is present as the sacrificed and crucified Lord. Third, the Eucharist is the commemoration in word and deed of Christ's sacrifice (*memoria passionis*). Fourth, Christ's sacrifice is currently present at the Eucharist (*repraesentatio passionis*). Fifth, the fruit, benefit and gift of Christ's cross are applied (*applicat*) to the believing recipients. Sixth, we sacrifice to God thanksgiving when we confess our sins, give thanks, pray and celebrate the Eucharist in accord with the First Commandment, the institution of Christ and the apostolic admonition (Rom 12:1). Seventh, the Eucharist constrains us to sacrifice ourselves to one another as an offering in mutual love.

Eighth – and maybe most importantly – Christ offers himself as a sacrifice prior to us, together with us and after us. He is not only the food and drink of the Holy Supper but also the host of the feast and the celebrant. The Catechism of the Catholic Church names Christ the real subject of the liturgy[18] and Martin Luther expresses the same thought in a different manner: "Christ is the chef, the waiter, as well as the food and drink of the Eucharist."[19]

---

[17] "Panis enim et vinum antea offerentur ad benedicendum, ut per verbum et orationem santificentur. Postquam autem benedictus et consecratus est, iam non offertur sed accipitur dono a Deo." WA 6, 525, 1-3.

[18] "Liturgy is an 'action' of the whole Christ (*Christus totus*)." *Catechism of the Catholic Church*, §1136. See also §1084-1090.

[19] "Denn her hats nicht alleine eingesetzt, sondern machts und helts auch selbs, vnd ist der koch, kelner, speise und trank selbs." WA 23, 270, 9-11.

The Holy Communion can well be termed a sacrifice, above all because "Christ appeared as a high priest of the good things to come" (Heb 9:11), giving himself to the Father and to us. Luther writes: "From these words we learn that we do not offer Christ as a sacrifice, but that Christ offers us. And in this way it is permissible, yes, profitable, to call the mass a sacrifice; not on its own account, but because we offer ourselves as a sacrifice along with Christ."[20]

The Holy Eucharist as a communal feast

On the basis of its name (*synaksis, communio*), the Holy Eucharist is a communal feast. St Paul writes: "Is not the bread which we break a sharing [*koinonia*] in the body of Christ?" (1 Cor. 10:16-17). The Holy Eucharist connects Christ and sinners, and the Christian to other Christians. Communion is not only a matter between God and the individual but a communal event with an ecclesiological and ethical dimension. Those who together share the consecrated bread and wine also share all joy and sorrow, victory and suffering, concern and comfort. Those who are joined to Christ in the consecrated bread and wine are also joined to one another in faith and love.

The communal nature of this Holy Supper is brought out forcefully in the theology of the Holy Communion of Martin Luther:

> Besides all this, Christ did not institute these two forms solitary and alone, but he gave his true natural flesh in the bread, and his natural true blood in the wine, that he might give a really perfect sacrament or sign. For just as the bread is changed (*vorwandelt*) into his true natural body and the wine into his natural true blood, so truly are we also drawn and changed (*als so warhaftig werden wir vorwandelt*) into the spiritual body, that is, into the fellowship of Christ and all saints and by this sacrament

---

[20] LW, 35, 99. "Auss welchen worten wir lernen, das wir nit Christum, sondern Christus uns oppfert, und nach der meyss is es leydlich, yha nuetzlich, das wir mess ein opffer heyssen, nit umb yret willen, sondern das wir uns mit Christo opffern." StA 1, 303, 11-15.

put into possession of all the virtues and mercies of Christ and his saints...[21]

Again through this same love, we are to be changed and to make the infirmities of all other Christians our own; we are to take upon ourselves their form and their necessity, and all the good that is within our power we are to make theirs, that they may profit from it. That is real fellowship, and that is the true significance of this sacrament. In this way we are changed into one another and are made into a community by love. Without love there can be no such change.[22]

The communal nature of the Holy Eucharist entails that in Luther's theology the celebration of the Sacrament of the Altar requires both priest and people, in other words a congregation. Luther did not approve of the thought of the head of a family celebrating Holy Communion for the family. Every adult Christian should be able to teach God's Word within the family and parish. But Christ has set this Sacrament as the common feast of the church for the public remembrance of his deeds. That is why a publicly ordained priest is needed for the Holy Eucharist.[23]

Nonetheless, Luther took a critical stance towards the Mass celebrated for the private devotion of a priest. The Common Feast always requires a priest who is responsible for his office, but it also needs a congregation which is thereby served.[24] Both on the bases of the presence of Christ and the communal nature of the Holy Eucharist, we Lutherans can boldly join in with the words of Pope John Paul II that the Holy Eucharist has a "unifying power."[25] Communion not only joins Christ and sinners, it also

---

[21] LW 35, 59 (StA 1, 279, 31 - 280, 4).

[22] LW 35, 58 (StA 1, 278, 34 - 279, 12).

[23] See for example WA Tr 5, 6361; WA Br 5, 528; WA Br 7, 339, 1-35.

[24] See WA Br 2, 372, 73; WA 39 I, 134-173 and the Smalcald Articles II, 2, 8-9.

[25] "Eucharistic communion also confirms the Church in her unity as the body of Christ. Saint Paul refers to this *unifying power* of participation in the banquet of the Eucharist... The argument is compelling: our union with Christ, which is a gift and grace for each of us, makes it possible for us, in him, to share in the unity of his body which is the Church. The

joins together Christians within the same church, young and old, priests and parishioners. It joins together dioceses and finally also local churches ministering to various parts of the world, churches confessing the same faith.

It is my fervent wish that we Lutherans could kneel together with our Roman Catholic and other Christian sisters and brothers at the common Communion table. We yearn for a common table because the Holy Eucharist is the feast of Christ's presence. There is, however, no shortcut to a joint Holy Eucharist. Unity does not endure without truth, we require "the truth in love," *veritas in caritate*. The goal of visible unity and of a common Communion demand that we dig deeper into the foundation of our Christian faith. We need patience to delve into revealed truth and we need the courage then to take decisive steps when adequate consensus is achieved. Prof. Eric W. Gritsch has for decades been practicing this patient research work, digging into the foundations of the faith.

Conclusion

In summary, may I dare to contend that Martin Luther, in his *Catechisms* and his writings on Holy Communion, speaks as *doctor communis*, not attempting to develop new doctrine but rather striving to express and interpret the common faith of the undivided Christendom. Thus his writings still bear ecumenical fruit. On the basis of Lutheran theology we have no difficulty in joining with those words which the Bishop of Rome, Benedict XIV, stated in his inaugural homily: "All of us belong to the communion of Saints, we who have been baptized in the name of the Father, and of the Son and of the Holy Spirit, we who draw life

---

Eucharist reinforces the incorporation into Christ which took place in Baptism though the gift of the Spirit (cf. 1 Cor 12:13, 27)...The seeds of disunity, which daily experience shows to be so deeply rooted in humanity as a result of sin, are countered by the *unifying power* of the body of Christ. The Eucharist, precisely by building up the Church, creates human community." *Ecclesia de Eucharistia, § 23-24.*

from the gift of Christ's Body and Blood, through which he transforms us and makes us like himself."[26]

---

[26] *Omelia del Santo Padre per il solenne inizio del Ministerio Petrino,* Domenica, 24 April 2005.

Some Remarks on the Ethical and Liturgical Distinction of Law from Gospel

Robert W. Jenson

Introduction

The famous Lutheran "distinction of law and gospel" is much treasured by Lutherans, and indeed provides powerful insight in certain contexts. But it is also one of the most variously and disastrously misused notions in the history of theology. Some mid-twentieth-century theologians even tried to spin it into an entire ontology - once upon a time, I tried that myself. But while some of the special Lutheran *theologoumena* do indeed have profound ontological consequences, this one cannot bear that weight. In a different key, the distinction has been used to atomize the Bible: "That passage is law, so it can't be used in this gospel-connection" and vice versa. Or even: "The Old Testament is law; the New Testament is gospel, so we don't need to refer much to the Old Testament when thinking about . . ." This *syllabus errorum* could be added to at length. At the moment, however, the most blatant misuse is in ethical and liturgical contexts. I shall discuss these matters here, and conclude by marking a limit of the distinction's applicability.

The Distinction between Law and Gospel in Luther

First, let me sketch what system I can discern in Luther's own use of the distinction, in order to show the general understanding behind the considerations that will be the bulk of the essay. "Law" and "gospel" functioned systematically - not always, I admit, rhetorically - for Luther not as labels for two subject matters or kinds of questions or bodies of authoritative writing, but as labels for the two ways in which the one God rules his creation.

According to Luther, God always creates and governs by speaking. When God rules by so speaking to us as to *mandate* righteousness, Luther calls that "law;" and when God rules by so speaking to us as to *share* righteousness, Luther calls that "gospel." If we wish to think with Luther, we will not sort out "law-issues" and "gospel-issues," since God can speak to any aspect of righteousness in either way, and even in both ways at once. As Luther wields the language, "the law" is not coterminous with ethics or "the gospel" with doctrine; these supposed equivalences were invented quite recently, to accommodate antinomian impulses by making it appear that ethical decisions cannot impact doctrinal faithfulness. Finally, since God rules by speaking, and since he speaks by the voice of creatures, by those to whom he commits his word, the occasions on which we are to observe the distinction of law and gospel are those when we are called to speak for him. It is preachers, teachers and judges who are to find guidance in the distinction.

Luther advanced the distinction primarily to protect the preaching of Christ's death and resurrection from exhausting itself in moralism, to guard "the gospel" from debilitation by mistaken deference to "the law." Well and good. But what is often forgotten, is that the distinction must necessarily also work the other way around: to guard the law from mitigation by the gospel. When Lutheran leaders[1] announce, "We are a church of the gospel, and not of the law" in order then to discount what Scripture mandates (e.g., sexual practices or the conditions of just war), they quite explicitly - if perhaps unwittingly - espouse Lutheranism's first home-grown heresy; a heresy which Luther himself denounced in terms as strong as those he used for late-medieval works-righteousness.

Something must indeed make wiggle-room in the practice of legal judgment, but this is not the gospel, but what Luther called *Billigkeit*, a kind of common sense that is appropriate to judges whether they believe the gospel or not, and is indeed simply an aspect of law itself. To be sure, it may be that the gospel instills in

---

[1] I do not of course suggest that only Lutherans do this. Lamentably, we do seem to have made converts to at least the antinomian part of the Lutheran tradition.

specifically ecclesial judges a special freedom to practice *Billigkeit* - then called "pastoral judgment" - but that again is another matter. In the famous and often cited instance when Luther advised Philip of Hesse to take a second wife rather than to proliferate adulteries, he was not led by the gospel, as is sometimes made out, but simply by judgment of how firmly law could hold in this case.

The gospel certainly does *not* obviate deontic paranesis based on Scripture in the life of the church or in the lives of individual believers -whether or not one counts a technically so called "third use of the law." This should be obvious; only blinding by culturally inflicted ideology can explain why it is not now apparent to many pious folk. We need only consider how Paul's letters end. Whatever he may have just said against *ho nomos*, he finishes with commands and exhortations, and however he may appropriate culturally going forms of moral instruction to do this, the deep text is always one or more of the biblical Ten Commandments. Or consider Luther's catechisms. It is not by accident that they begin with those same commandments: the first thing[2] Christians need to know is how God expects us to conduct ourselves, and the texts in which he tells us this. Nor *in this context* do we encounter those Lutheran profundities about freedom from the law or the law being impossible to fulfill or its always working death. On the contrary, when we come next to Luther's exposition of the creed, we read that the very purpose of the gospel is to awaken *Lust und Liebe*,[3] "desire and affection," for the commandments just expounded. Outside certain extreme contexts, Luther was at one with the psalmists and wise men of Israel about the pleasures of God's commands.

We cannot use the gospel to escape the commandments. And correlatively we cannot derive ethics from the gospel. Indeed, insisting that we cannot do that is one half of the law-gospel distinction's very purpose. Antinomians often - more or less - quote Augustine: "Love God and do as you see fit." Following this maxim, "situation ethics" once dispensed with the law altogether,

---

[2] In the post-apostolic situation, the order reverses itself: what in Paul was conclusion is for the later church opening statement.

[3] "Lust" is of course German for *eros*. Luther does not here seem to share the disavowal of *eros* in favor of *agape.*

relying only on the leading of the gospel in each situation. One does not now hear much about "situation ethics," but this may only be because its principle has been adopted by the Protestant mainstream. As for Augustine, we should remember how strenuously he understood that command (!) to love God. In his understanding, loving God had to be learned, indeed it was a life-long discipline; and as Augustine himself grew more and more into the love of God he understood this discipline more and more as a living in "the strange new world of the Bible,"[4] which he certainly read without dissecting it into legal bits and gospel-bits.

At this point, it may be urged that gentile Christians - and Jewish Christians previously alienated from Judaism - did and do regard themselves as authorized to discount certain scriptural commands, and that this is no antinomian development, since it dates back to Peter and Paul, and "the apostolic council," and to the momentous decision when Christians stopped keeping Sabbath and substituted Eucharist on the first day. Is it not the gospel that allows us to make such judgments?

The account is plausible, but wrong. To see why, perhaps we may begin by noting that Judaism makes similar judgments. Thus the great bulk of Old Testament law mandates a specific sacrificial cult, which nevertheless has been in abeyance for two millennia and which rabbinic Judaism feels no urge to restore. Obviously, the rabbis make such judgments without permission from the gospel about Jesus. May it not similarly be other than gospel-considerations that, e.g., allow Christians to eat pork while remaining bound not to eat flesh while the blood lives in the animal? How after all did the "apostolic council" decide that of the Old Testament's food prohibitions only this one applied to gentiles? Lines from the *gospel* to that decision are not easy to discern; while lines from general considerations of humanity are plain.

It is simply a particular sort of *Billigkeit* that leads us to judge both that God explicitly commanded his people to abstain from certain foods, and that he does not command the gentiles grafted into his people to maintain all the same abstentions. What sort of

---

[4] Karl Barth.

Billigkeit might this be? How does it work? Perhaps a famous passage may help: Peter's vision of a banquet of abhorrent species instructed him that gentiles could indeed receive the Spirit without keeping kosher, because the division of permitted and forbidden foods was not a universal or permanent rule for God's people.

The judgment that gentiles can indeed belong to God's people without obeying the Jewish dietary restrictions is thus indeed a *judgment*; that is, there is a reason for it, the stated limited applicability of those rules. In general, judgments shaped by *Billigkeit* begin with presumption of some mandate or prohibition, and then when a case or range of cases comes up ask whether or how strictly the command should here be enforced. The point is: there has to be a *reason* for a decision to enforce not at all or only in part. There has to be a reason why grafted gentiles are exempt from circumcision, are allowed to work on Saturday, etc.

Of course, according to Paul, not only are gentile converts not obligated to keep kosher or be circumcised, but they endanger their relation to Christ if they do. We are in deep exegetical waters here, but Paul's argument seems[5] to be something like this: gentile converts' only reason to have themselves circumcised or to celebrate certain festivals, or to keep kosher, would be that they thought their relation to the chosen people - and so to God - depended on it, while in fact that relation depends only on faith. So with respect to the definitive relation to Christ there is indeed a connection between the gospel and our relation to the law. But justification is not the context of the present discussion, since at least in Christian understanding Jew and gentile alike are free from the law in *that* context.

What then is the reason for gentile exemption from some of Scripture's law? If we look at the actual commands from which Paul exempts gentiles - and not first at his not altogether consistent general statements on the subject of *nomos* - the answer springs to the eye. Circumcision, certain festivals, abstaining from certain foods - these are all laws obedience to which distinguishes Jew

---

[5] It is, I think, wise never to be absolutely certain how Paul intends his arguments to run.

from gentile. A Jewish theologian friend of mine[6] once remarked, "Why can I not eat shrimp? To make me seem peculiar, both to gentiles and to myself." But now, Paul and some others believed, the time had come for the prophetically promised ingathering of the gentiles, precisely *as gentiles*. Thus, for gentile converts to submit to the laws that distinguish Jews *from* gentiles meant renouncing the very title under which they now were to be brought in. But suppose some erstwhile gentile had actually gone through the process of proselytism, was now in fact a Jew and not a gentile, and *then* applied for baptism, would Paul denounce *his* circumcision?

So if we want to say, for instance, that scriptural prohibitions of some sexual practices do not apply to Christians, we have to provide specific reasons why they do not. As we have seen, there is exegetical reason to think that God mandates circumcision for the Jews as God's people but not for those to whom the Resurrection opened a new way into that people. Whenever someone wants to discount a biblical command, he or she has to provide a reason of that sort. If someone wants to argue that bestiality might be sometimes a good thing, they have to provide exegetical argument to the effect that abstention from the practice marks Jews, but that Scripture does not see anything intrinsically wrong with it. The objection that is now often instant in our minds, "But would the God of the gospel actually forbid . . .?" is not enough - and indeed it is itself a blatant confusion of law with gospel. To find out what that God would actually forbid we have to look and see the actuality, and what we find may not please our gospel-inflated souls. The God of the gospel forbids murder, and most of us are happy that he does so, but this God may and does give commands and prohibitions with which some or all of us will be very unhappy.

Finally, one must note that antinomian misuse of the distinction regularly has a paradoxical result: a crushing legalism. When God's law is expelled, human moralism fills the vacuum. Thus many a sermon that begins by denouncing "the religious right" for its clinging to one or another biblical admonition, "from which

---

[6] David Novak, no mean Jewish theologian.

surely the gospel has set us free," expends itself in grim and minute enforcement of "peace and justice concerns."

In sum, what the distinction of law from gospel does for ethical reflection, is to allow us to consider God's commands, in Scripture and perhaps elsewhere, for their own sake and in their own coherence and - indeed situationally - varying stringency. Far from prompting us to think "But the gospel . . .", the law-gospel distinction reveals this move as a distraction from careful exegesis of and obedience to God's law, and relieves us of it.

The Distinction between Law and Gospel in the Liturgy

Then there is the particular lot of works we call liturgy. Misuses of the "law and gospel" distinction with respect to liturgical work run parallel to those we have just more generally noted. There is, to begin, simple liturgical antinomianism. Lutherans love to say that the choice of liturgies and prayers, the establishing of rules for admission to communion or the age of confirmation, and all such things, occur in the land of *adiaphora*, of things that make no difference. Now there may indeed be *adiaphora*, but if there are, the line between them and things that do make a great deal of difference cannot be drawn by the law-gospel distinction itself, and in fact properly shifts from context to context. I well remember the time when the friend for whose *Festschrift* these remarks are written refused to preside at the Supper at all so long as he was forbidden to commune "infants" - adiaphoristic though one might think the age of admission to communion would otherwise be.

When it is supposed that the line between *adiaphora* and *diaphora* can be drawn by the distinction between law and gospel, the line is sooner or later not drawn at all, and all or nothing is permitted. Consider, for a central case, the way many Lutherans - and others - treat the commandment to celebrate the Supper - for of course "Do this" is the very model of a straightforwardly deontic commandment. The dominical command is plain enough: we are to give thanks to God for his benefits, expressly adducing the benefit of Jesus' life and death, and uniting in this thanksgiving by sharing bread and a cup of wine. One would think that no pastor or congregation would dare to disobey this command when the bulletin announces "the Lord's Supper" or "Communion" or "Eucharist." But of course Lutheran - and other - congregations regularly and blithely offer no thanksgiving at all, or emulate Burger King in inviting individuals to "have it your way" with the bread or cup and its contents. "Can it really make any decisive difference?" we rhetorically ask, if we prefer sanitation to fellowship in the cup? The obvious answer to which is: it makes all the difference between obedience and disobedience - and if we think *that* difference unimportant, we have carried antinomianism beyond the bounds of Christianity.

As with biblical laws generally, the line between liturgical *adiaphora* and *diaphora* is not to be drawn by the law-gospel distinction itself, but by the appropriate kind of *Billigkeit*, by the making of judgments for which indeed it is the *gospel* that is *adiaphora* and gives no guidance. Must the cup be plated with a noble metal? Well, it would be nice, but no. Must the thanksgiving follow the Trinitarian order of the fourth-century prayers? Well, it surely would be best, considering the church's long pondering of this prayer, and the generally Trinitarian shape of Christian prayer, but another ordering would not invalidate the sacrament. Can we use popcorn instead of bread? Well, no, not if we want to celebrate the Supper the Lord in fact commanded.

In fact, there are few if any liturgical decisions which truly make *no* difference at all. This extends to the choice of music, seating arrangement, clerical vestments, etc. Thus God undoubtedly accepts "praise-songs" along with Palestrina, but the choice does make a difference to *something*, and indeed to an aspect of our relation to that God. For why do we sing our prayers at all? Because beauty is with truth and goodness "transcendental," and because the transcendentals are "convertible" with one another: whatever is true is also beautiful and good, and whatever is beautiful is also true, and so on, *and* whatever is not beautiful is not true, and so on. Ultimately, God is true and good and beautiful just because he is God, and in him truth *is* goodness and beauty, and goodness *is* truth and beauty, and beauty *is* truth and goodness. Thus the soaring melody and guiding counterpoint of a Palestrina setting of a prayer belong also to the prayer's truth and goodness, not indeed to the sincerity or virtue of the one praying but nevertheless to the truth and goodness of the prayer itself. And again, if we think the truth and goodness and beauty of the prayers we offer to God are unimportant, we have carried antinomianism beyond the bounds of the faith.

What we offer to God should be as true and good and beautiful as the circumstances of a time and place make possible for us; we need to exercise liturgical *Billigkeit*. We must ask: Within the range of the here and now possible, what is most appropriate to the God who is supreme truth and goodness and beauty? If we think it is the gospel itself that will provide the answer, we will finally not find any answer at all.

Does it make any difference if the pastor - or "worship-leader" - leads the service in shirt-sleeves from a platform adjacent to the parking lot, with a rock band for backup? Of course we must start with, "That depends." *Billigkeit* must inquire: perhaps a shirt is all the pastor or congregation can afford, the church-building is ugly inside, and rock is the only kind of music anyone in the congregation can make. But if such circumstances do not obtain, then we must judge that pastor and congregation should stop indulging themselves: they should adopt the vestments which within their tradition mark continuity with the church through its history of beauty, acknowledge that a picnic is not usually a promising milieu for a solemn meal of fellowship with God, and attempt some music with more than three chords.

Finally, also liturgically there is a way in which misuse of the law-gospel distinction opens a disastrous legalism. In my observation, this takes two forms. The crudest and now most common is merely a version of a phenomenon noted above: where the founding liturgical mandates are shaken off, human moralisms fill the vacuum. Thus the Lord says, "Wash initiates in the name 'Father, Son and Holy Spirit.'" So long as we simply obey, the celebration is simple and free. But as soon as we ask, "But does it really have to be this very phrase, 'Father, Son and Holy Spirit'?" all manner of moralisms rise up to enslave us. How can we turn those who had abusive fathers over to an omnipotent "Father"? How can women identify with a Savior called "the Son"? Perhaps "Creator, Redeemer and Sanctifier" can be an equivalent? But how can we know whether or not it is? Conducting a baptism becomes a burden of legalistic negotiation and high soteriological risk.

A few years ago, misuse of the law-gospel distinction produced in some circles of Lutheranism a second and quite different liturgical legalism. It is not often observed now. I will nevertheless describe it, since its tangles mark something theologically vital, the limit to the applicability of Lutheranism's related dichotomies of law and gospel, faith and works, etc. There is a tradition of considering liturgical actions under the paired rubrics "sacrament" and "sacrifice." The distinction itself is harmless and often pedagogically helpful, so long as we remember what "sacrifice" was when actually practiced, and is in the New Testament or in the discourse of the ancient church. Intrinsically, and in original churchly discourse, a sacrifice is an obtrusively embodied and visible prayer. If sacraments are visible proclamation, sacrifices are visible prayer; and indeed verbal prayers are just more verbal and less visible sacrifices - as appears in a universal use that speaks of "offering" prayer.

So far, so good. But the discourse of "sacrament" and "sacrifice" becomes ominously freighted when correlated to the distinction of gospel and law. Sacramental actions are, in the Lutheran adaptation of Augustine's phrase, visible gospel-words, and are therefore actions of God toward us. Sacrificial actions must then, it seems, be our actions toward God. Thus sacrament seems to be gospel, whereas sacrificial actions are works and so must be correlates of law. Therefore, it was said, sacrament and sacrifice must not be mixed lest we mix law and gospel; no action dare be both at once. But how avoid mixing them, in any actual liturgical action?

The distinction of law as mandating sacrifice and gospel as embodying itself in sacrament can only be maintained liturgically, it works out, by rigorous policing. Consider the pitfalls attendant, from this point of view, on the simplest arrangements for the Supper. The bread and cup are to be the visibility of the gospel "Given and shed for you," so they have to be on the altar to be consecrated and distributed. But how are they to get there? Plainly, somebody will have to put them there. But this human work must not be mixed with God's sacramental work. Therefore the elements must be put there before the service ever starts: there must be no offertory procession or other offertory action involving them, despite the unanimous tradition of the church and indeed the circumstance that the gift-giving practiced in the apostolic church included the gifts destined for the altar. Or again, in the verbal actions around the bread and cup, gospel-speaking and prayer must always be separated by clear linguistic markers. If the consecration is effected by the "words of institution,"[7] these words dare not be grammatically or rhetorically embedded in prayer; even the ". . . who in the night in which he was betrayed . . ." is prohibited, on account of the grammatically linking pronoun.

We have plainly reached a *reductio ad absurdum*,[8] whether by the standards of liturgical common sense or by the standard of what the New Testament actually displays of liturgy and says about it. What is blocked by this *reductio* is the attempt to carry the distinctions of law and gospel, and of faith and works, past their application by dividing faith and prayer. Prayer, whether maximally or minimally embodied in visible acts, is a "work" beyond the distinction of faith and works; and the mandate to pray is beyond the distinction of law and gospel. For prayer is the very work of faith itself. It is not a work we do because we have faith or to which we are enabled by faith; it is what we do as being faithful. Faith, it is ecumenically agreed, is above all trust; but trust between persons is a verbal phenomenon. We believe precisely *as* we pray. Thus when we come to the prayer of the liturgy, and to the sacrifice that is its maximally embodied form, we are beyond the distinction of faith and works. Many, perhaps all liturgical actions are in one or another way, and in one or another balance, at once sacrament and sacrifice.

Conclusion

I may close by noting the ecumenical importance of this result. Catholic theology tends to begin from sacrament, and indeed from the Eucharist, and to face something like a near-vacuum of

---

[7] It is perhaps worth noting that the doctrine that the Words by themselves are the mandated consecration is a late-medieval development that was unthinkingly taken over by the Lutherans, and that it has no biblical support.

[8] Though that has not prevented these absurdities from having disastrous influence in Lutheran liturgical orders.

practice when it turns to consider preaching and teaching. Thus Catholic theology tends to assume the unity of sacrament and sacrifice, and to be puzzled by Protestant insistence on a momentous distinction to be made within the discourse of proclamation. Protestant theology tends to begin with analysis of "the Word," of the law-gospel hermeneutics and rhetoric of proclamation, and to face a near-vacuum of practice when it turns to consider embodied prayer and sacrament. Thus Protestant theology tends to assume the distinctions which indeed must control proclamation, and to be offended by Roman Catholic assumption of unities to be celebrated in the discourse of liturgy. What if both should adopt the insight of the other?

Contemporary Implications of Luther's Ethical Teachings

William H. Lazareth

In my text "Christians in Society," Eric Gritsch is recognized appreciatively as being among those leading scholars whose impressive historical and theological research helped to apply the insights of the Luther Renaissance to 21st century American Lutheranism.

In this additional tribute, I will first sketch the theological ethic of Luther and some other Reformers in early Lutheranism. Then I will briefly demonstrate its contemporary relevance for guiding the evaluation and regulation of homosexual orientation and practices within the church, as witnessed recently by the official 2005 stance of the Evangelical Lutheran Church in America. As circulated during the preceding church wide debate on this controversial ethical issue, earlier versions of this since-updated article were printed in the Winter 2002 edition of the LUTHERAN FORUM and electronically posted in the September 2005 edition of the "Journal of Lutheran Ethics."

Fortunately, there have been no major attacks on the development of Luther's theological ethic in the central body of my cited book itself. As a Biblical and systematic rejoinder to anti-Lutheran critics, there seems to be a broad consensus in approval of its densely-documented central thesis: Historically, it was in meeting the challenges of the chaotic mid-1520's that Luther increasingly supplemented—not replaced—(1) his earlier Biblical dualistic-eschatological model (the "two kingdoms" of God or Satan) by (2) his later Biblical dialectical-historical one (the Triune God's "twofold rule" of creation and redemption by Law and Gospel through Caesar and Christ, with their intersecting powers directed against the forces of Satan both temporally and spiritually, both within society and before God) .This book intentionally integrates both these Biblical norms of Luther's theological ethics.

The initial reviewers' intra-Lutheran dialogue centers instead on my own relation to past and present schools of Luther research and Lutheran church implementation. These queries and comments are based on either (1) my introductory chapter's comprehensive survey of some 200 texts and articles in the twentieth century before and after the Nazi tyranny in Germany; or (2) my Afterword's claim that the Biblically-coherent climax of Luther's theological ethic of sanctification is better expressed by the ethical function of God's Gospel rather than by the didactic function of God's Law.

For guiding and instructing the ethical lives of Christians, *insofar as they are already righteous (nota bene)*, I advocate God's sanctifying love command (*Gebot*), in what I have called "the second or parenetic use of the Gospel" as a superior alternative to any later-designated "third or didactic use of the Law" (*Gesetz*) (cf. below, Formula of Concord, Article VI).

These issues deserve a well-documented summary response for the interested pastor-theologian. Moreover, the legitimate request for some normative direction in addressing current *social* ethical controversy should also be honored, especially in view of my book's misleading (publisher-imposed) subtitle. One such paradigm on current sexual ethics will be offered below, to be added to another earlier one on military ethics written soon after the September 11, 2001 Al Qaeda attack on the United States and before the 2002 confrontation with Iraq. That article has already been published as "Christians in Society: Implications of Luther's Theological Ethics for the War on Terrorism" in LUTHERAN FORUM (Winter 2001).

Consequently, my aim here is to provide a Biblical-theological "paper trail" that begins and ends in ethical controversy—from Luther and other Reformers down to the ELCA's 2005 Assembly action regarding proposed changes of its traditional official standards for both the ordination and the union blessing of committed same-sex partners in this Church.

Luther on the Uses of the Law

The twentieth-century Luther Renaissance analyzed at length Luther's Pauline paradoxical approach (es) to God's holy will. On the one hand, Luther explicitly summarized his own support for only "two uses" of God's sin-oriented Law (Nomos/ Gesetz); both civilly and theologically, after the Fall and before the Resurrection, in both his magisterial Lectures on Galatians (1535) and his theological "last will and testament" in the Smalcald Articles (1537). Before God, the Law always accuses rebellious persons of idolatry, and in society it also struggles against corrupted disorder and suffering injustice.

On the other hand, Luther also followed Paul in his evangelical interpretation of God's grace-grounded Ten Commandments (Torah/Gebot); highlighting gospel-enriched "meanings" for righteous believers, both before the Fall and after the Resurrection), especially following the proclamation of the Apostles Creed in both of his Small and Large Catechisms (1529). This is because it is only through knowledge of the Apostles' Creed that pardoned and renewed sinners in the Spirit "come to love and delight in all the commandments of God" (Large Catechism, p. 440. II, 69). As at once both righteous and sinful, Christians do not legalistically perform ethical works of love and justice in order to be saved, but they may now do so freely to God's glory because they have already been saved by Christ alone.

This international scholarly consensus on Luther and the Law was summarized in 1965 by Wilhelm Maurer. In contrasting Luther's approach with the title and parts of the later Formula of Concord (1577), Maurer judged: "In Article VI, however, the Gospel is actually subordinated to the Law....Recent Luther research has adduced the evidence that the doctrine of the third use is foreign to Luther; nor is it set forth in the Augsburg Confession [1530] or the Apology [1531]" (Bodensieck II: 873). This authoritative evaluation covered the published research of such celebrated Luther scholars as Paul Althaus, Heinrich Bornkamm, Gerhard Ebeling, Werner Elert (Germany); and Ragnar Bring, Anders Nygren, Lennart Pinomaa, Regin Prenter, Gustaf Wingren (Scandinavia).

Then at the end of the twentieth century, this preponderant academic viewpoint was once again corroborated by Karl-Heintz zur Mühlen as follows: "This understanding of the distinction between Law and Gospel led Luther to the doctrine of the *duplex usus legis* (the twofold use of the Law)," the civil use to promote temporal peace and justice, the theological use to accuse and torment spiritual sin and unrighteousness. He concludes:

> A third function of the Law that followed upon this two-fold function—as an instruction on living for believers or those who have been reborn—was rejected by Luther, because living faith spontaneously fulfills the demands of the divine law which coincides with the *usus civilis legis* [the civil use of the Law] as to its content" (Hillerbrand II: 405)

Some of the additional approving Luther researchers now cited are Oswald Bayer, Bengt Haegglund, Lauri Haikola, Gerhard Heintze, Wilfried Joest, and Martin Schloemann.

The Sixteenth-Century Antinomian Challenge

Luther's position was also endorsed for over a decade by Melanchthon until the latter wrote his own later Commentary on Colossians (1534) and a revised edition of the *Loci communes* (1535). Melanchthon's new position—following the shocking experiences of the 1527 Saxon visitations—was to broaden the Law's coverage to include an additional didactic or "third use", that is, permanent moral instruction for Christian believers, not solely insofar as they are still sinful, but now also insofar as they are already righteous. John Calvin promptly followed suit in Geneva—for different reasons, viewing the Gospel as illumined Law—and also taught "three uses" of the Law, with the third as the "principal one" of them, in order to instruct Christian sanctification in all the post-1535 editions of his *Institutes of the Christian Religion.*

The second generation of the Reformation was thereafter plagued by a series of resultant antinomian controversies led by John Agricola over the Biblically- legitimate uses of God's Law. (See Timothy Wengert's lucid survey on "Antinomianism" and its antecedents in Hillerbrand II: 51-53.) Unfortunately, most of the relevant academic disputations by the Reformers are still not translated into English (see *Luther's Works* 47: 101-106 and "Against the Antinomians" 107-119).

Of special significance for us, however, is how Luther and Melanchthon were consistently united in rightly opposing Agricola's proposed abolition of all law in the church—*antinomos* being Luther's derogatory appellation of this neo-Marcionism. Whatever differences the two major Reformers may have taught on the uses of the Law in the life of the redeemed (twofold or threefold), they nevertheless joined ranks to oppose Agricola's rejection of both the theological and didactic functions in the pulpit, while relegating its only remaining civil function to the town hall.

There were, nevertheless, repeated antinomian controversies (1527-1528, 1537-1540, and 1550-1577) that threatened to mislead Lutheran Christians with over-assured consciences into unethical behavior. Confusing for many ever since, the disciples of Luther and Melanchthon earnestly carried on concurrent wars on two fronts: strategically united against Agricola's antinomianism, while remaining tactically divided on their own distinctive grounds of opposition.

The Formula of Concord (1577) addressed these and related issues in Articles V ("Law and Gospel") and VI ("Third Use of the Law"). The Formula's irenic purpose was to try to interpret pertinent articles of the Augsburg Confession and its Apology after four decades of Lutheran internecine strife. Worthy of our special attention in Article VI are: (1) the issue, (2) the condemnation, and (3) the supporting theological foundations for the condemnation on the issue. The new Kolb and Wengert edition of the *Book of Concord* (Fortress, 2000) supplies helpful accompanying footnotes to clarify the text's complex situation.

1. The chief issue at stake centers on the alleged validity of a "third and final use" of the Law. It is described as taking place "when those who have been born anew through God's Spirit, converted to the Lord, and had the veil of Moses removed from them, live and walk in the Law" (Solid Declaration VI.1). In the Epitome, it is amplified further that the Law is to be urged upon reborn Christians

"since nevertheless the flesh still clings to them—that precisely because of the flesh they may have a sure guide, according to which they can orient and conduct their entire life" (VI.1).

2. The concluding condemnation rejects the disputed teaching "among a few theologians":

> Therefore, we reject and condemn as a harmful error, detrimental to Christian discipline and true godliness, the teaching that the Law is not to be urged in the way just described upon Christians and those who believe in Christ but only upon unbelievers, non-Christians, and the impenitent (Solid Declaration VI.25).

A footnote asserts that the condemnation is directed specifically against "the position of John Agricola; this viewpoint was not advocated by any of the so-called antinomians of the 1550's and 1560's, neither by Musculus nor by Amsdorf, Poach, Otto, and Neander" (*Book of Concord* 591).

3. With regard to its theological foundations, the most current editors of the *Book of Concord* also explain (p. 587, f.n. 165)) that the Formula's mutual accommodation between the Gnesio-Lutherans and the Crypto-Philippists was accomplished by the original co-authors—Andreae, Chemnitz, Chytraeus, Körner, Musculus, and Selnecker— only when they editorially interpolated in the Second Declaration, directly alongside each other, the differing views of Luther via Musculus (paragraphs 15-19) with those of Melanchthon via Andreae (paragraphs 1-14, 20-25).

Understandably, therefore, theological tensions continue to coexist therein for those who believe that God uses the Law to serve the Gospel, and others who affirm rather that God's Gospel is to serve the Law. Nor is this merely an overblown clash over words: one's coherent views of Christ's vicarious atonement and Christian justification and sanctification are radically affected accordingly, as amply demonstrated in centuries of subsequent Lutheran church history and social ethical activity (or inactivity).

Why did Luther also have serious reservations about an exclusive Latin view of the atonement (Anselm), where there must be a "vicarious satisfaction" paid by the Cross of Christ to meet the just demands of an alleged "eternal law" (lex aeterna) in an ideal cosmic order governing the legal relation between God and humanity? How are we to relate the Formula's exclusively forensic (legal) model of justification to other major but non-legal metaphors of redemption also stressed in the New Testament? Is sanctification the ground or the goal of the Christian's growth in grace? And how do we reconcile the Law's "third use" with all the grace-based parenetic commands and exhortations for Christian ethics at the conclusion of the Pauline epistles and throughout the Johannine corpus? In my own book I suggest:

> At best, if consistently understood as the Pauline *nomos*, the Law's 'third use' in Article VI can rightly refer only to the legitimate application of these first two uses to the *persisting sin* ("like a stubborn, recalcitrant donkey") of imperfect Christians, as well as elsewhere to non-Christians. However, that is not a new "third use" in kind, but solely a different area of the first two functions' implementation (Lazareth 243).

In other words, Christian ethics involves action that is based not merely on a new use of the Law, but rather on a new user of the Gospel—the Holy Spirit! Only by allowing such complex questions to remain incoherently unanswered were both contending parties finally able in 1577 to converge in reconciled diversity and join together to denounce the perfectionistic views of their far more dangerous common theological foe: the indiscriminate lawlessness of Agricola's antinomianism.

The Twenty-First-Century Antinomian Challenge

Turning now pastorally to our own day, a variety of theological ethical stances tried to witness to the multiform American Lutheran legacy in the ELCA symposium edited by Karen L. Bloomquist and John R. Stumme, *The Promise of Lutheran Ethics* (Minneapolis: Fortress, 1998). In my judgment, the most promising way forward is proposed by Reinhard Hütter's essay, "The Twofold Center of Lutheran Ethics: Christian Freedom and God's Commandments" (pp.31-54).

In championing Luther's law-free Gospel, Hütter seeks to combat current Lutheran antinomianism without resorting to legalism. In doing so, he also generously alludes to my own further development of views on Luther that were already well researched by Paul Althaus, Wilfried Joest, and Helmut Thielicke. Earlier I had published *Luther on the Christian Home* (Philadelphia: Muhlenberg Press, 1960); written an extended introduction to the English translation of Paul Althaus' *The Divine Command* (Philadelphia: Fortress, 1966); and also edited the English translation of Helmut Thielicke's *Theological Ethics: Foundations* (vol. 1) and *Theological Ethics: Politics* (vol. 2) (Philadelphia: Fortress, 1966, 1969).

Their collective impact may be traced especially in the refined theological structure (chapters 3 and 8) of my recent *Christians in Society*. Luther's Biblical construal of God's pre-Fall and post-Easter "command of grace" (*Gebot*) both precedes and succeeds the interim soteriological dialectic of God's judging and preserving "law" (*Gesetz*) versus saving and serving "gospel." The "Law" (Pauline *nomos*) joins sin, death, wrath, and Satan as opposing powers of divine-human alienation and rebellion until the final judgment. Therefore, it should never be allowed to replace God's gracious and loving command (Psalmic *torah*) in both the original Garden of Eden and in the presently breaking in of the fulfilling reign of God.

It is the unique Biblical witness to the history of salvation that provides the theological foundations for the Spirit's "imperatives of grace" to guide and instruct the ethical life of Christians insofar as they are already righteous (Christian righteousness). This is above and beyond the still applicable compulsion of "imperatives of law" insofar as these same Christians are still sinful (civil righteousness). To highlight Luther's distinctive evangelical difference, I consciously chose to call the underrated Spirit's divine sanctifying activity the "second or parenetic use" of the Gospel (*Gebot*) rather than any "third or didactic use" of the Law (*Gesetz*).

Reinhard Hütter aptly summarizes this Pauline and Johannine ethos for ethics:

While I agree with the insight that the "third use of the law" intends to maintain, it is crucial to distinguish between "law" on the one hand, and "commandment," "mandate," "torah" on the other hand. Due to the condition of sin, "law" in both its first and second use has an enforcing, restraining, and convicting character. This is not inherent in God's Law, but is the result of the radical human estrangement from God. As the *Gestalt* (form) of the way of life with God – the embodiment of genuine human freedom – the enforcing, restraining, and convicting elements are lost.

Hutter continues:

The "commandment" in distinction from "law," as suggested by Paul Althaus, embodies the goods constitutive of the way of life in communion with God. It is the *usus practicus evangelii* (in Wilfried Joest's terminology) or the "second use of the gospel" (in William Lazareth's words) . . . By grasping Christ in faith . . . Christian freedom receives its distinct *Gestalt* (form) through a way of life according to the commandments: the Decalogue, the Sermon on the Mount, and the double love commandments. Here I am basically drawing upon Article VI of the Solid Declaration, Formula of Concord.

Hütter's discerning essay serves accurately to present and to locate my own position within a prominent strand of post-Nazi Luther research. In the United States, it also simultaneously highlights the doctrinal basis of my own continued social ethical opposition to the proposed ordination of practicing homosexual pastors and the blessing of committed same-sex unions. These proposals were earlier critiqued (when they were first proposed and then postponed at the 1995 ELCA Churchwide Assembly) in my article entitled "ELCA Lutherans and Luther on Heterosexual Marriage" in *Lutheran Quarterly*, VIII/3 (Autumn 1994).

A Summary Response

The authentic Lutheran Reformers were never unethical antinomians. An antinomian is opposed to all law in the Christian life. Luther, following Paul, taught rather that the Christian is (1) wholly free from the Law as a way of salvation, but also (2) still bound to the Law both religiously insofar as one acts sinfully, and ethically insofar as one acts civilly. Existing at once both righteous (in Christ) and sinful (in self), a Christian is divided into two times: "To the extent that he is flesh, he is under the Law; to the extent that he is spirit, he is under the Gospel" (*Luther's Works* 26: 342).

In harmony with these basic norms of Luther's theological ethic, I again contend that the ELCA should now preach and teach God's whole Word:

- Homosexual citizens should benefit equitably from the government's provision and protection of the Constitutional non-discriminatory rights and justice of all persons created in God's image (Gen. 9:1ff.) within the present legal structures of our own modern democratic and pluralistic society (Law's civil function);

- Homophobic prejudice (attitude) is sinful; just as homosexual practices are also the Biblically-censured acts (conduct) of an intrinsic human disorder (orientation) that departs from Christ's normative teaching (Mt. 19:4-6) on God's mandate for our essential heterosexual complementarity "from the beginning" (Gen. 1:27; 2:24) of co-human creation (Law's theological function);

- Homosexual persons are also justified as saints by God's grace, for Christ's sake, through faith alone (Rom. 3:21-28), and are to be fully welcomed into the worship and witness of the forgiven sinners who compromise the communion of saints in Christ's Church (Gospel's salvific function);

- Marriage is God's holy ordinance for one man and one woman to live together personally and sexually as "one flesh" in a lifelong covenant of fidelity that analogously resembles the unity between Christ and the Church (Eph. 5:28-33), and also blesses Spirit-guided Christians (Eph.6: 1-3) both as a "remedy against sin" (Law) and as an "estate of faith" (Gospel) for their shared service in sanctified love and responsible nurture of children in family life and society (Gospel's parenetic function).

We turn now finally to the ELCA Assembly in 2005 which followed an extensive and years-long process of study and discussion throughout this denomination's congregations, synods, seminaries, boards and agencies. After hours of climactic deliberation that centered largely on this church's pastoral and disciplinary policies, the delegates voted to reject a proposal that would have allowed gays and lesbians in committed same-sex relationships to serve in exceptional circumstances as ordained clergy.

ELCA delegates also endorsed the Lutheran church's traditional theological and ethical position on marriage as summarized in Recommendation #2:

"WHEREAS, this church holds that "marriage is a life-long covenant of faithfulness between a man and a woman" (Message on Sexuality: Some Common Convictions (1996, page 3); and WHEREAS, the Conference of Bishops in October 1993 stated., "We, as the Conference of Bishops of the ELCA, recognize that that there is basis neither in Scripture nor tradition for the establishment of an official ceremony by this church for the blessing of a homosexual relationship. We, therefore, do not approve such a ceremony as an official action of this church's ministry. Nevertheless, we express trust in and will continue dialogue with those pastors and congregations who are in ministry with gay and lesbian persons, and affirm their desire to explore the best ways to provide pastoral care for all to whom they minister" CB93.10.25); therefore, be it RESOLVED, that the Evangelical Church in America continue to respect the guidance of the 1993 statement of the Conference of Bishops; and be it further RESOLVED. that this church welcome gay and lesbian persons into its life (as stated in Churchwide Assembly resolutions from 1991, 1995, and 1999), and trust pastors and congregations to discern ways to provide pastoral care to all to whom they minister".

In conclusion, I contend that the ELCA's official reaffirmation of such updated ecclesiastical applications of Luther's historic theological ethic might greatly contribute to authentic signs of piety within the already-reconciled Church of Jesus Christ. In Christian ethics, baptismal vows must precede and govern our subsequent marital and ordination vows. Unless present-day followers of Luther and Melanchthon, through their disciples Musculus and Andreae, can now likewise collaborate in doctrinal orthodoxy and pastoral compassion, the antinomian adherents of Agricola could soon carry the day politically in reflecting our morally autonomous and secularized society.

Sources Cited

Bodensieck, Julius (Ed.). *The Encyclopedia of the Lutheran Church* (Ed. for the Lutheran World Federation). Minneapolis: Augsburg Publishing House, 1965.

Bloomquist, Karen L. & John R. Stumme (Ed.). *The Promise of Lutheran Ethics*. Minneapolis: Fortress Press, 1998.

The Book of Concord (Ed. & tr. by Robert Kolb & Timothy Wengert et al.). Minneapolis: Fortress Press, 2000.

Hillerbrand, Hans J. (Ed.). *The Oxford Encyclopedia of the Reformation*. New York: Oxford University Press, 1996.

Lazareth, William H. *Christian in Society: Luther the Bible and Social Ethics*. Minneapolis: Fortress Press, 2001

The Theology of the Cross: A Usable Past

Douglas John Hall, *McGill University*

Among those who have read some of my work it is fairly well known, I think, that I am an admirer of Martin Luther. I have even been introduced – in print – as "a Lutheran theologian." Alas, I am not a Lutheran. Insofar as these distinctions are still relevant and meaningful, I am a member, minister and theologian of the United Church of Canada—which, historically, ought to bring me closer to the Reformed than to the Lutheran side of the Reformation, since the union of churches that brought my denomination into being in 1925 included both Presbyterian and Congregational components. But somehow these distinctions, while not meaning*less,* are far less meaningful than they were even two or three decades ago. The question today is not what confessional tradition we adhere to but whether we are able – in the face of the many problems that confront our species – really to *confess* the faith at all: not merely to *profess* it. We must confess the faith; that is, to engage the world at the level of its real crises and to confer upon it the blessings of both truth and hope.

Two Preliminary Observations

My topic is "The Theology of the Cross: A Usable Past," and before I turn to the primary substance of my presentation I would like to make two preliminary observations.

First, let me offer a brief comment on the term, *theology of the cross*. It was part of the genius of Martin Luther that he detected, quite brilliantly, the difference between this biblically-based conception of the theology appropriate to our faith, and the culturally and philosophically-based *theology of glory* that has colored most of the history of Christendom. Luther named this distinction, and the naming of things is of vital importance for the corporate thinking of the church. But of course he did not invent the theology of the cross. He himself depended, as we must, upon a tradition: the tradition particularly of Paul, but behind that the tradition of the Hebraic prophets and poets who understood the highest consciousness of Hebrew faith to consist in the awareness of the "pathos of God" – as Abraham Heschel insisted.

But when we ourselves want to draw upon the tradition named *theology of the cross* we – if we go deeply enough – will find ourselves drawing not only on this biblical and classical past but, in addition to Luther himself, on a modern host of exemplars of this tradition that is both numerous and impressive. It includes, certainly, Kierkegaard, the early Karl Barth, Paul Tillich, Reinhold Niebuhr, Dietrich Bonhoeffer, Kazuo Kitamori, Kornelius Miskotte, Hans-Joachim Iwand, Juergen Moltmann, Kosuke Koyama, Dorothee Soelle, Elisabeth Moltmann-Wendel, and many others – persons who, in their particular times and places, have grasped essential aspects of this theological tradition and applied them to their analyses of and messages to their social and ecclesiastical contexts. Luther in many ways stood alone when he first introduced this term and this distinction, though the German mystics Tauler and Nicholas of Cusa and others were certainly there in the background, along with Augustine of Hippo; but Luther has not been alone in the exemplification of this tradition in subsequent centuries, and I will draw upon some of these in what follows.

The second preliminary observation concerns Luther himself, or rather our appropriation of his thought – though it could be applied to any great thinker of the past (for instance, Karl Rahner applies something like this same observation to St. Thomas Aquinas). When as Christians in the here and now we turn to the great figures of our faith's past, there are two attitudes that can be taken: one is a strictly historical attitude which asks, "What did this thinker actually say and do?" The other is an attitude which, whilst wishing to take history seriously, is asking for something more than history alone can give. Standing in the present and wanting to be a faithful witness in that present, this second attitude asks "What would this thinker say and do if he or she were here with us?" Here, therefore, as one conscious not only of the

179

problems and possibilities of the past to which he or she belonged, but conscious also of our present-day context in all its specificity.

My interest in Luther is chiefly of this second type. In fact, I have found Luther as interesting as I have (for decades now) because from the first I sensed, in what I learned of him, that this was indeed a figure from our common Christian heritage who could understand something of our present situation, and who could be shown to have some very important things to say to us. In short, his life and work was such that it could constitute for us "a usable past." Not all that makes up the past of the Christian sojourn through history is usable today. In fact a great deal of it, when not simply use*less*, is positively misleading for us, and a hindrance. For instance (to consider a recent period) nineteenth-century utopian liberalism is at least misleading today, and the nineteenth-century Fundamentalist reaction to that liberalism and modernism is more than misleading, it is dangerous – a fact that is illustrated for us on this continent daily, in spades. The need for a past, which is an *essential* need for Christians (for we do not invent our message arbitrarily as we go along!), cannot be satisfied with any and every testimony from the past. Theological judiciousness is nowhere more vital than in our choice of pasts on which to meditate in our search for foundations. I have found Luther a trustworthy guide in most things; but my interest in him is not that of an historian, who only wants to know what Luther did and said then; I want him to help me know what to do and say now. I hope to have grasped his own person and thought with something like a reasonable intuition, but my purpose is quite clearly not that of the historian or Luther scholar, but that of the theologian; and (linking this with the first observation), as a theologian I am bound to hear his 'theology of the cross' (which is a term I would apply to his theology as a whole) in tandem with those later and earlier witnesses to this tradition who tried in their own times and places to comprehend and apply this tradition.

A Spirit and Method

This being said by way of presupposition, I turn now to the main part of this address. If our purpose is to find in the theology of the cross such a "usable past," it is essential that we attempt to achieve some grasp of this theology that can be shared by as wide a spectrum of Christians as possible. It is certainly not a theology that lends itself to popularity – as Juergen Moltmann said of it, "There is a good deal of support in the tradition for the theology of the cross, but it was never much loved." But while it will likely never be a theology with wide popular appeal, neither ought we who feel its power and relevance imagine, in our pride of ownership, that it is so far above the ordinary grasp of church folk that it is unprofitable to make the attempt. The truth, as I have experienced it, is that minorities within all the once-mainline churches of this continent, disillusioned with the pompous Christian triumphalism of popular religion and sickened by the religious and cultural imperialism that that triumphalism inevitably begets, are extraordinarily open to the alternative that this submerged theological strain represents. But of course it needs to be cast in language that can be grasped by persons without a great deal of theological and historical background, and above all it needs really to engage the real problems and possibilities of the present.

What is, then, the theology of the cross? I have tried on many occasions, in both sustained argument and more metaphoric ways to describe this "thin tradition" – as I called it in my first book on the subject, *Lighten Our Darkness.* I know that I will never do justice to it because, to begin with, the theology of the cross is not an "it"; not a specific and objectifiable set of teachings or dogmas; not "a theology" – it is, rather, a spirit and a method that one brings to all one's reflections on all the various areas and facets of Christian faith and life. I have never been able to improve on Moltmann's metaphor when he says that the theology of the cross is "not a single chapter in theology, but the key signature for all Christian theology." This is a theological approach that is not easy to pin down, as one can (with care) pin down terms like "orthodoxy," or "neo-orthodoxy," or "liberalism," or "fundamentalism." But *theologia crucis* as a spirit and method of theological thought cannot be stated in a formula. It may, however, be *recognized* when it is heard or experienced, whether in sermon, serious theological writing, or artistic expression. With regard to the latter, I have found it interesting that some of the best expressions of this very classical Protestant approach to the

Christian message are found in plays and novels by Roman Catholics – like Shusaku Endo's *Silence,* Graeme Green's *The Power and the Glory,* or George Bernanos' *Diary of a Country Priest.* It is also representable in art. The great figure of modern ecumenism, W.A. Visser t'Hooft, wrote a beautiful book about his countryman, Rembrandt, in which he presents Rembrandt as an "artist of the cross," and in letters to me he reinforced this connection between Rembrandt's painting and sketches and the theology of the cross. I think one could make a similar observation about Georges Roualt, Kaethe Kollwitz, Ernst Barlach, and many other artists.

If one cannot exactly codify the theology of the cross, what one can perhaps do is to identify certain informing or overarching principles that inform this "thin" tradition. And in what remains of my presentation I should like to attempt just that.

Informing Principles of this Theology

1. The Compassion and Solidarity of God

This must be thought the 'first principle' of this theology. The christological basis of the theology of the cross is at the same time its Theological basis [and I am using Theology here in the more restrictive sense, meaning our understanding of the nature of the deity]. For this theological approach, the cross of the Christ is not only Jesus' cross, it is also and simultaneously God's cross. As Jon Sobrino writes,

> Our theology of the cross becomes radical only when we consider the presence (or absence) of God on the cross of Jesus. It is at this point that we face the alternative posed by Moltmann: Either the cross of Jesus is the end of all Christian theo-logy [by which he means the end of speculation concerning the being and acting of God] or else it is the beginning of a truly Christian theology.

This is indeed a radical affirmation in the light of the entire Theological background of the church triumphant, especially from the time of its Establishment in the fourth century. The need of all self-declared "high" religion, particularly when it is politically and culturally "established," to keep God absolute in power and transcendence, and therefore free of contamination by earthly involvements and passions, is so strong in the whole history of Christian Theology – also today! – that it is astonishing and unacceptable to many Christians whenever God is too closely associated with His crucified son. Curiously, especially in the Christian West, we characteristically accentuate the second person of the Trinity – to the point, as H. Richard Niebuhr complained, of ending with a "unitarianism of the second person of the trinity"; and yet when it comes to assumptions about God "the Father," we fail to apply this same christomonistic tendency and accentuate attributes of magnificence, especially of power, that scarcely reflect either the God of Israel, who is so deeply involved with his people, or the God and Father of Jesus, the Christ.

Luther (and in this I think he has been followed by all who took up the theology of the cross subsequently) dared to break with this hold of classical philosophic-theology, as it was held especially by the school of Alexandria, and in the spirit of the school of Antioch accentuated the themes of compassion and solidarity. One could say, using other terms, that he christologized the Deity, even going so far as to speak of "the crucified God." As Moltmann characterizes this:

> Christian faith stands and falls with the knowledge of the crucified Christ, that is, with the knowledge of God in the crucified Christ, or, to use Luther's even bolder phrase, with the knowledge of the 'crucified God.'

The implications of this radical identification of God with the crucified Christ are manifold, for it means not only that the famous 'distinctions' between the persons of the Trinity are radically qualified and their tendency to devolve into tritheism checked, it means also that theories of the *work* of Christ (soteriology) that depend upon these distinctions, as does that of Anselm of Canterbury, are implicitly called in question. And in that connection I think that Gustuf Aulen was entirely justified when – in his famous little study, *Christus Victor*, he affirmed that Luther did not follow the general tendency of the Christian West in picturing Christ's work as satisfaction offered to a holy, remote and implacably righteous God for the sins of the many. Such a conception of the atonement depends upon keeping God strictly differentiated from the substitutionary victim, Jesus; and it is one of the anomalies of Western Protestantism that most of it has nevertheless clung to an Anselmian soteriology indistinguishable in essentials from the very Catholic Theology (doctrine of God) that Luther questioned. Calvin, of course, did not help very much in this process!

2. The Cross as World-Commitment

If the cross of Jesus is first of all a statement about the nature of the Deity, it is in the second place – but not even as a second step, but implicitly and necessarily – a statement about the world and God's abiding love for the world and all its creatures. It is not strange to faith, however astonishing or incredible it may seem to unbelief (which is always at base cynicism about the worthiness of the world), that when the author of the fourth Gospel, allegedly the most Hellenistic of the four gospels, wished to state in a sentence the whole intention of God in the Christ, he wrote, "For God so loved the world that he gave his only Son, so that everyone who believes in him may not perish but may have eternal life."[John 3:16, NRSV]. Nor is it surprising that this same verse of scripture is the best-remembered New Testament sentence of them all; for despite the rhetoric and the activity of Christians and churches, which often betray precisely such a sentiment, that which is best in all of us remembers that at the center of this faith there is an extraordinary affirmation of creation. Doctrine must never become so drunk on redemption, or rather on its own superlatives and exaggerations of the redeemed estate, that it ends by denigrating the creation that God "so loved" and loves.

The cross is at once, for Christians, the ultimate statement of humankind's movement away from God and of God's gracious movement towards fallen humankind. I think of the cross of Golgotha as the divine determination to *claim* this world, however wretched its history and however costly its redemption. "I will be *your* God and you will be *my* people!" Against the clear tendency of the creature to degrade itself and abuse its environs, God in Christ reinstates the divine ownership of creation and commits God's self to creation's fulfillment, its flourishing.

It was this sense of the divine commitment to the world that made the young prisoner, Dietrich Bonhoeffer, perhaps the best advocate of the theology of the cross in our epoch, call in question the interpretation of Christianity as a religion of 'redemption'. "The redemption myths," he writes,

> try unhistorically to find an eternity after death . . . ..[For them] redemption . . . means redemption from cares, distress, fears, and longings, from sin and death, in a better world beyond the grave. But is this really the essential character of the proclamation of Christ in the gospels and by Paul. I should say it is not. The difference between the Christian hope of resurrection and the mythological hope is that the former sends [a person] back into . . . life on earth in a wholly new way. . . . The Christian, unlike the devotees of the redemption myths, has no last line of escape available from earthly tasks and difficulties into the eternal, but, like Christ himself . . . he must drink the earthly cup to the dregs, and only in his doing so is the crucified and risen Lord with him, and he crucified and risen with Christ. This world must not be prematurely written off; in this the Old and New Testaments are at one.

3. Honesty about Experience (Christian Realism)

As a third principle at work in the theology of the cross I would name an extraordinary commitment to truth-telling, a rare determination to be honest in one's faith-claims – rare, I mean, in the whole realm of "religion." For me at least, the twenty-first thesis of the Heidelberg Disputation has been vital:

> *Der Theologe der Gottes unverborgene Herrlichkeith sucht, nennt das Uebel gut und Guttes uebel; der Theologe des Kreuzes nennt die Dinge beim rechten Namen [The theologian who seeks God's unconcealed glory names evil good and good evil; the theologian of the cross calls things by their proper name.]*

This is in some ways an enigmatic statement, but only if we fail to grasp the critique of religious triumphalism that is being contrasted with the theology whose character Luther is attempting to depict. A theology that seeks to show the obviousness of the divine power and glory has to end in exaggeration and untruth.

Why? Because in order to uphold its exaggerated positive it must downplay or neglect everything by which that positive is negated or called in question – which is to say, the "evil" that manifests itself in everyday life. By contrast, he says, the *theologia crucis* names the negating realities openly, beginning with the cross of Christ itself: the cross and all that it stands for by way of human degradation and suffering is not good, not *in se* – in itself! We are not called to laud and embrace this symbol of violence and torture and death as though it were something splendid. What is good lies hidden underneath or behind this dreadful reality: namely, God's concealed presence and determination to mend the creation from within. The theology of the cross is thus not only allowed but commanded to draw the attention of church and world to that, in both, which contradicts and demeans the glory of God. The theologian of the cross is not (as is childishly alleged) a pessimist, but he or she is also not the congenital optimist who must repress every thought of doubt, despair, the demonic and death. The theology of the cross therefore leads to a *prophetic* stance on the part of the church, a boldness which "calls a spade a spade." It is here that Reinhold Niebuhr's 'Christian realism' has its foundations.

But thesis twenty one has another connotation that is easily overlooked. It means not only that faith is called upon to be *honest* about the reality of historical experience but that it must be *modest* about its own claims. For if God's triumph is indeed 'hidden beneath its apparent opposite', we dare not imagine that we have captured the truth of God in our theology! That is precisely the error of the theology of glory! Rather, we who live "under the cross," are able only to point to the mystery of the divine *agape* that is manifested in this strange, paradoxical manner. As von Loewenich writes in his biography of Luther,

> Luther's view appears to be complex, but basically it is quite simple. The apparent paradoxes prove to be true in experience. It is a question of honesty whether we acknowledge the reality of this experience or whether we reject it. Luther calls this honesty *humility.*

This "humility" has always been mandatory for those who have grasped the fact that God is *Person*, "Thou" (in Buber's terms), and who contemplated in all seriousness the mystery of God's compassion and solidarity with us *en Christo*. But today it is of the very essence of Christianity, for like all religion our religion too, as religion, is sorely tempted to make grandiose claims for itself, and in that direction – in our pluralistic world – lays violence and death. Whatever else may be said of the monumental theology of Karl Barth, his ties with Luther's *theologia crucis* are no more clearly in evidence than when, in his *Evangelical Theology*, his Chicago lectures, he insists: "Evangelical theology is *modest* theology, because it is determined to be so by its object, that is, by him who is its subject."

4. The Contextual Character of This Theology

In my book, *The Cross in Our Context,* I argued that the theology of the cross is inherently and fundamentally a contextual theology. I suppose such a claim could be interpreted as an attempt, on my part, to justify by reference to an authority-figure whom I respect, a predilection of my own for contextuality in theology. I am a sinner, also intellectually, and therefore I shall not seek to argue for the purity of my motives. Yet I do not see how one can immerse oneself in this theological tradition, not only Luther but the whole tradition, without coming to that kind of conclusion. As for Luther himself, it is of course perfectly obvious that he did not think of his work in modern contextual terms. Contextuality in theology is a by-product – rather late in time, actually! – of historical consciousness, which is a Modern mindset. Nevertheless Luther *acted* in a contextual manner, as one intensely aware of the fact that he was—for instance, a German; an Augustinian; and a critic of Aristotelianism and its ascendency in the official theology, and so on. That Aristotelianism, as James M. Kittelson notes in his biography of Luther, assumed as its primary methodological presupposition, that "all important truths . . . were universal. Circumstances of time and place made no difference to the truth of propositions that could be developed by the exercise of right reason." Precisely that assumption, which in the hands of religious authority was no innocent teaching but a potent tool for the suppression of difference, was what Luther had to challenge – and not only because he had been influenced by the so-called *via moderna,* but because as a German conscious of his own and his people's particularity he simply could not accept as binding truths that were "made in Rome," a quite different context from his own. One could argue, surely, that the whole Reformation was steeped in a place-consciousness that could not be fitted easily into the religious ideology of external authority.

But in addition to such *historical* reasons for concluding that this theological approach is inevitably contextual, there are solid *theological* grounds for such a conclusion. It follows irrevocably from all three of the previous principles: (1) A conception of God as one having compassion for, and desiring solidarity with the creature would be an empty sentiment unless "the creatures" for whom such love is intended were seen in all their particularity – which only represents, in fact, a return to the tradition of Jerusalem, with *its* historical consciousness, and away from the kind of abstractionism belonging to that side of the tradition of Athens that loves universals at the expense of particulars. (2) To speak of the cross of Christ in terms of God's world-orientation and commitment could only be an empty claim if "the world" remains at the level of an intellectual construct and does not become explicit. The "world" that God loves is not a construct but a reality, constantly in flux, rich in variety, old in sin but redolent of potentiality. Love itself, whether divine or human, is never love for generalities but for specifics; and it becomes an absurdity and a pretense if it indulges in generalities that defy specificity, which unfortunately happens all too often in religion ("I love the world, it's only these wretched people I can't stand"). (3) A theology that is committed to truth-telling, realism about evil, modesty about itself, can only be a contextual theology. Its honesty (*Wahrheitso-rientierung*—its orientation towards truth) is nothing but a determination to pay "attention" (in Simone Weil's sense) to what is actually there in front of it. It is not permitted to contemplate an ideal that is wholly unrelated to the here and now. It entertains change, certainly, and even strives for change with every fiber of its being, but it wishes to change what actually is, and (as in the famous serenity prayer of Reinhold Niebuhr) "can be changed."

To translate all this into other terms, the theology of the cross is at base a *practical* theology. It is not interested in pure theory. It is inherently critical of ideology. It drives always towards incarnation, towards enactment. This at least it has in common with liberation theology, that it is never satisfied with being theology but must become an ethic; yet, never an ethic separable from its own theological base and point of departure. Bonhoeffer, the Lutheran, complained about the Lutheranism that nurtured the theology of justification because it did not find its inherent goal in just action but rested in the security of a doctrinalized grace. One could complain just as appropriately of the Christian activism that never ponders the why of the act and therefore, perennially complicates the very problems it would address.

5. The Refusal of Finality

It would be difficult to grasp the character of this theological tradition without paying a good deal of attention to the eschatological dimension that runs through its length and breadth. One could even say that the chief difference between the theology of the cross and the antithesis that Luther uses as his contrast, the *theologia gloriae*, is their eschatology. The theology of glory depends on an eschatology that is fully "realized" – namely, realized in the church, realized in theology as true and irrefutable doctrine. There is a "realized" dimension in the theology of the cross, too; but it is not a realization to which the church and its theology can lay claim. The purposes of God are realized *in Christ*, and faith looks to God in trust and hope. But the faithful live without finality, without closure, without certitude. All our ancestors were "under the cloud," says Paul. "Nevertheless with most of them God was not pleased; for they were overthrown in the wilderness. . . . Therefore let anyone who thinks that he stands take heed lest he fall." [I Corinthians 10:1ff.] In confidence [*con – fide*] we may feel that we are on the right road, but woe to any who imagine they have arrived. The following statement seems to me typical of Luther:

> Christian living does not mean to *be* good but to *become* good; not to *be* well, but to get well; not *being* but *becoming*; not rest but training. We are *not yet*, but we shall be. It has *not yet* happened, but it is the way. Not everything shines and sparkles as yet, but everything is getting better.

This kind of statement does not deny progress or betterment, but neither does it affirm the kind of perfectionism that John

189

Wesley courted. We are living, it is true, after the victory of God in the risen Christ; but while the Christ is risen we ourselves live in hope and not fulfillment – we live, as the late Alan Lewis put it, on holy Saturday, between cross and resurrection.

And this is perhaps the best place to address the question, "what is the relationship of the resurrection to the theology of the cross"? Contrary to many critics of the theology of the cross, this theology does not overlook or downplay the victory of the third day; what it critiques is the use, or rather the misuse, of the resurrection to render the cross null and void. And that misuse is by no means a minor thing. Especially in North American popular Christianity the resurrection – or what I call resurrectionism – functions to turn the religious away from the cross as a thing well and truly overcome. And that means not only the cross of Jesus, but the cross of reality; so that the religion thus mythically bolstered becomes a primary factor in the deadening of otherwise sensitive people to the pain of God in the world.

I suspect there is no greater theological task in North America today than to refuse and redirect this false and dangerous functioning of Easter in this society. Rightly to grasp the meaning of Christ's resurrection is to be turned towards the cross, with understanding, not away from it. Moltmann puts it this way:

> [Easter] does not overcome the story of Christ's passion so that we no longer remember it. Rather, it establishes Christ's cross as a saving event. The one who goes before us into the glorious and liberated future of God's resurrected is also the one who died for us on the cross. We come face to face with the glory of the coming God beholding the features of the crucified and not through infinite demands or flights of fancy.

Being turned by resurrection faith and hope towards the cross of Jesus is not merely an act of piety; it is also an act of human and ethical solidarity with all who suffer. For Jesus is never alone, never "just Jesus." He is this representative of the suffering God and of suffering creation and creatures. A religion that in the name of faithfulness to Jesus turns away from, or becomes smug and indifferent in relation to the world, is a blasphemy in the service of false religion, the religion of glory without the cross. We are living in a society that walks very close to this blasphemy.

Conclusion

I must bring this lecture to an end, and I can only do so reluctantly, for I could have wished to cover all the aspects and facets of this theological tradition in a persuasive and final way. But that too indicates the temptation of theology always to covet glory for itself. If it is the theology of the cross that we are treating, there can be no final statement. Final statements in Christian theology are invariably to be mistrusted. That is the frustration of this discipline whenever it wishes to be a theology of the cross.

In concluding, I will leave you once again – as I did in *The Cross in our Context* – with a kind of meditation on the three Pauline virtues, faith, love and hope. The best way that I have found of conveying what I think this theological method and spirit is all about is by considering these so-called virtues in the light of what they are each negating. Unless the negation of each is understood, the positive statement (the "virtue") of each is cheapened and made into a cliché. We do not have to speculate about what these virtues negate, for in each case the negation is clearly present in the collected works of Paul; and as the New Testament's chief exemplar of this "thin tradition" Paul speaks, I believe, not only for Luther but for all who have been grasped by the principles of this tradition.

Faith: What does this term negate? The metaphor that crops up time and again in Paul's writings is "sight." Faith "comes by hearing" and is precisely a not-seeing. "Now faith is the assurance of things hoped for, the conviction of things not seen," – one of Luther's favorite texts. The eschatological element – especially the "not yet" side of Christian eschatology – is here strongly present. The theology of the cross is a theology of faith, and while faith is certainly a positive term for Luther it must not be elevated beyond its proper limit. In the act of trusting, the One trusted is glimpsed – as through a glass darkly; but not seen. Faith that is not sight is thus a faith warned against presumption. It is also a faith that is able to live with its antithesis, doubt, and that is in fact dead faith (as Unamuno said), when doubt is no longer allowed a hearing.

Hope: Hope is at once an orientation to the future and a recognition that the present is still lacking its promised fulfillment. Hope realized is no longer hope. The stance that we call hope is one constantly made conscious of the fact that the present, the *hic et nunc*, is a falling-short of what is most to be desired. So the hope that is faith's future dimension is always "hope against hope" [Rom. 4:18]. As faith must live with doubt, so hope must live with its antithesis, hopelessness, despair. What is hoped for must not be taken for granted, as though it were already experienced reality, already "seen" – for here too Paul resorts to the metaphor of sight: "For in hope we were saved. Now hope that is seen is not hope. For who hopes for what is seen? But if we hope for what we do not see, we wait for it with patience" (Rom. 8:24-25).

Love: Love negates many things, as Paul makes plain in the famous hymn to love in I Corinthians 13. But I think that what must receive priority where this discussion is concerned is power, "Love does not insist on its own way" [13:5]. "The crux of the cross," wrote Reinhold Niebuhr, "is its revelation of the fact that the final power of God over man is derived from the self-imposed weakness of his love." This, I think, is of the essence of this theology, and it is hard for all to accept who think of deity chiefly in terms of power – *omnipotence*, almightiness. But if God is love, then the divine power must accommodate itself to divine love, and not vice versa. And that, for the theology of the cross, is basic. Paul Tillich writes [and I will quote the entire thought because I think it is wonderfully illuminating]:

One of Luther's most profound insights was that God made himself small for us in Christ. In doing so, He left us our freedom and our humanity. He showed us His heart, so that our hearts could be won.

When we look at the misery of our world, its evil and its sin, especially in these days which seem to mark the end of a world period, we long for divine interference, so that the world and its daemonic rulers might be overcome. We long for a king of peace within history, or for a king of glory above history. We long for a Christ of power. Yet if *He* were to come and transform us and our

192

world, we should have to pay the <u>one</u> price we could not pay: we would have to lose our freedom, our humanity, and our spiritual dignity. Perhaps we would be happier; but we should also be lower beings, our present misery, struggle and despair notwithstanding. We should be more like blessed animals than men made in the image of God. Those who dream of a better life and try to avoid the Cross as a way, and those who hope for a Christ and attempt to exclude the Crucified, have no knowledge of the mystery of God and of man.

To summarize: the theology of the cross is a theology of faith (not sight; a theology of hope (not consummation); and a theology of love (not power). And if you want to understand what the theology of glory is you just have to turn this ordering of the virtues around: it is a theology of sight (not faith), of consummation (not hope) and of power (not love).

The one aspect of the theology of the cross that I have omitted from this characterization concerns its consequence as an <u>ecclesiology</u>. This is a serious omission, because the *theologia crucis* is only a viable theology as and when it expresses itself in an *ecclesia crucis*. To make up for this omission, besides referring you to Part three of my book *The Cross in Our Context*, I want to quote the final paragraph of Paul Tillich's best-read book, *The Courage to Be:*

> . . . . a church which raises itself in its message and its devotion to the God above the God of theism without sacrificing its concrete symbols can mediate a courage which takes doubt and meaninglessness into itself. It is the Church under the Cross which alone can do this, the Church which preaches the Crucified who cried to God who remained after the God of confidence had led him in the darkness of doubt and meaninglessness. To be as a part in such a church is to receive the courage to be in which one cannot lose one's self and in which one receives one's world.

PART III

Lutheranism around the World

Lutheran Churches in Eastern Europe: The Burden of History

David P. Daniel, Evangelical Theological Faculty-Comenius University, *Bratislava*

Lutheranism in Eastern Europe: Some General Statistics

According to information published for 2005[1] by the Lutheran World Federation, about 55% (38,935,938) of the 69,757,570 Lutherans in the world lived in Europe. 1,586,203 or roughly 2.27% of Lutherans in the world or 4% of those in Europe live in what traditionally has been considered "eastern" Europe. The 471,000 Lutherans in the Baltic states of Estonia, Latvia, and Lithuania comprise about 30% of Eastern European Lutheranism but just 1% of European Lutherans. In the successor states of the former Soviet Union (including Russia, the Ukraine, Belarus, Kazakhstan and Siberia) there are 91,000 Lutherans; in Poland 77,500, that is about 23% and 11% of European Lutherans and 5.7% and 4.8 % of Eastern European Lutheranism respectively.

Slovak Lutherans comprise the largest community of Lutherans in Eastern Europe. There total number is estimated at 430,000 or about 1.1% of European and 27% of Eastern European Lutherans. They are scattered throughout the Danube basin in the successor states of the Austro-Hungarian dual monarchy. The largest group is the Evangelical Church of the Augsburg Confession in the Slovak Republic, which reported 372,858 members in 2005. The Slovak Evangelical Church of the Augsburg Confession in Serbia and Montenegro numbers about 49,000. Another 9,000 to 10,000 are scattered throughout Hungary, in southwest Romania, in the Czech Republic and

---

[1] http://www.lutheranworld.org/LWF_Documents/LWF-Statistics-2005.pdf

Austria. In Romania the Slovaks are a minority within the largely Magyar Evangelical Lutheran Church in Romania that has about 32,500 members. The 14,460-member Evangelical Church of the Augsburg Confession in Romania is a remnant of the once substantial German Lutheran community in Siebenbürgen (Transylvania). About 20,000 Lutherans live in Slovenia and 3,500 in Croatia. The Lutheran Church in Hungary has about 305,000 members. Although the LWF statistics list 149,445 Lutherans in the Czech Republic, 114,445 are members of the Evangelical Church of the Czech Brethren, an ecumenical church formed after World War I when the Czech Reformed and the Czech Lutheran churches merged. This newly-united body is a member of the Reformed World Federation and aligns itself primarily theologically and ecclesiastically with the churches of the Helvetic Reformed tradition.[2] The Silesian Lutheran Church, located in northern Moravia has 35,000 members. Finally, although not usually considered "eastern" European, by virtue of location and history, the Evangelical Church of the Augsburg Confession and the Helvetic Confession in Austria, with 325,429 and 19,000 members respectively, is closely linked to the Protestant communities in Eastern Europe. As the name implies, two separate and distinct confessional groups and administrations share a common parliamentary instrument and legal corporate status.

It is clear that, with the exception of the Lutherans in the Baltic states of Estonia and Latvia, Lutherans in the countries of Eastern Europe are members of minority churches and most consider themselves to be "diaspora" or "dispersed" churches. Today Lutherans make up 7% of the population in Slovakia, 5% in Austria and a little over 3% in Hungary. On the other hand, Lutherans in these three countries comprise a greater proportion of the population than in the United States of America where they are just 2.7% of the population, or in Great Britain, France, Switzerland or anywhere in southern Europe. Collectively, Lutherans in the so-called successor states of the Austrian-

---

[2] Jiří Otter, Evangelical Church of Czech Brethren in the ČSSR, Prague: 1985, 3-4.

Habsburg monarchy today number about 803,767, that is, 2% of European or 50.6% of east European Lutherans.

New Political Situations; Old Challenges

In 1989 few were prepared for the dramatic transformation that took place in Eastern Europe. The communist regimes that had appeared entrenched and intractable collapsed like a house of cards. The physical "iron curtain" was dismantled. The Warsaw Pact alliance dissolved. Artists and academics, students and trade unionists, former political prisoners and recent converts to democratic changes became the new leaders of government, industry and non-governmental, not-for-profit organizations. They confronted monumental challenges and often disparate demands for change and reform. This task was complicated by the collapse of bloated, stagnant state industries, the need for massive infusions of capital and technological innovation, as well as by naiveté, corruption, and the personalization of political disagreements. They received political and economic guidance from western governments, aid agencies and from well-meaning amateurs. Assistance frequently was accepted uncritically. The "new democracies" wanted "in." They wanted to become part of the economic, political and security structures of "western" Europe as quickly as possible. Eastern European wanted the freedom, wealth, and mobility they identified with the West. This, however, required difficult structural changes in government and business, the adoption of new, often unfamiliar responsibilities and obligations, and a fundamental transformation of social expectations and attitudes. Foreign influences that penetrated the newly "open" societies were received with mixed feelings while the "old" European Union countries quickly tempered their initial enthusiastic expressions of welcome to the "new" democracies. A more cautious, sometimes suspicious, but certainly more realistic understanding of what the "unification" of Europe will bring and mean has developed during the past decade and a half.

The Lutheran churches of Eastern Europe were equally if not more surprised by the collapse of the regimes to which they had, more or less, become accustomed and with which they had established their own specific *modus vivendi*. The communist states mistrusted and resented the influence of Christian churches as incompatible with the new official ideology of state and society. But they were willing to tolerate them, if only temporarily, as agents of social control as long as they did not challenge the hegemony of the state or its political, economic and social omnicompetence. In exchange for official declarations of religious freedom and minimal but regular financial support, church leaders and members gradually became accustomed to and tolerated the new system of state influence, supervision, and control; most grudgingly, a few enthusiastically. Clergy were expected to become partners in social control or even agents of state security. Those who refused to cooperate were removed, imprisoned, executed, banished, or "allowed" to retire. The churches might seek to ameliorate the worse abuses of state power. They did not dare to challenge it directly. They neither anticipated nor believed that the system would change substantially, much less disappear.

Caught unaware, the churches of Eastern Europe have had to respond to unexpected and unfamiliar changes of political, social, and cultural structures, realities, expectations, and attitudes. In many ways the revolutions of 1989 were a mixed blessing for the churches. New opportunities abounded. But human and material resources were few. The toll taken by forty years of control by governments officially dominated by the atheist communist party became painfully evident as Christian churches in Eastern Europe sought to cope with and respond to new circumstances.

Early Historical Relations between the Church and State

What is frequently overlooked or too often forgotten, however, is that the subordination and politicizing of Christianity was not peculiar to the communist era. In most regions of Eastern Europe the control and even exploitation of Christian churches by the state is an ancient tradition, almost as ancient as the attempt by churches to influence and exploit political and national sympathies for ecclesiastical and confessional benefit. As the second millennium of Christianity came to an end, Eastern European Christians had to come to terms with a consciously and subconsciously engrained burden — the burden of their identity, of their own history, both immediate and distant.

It is in eastern Europe that the oldest, most durable border, some would say barrier, between "East" and "West" was established by the confrontation of eastern (Greek or Slavic) Orthodoxy and western Latin Christianity, differentiated by ecclesiastical orientation or loyalty, theological attitudes and traditions, liturgical languages and even alphabets. It was reflected in the encounter of eastern and western Christianity during the ninth-century mission of Constantine (Cyril) and Methodius to the short-lived principality of Great Moravia. Invited by Rastislav, the nephew of its founder Mojmír, the brothers from Salonika developed the Glagolitic script (the ancestor of Cyrillic letters), which they used to translate parts of the Bible and to prepare a liturgy in the old Slavic language. A code of laws was prepared in the language and a school established for training clergy, who also served the prince as clerks. The attempt to create an independent Slavic province within Latin Christianity, however, was thwarted almost immediately by the eastern Franks or Germans. After the death of Cyril and Methodius and the expulsion of their students, Latin Christianity was re-imposed in east-central Europe, in the Baltic countries, Poland, and in the Danube-Carpathian basin. It became a unifying force in the kingdom of Bohemia, the principalities of Austria, the Polish-Lithuanian monarchy, and in the kingdom of Hungary that was interposed between the western and southern Slavs, and formally established by the Magyar King Stephen on December 25, 1000. Western Slavs became Latin Christians, Northern and most Southern Slavs adopted eastern Christianity.[3]

As elsewhere in Europe, the churches in Eastern Europe claimed and endeavored to secure independence of secular authority or obligations. But they performed functions essential for the administration of the state. For centuries the chancellors and other clerks of the royal and noble courts were clerics. Religious orders and monastic houses provided utilitarian services. Monks taught, prepared documents, copied books, maintained libraries

---

[3] Francis Dvornik, *The Slavs in European History and Civilization*, New Brunswick, NJ: Rutgers University Press, 1962, 1-8. Ján Lukačka, Ján Steinhübel, "The History of Slovakia up to the Beginning of the 10th Century" in Elena Mannová (ed.), *A Concise History of Slovakia*, Bratislava: Historický ústav, Slovenskej akadémie vied, 2000, pp. 19-27.

and archives, established hospitals and orphanages, organized poor relief, were agricultural entrepreneurs and innovators, apothecaries and land-lords.

What was initially mutually beneficial, ultimately engendered tension as state and ecclesiastical institutions, interests and authority became almost inextricably intertwined, commingled, confused and abused. Even within the Church, secular and spiritual activities collided. This was manifested by the schism between eastern and western Christianity and within western Christianity, the conciliar movement of the fourteenth and early fifteenth centuries, theological dispute and diversity, and the emergence of heresy but especially by repeated calls to reform the church in its head and members.

The Protestantism in Eastern Europe: Sixteenth through the Nineteenth Century

The reformers – John Wycliffe in England, Jan Hus in Bohemia, Martin Luther in Germany, Ulrich Zwingli, Heinrich Bullinger and John Calvin in Switzerland – transformed and diversified the religious life and structures of Europe that resulted in fragmentation of Latin Christianity. The hegemony of medieval Catholicism was challenged by the Reformation movements. The understanding of Christianity became more diverse, ecclesiastical structures were particularized. By the end of the sixteenth century the reformation movements had not just penetrated much of Eastern Europe, they were dominant in kingdoms of Bohemia and Hungary and a significant minority in Austrian patrimonial lands ruled by the Austrian line of the Habsburg family.

The Czech Hussite tradition, either in the dominant Utraquist form or the more radical tradition represented by the *Unitas Fratrum* (Unity of the Brethren) had been established in the fifteenth century. Lutheranism, therefore, did not become firmly rooted in Bohemia.[4] It was, however, accepted primarily by some

---

[4] Jiří Otter, *The Witness of Czech Protestantism,* Prague: Kalich, 1970, pp. 32-46. Rudolf Říčan, *The History of the Unity of Brethren,* C. Daniel Crews (tr.), Bethlehem, PA: The Moravian Church in America, 1992. Ferdinand Hrejsa, "Kirchengeschichte Böhmens," in Friedrich

nobles and the German population in the border regions and some of the major cities in Bohemia, in parts of Moravia but especially in Silesia. On the other hand, its confession of faith did serve as a model for the *Confessio Bohemica* of 1575, which was an attempt by Bohemian non-Catholic churches to present a united front in seeking legal toleration from the Habsburg monarch.[5] In the Austrian patrimonial lands, subject to the direct hereditary rule of Habsburg princes, Lutheran ideas and worship spread during the second half of the sixteenth century largely due to nobles and townspeople who used their right of ecclesiastical patronage –the right to name the clergy serving on their estates or for churches they had built – and the threat of a Turkish invasions to wrest tacit toleration from the Habsburgs.

Reformation Lutheranism and Calvinism had a much greater impact upon the kingdom of Hungary.[6] This was made possible in part by the division of the kingdom into three parts after King Louis Jagellon, more than 500 nobles, two archbishops and five bishops, and over 80% of the Hungarian army were killed by the Turks at Mohács in August of 1526. For 175 years a triangular struggle between the Habsburg kings, Transylvania princes, and

---

Siegmund-Schultze (comp), *Ekklesia, eine Sammlung von Selbstdarstellungen der Christlichen Kirchen, V. Die Osteuropäischen Länder, Die Kirchen der Tschechoslowakei,* Leipzig: Leopold Klotz Verlag, 1937, pp 31-76. Winfried Eberhard, "Bohemia, Moravia and Austria", in Andrew Pettegree (ed.), *The Early Reformation in Europe,* Cambridge: University Press, 1992, pp. 23-48.

[5] Zdenìk V. David, "Utraquists, Lutherans and the Confessio Bohemica of 1575", *Church History* 68, 2 (June, 1999): 294-336. Ferdinand Hrejsa, *Česká konfesse. Její vznik podstata a dějiny,* Prague: Ceská akademie pro vědy slovesnost a umìní, 1912. David P. Daniel, "Ecumenicity or Orthodoxy: The Dilemma of the Protestants in the Lands of the Austrian Habsburgs", *Church History* 49.4 (Dec., 1980): 387-400.

[6] See Ivan Mrva, David P. Daniel, "Slovakia during the Early Modern Era, 1526-1711", in Elena Mannová (ed.), *A Concise History of Slovakia,* Bratislava: Historický ústav Slovenskej akadémie vied, 2000, pp. 105-154. David P. Daniel, "Calvinism in Hungary: the theological and ecclesiastical transition to the Reformed faith", in Andrew Pettegree, Alastair Duke and Gillian Lewis, *Calvinism in Europe: 1540-1620,* Cambridge: University Press, 1994, pp. 205-230.

Turkish sultans devastated the kingdom. But this also allowed the practically unfettered spread of reform. By the beginning of the seventeenth century, only about 10% of the population remained Roman Catholic and the bishops complained about the shortage of priests. Most of royal Hungary, that is western (today the Austrian Burgenland and western Hungary) and northern Hungary (roughly congruous to today's Slovakia) became Lutheran. So did the majority of the German population of Siebenbürgen or Transylvania (today the western part of Romania). Lutheranism initially attracted the German towns' people, intellectuals and some of the middle- and upper-nobility. After mid-century, Helvetic Reformed practices and theology proved more attractive to the majority of the Magyars in Turkish occupied Hungary and Transylvania. By the beginning of the seventeenth century, non-Roman Catholics made up about 85% of the population of the divided kingdom.

The Habsburgs and post-Tridentine Catholicism made a common cause and created a "union of altar and throne" that sought to halt and then reverse the spread of Lutheran and Reformed influences throughout their lands. By the beginning of the seventeenth century the reinvigorated episcopacy were using monastic orders (especially the Jesuits, Franciscans, and Piarists), anti-Protestant regulations and the police power of the state, visitations, persuasion, free education and even bribes, to try to regain the allegiance of the nobility, bourgeoisie and the political elite.

The Fifteen Years' War (1593 – 1606), also known as the Long War with the Turks, the revolt of the Calvinist Stephan Bocskai in Hungary, and conflict within the Habsburg family made it possible for Protestants in the Hungarian and Czech kingdoms as well as in upper Austria to obtain promises of toleration in 1608/9. But the uprising of the Protestant estates of Prague in 1618 and their subsequent defeat in 1620 doomed the Reformation movements in not only in Bohemia but also in the Austrian patrimonial lands and plunged Europe into thirty years of war. After 1628, Austrian and Czech Protestants were forced to convert or go into exile in Hungary or in Protestant states in Europe or go into hiding. In Hungary, however, the nobility employed their legal right of armed resistance to force the

Habsburgs monarchs to assent to the treaties of Vienna (1606), Mikulov (1622) and Linz (1645). These granted the Lutheran and Reformed churches in Hungary the right to exist, their own ecclesiastical administrative structures and to self-government and extended to the serfs freedom of worship. The Catholic hierarchy, however, argued that the monarch had been coerced to agree to these treaties and thus they were illegal.[7]

It was a conspiracy led by the Catholic viceroy and the archbishop of Esztergom that ultimately resulted in the Lutherans and Reformed in Hungary being accused of treason. During the second-half of the sixteenth century, the Protestants of Hungary were subjected to a process of "confessional cleaning." Lutheran and Reformed churches and schools were confiscated. Their pastors and teachers were summoned to appear at extraordinary tribunals where they faced the death sentence if they did not abjure their faith or resign their office. Those who refused to convert were immediately exiled. The recalcitrant were imprisoned or sold as galley slaves. Ultimately, despite all constitutional guarantees, the Protestant churches were forbidden to function during the "tragic decade" (1670-1680). This banning of Protestant led to protests from abroad, by fellow Protestants and foreign rulers and to another revolt, to which the Turks tacitly consented, this time led by Imre Thököly. This forced the king to convene of the Diet of Sopron in 1681. It saved Protestantism from extinction in the kingdom of Hungary. But it transformed the earlier *right* of the Lutherans or Reformed to worship as they wished into a *privilege* granted by the king. In article 26/1681 the diet designated two specific places in each county where new protestant churches – the so-called "articular" churches – could be built to replace the many churches that had been confiscated by the Catholic landlords, bishops or royal agents. Even then Protestant churches were few. Moreover, the property rights and civil liberties of Protestants

---

[7] Márta Fata, Ungarn, das Reich der Stephanskrone, im Zeitalter der Reformation und Konfessionalisierung, Multiethnizität, Land und Konvession, 1500 bis 1700. Münster. Ashendorfische Verrlagsbuchhandlung. 2000. Peter Kónya, "Dejiny ECAV na Slovensku v rokoch 1610-1790", in Pavel Uhorskai and Julius Alberty (eds.), Evanjelici v dejinách slovenskej kultúry III. Lipt. Mikuláš: Tranoscius, 2002, pp. 26-61. See also Mrva and Daniel as above in n. 6.

were steadily encroached upon. The constant pressure of "bureaucratic" persecution during the reign of Maria Theresa proved even more effective than the earlier use of armed force. Catholic bishops and local priests received payment for religious acts performed by Protestant clergy. Questions of marriage, inheritance, and public morality were governed by Catholic regulations. From being a bare majority of the population even at the end of the seventeenth century, Protestants were reduced to about 10% of the total population of Hungary and less than 1% elsewhere in the Austrian Habsburg lands.[8]

The edict of toleration issued by Joseph II in 1781 restored many of the civil rights of the Protestants and Greek Orthodox and made possible a broader public exercise of non-Catholic worship than heretofore. The emperor did not intend to encourage Protestantism and preferred that it would disappear. But he believed in the social utility of religion and required that all churches, including the predominant Roman Catholic Church, were to serve the public interest of the state and likewise be supervised by the state. Legal organizational equality of the churches before the law was achieved only after the "national" revolutions of 1848/9. However, the majority Roman Catholic Church continued to enjoy special privileges and exercise considerable influence throughout the region.[9]

During the nineteenth century, Protestants were in the forefront of shaping and marshaling the national consciousness of the various ethnic groups in the Austro-Hungarian monarchy. National and confessional identity or consciousness increasingly interacted and intertwined. Some leaders of minority "nations" in

---

[8] Mihály Bucsay, Der Protestantismus in Ungarn, 1521-1978, Ungarns Reformationskirchen in Geschichte und Gegenwart. I, Im Zeitalter der Reformation, Gegenreformation und Katholischen Reform, Wien-Köln-Graz: Verlag Hermann Böhlaus Nchf., 1977, pp. 193-222.

[9] Libuša Frankova, "Dejiny ECAV na Slovensku od osvietenstva po cisársky patent" in Pavel Uhorskai and Julius Alberty (eds.), *Evanjelici v dejinách slovenskej kultúry III.* Lipt. Mikuláš: Tranoscius, 2002, pp. 63-109. Tibor Fabiny, *Bewährte Hoffnung, Die Evangelisch/Lutherische Kirche Ungarns in vier Jahrhunderten,* Erlangen: Martin/Luther/Verlag, 1984, pp. 39-55.

the dual monarchy attempted to create a "federal" monarchy. Some Czech and Slovak Lutheran leaders agitated for the creation of joint state of Czechs and Slovaks. Others looked to Russia as a possible "defender" of Slavic interests. In the almost autonomous Kingdom of Hungary, the Magyars (the largest ethnic/national group, which actually were a minority of the population of the whole kingdom) were the dominant political and cultural force. They sought to transform the kingdom into a unified national monarchy (with a unified Protestant Church) through forced "Magyarization." World War I, however, resulted in the dissolution of Austrian-Hungarian monarchy and the creation of the national states of Austria, Czechoslovakia, Hungary, Romania and the United Kingdom of Serbs, Croats and Slovenes.[10]

Enduring Two World Wars

The twentieth century was not kind to the Lutherans in the former Habsburg lands, nor elsewhere in Eastern Europe. The Lutheran and Reformed churches had to reorganize within new state structures. In Austria, the Catholic Church exploited its substantial influence and government weakness. Nevertheless, the annexation of the Burgenland increased the membership of the Lutheran church as did the "Away from Rome" movement of former Catholics that also brought about 100,000 Catholics into the newly established Evangelical Church of the Czech Brethren. But theses churches had far too few human and financial resources, far too little time and far too little spiritual vigor to prepare for the onslaught first of Christian Socialism and then National Socialism. The annexation of Austria by the Nazi "Third Reich" in March 1938 and the dismemberment of Czechoslovakia in March 1939 were accompanied by anti-church measures. Schools were closed, pastors expelled from office or imprisoned, religion was not to be taught in the schools, diaconal or social work was restricted and state subsidies ended. Yet the very

---

[10] Elena Mannová and Roman Holec, "On the Road to Modernization, 1848-1918, Elena Mannová (ed.), *A Concise History of Slovakia*, Bratislava: Historický ústav Slovenskej akadémie vied, 2000, pp. 185-240. Tibor Fabiny, *Geschichte der Evangelischen Kirche in Ungarn*, Budapest, 1995, pp. 27-33.

hardships faced by the churches forced them to cooperate and strengthened the focus on the spiritual needs of its members.[11]

After World War I, in December 1918, the Evangelical Church of the Czech Brethren was established by a merger of Czech Reformed (126,000 members) and Lutheran (34,000) Lutherans.[12] It identifies itself with and has sought to reinvigorate the Czech Hussite tradition and adopted four Reformation confessions.[13] The old Silesian Lutheran Church in northern Moravia in the districts of Ostrava Karvin and Český Těšín was re-organized in 1923 after most of the Czech Lutherans had joined the newly founded, largely Reformed Evangelical Church of the Czech Brethren. A separate German Lutheran Church continued to exist in Bohemia and Moravia. After the region was annexed by Poland in 1938, it was briefly placed under the jurisdiction of the Lutheran consistory in Warsaw. But with the German invasion of Poland, the church was subsumed by Evangelical Union Church in Breslau. It suffered considerably as almost all of its pastors of Czech, Slovak or Polish nationality were deposed and replaced by German-speaking clerics. It was restored again as an independent Lutheran Church with its own ecclesiastical administration in the Czechoslovak Socialist Republic in 1948.[14]

In eastern Czechoslovakia, after centuries of being a part of the Lutheran Church in the kingdom of Hungary, the Evangelical Church of the Augsburg Confession adopted a new constitution in 1921 and became a primarily Slovak Lutheran Church. It took

---

[11] Grete Mecenseffy, Geschichte des Protestantismus in Osterreich, Graz-Köln, Hermann Böhlaus Nachf. 1956, pp209-223. Gustav Reingrabner, *Protestanten in Österreich, Geschichte und Dokumentationen.* Wien-Koln-Graz, Verlag Hermann Böhlaus Nchf. 1981, pp. 236-275.

[12] Jiří Otter, Evangelical Church of Czech Brethren in the ČSSR, Prague: 1985, 3-4.

[13] The Augsburg Confession of 1530, The Bohemian Confession of 1535 as revised by John Amos Comenius in 1662, the Second Helvetic Confession of 1566, and the Bohemian Confession of 1575. *Čtyři vyznání*, Praha: komenského evangelická bohoslovecká fakulta, 1951.

[14] E. Theodore Bachmann, Mercia Brenne Bachmann, *Lutheran Churches in the World, A Handbook*, Minneapolis: Augsburg, 1989, PP. 307.

control of theological training, diaconal work and schools that had existed in the Slovak area of the kingdom of Hungary during the nineteenth century and began new work. After Bohemia became a protectorate of Nazi Germany, Slovakia became an independent Slovak republic led by the Hlinka's Slovak Peoples Party. The priest Jozef Tiso became the "Leader" of the party, the Slovak state and Germany's ally. Priests were strongly represented in the party, state council and parliament supported the social, cultural, and educational polities of the government. But there existed internal disagreements between Tiso and the more radical Slovak national socialists. During World War II, some of the German congregations seceded from the Evangelical Church of the Augsburg Confession in Slovakia and Germans held a special (though irritating) position within the state. There was less direct interference in the religious life of the Lutheran Church by the Catholic leadership of the Slovak state. However "unofficial" attacks by para-military Hlinka Guards on individuals and groups of Lutherans were not rare. Significant differences in political attitudes emerged. The Lutherans who had held influential positions in the economy, cultural institutions, and state administration during the Czechoslovak Republic felt marginalized.[15] This resulted in conflict between the government and Lutherans. The number of restrictions intended to control the public activities and leadership of the Lutherans Church increased. Some leaders were imprisoned several times for anti-state activity when they protested the abuses of those in power.[16] Not a few Lutherans actively protected the Jews and many played important roles in planning and leading the uprising against the Nazi dominated state in 1944, the largest anti-fascist national uprising during World War II.[17]

---

[15] Ondrej Žilák, "Dejiny ECAV v rokoch 1918-1948," in Pavel Uhorskai and Julius Alberty (eds.), *Evanjelici v dejinách slovenskej kultúry III.* Lipt. Mikuláš: Tranoscius, 2002, pp. 110-125.

[16] Yeshayahu Jelinek, *The Parish Republic: Hlinka's Slovak People's Party, 199.1945.* Boulder: East European Quarterly, 1976. p. 50.

[17] Ján Ušiak, "Evanjelická cirkev a slovenský štát" in *Sbornik Ústavu dejín KSS. Poboèký ÚD KSÆ*, 8,2 (1967): 5-53.

Ethnic tensions and the loss of over two-thirds of the territory and 40% of the population of the former kingdom of Hungary and incorporation of about 8% of the Magyars population into the successor states greatly affected political, national and even religious relationships and organizations in the region. Nationalism and irredentism infected even the theology of churches of Hungary and a "Hungarian Creed" was recited in schools.[18] The state cooperated with Nazi Germany and received much of southern Slovakia as a result of the Vienna Award in the fall of 1938. The three major churches, the Roman Catholic (with about 70% of the population), the Reformed, and the Lutheran all had representatives in parliament. Attempts to create a unified Hungarian Protestant Church at the turn of the century were gradually abandoned in favor of the renewal of confessional identity in both the larger Reformed (1,632,852 members) and the smaller Lutheran (485,219 members) churches in Hungary. On the whole church life was not substantially hindered in the Hungarian state. A Lutheran theological faculty was established in Sopron to replace those that had been in Slovakia and subsequently abolished and replaced by the theological school (now university) in Budapest. Revival movements were extremely popular during the inter-war period and the Lutheran Church in Hungary developed diaconal work and a large network of primary, secondary, and higher schools.[19]

In 1940, two-fifths of Transylvania was returned to Hungary only to be returned to Romania after the war ended. The war was followed by the introduction of communism and the continued marginalization of the once substantial Magyar, Slovak and German Lutheran communities. But despite severe restriction on their activities and the loss of most of their property, leaders and members, through emigration or death, two Lutheran Churches, one Magyar and Slovak, the other German continue to function in

---

[18] Mihály Bucsay, Der Protestantismus in Ungarn, 1521-1978, Ungarns Reformationskirchen in Geshichte und Gegenwart, Part 2. Von Absolutismus bis zur Gegenwart. (Wien/Köln/Graz: Hermann Böhlaus Nachf., 1979), p. 138

[19] *Ibid.* pp. 132, 143-147. Tibor Fabiny, *Geschichte der evangelischen Kirche in Ungarn*, pp. 34-41.

post-Communist Romania and actually exhibited some signs of renewal.[20]

Protestantism Under the Communist Regimes

After World War II, the Lutheran Church in the occupied second Austrian Republic began its renewal under the leadership of Bishop Karl May and then Oskar Sakrausky.[21] The Austrian state treaty affirmed the country's perpetual neutrality as a condition for ending occupation. A new constitution for the church was drawn up and approved in 1949 while the so-called Protestant Law of 1961 regulated the relationship between the state, the Evangelical Church of the Augsburg Confession and Helvetic Confession on the basis of a "free church in a free state."[22] The two churches work closely together, have adopted the Leuenberg Concord and enjoy legal parity with the Catholics. The Lutheran church is in the foreground of defending human rights, opposing racism and chauvinistic nationalism and works especially with refugees and émigrés, and international relief agencies. It is active in international ecumenical activities. During the communist era in Czechoslovakia and Hungary, the Austrian Church developed closer ties with the Czech and Hungarian Churches, but began to be actively engaged with the Slovak Lutherans only after 1989. As new religious communities began to seek recognition in Austria during the final years of the twentieth century, a new law on religious associations was passed 1998. It distinguishes between recognized religious communities and new confessional communities or religious societies. Confessional communities may obtain legal corporate status after the government investigates their operations and teachings. Even then, they do not obtain the

---

[20] E. Theodore Bachmann, Mercia Brenne Bachmann, *Lutheran Churches in the World, A Handbook*, Minneapolis: Augsburg, 1989, PP. 318-321.

[21] Karl May (ed.), *Die Evangelische Kirche in Österreuch*, Göttingen: Vandenhoeck & Ruprect,, 1962.

[22] Gustav Reingrabner, *Protestanten in Österreich, Geschichte und Dokumentationen*. Wien-Koln-Graz, Verlag Hermann Böhlaus Nchf. 1981, pp. 275-300.

right to provide religious instruction in schools nor to invite religious workers from abroad to assist them. On May 17, 2005 the Evangelical Church of the Augsburg Confession and Helvetic Confession in Austria adopted a new constitution that went into effect on January 1, 2006.

The defeat of Nazi Germany was followed by the restoration of the Czechoslovak state which had most of its confiscated territory returned. President Eduard Beneš applied the principle of "collective guilt" and ordered the wholesale deportation of nearly 2.5 million ethnic Germans from restored Czechoslovakia as "collaborators." According to the Potsdam agreement, Hungary and Czechoslovakia agreed to exchange populations. This destroyed the viability of many formerly large Slovak congregations in Hungary.[23] Slovaks were encouraged to immigrate to Slovakia; Hungarians from Slovakia were to go Hungary. About 500,000 Hungarians remain in southern Slovakia and the Reformed Church in Slovakia is largely Hungarian. The once significant German Evangelical Church disappeared.

During the communist era, the fate of the Lutheran churches in Czechoslovakia and Hungary and Romania were similar. The Catholic Church, because of its position in the war-time republics, were the initial targets of property confiscations and those who openly refused to cooperate with the new authorities were excluded from office. The Lutherans, however, were also quickly confronted with the hostility of the new regimes. They were, to be sure, legally recognized and the freedom of religion was incorporated into the new state constitutions. New constitutions were prepared for the churches that severely restricted the scope and competencies of pastors and congregations. School buildings, hospitals, orphanages were confiscated, church schools and diaconal work ended, the teaching of religion excluded from the curriculum. The theological academies were likewise purged of

---

[23] For example, the second largest protestant church building in Europe, after the Ulm cathedral, is the Large Lutheran Church in Bekescsaba with a capacity of 3,500 worshipers that had a congregation of about 10,000. Today barely a score attend Slovak services. See. Balázs Dercsenýi and others, *Lutheran Churches in Hungary*. Budapest, Hegzi a Company Publishing House, 1992, p. 131.

faculty and students whose loyalty or willingness to cooperate with the new order was suspect. The government did everything it could to marginalize the church, limit its sphere of activity to "spiritual" matters, strip it of most of its assets, intimidate the clergy, subordinate them to strict state control, and employ compliant ecclesiastical and lay leaders. Pastors were rewarded for inaction, active evangelization or formal work with youth discouraged or banned. Church publications were censored and paper stocks limited. New secular rites for the new-born, for adolescents, marriage and burial were designed and encouraged as replacements for baptism, confirmation, weddings and church funerals. Open criticism of the leadership of the church or state would have serious consequences.[24] In Hungary Bishop Lajos Ordass[25] sought to defend (as did Vladimír Pavel Čobrda and Fedor Fridrich Ruppeldt in Slovakia) the integrity and independence of their respective Lutheran churches during World War II as well as under the communist regime for which they deposed and imprisoned. Cooperation with the agents of state security was expected, especially for those who had contacts with foreigners. Bishops were elected for life and the senior or general bishop was entrusted with the responsibility of representing the Church abroad. The communist government approved but also controlled the involvement of selected clerics in international organizations such as the World Council of Churches, the Lutheran World Federation, the European Church Conference as well as the Christian Peace Conference whose founding president was Jozef Hromadka. He was the leading theologian of the Evangelical Church of the Czech Brethren and an advocate of adapting theology to meet the new social and political realities.

---

[24] Jan Pešek, "Dejiny ECAV na Slovensku v rokoch 1948-1990" in Pavel Uhorskai and Julius Alberty (eds.), *Evanjelici v dejinách slovenskej kultúry III.* Lipt. Mikuláš: Tranoscius, 2002, pp. 162-175. Jan Pešek, Michal Barnovský, *Cirkvi na Slovensku v rokoch 1953-1970*, Bratislava, VEDA, 1999. Pavel Uhorskai, *Uncompromising Faith, One Man's Notes From Prison*, Jaroslava Vajda (tr.), St. Louis, MO: Concordia Publishing House, 1992.

[25] Laszlo G. Terray, Eric W. Gritsch (tr.), *He Could Not Do Otherwise: Bishop Lajos Ordass, 1901-1978*. Grand Rapids, Michigan: Eerdmans, 1997.

There were two great waves of repression in the churches in the region. The first began in 1948 and concluded after the death of Stalin in 1953. The communist regime attempted to crush open opposition within the churches.[26] After a brief period of respite a second wave of repression began, first in Hungary and then in Czechoslovakia, after attempts to ameliorate the abuses of the Communist regimes were forcibly brought to an end.

In Hungary, this second wave of repression followed the suppression of the Uprising of 1956 and the occupation of Hungary by Soviet forces. The briefly rehabilitated Ordass was replaced by Zotán Kaldy as bishop of the southern diocese. Kaldy developed a "theology of diaconia"[27] which held that service to others is the heart of the Gospel and that the church should be involved in the political realm. Even more radical was the Professor Erno Ottlyk, elected bishop of the northern diocese in 1967. When it was decided that the seventh Lutheran World Federation Assembly would be held in Budapest in 1984 (the first time in Eastern Europe), Ottlyk was replaced by the more sophisticated and trustworthy Gyula Nagy who had spent time working in Geneva at the LWF.[28] The LWF Assembly ignored criticism of Kaldy and elected him President. Eric Gritsch notes that the "final message of the Budapest Assembly disclosed the LWF's darkest hour."[29] During the 1980s the control of the state over the church began to be relaxed.[30] In Czechoslovakia, the

---

[26] Magdalena Forgacova, "Slovak churches and proselytism", *Journal of Ecumenical Studies* 36, 1/2 (Winter/Spring 1999):116 -144, here 129-128.

[27] János Pásztor, "The Theology of the Serving Church and the Theology of Diaconia in the Protestant Churches and their Consequences," Religion in Eastern Europe.
http://www.georgefox.edu/academics/undergrad/departments/soc-swk/ree/ PASZTOR.doc

[28] Tibor Fabiny, jr. "Theologies of Church Government in the Hungarian Lutheran Church during Communism (1945-1990). *Religion in Eastern Europe 24,4* (August, 2004): p 11-27.

[29] Eric W. Gritsch, *A History of Lutheranism,* Minneapolis: Fortress Press, 2002. p. 235.

[30] Tibor Fabiny, *Geschichte der evangelischen Kirche in Ungarn*, pp. 46-48.

second wave followed the Prague Spring of 1968 and the attempt Alexander Dubcek to create "socialism with a human face." During the normalization of 1970s, Bishop Ján Michalko and General Supervisor Andrej Žiak (the highest lay leader) assured the docility of the church in an attempt to avoid any conflict with state power. Open dissent was not tolerated.[31] In the eyes of the regime the Lutheran Church in Slovakia was no longer was a problem.[32] But beneath the surface and away from the eyes of the general public, opposition was growing within the church. It erupted after November 17, 1989 when the gentle revolution in Slovakia began.

Protestantism since 1989

During the fifteen years following the dissolution of the communist regimes in Eastern Europe, much has changed.[33] What is interesting is that, from an historical point of view, it is following a rather traditional pattern. The churches look for new leaders. They reorganize and prepare new constitutions.[34] They seek to regularize and improve the state subsidies and improve financial management. Part of this has been to seek a continuation of the assistance that was provided to the Lutheran churches in this region from the west, especially through the LWF and WCC. But

---

[31] Daniel Vesely, "Evanjelici za vlády komunistov". Mss in possession of author.

[32] Jan Pešek, "Dejiny ECAV na Slovensku v rokoch 1948-1990" in Pavel Uhorskai and Julius Alberty (eds.), *Evanjelici v dejinách slovenskej kultúry III.* Lipt. Mikuláš: Tranoscius, 2002, pp. 188.

[33] One of the quickest and quite reliable ways of following the changes that have taken place is to utilize the Annual International Religious Freedom Report of the United States Department of State available electronically. (http://www.state.gov/g/drl/rls/irf/2005)

[34] For example. Cirkevný ústavný zákon č. 1/1993, Evanjelickej cirkvi augsburského vyznania na Slovensku (http://www.ecav.sk/archiv/ dokumenty/ustava.htm). Verfassung der Evangelischen Kirche A.u.H.B. in Österreich einstimmig beschlossen von der Generalsynode am 17. Mai 2005 (http://www.evang1.at/fileadmin/evang.at/doc_rechtsdatenbank/gesetze/k v.pdf).

they also have sought out and received substantial assistance from partner churches, various ecclesiastical aid organizations, foreign congregations, and individuals. The churches have sought the return of property alienated during the communist era. This has proven to require difficult negotiations and precise documentation, especially when legally documented transfers took place, no matter how suspicious the circumstances may have been.

Church schools have been established or reorganized and refurbished. This has been a particularly successful undertaking of the churches in Eastern Europe, especially when the church schools provide bilingual instruction. While the number of theological students enrolled at theological faculties initially increased significantly in the early 1990s, the number of those enrolling annually has begun to decline or stabilize. A new generation of young theologians, many of whom have studied or are studying abroad, is being created. They will be the ones who will determine the future of theological training and thus the theological orientation of the churches. The status of theological schools is also being regularized and they have become theological faculties of established universities or recognized as independent university level schools granting officially recognized degrees. The question of religious education for those enrolled in state schools is one that engenders much discussion. The most extensive requirements are probably in Slovakia where religion or ethics is a required subject in elementary schools and is in accordance with the treaties signed by the Slovak government with the Vatican and also with churches of the Ecumenical Council. The Lutheran churches in Eastern Europe also have developed or expanded their diaconal or social service work. An important aspect of this is work with refugees and immigrants, both legal and illegal, the number of which has grown substantially.

However, the most significant challenges facing the Lutheran churches are not the number of members, students, teachers, pastors, or congregations. Nor is it primarily that the churches lack resources. To be sure, there are often problems with the effective identification and utilization of human or material resource and modern management skills are in short supply. But even there the situation is improving.

The most difficult burden or challenge facing Lutherans, as well as other Christians in Eastern Europe, is come to terms with their own common history and to clearly define who and what they are. The traditions that characterize and the tensions that divide Christians in Eastern Europe are deeply engrained in the churches. They consider themselves "diaspora" or widely dispersed churches. But are they any more so than churches elsewhere in the world? They emphasize the very significant contribution they have made to the development of national cultures. But this can easily lead to a religion of culture and or national allegiance and its corollary, national antipathies and suspicions. They are deeply proud of the history of their churches; but can the history of the church be known if there is a lack of commitment to preserve the very substance of history, the written and other material monuments of the past? They emphasize that they are ecumenically active, confessional churches. But can a church seek honest ecumenical understanding and cooperation if its members or pastors are unsure of their confession?[35] They look to the state for support and protection. But has not their history in Eastern Europe shown the dangers lurking in state support? When the state becomes a protector of ecclesiastical interest it seeks to realize the interests of the state for reasons of state? These are the burdens that Eastern European Lutherans now are facing and must face. How they will face them, is a tale that will be told ages hence.

I offer three observations in conclusion. In 2001, in the chapel of the presidential palace, the Roman Catholics and Lutherans signed a six-point agreement to recognize each other's baptism. Whatever the merits of the agreement – and there are those who oppose it as unnecessary – what is striking is where it was signed and that in Slovakia such an agreement seemed necessary. As these lines were being written, the government in Slovakia was forced to call for early elections when the Catholic Christian Democratic Party resigned from the governing coalition. The cause was a dispute over a corollary to the state treaty between

---

[35] Lubomír Batka, "Does the Lutheran Church Have a Future? A Contribution From a Central-European Lutheran", Mss. of an article scheduled for publication in Lutheran Quarterly.

Slovakia and the Vatican. The corollary would incorporate into state law the "right of conscience;" that is, a person could not be forced to perform an act that conflicted with his conscience. The point of conflict is that the definition of what constitutes a legally recognized "act of conscience" are by implication the ethical standards established by the magisterium of the Catholic Church. According to one legal historian at the Institute of State and Law of the Slovak Academy of Sciences and to some representatives of the European Union, the treaty does not conform to the Charter of Human Rights of the EU or to other previous negotiated human rights agreements[36] and inadequately considers the rights of those who do not recognize the teaching authority of the Catholic Church. It has called attention to the political influence of the Catholic Church in central European and re-opened the neuralgic question of a possible separation of Church and State.

Thus, at the dawn of the twenty-first century, Lutheran churches in central Europe are being confronted both by rapid and unexpected changes and by the burden of their history. Initially they seemed stunned by the political, economic, social, and cultural changes effected by the collapse of communism. They became almost like strangers in a once familiar land. The landscape and the people seemed familiar but they definitely were no longer the same. Nor had their history changed. But its significance certainly is being critically re-examined and re-interpreted. Traditions and relationships are changing and being redefined – within the Lutheran community, in dealing with other ecclesiastical and confessional groups, with the state, and with society as a whole. How Lutherans and Lutheran churches respond to these changes, how they understand and utilize their own recent and more distant past experience, and how they define their own identity will significantly affect the shape and vitality of Lutheran churches in Eastern Europe during the third millennium.

---

[36] "Zdesená", *Plus 7dni,* 16, 9 (24 February 2006): 24-26. An interview with JUDr. Katarína Zavacka.

Lutheran Church in Africa

Wilson B. Niwagila, *ELCT- Northwestern Diocese, Tanzania*

1. Introduction

The history of the Lutheran Church in Africa is an interesting study. It is interesting because of the ways it was introduced in the Continent. The Lutheran Churches in Africa are found in Namibia, Liberia, Nigeria, Ethiopia, Tanzania, Malawi, Zimbabwe, Zambia, Madagascar, Botswana, Mozambique, Kenya, Rwanda, Congo and South Africa. These churches are autonomous but also working together with other Lutheran bodies such as The Lutheran World Federation.

To write about the Lutheran Church in Africa in such a short paper will not give a clear picture. I have, therefore decided to write specifically on the Lutheran Church in Tanzania. This will serve as an example since it is the biggest Lutheran body in Africa.

2. Historical Background

Writing about African Church History one has to look into the History of Missions, which have made a big impact on the development of the African Church and African Christianity. African Christianity has undergone four major exciting periods of missionary activities. As John Baur indicates, Christianity in Africa is not a recent happening, nor is it a by-product of colonialism. Its roots go back to the very time of the Apostles. In this study we have to examine in short these early years of Christianity in Africa in order to get an idea of the 19th-20th Century Mission History in Africa.

During the first six centuries Egypt and North Africa formed one community with the other countries around the Mediterranean Sea. These countries were bound together by the Greek-Roman cultures from which historians base their argument in excluding North Africa from the rest of African countries. This influence does not change the fact that this part of Africa has for so many years interacted with the rest of African countries. The scientific study of the languages has proved this to be beyond doubt.[1] In North Africa the society was divided into three groups, and the respond to Christianity varied from one group to another. The first group belonged to Romans, the ruling class comprising of imperial officials and wealthy retired colonialists, the soldiers whose prosperity depended on Rome's economic strategy. These were reluctant to accept Christianity because of the Emperor Worship cult, which they cherished. The second group comprised of traders and business people mainly of Semitic and Punic origins. These accepted Christianity without difficulties provided there was no interference with their trade. The third group are of those who suffered most from the Roman's colonial conquests. Most of these were the indigenous Berbers, who were taken captives or they had to flee in the mountains for their survival. These were not very much enthusiastic with Christianity because the language spoken was Latin, a language of the colonizer. The birth of the Church in North Africa has been possible because of the following factors:

a) **Geographical Position:** The good communication of that time-the sea routes. The Mediterranean over which St. Paul sailed to Rome and perhaps to Spain served also as a route for the Christian message to reach North Africa. The role of the waters in the propagation of the Gospel has been tremendous: the oceans, the seas, the lakes and rivers are highly regarded in this endeavor.

b) **Political Influence:** The growth of the North African Christianity can only be understood against the background of the Roman rule, which began with the sack of Carthage in 146 BC and was completed with the conquest of Mauritania (north of Morocco) in AD 40. North Africa

---

[1] Read, Oduyoye Modupe, *The Sons of God and the Daughters of men;* Greenberg, J. H, *The Languages of Africa*, The Haque 1969.

underwent a process of Romanization that had no parallel in Egypt. New provinces were founded, Mauritania, Numidia (northern Algeria), and Africa in Tunisia, which received its name from the local Afri, whose name has become the name of the entire Continent. Many former Roman soldiers were given land to settle and became colonists. Local notables and whole the township were given Roman citizenship. The local languages were discouraged and Latin became the official language.

c) *The Influence of Big Cities:* Nobody can ignore the fact that big cities became main centers of new ideas and new learning. In this regard Christianity did not move to the rural areas as such but remained a religion of the city dwellers. Big cities were a meeting place of scholars, traders and merchants who also came into contact with the Christian faith.

The history of the church in Africa has proved to us that the early beginning of Christianity in Africa was successful in the first six centuries. The Church in Northern Africa was growing and expanding from the Red Sea to the shores of Mauritania, from the Mediterranean Sea to the high mountains of Ethiopia and from the deltas of Egypt to the White Nile. The coming of Islam in Northern Africa seven years later after the death of Mohammed in 632 AD changed the whole history of Christianity in Africa. Islam was able to strangle the Church that after some years there was no trace of Christianity in North Africa, except in Egypt, Ethiopia and some parts of Sudan.

For at least 6 Centuries the church in Northern Africa could survive the persecutions of Emperor Diocletian, it could stand against heresy and church division, but the dawn of Islam on North Africa had succumbed the church to death. In some areas like Egypt, Abyssinia and Nubia the church survived due to the following reasons.

In Egypt:

In Egypt the Coptic Church was able to remain independent and continued to serve its members during the Muslim occupation. We have nevertheless to remember that membership was not

221

allowed and evangelism was forbidden. The Church had legal status. It continued her ministry under the Patriarch. Three things helped the Church in Egypt to survive:

* The national character of the church.

* The use of the Bible in the Coptic language.

* The unity of the church under one leadership-the Patriarch.

In Ethiopia:

In the beginning of Muslim invasions, Ethiopia was the only country in the Northern part of Africa, which enjoyed a friendly relationship with the Muslims. The persecution of the first followers of Mohammed in Mecca, made them to take refuge in Ethiopia, due to this fact the Qur'an forbade *jihad* against the Ethiopians, calling them, "a humble people of priests and monks." Later this relationship was destroyed when the Arabs took control of the trade route along the Red Sea and cut off Ethiopia from the outside world

* From 1270-1527 Christian Emperors of Ethiopia were in charge of Christian presence in Ethiopia. They felt it was their divine duty to defend Christianity with all their might against Muslim invasion.

* Ethiopia's geographical position prevented Muslims not to make easy attacks. This helped Ethiopia to play a big role in cultural, economic and spiritual developments.

* In order to preserve the cultural, religious and economic heritage the city of Axum was transferred to the Southern Province, because it was vulnerable to the Muslim invasions.

* The Emperors of the 14th and 15th Centuries made use of Christianity as a unifying factor. The saint of Ethiopia Tekle Haimanot helped the Church to undergo a revival. The Church and the State stood together for religious and national preservation against Muslims who made several attempts to conquer Ethiopia.

In Nubia:

In spite of being surrounded by Muslims and being limited to have contacts with the Mediterranean world, Christianity had the chance to survive in Nubia. The reasons for this survival are as follows:

- The ministry of the monks at Dongola was quite influential to the church and its existence.

- There was close cooperation with Ethiopia. The emperor was able to support the Church that it survived until 1504. The survival of Christianity in Nubia for 1000 years could be credited to the following:

  a) Christianity was deeply rooted among the Nobadae and the Makorites.

  b) The use of Nubian language for the production of the Christian literature.

3. Christianity South of the Sahara 1500-1700

We call this period a time of Imperialism and Missionary attempt to Christianize and colonize some areas of Africa. A tide had changed. Islam occupation of the Middle East changed also the situation of the world. The route to the Far East was blocked, the Crusades waged by Church failed completely to get rid of the Moslem occupation. This caused many changes. Henry the Navigator had invented the Compass, which opened a new chapter in the navigation history. A new route to the Far East was to be discovered. Columbus, Vasco da Gama and their friends devoted themselves to find the routes for their people to continue seeking ways of trading with the Far East people. For the first time Europe through these navigators got the opportunity to go to many places seeking for wealth, riches and new settlements. Since the Portuguese and the Spaniards were the first people to do such adventures the Pope had to assign the king of Spain and the King of Portugal to establish colonies with the goal of converting the natives into Christianity. It has been a widely held idea that Christianity south of the Sahara is a by-product of the Portuguese maritime trade empire, built up in the so-called Age of Discoveries of Christopher Columbus to the west and Vasco da Gama to the east. Portugal of course played a decisive role in establishing communication between four continents as well as in planting of the Christian faith in all the places visited by its navigators.

3.1. Christianity in the Congo Kingdom-King Alfonso Mbemba Nzinga's contribution

The first Portuguese vessel led by Diago Cam anchored off the Zaire river known as Congo river in 1483. Diago met friendly Africans who impressed him. The Congo kingdom welcomed the Portuguese and Christianity, in spite of its objectives and aims as described in papal bulls. There are some speculations that at first the Congo people welcomed the white Portuguese because according to their tradition the white people were simply the living dead ancestors of each clan and family. It gave the Congo people as they saw the Portuguese the impression of having the right message from the spiritual world of the ancestors. Later this positive picture disappeared after the Portuguese misbehaved contrary to what they were expected to be. This welcome made Diago Cam to take a few Africans to Portugal. In order to prove to the King of Congo and the relatives of the men he left few Portuguese seamen behind as a proof that he was not going to make Africans slaves.

The Congo Kingdom was well established with its capital at Mbanzakongo which is now the city San Salvador in the Northern Angola. In 1485 the Africans who went to Portugal returned. They had learnt the language and basic facts of Christianity. The King of Portugal sent presents to King Nzinga a Nkuwu (Mani Kongo)- the powerful king of the Bakongo. The King was impressed by the report of his men and the presents they brought with them from the King of Portugal. King Nzinga, therefore, took the initiative to ask the Portuguese to send missionaries to his Kingdom. The first missionaries arrived in 1491 and he was baptized in the same year being called Joao I.

The missionaries who arrived were of mixed capabilities, masons, carpenters, craftsmen who were ready to build mission stations and the capital. His wife and his oldest son were also baptized. His first son Alfonso was sincere and he was made governor of the province of Nsundi in 1504. His younger brother was not interested in Christianity. Alfonso invited teachers and music directors in his province. His son Henry was sent to Portugal for further studies in theology and music. When his father Joao I died in 1506 he was made King of Congo in 1507. He encouraged missionaries to build up Christianity in his Kingdom. His son Henry, after finishing his theological studies in Portugal, was made the first African Bishop in 1518. He returned to his country in 1521 as Vicar apostolic of Congo. Due to ill health he died in 1530. Few Africans were ordained priests but the effort to create an indigenous clergy was unsuccessful.

The history of Christianity in the Congo will always be linked with the name of Mbemba Nzinga, baptized as Alfonso. He became king after a civil war, after the death of his father Joao in 1506 and ruled until his death in 1543. According to one tradition, Mbemba was the son of Nzinga Nkuwu who was the son of the founder of the kingdom, Ntinu Wene, came to power after two of his cousins. Ntinu Wene, the King of Kings (literally Ruler and Lord, the supreme wielder of authority), coming from Mbungu, north of the river, had conquered the country and was recognized by the local people as Mani Kongo (Lord of conquest or governor of the conquered people). The Mani Kongo in accepting the strangers was pleased to learn that the king of Portugal was in recognition of his kingdom and because of this, he accepted Christianity and asked the Portuguese to train some of his people in Portugal. Mbeba Nzinga and his father Nzinga Nkuwu were baptized on the same day on March 3, 1491.

Alfonso attributed his conversion to a special divine grace. Twenty years later he wrote, *"The grace of the Holy Spirit enlightened us by a unique and special favor, given to us by the Holy Trinity. We received the Christian doctrine so well that, by God's mercy, it was from hour to hour and from day to day better implanted in our hearts. We definitely renounced all errors and idolatries which our ancestors thus far had believed in"* (Letter 13, 1512). Alfonso's words were in practice refuted by the members of his family and his own subject- a question which is also posed today whether our Ancestors lived without the knowledge of God. Alfonso was opposed by his brother Mpanzu Nzinga who denounced the new believers as dangerous sorcerers and puppets of the foreigners. Alfonso was exiled to Nzundi and became there as Mani Nzundi. But when he heard that his father had died he waged war against his rivals through a big support of committed Christians. He fought and won the war. His brother was captured and executed but the rest were pardoned. Alfonso's position as a Christian king became endangered after the Portuguese missionaries began to misbehave. And this eventually led to the downfall of Christianity in this particular area of Africa.

3.2. *Christianity in East Africa.*

I need to mention one fact that Moslem settlements in East Africa came earlier than Christianity. These settlements were along the East Coast. The coming of the Portuguese changed the whole atmosphere. There was suspicion among the Moslems of the new comers to East Africa from Europe who had killed two young Moslem men who were asked by the Portuguese to show them the way to India. They picked them from Lindi but after the ship arrived in Mombassa the two Moslems were killed. The distrustful situation of the Moslems about the new comers proved to be true because the Portuguese were able to colonize the East Coast of Kenya between the 15th Century and the 16th Century. The Portuguese Christians were cruel to Moslems inhabitants who refused to be converted into Christianity. The Portuguese were still occupied with the memories of defeat and the blockade of Middle East by Moslems. Because of this they vowed to fight against every Moslems they come across. They understood and were convinced that they were doing great service both to God and the Portuguese sovereign. One of the Portuguese viceroys of the Indies wrote the following as his plan to capture Malacca in 1511:

> *The first aim is the great service which we shall perform to our Lord. . .quenching the fire of the sect of Mohammed. . .The other is the service we shall render to the monarch. . . in taking this city, because it is the source of all the spices and drugs. . . For I hold it certain that if we take this trade of*

Malacca away from them, Cairo und Mecca will be entirely ruined.[2]

The Portuguese destroyed many Moslems mosques and Fort Jesus on Mombassa Island was a slaughter jail for dissident Moslems. The Portuguese occupation of the East African Coast led the Oman Moslems rulers to wage war against the Portuguese that drove them out of the territory in the 1720's. In revenge, those converted African Christians who refused to become Moslems were butchered by Oman rulers and worked towards destroying Christianity and its elements in the area. We therefore find no trace of Portuguese Christianity in Kenya except the monuments of old Mombassa Cathedral and the Fort Jesus.

4. The New Period- The Eve of Protestant Missions (Lutheran Missions in Tanzania)

We have just seen the rise and fall of the Portuguese Missions along the west coast and the east coast of Africa. Just like in the northern part of Africa during the invasion of Muslims, Christianity did not hold its strength during this time. Christians who remained in those areas were only the minority. Many left Christianity and started practicing their traditional "religion." We have therefore a period of silence until the time when the Protestant missions came in Africa. With the exception of the Coptic Churches in Egypt, and Ethiopia and the Churches established by the Portuguese, contemporary Christianity of our time goes back to the 19th Century. The conversion took a dramatic and astonishing short time but most complex filled with opportunities and challenges embracing large areas of the population.

4.1. European Exploration.

One of the factors, which gave a good beginning for the missionary activities, was the extensive adventure of the European explorers who tried to find the unknown areas in the interior of

---

[2] Richard L. Greaves, Robert Zaller, *Civilization of the World,* New York, N.Y. 1990, p. 411

Africa. The explorers paved the way for the intensive work of the missionary activities in the interior of Africa. New maps were made to show the major ways of communicating with the interior. They made friendship with the kings of different African ethnic groups and devoted their time to fight against slave trade that was predominant in East Africa. In this case they won many friends in order to influence the people. In East Africa new alliances called *treaties* were made between the Imperialist explorers and the African chiefs and kings. The major goal was a promise for the security of the king or chief, who was promised to be defended from his rivals; on the side of the Imperialist, he was securing an area for his country, which was to make that area a colony. This was done on a competitive spirit. Where the British entered and made treaties with the natives did not like to see that the Germans or French or Belgians put in their noses. This was the same also in the missionary enterprise. The missions in fact followed the path where the explorer or Imperialist of his country passed. It was therefore important to make such treaties with the kings and with the chiefs. There were strong intra-imperialist struggle for the African countries and sometimes brought some conflicts between the natives and the Imperialists.

4.2. The European Colonization and the Establishment of Missions.

When we talk about the Church in the time of colonization, we are simply talking about the planting of the Church during the colonial era. A hundred years ago colonization and the planting of Christianity south of Sahara went hand in hand. During this time missionary activities were followed by colonization and expansionism or vice versa. Many people, as I have pointed out earlier have evaluated this period, the most successful period in the history of the Church in Africa.

The problem of this period is that Mission expansionism was in one way or another identical with colonial expansionism because it took place within the context of European colonial conquest, which crept into missionary vocabulary. Robert Schreiter makes a point in his book- *Reconciliation as a Model of Mission* when he points out that missionaries frequently shared the colonizer's view of the otherness of the people they encountered, seeing them as inferior people, savage without a culture, a history and knowledge. They saw them as people who needed education and western values.

At the same time, the African made also his own evaluation about the missionary and the colonizer; he remarked that the White man's building had two domes *colonialism and missions.* One dome - colonialism was collapsing while the other one-mission was continuing to flourish. The Church planted through missions from Europe was to survive by being planted in the African soil otherwise it faced the same danger as colonialism.

It was clearly understood in those days that the colonial government could do nothing without the help of the missionary activities. In one of the Colonial Congress, which took place in 1902, a missionary called A. Marensky advocated the collaboration of the colonial government with the mission societies as follows: *"The state can bring external order by forcing people to accept it, but it cannot bring peace, love and the moral ethical life of the heart. The state, therefore, needs the help of the sion"*[3] This proved the fact that without the help of the missions the colonial government could not have succeeded in implementing the work among the Africans.

On 14th May, 1886 a Missionary Society was founded with the name *Evangelische Missionsgesellschaft für Deutsch Ostafrika* whose aims and objectives were the following:

a) The Missionary Society was to preach the Gospel of Christ to the "pagan" in the German East African Colony.

b) Was to take the Spiritual care of the Germans who worked and lived in this part of the world.

c) Was to provide medical care of the German citizens and for the natives.

d) Was to begin Christian Schools for the natives.

Carl Peters, who first came to East Africa with the *German Company for East Africa*, was the one who founded this mission

---

[3] C. Mirbt; Mission und Kolonialpolitik in den deutschen Schutzgebiet, Tubingen 1910, p89

society. Carl Peters is also given credit for convincing Bismarck through the business people of Hamburg, Bremen and Berlin, to start securing colonies for the Germans. It is also known that Carl Peters convened Christians in southern German to start a Mission Society, which could work well in Deutsch Ostafrika colony known as *"Die Evangelisch-Lutherische Missionsgesellschaft für Ostafrika.*[4] Carl's ideas were based from the fact that no other mission societies besides the German Mission societies were to take this opportunity in the German Colony. Being a man with great ambition to conquer and win East Africa for the German people, he felt that the Germans were under the threat of the British Missionary presence that were already established in Zanzibar and on Tanganyika mainland. His great effort in making treaties with the chiefs and the Sultan of Zanzibar along the coast and mainland Tanganyika was to get rid of the British presence in the German sphere of influence. He made several speeches contending to his audience that the German Mission Society could influence the German Missionaries[5] who were working for the British Mission societies to stop doing so and instead be convinced to be incorporated in the German Colonial Movement and work in the German national spirit.[6] And above all teach the natives to work in the German plantations.[7] Carl Peter's ideas were overwhelmingly taken but few people like Gustav Warneck were not in favor of Peter's ideas. Warneck did not like to see Christian Mission Societies being interpreted in the same language as "promoting the German colonial spirit"[8]

Warneck's argument was simple and clear that if the missionary societies worked independently of the Colonial Government they would have the opportunity of helping the colonial

---

[4] Carl Helberg, Mission on Colonial FrontierLund p.91

[5] Krapf and Rebmann were Lutherans sent by the British Mission society to East Africa.

[6] NB. After the formation of a German Empire in 1871 the spirit of Nationalism was very strong and this encouraged Germans to strive for more economic power.

[7] Roland Oliver; The Missionary Factor in East Africa, London 1967; pp, 94f.

[8] Gustav Warneck; In: AMZ, 1891, pp120f.

government to fulfill her duty properly, because they could raise constructive criticisms against the government more freely than if they were incorporated in it. Nevertheless Warneck's criticism did not convince a good number of missionaries. Carl Peter's Company was taken over by the German colonial government after 1885 when the entire Continent of Africa was divided into European colonies. Tanganyika became a German Colony and this was the beginning of missionary activities in Tanganyika with a Lutheran identity.

5. The Historical Background of the Evangelical Lutheran Church in Tanzania

The Evangelical Lutheran Church in Tanzania originated from different Mission societies of different background and traditions. In order to get a clear picture of this Church we need to observe the following periods:

5.1. Mission Societies during the time of German Colony-1885-1914

The shape of the Evangelical Lutheran Church in Tanzania of today is a testimony of the great work of the different groups of Christians, both from Germany and Tanganyika, who devoted their time to make Christ known to the Tanzanians. We can divide these groups into four categories:

a) The Leipzig Mission that worked in the Northern and Central Tanganyika.

b) The Berlin I Mission, which came from South Africa and worked in the Southern part of Tanganyika

c) The Berlin III which first worked in Zanzibar and later moved to Dar es Salaam, Kisarawe and Usambara-Digo. This Mission society was replaced by Bethel Mission and Berlin I after getting financial difficulties and lacking of personnel to work in Zanzibar and in Tanganyika main-land[9].

d) Bethel Mission, which worked in Usambara-Digo, Buko-ba, Karagwe (West of Lake Victoria) and Rwanda.

e) African Group Initiatives, which worked in North West of Tanganyika after being baptized in Uganda.

5.2. Missionary activities during and after the First World War.

The defeat of German Colonial Government during the First World War affected the work of the German Mission Societies already established in the *Deutsch Ostafrika* colony. After the Germans lost the War all German missionaries were repatriated and their work was either taken over by newly converted African Christians or by other mission societies from other countries. The League of Nations entrusted Tanganyika to the British Govern-ment until the time of its independence. The British Mandate Government in seeing that the former German "mission fields" were taken care of by other Mission societies. The following groups became responsible in taking over the work of German Missions:

a) **Missionaries from the Anglican Church of Uganda**-The Bishop of Uganda sent three missionaries after being asked by the Christians from Buhaya and Karagwe (North West of Tanganyika) to assist the African Christians who worked with German missionaries. The three missionaries from Uganda comprised of 2 Africans and 1 British. These three worked with African Christians for a short period and were called back by the Bishop.

b) **Missionaries from the Methodist Church in South Africa**- After calling back the three missionaries from Uganda the Bishop of Uganda advised the Methodist mis-sionaries from South Africa to take over the work in North West Tanganyika without consulting the African Chris-tians from that area. This move of the Bishop did not

---

[9] Wilson Niwagila, *From the Catacomb to a Self-governing Church*, Verlag an der Lottbek, Second Editon, Hamburg 1991 pp. 112-116

please the Africans from North West of Tanganyika. The Methodist missionaries moved in the area and worked hard. In spite of hard work the African Christians, who became used to Lutheran theology became strongly opposed to the Methodist presence in the area and all their teachings. The Methodists discontinued the missionary activity but left African Christians divided into two groups who later belonged to Lutherans and Anglicans.

c) **The Augustana Mission from United States of America.** In 1926 the Augustana Mission got permission from the British Mandate Government, which was in charge of Tanganyika, to take care of the "mission fields" of the Leipzig Mission in Kilimanjaro and Singida areas.

5.3. The Return of German Missions in Tanganyika.

It is interesting to note that the African Christians who could not cope with the Methodist missionaries took the initiative of writing letters to the Bethel Mission Director in Germany to think about returning to Tanganyika. The reason given was that the Bishop of Uganda had betrayed them by sending the Methodist missionaries without their consent.[10] On the other side other German Missions had the desire of returning to their former "Mission fields" in Tanganyika. But since Tanganyika was under the British Government it was clearly stated at the Versailles Peace Conference that the Germans should not be allowed to come back to their former "mission fields". The appeal of Mr. Oldham, the General Secretary of the International Missionary Council, and the Conference of the British Missionary Society moved the British Parliament on 1st July 1924 to pass an Act allowing German Missionaries to return to their former "mission fields" in East Africa- Tanganyika.[11] This was a big opportunity for Germans to continue their missionary activities in their former German Colony. They knew that their rights were limited under

---

[10] Ernst Johanssen, *Führung und Erfahrung.* Vol. III Bielefeld 1931-1934 p.135f

[11] G.P.Groves, *The Planting of Christianity in Africa.* Vol. IV London 1958. Read also: *International Review of Missions* 1924 p 496.

233

the British Mandate Government. After their arrival they discovered that the churches had grown fast under the African leadership. This challenge made the Germans not to take the African for granted. The first step they did was to ordain the African leaders as pastors. This gave the African pastors the opportunity to participate in the decision making of how the young churches in Tanganyika could make Christ known to many people who have no idea about the love of God.

New strategies were developed in order to make the young churches grow to full self-governing churches. In 1938 all mission societies together with African leaders met together in Kidugala, South of Tanganyika, and formed a Federation. The objectives of this federation were as follows:-

a) To work together as Lutheran Christians

b) To work together in preaching the Gospel

c) To have one voice in approaching the British Mandate Government

d) To co-operate in building schools and health care centers

e) To work together in promoting self-support, self-governing and self-propagation.

These objectives were interrupted by the outbreak of the Second World War that also made the German missionaries to leave the country. At this time it was obvious that "orphan" churches were to be under the Augustana Mission as the custodian of the German property. The Federation comprised of seven churches:

a) The Lutheran Church of Iraqw (Among the Mbulu people in Northern Tanganyika)

b) The Evangelical Church of North western Tanganyika (West of Lake Victoria)

c) The Lutheran Church in Northern Tanganyika

d) The Lutheran Church in Central Tanganyika (Singida area)

e) The Lutheran Church of Ubena-Konde (Southern Highlands of Tanganyika)

f) The Lutheran Church of Usambara-Digo (Usambara and Tanga area)

g) The Lutheran Church of Uzaramo-Uluguru (The Eastern coast of Tanganyika)

5.4. Missionary activities after the Second World War until 1963

The effects of the Second World War were great. In order to face the challenges of the war the young churches within the federation needed more support, both personnel and financial, from mission societies. Swedish, Danish, Finish and Norwegians from Scandinavian countries were accepted to work in Tanganyika in support of these young churches. In the 1950's few German missionaries were also allowed to join other missionaries in support of the young churches. During this period we have, therefore, missionaries from United States of America, Scandinavian countries and from Germany who joined the Africans to make the Lutheran Church in Tanzania grow. The following strategies were laid down in order to make these churches grow and become self-support.

a) To give strong support to the federation after the damages made by the war.

b) To make sure that these young churches work towards becoming independent.

c) To promote self-support and to work towards Christian unity that crosses the tribal boundaries and national borders?

d) To prepare African leaders with high theological education.

e) To build the Lutheran office center of the federation in Dar es Salaam.

f) To form new strategies of preaching the Gospel.

g) To build schools, colleges and hospitals.

235

It is worth noting that in this period there was a tremendous growth of church members, many schools were established. Teachers colleges, Medical School and a theological Seminary were established. More African pastors were educated both in the country and abroad. This was the time of preparing the birth of the Evangelical Lutheran Church in Tanzania.

6. The Birth of the Evangelical Lutheran Church in Tanzania

One of the objectives of the Federation of the seven churches was to make sure that in future the seven churches would become one united Lutheran church with full responsibilities. This dream became a reality on the 19th June 1963 when the federation was dissolved and the Evangelical Lutheran Church in Tanzania was born. This unity was necessary because of the following reasons:

a) It is the wish of the Lord of the Church that all may be one.

b) This unity gives more strength to the Christians in preaching the Gospel.

c) This unity opens the door for working towards a wider unity beyond the Tanzania borders.

d) It is the wish of the Lord that this kind of unity will motivate all church members to open mission work within and outside Tanzania.

6.1. The Structure of the Evangelical Lutheran Church in Tanzania

The former Seven Churches have grown into twenty Church units known as Dioceses. Each Diocese has its own constitution and diocesan leadership. These twenty different dioceses make a Lutheran Church in Tanzania, which has a membership of about 3 million members, the second largest Christian body in Tanzania and the first biggest Lutheran body in Africa. The Head of the Church, called Mkuu wa Kanisa[12], is elected from the twenty

---

[12] Mkuu wa Kanisa is a Swahili title meaning the Presiding Bishop

bishops. The first Mkuu wa Kanisa was the late Bishop Dr. Stefano Moshi from Northern Diocese who was succeeded by the late Bishop Dr. Sebastian Kolowa from the North Eastern Diocese who was also succeeded by Bishop Dr. Samson Mushemba from the North Western Diocese. The Church has a General Secretary working together with Executive Secretaries of different Departments. There is a General Assembly, which meets every four years and the Executive Council, which meets four times a year. The Church Headquarters are in Arusha, one of the growing cities of Tanzania in the northern part of the country.

6.2. The Mission of the Church

From the beginning this church has been involved in mission work. It has mission frontiers within the country and outside the country. In the 1960's and 70's it worked in Kenya and Congo. In the 80's it worked in Malawi, Zambia and now in Mozambique through the support of LWF and Uganda. Within the country it has established new mission areas. The work of diaconal is very strongly emphasized. Education has become number one priority. It has established secondary schools, colleges and a University to make sense of its Missionary task. I would like to point out that the members of this church have been very active in supporting the mission activities of the church. This is what we call *Evangelistic Dynamism*.

A classic example from the present writer's experience is the mission initiative carried out by Tanzanian lay Christians who move to new areas for new settlements or who move to new areas because of being civil servants or because of doing business in that area. These lay Christians come together and form a small congregation without a pastor or an evangelist. They choose their leader and meet together in one of the member's home. There they read the Bible and encourage one another to look for new members. Much of the teaching and preaching takes place in these centers. The congregational servants are needed in these centers for the nurture and equipping of the people of God. As a rule the request for a pastor or evangelist goes to the Headquarters in Arusha. Department for Mission and Evangelism takes the responsibility to look for a talented pastor or evangelist to work in the new congregation. Here evangelism is not a one person's show

237

but a fellowship in prayers, giving testimonies of their experiences through reading the Bible.

The growth of the Lutheran Church in Tanzania, which is about 10% a year, has been the result of a joint effort in evangelism by lay Christians, evangelists, pastors, deacons, deaconesses, parish workers, Sunday school teachers and bishops. In other places other denominations have assisted in supplying worshipping places, exchange of preachers and conducting interdenominational fellowship Bible study groups and evangelism programs.

6.3. The Relationship with other Christian Church Bodies.

In continuing the longstanding relationships with the former Mission societies a Lutheran Christian Service body (LCS) was established in 1973 and in 1998 became the Lutheran Mission Cooperation (LMC) whose office is within the ELCT Headquarters in Arusha. This body works together with the Evangelical Lutheran Church in Tanzania to fulfill her Mission objectives. The ELCT is a member of Christian Council of Tanzania, All African Conference of Churches, Lutheran World Federation and World Council of Churches. It has shared its leadership talents with the World Christian Community. One of the Presidents of the LWF is the late Bishop Dr. Josiah M. Kibira (1977-1984) who was also a bishop of one of the church units of the ELCT.

7. Challenges and opportunities.

Africa is undergoing tremendous social, political, religious and economic changes. This situation gives the churches great challenges but also new opportunities to create new strategies in facing these challenges. The Evangelical Lutheran Church in Tanzania is trying to face the challenges with the following programs:

7.1. Opening new Areas of Mission.

Tanzania comprises of more than 126 ethnic groups who previously were living as individual small nations divided according to their tribal identity. Since Independence the political exercise created the consciousness of unity. This has resulted in breaking down the tribal barriers. People have the freedom to move to any place in Tanzania and make new settlements. This is a big challenge to the Church to establish programs which will equip the people of God in making Jesus Christ known to all Tanzanians. New Areas of Mission are both geographical and the programs that meet the needs of the people such as health care, assisting the government in providing basic needs of the people.

7.2. Evangelism through Music.

It is very interesting to note that music has been an instrument of communication in the history of African culture. Africans are gifted in singing and dancing. Their dances and the singing communicate the message better than mere words.

The singing of African songs in the ELCT has developed from the initiatives of individual African Christians, especially pastors, evangelists and theological students from Makumira University College. In the 50's, Pastor Sila Msangi from Pare Diocese in North Tanzania was the first to compose and write Christian songs from African Melodies. Before his death, he had already composed and written more than 300 songs. Many of his songs have been widely sung by many congregation choirs in the Lutheran Church and even among the Anglicans and Moravians. Some of his songs have been included in the ELCT Hymn. The revival Movement, which began in 1935 in Bukoba, attracted many pastors and evangelists to compose revival songs, which became popular in the revival meetings. Pastor Ernest Kalembo and Evangelist Sylvester Machumu composed songs from African traditional melodies, expressing the cross and the blood of Jesus as the only means to bring people to repentance and reconciliation with God. In the southern part of Tanzania the Wabena and Wanyakyusa attempted to compose Christian songs, some of which were later adopted and included in the ELCT Hymn Book.

In 1964, Makumira Theological College launched a research on collecting African melodies from different ethnic groups in Tanzania and beyond. Theological students who belonged to the ethnic groups were able to collect the melodies and composed songs. This venture accelerated the art of singing in the entire Lutheran Church in Tanzania. The use of African music instruments and the composition of songs from African traditional melodies was a new revolution in the history of the Lutheran Church in Tanzania. Theological students in Makumira including the writer of this article determined to use the drum in the services, especially in the choir. The Makumira Student Choir recorded songs, and sent them to the LWF Radio Voice of the Gospel in Addis Ababa Ethiopia. This radio was a key instrument to make the new African songs and melodies become known to all parts of Africa. Each week in the evening, the Voice of the Gospel Addis Ababa transmitted the songs from Makumira to East and Central Africa. Some of these songs became also known in Germany in the 1970's through the initiative of Pastor Gerhard Jasper. The way of singing from Makumira set forth a new understanding of praising God with voices, melodies and music instruments from the African heritage. Early 1968, one could hear from all corners of Tanzania a new way of singing. One choir from Singisi congregation in Meru Diocese became very popular in singing Christian songs composed from the Wameru-Waarusha ethnic groups. The choir toured the whole East Africa doing evangelism. The use of African melodies impressed and motivated many people.

Already in 1964, the ELCT-North-western Diocese had started plans to build a music school at Ruhija Evangelical Academy. The objectives of the school were three, first, it was to research and write Christian songs from the African melodies. Second, it was to teach young musicians who were to become responsible in forming choirs and improve the way of singing in the congregations. Third, it was to teach music students how to make African music instruments and learn how to play them. The use of African music instruments in the church was necessary because it changed the existed mentality that piano and organ were the only instruments to be used in the worship services. These measures brought great changes in the church. The way of singing has improved to the extent that every congregation, small or big has a youth choir. Every year there is a choir competition in many of the ELCT-Dioceses. Young people are encouraged to compose two songs. The music institutions give a set song from which the judges could determine which group has been able to sing better the song.

In recent years the churches in Tanzania have discovered this gift as a new way of communicating the Christian faith today. Choirs and individual composers of songs have attracted many people, especially the youth. The music industry has also helped the churches to record the songs on tapes, Video Cassettes and CDs and distribute them to the customers. These songs are heard in the market places, in towns and big cities, in the families and in the villages.

7.3. Evangelism and the Poor.

Tanzania is one of the poorest countries in the world. The effects of poverty in Tanzania are overwhelming especially among the widows, orphans and old people. In spite of limited funds the church has tried to meet this challenge. The Christians are committed to share what they have with these people. In the Evangelical Lutheran Church in Tanzania, North-western Diocese, there are three projects run by the diocese. **a) Igabiro Home for Disabled**-This was started in 1968. Apart from financial support of the government and families many congregations and individual Christians have given their full support, with money, food and materials. **b) Ntoma Orphanage**-This is the oldest institution which receives babies who have lost their parents. The Kanyange-reko congregation, where this institution is situated, has committed herself every month to assist these children with money and food. The Christians of Kanyangereko understand that it is their obligation to share their Christian faith with these children. **c) HUYAWA** –The HUYAWA program was started in recent years to meet the challenges of HIV and AIDS. This program supports widows and children who have lost their parents because of HIV and AIDS. The Diocese advocates for the rights of the widows and children who are unjustly treated by the relatives of the deceased, especially in matters of inheritance.

7.4. Peace and Justice.

In each age, time and place the issues of Justice and Peace dominate the whole sphere of life. The meaning of Justice is

241

simply caring for God's created being. Justice is very much concerned with interpersonal relationships. This relationship is not just limited to human beings only but also between humankind and his environment. The function of Justice is to heal the wounds caused by hatred and bring harmony, peace and tranquility among individuals, families and nations. Justice mends the broken relationships. The church as the instrument of justice and peace is challenged by the situation in Africa to be more prophetic. The alarming social injustices and the unbalanced economic order in African countries is causing the majority to undergo many sufferings. Some years ago I read a Kenyan newspaper - *Daily Nation* - with a subtitle, "Culture corruption in Kenya." The paper was revealing the evils done by a handful of people who take the advantage of their power to accumulate wealth through corrupt means and leaving the majority to live in "grinding squalor and poverty." In Tanzania, the situation is not different. The rise of prices of different commodities does not affect the well paid middle class people but it affects the majority of Tanzanians living in rural areas whose income cannot buy one bag of maize. It is only the elite and people in power who will have the opportunity to send their children to colleges and universities, but the majority of Tanzanian parents have no chance. The uncertainties of educational programs are leaving many young people to capitulate to other forces such as drug abuse, criminality and dirty business.

As far as medical care is concerned I can say that it is a scandal to see children, pregnant women and the majority Tanzanians dying from all kinds of diseases because they cannot afford to pay for the treatment. It is quite obvious that few people - of course those who have accumulated wealth on the sweat of others - will be able to pay for medical treatment and even, on the expenses of tax payers, will be referred to expensive hospitals.

African countries are experiencing a wave of greedy politicians and business people. From all corners of Africa we hear cries of poor people whose vineyards have been confiscated by those in power and by rich people. The story of Loliondo in Maasai area is a vivid example of social injustices based on economic injustices which are currently taking place in our countries. The peasants of Tanzania and other African countries are no longer the owners of the land and crops they produce but are becoming servants of the big Boss from somewhere; a new type of slavery Africa is again experiencing. Because of this situation people live from hand to mouth. Money has become a small god/goddess who is driving everybody crazy. Think of what we are producing in our countries! The best quality is sold outside in order to get foreign currency and the entire population is left with the leftovers which make you think twice before you use them. One theological student exclaimed, "We import what we do not produce and we export what we do not use." It is a scandal to sell the best food outside and leave the population with the imported left-over and expired food commodities from outside.

In the 1950's and 60's many African countries became independent. People laid down political ideas, and the political leaders promised to lead their countries towards peace and prosperity; they promised the long colonized Africans to lead them into the land "full of honey and milk." But before a real settlement in these lands could be established, these same political leaders became the first to grab the land, monopolizing honey and milk with greed leaving the majority in the shadows of poverty and death. The Exodus to freedom turned to be an exodus to bewilderment; honey and milk turned to be hunger and poverty; harmony, peace, joy and prosperity turned to be agony, killings and hatred. Many have been left in the wilderness to die as refugees and misplaced people. We are told that since the era of Exodus to Freedom, Africa has had about 6 million refugees and 14 million displaced people. Africa, which used to be a sanctuary for refugees (story of Abraham, Joseph and Jesus), has recently become the killer and letting her own people to flee the country because of the terrible genocide among different ethnic groups. Since the 1990's Africa has experienced another political Exodus of political parties. Few people are just optimistic but the majority are asking one question: if the first Exodus ended up in this turmoil, how can the second exodus succeed?

Working for Justice and Peace is not simply a humanitarian business whereby the world community becomes active when there is a catastrophic situation. Working for Justice and Peace is an ongoing activity. In this case the Church is called to follow the footsteps of its Master, to be a forerunner of Justice and Peace. The Church in Africa is called to be a spokesman of Justice and peace, a prophet of hope, love and reconciliation. The history has taught us not to keep silent when injustices are exercised in our societies. The atrocities in Rwanda, Somalia, Sudan, Sierra Leone and Darfur are challenging the Churches in Africa to work tirelessly towards Peace and Justice. The prophetic function of the Church is to speak out, loud and clear.

7.5. Relations with People of other Faiths.

Tanzania is a pluralistic society. Christians and Moslems live side by side and share common family ties. It will be a disaster if both Christians and Moslems create an atmosphere of hatred. Both African Moslems and Christians value highly the sense of belonging in a community. The African understanding of human life is a life in a community that leads to courtesy, tolerance and forbearance when religious differences are being discussed. African family ties were more binding than separating. This does not affect the deep commitment of Christians to confess their faith nor does it prevent Moslems from being confident about their religion and faith.[13] The African understanding of the wholeness and vocation of care challenges both Christians and Moslems to understand themselves in the context of the wholeness, oneness and the interrelatedness of life as far as traditional African values are concerned. The circumstances compel both Christians and Muslims to live a life of a caring community, a healing community, and a life of fellowship. The primal ties of clan, neighborhood and age group assert the importance of fellowship regardless of which religious group one belongs.

Through the Ki-Swahili culture there has developed a new sense of unity. The Swahili language has created a common ground for good relationship between ethnic groups and between Moslems and Christians. The Ki-Swahili vocabulary used in religious language is the same and sometimes you cannot tell the difference when Moslems and Christians deliver their religious messages. The Ki-Swahili culture has in one way brought Christians and Muslims in East Africa closer than in any other

---

[13] T.G.O. Gradamosi, The Growth of Islam among the Yoruba, 1841-1908, London, 1978 p. 146f.

African countries. Due to these facts the Lutherans and the Moslems of the BAKWATA[14] group in Tanzania have formed a committee with the following objectives:

7.5.1. Learn to live together in Peace.

Both Christians and Moslems have had enough time of conflicts and tensions. We remember the Middle Ages military confrontation which occurred in two areas: in the West- the *Reconquista* of the Iberian peninsula- and in the East- the crusades in the Middle East that went hand in hand with anti-Islamic propaganda. The Moslems like the Jews were categorized as "enemies of the cross." The result of this confrontation led the Moslems to develop an **ideology** of **defense** and **resistance** which of course was implemented through a political ideology. We need to understand that such conflicts and tensions are an alienation of our religious beliefs. It is pure idolatry and blasphemy to wage wars against humankind in the name of religion. We should be aware of the fact that in Africa we live in pluralistic societies in which there is no room for entertaining tensions and conflicts. To live in peace is the divine message to all people including Christians and Moslems. Religious groups should not claim their superiority over other religions but on the contrary, they should work as caring and **just** religious communities in the society. John Baur thinks it is wrong to think of modern Islamic-Christian relations in terms of *jihad* and *crusade*[15]

7.5.2. It is high time for Dialogue.

For a long time most of the talk has been <u>about</u> each other, but now it is high time we talk <u>to</u> each other. It is quite obvious that Christians would like to speak to Moslems about Jesus, but how? By confrontation? The Moslems likewise would like to make Mohammed, the prophet, known to Christians but the question is how? No one will accept the message which is delivered through

---

[14] BAKWATA is a Moslem recognized organization in Tanzania, which unites all moderate Moslems

[15] John Baur, op. cit., p. 366

forces and violence. Religious tensions and conflicts bring always misunderstandings and even violence.

Dialogue is defined in the Dictionary as "Interchange and discussion of ideas, especially when open and frank, as in seeking mutual understanding and harmony."[16] In exchanging and discussing about our faiths, "we shall find much we have in common, but also much which is peculiar and unique to our religion as well as to the other religion."[17] The Moslems and Christians are challenged by what is happening in the continent. Africa has become a continent of crisis. The most serious crisis has developed through all the years of independence and is now breaking out like a bursting ulcer, revealing the bankruptcy of the political leadership, the impoverishment of the masses that provoke the people's cry for democracy, peace, justice and equality. Through dialogue both Moslems and Christians have to find answers to the cries of the time. The future of Africa depends on the role played by the religious communities in minimizing tensions and conflicts and work towards mutual understanding.

7.6. Striving for Higher Education.

The Evangelical Lutheran Church in Tanzania has been on the forefront in promoting education in Tanzania. Many schools and colleges of the church have promoted education in the country. Since 1997 the ELCT has opened a University called TUMAINI (hope). The University has four campuses, which prepare Tanzanian students in Theology, Law, Medicine, Education Journalism, Economics, Engineering and Computer Science. As the name of the University indicates, this gives opportunities and creates hope to the young people of Tanzania to become better leaders.

---

[16] Webster's New Word Dictionary.

[17] Christian-Muslim Relations -Report of workshop by National Council of Churches of Kenya, Limuru 1985, p. 11.

8. Conclusion

In recent years there have been some discussions concerning the structure of the Evangelical Lutheran Church in Tanzania. Since 1963 the Presiding Bishop who is at the same time bishop of the Diocese has headed this church. The ELCT has 20 Dioceses and each Diocese has its own constitution, which at the same time must comply with the common constitution of the entire ELCT. The recent discussion has been to have a Presiding Bishop whose powers are not shared with the office of the Diocese, which means that the Presiding Bishop has to be given more powers as the head of the Evangelical Lutheran Church in Tanzania. The study conducted in 2006 shows that many members of the church are in favor of having a Presiding Bishop who is in charge of the entire ELCT without being a bishop of the diocese. Some bishops and few lay people would like to see that the present structure continues. This debate has also stimulated the idea of having a Presiding Bishop with Apostolic Succession in order to solve the problem of having two types of bishop's office. Nobody is quite sure whether this idea will be accepted. We have to wait and see how these debates develop.

The ELCT has come a long way. She has enjoyed the participation of foreign missions and she has done missionary activities within and outside Tanzania. Her service to the Lutheran world community and to the people of Tanzania has received great appreciation. We hope and pray that the Future of the Evangelical Lutheran Church in Tanzania will depend on her commitment to serve as a witnessing, prophetic and sharing community.

Lutheranism in Asia: Challenges and Contributions

Yoshikazu Tokuzen, *Japan Lutheran Theological Seminary*

Lutheranism in Japan: The Historical Development and Legal Situation

It is well known that the sixteenth century Roman Catholic missionary efforts were carried out by the Society of Jesus (the Jesuits). Francis Xavier, a cofounder of the Society, came in 1549 to Kogoshima, Kyushu. There he met with much success, drawing many people from diverse social strata of Japanese society; from nobles to the simple peasants. It is estimated that in 1598 there were as many as 300,000 Japanese converts to Christianity. On account of a growing anxiety over the ever-increasing influence of European colonization, in 1612 the Shogun suddenly forbade Christian missionary activity. Many years of hardship and persecution followed. After the modernization of Japan, only a small remnant of these early Christian communities on the tiny island of Kyushu could be found. Interestingly, when the government relaxed its persecution of Christians, some of this group returned to the Roman Catholic Church while the others retained the particular syncretistic practices developed over the centuries of isolation.

In 1892, the first two Lutheran missionaries in Japan came in succession from the United States. They had been sent by the United [Lutheran] Synod of the South (which covered Virginia and West Virginia, and North and South Carolina). After language training in Tokyo, they arrived in the city of Saga on the southern island of Kyushu. They held their first Lutheran service on Easter Sunday of 1893. This event came just twenty-five years after the start of Japan's modernization. The imperial government created a modern constitution along western ideals. Nevertheless, the Emperor was unchallenged head of state and Shintoism (according to which the Emperor was both a god and high priest) remained deeply woven into the social fabric of Japan. At this time, the government also sought a complete overhaul of the military, educational, parliamentary, and economic systems. Missionary work still held a tenuous place within the newly modern Japan and missionaries were often compelled to compromise and justify their existence. Often the only response to their proclamation was a pelting by rocks and dung. They could only wait in hope for harvest of the seeds they had planted.

In 1900, the Lutheran Evangelical Association in Finland joined the missionary effort in Kyushu. However, with the start of the Russo-Japanese War, they were forced to leave and so began their work in Nagano and Tokyo. Until 1945, they developed Christian communities in Tokyo, Nagano, and Hokkaido.

The American missionaries expanded their field to include Kumamoto, Kurume, and Hakata on the island of Kyushu; and later even further to include Osaka, Tokyo, and the cities in between. These efforts resulted in the formation of a native, independent church, the Japan Evangelical Lutheran Church (JELC). With the beginning of the Second World War, all Protestant denominations were forced by military order into one association: the United Church of Christ. Soon after the war, however, the Lutheran churches left this association. At this time, both the Augustana Synod and the Lutheran Church in America sent missionaries as workers for the JELC. The first German missionaries after the war arrived in the 1960s when the North German Missionary Society (*Norddeutche Missionsgesellschaft*) sent two deaconesses to work for the JELC. Since the 1970s, under the auspices of the VELKD, the Lutheran Church of Braunschweig has provided for not only the financial but even the pastoral and staff support of the German missionaries there.

When China began to embrace Communism at the end of the 1940s and early 1950s, many missionaries of various denominations fled to Japan. Among the Lutherans of the former mission to China, the Lutheran Church – Missouri Synod (LC-MS) founded the Nippon Ruteru Kyokai (NRK, or the Japan Lutheran Church) and from two Norwegian missions were formed the Kinki

Evangelical Lutheran Church (KELC) and the West Japan Evangelical Lutheran Church (WELC).

Despite attempts to unite these four church bodies in the early 1960s, the plan failed. However, they have created a formal National Committee and their Presidents and General Secretaries meet throughout the year to discuss cooperative efforts in the church's mission and services. In particular, these bodies worked together until the 1990s with the Seibunsha publishing house (Lutheran Literature Society). Together, they published many books on the Lutheran tradition, including the Lutheran confessional texts and works by Martin Luther (which to date stands at sixteen volumes). Since the 1990s, the publications of these works have been carried out by various Christian publishing houses. The JELC and the NRK have joined together in order to provide a theological seminary (a four-year program) with the Japan Lutheran College/Seminary in Tokyo, and the KELC and WELC have established their own theological seminary (a three-year program) in Kobe.

It might help to view their theological cooperation in context to their overall place with other Lutheran and Christian denominations within Japanese society. According to statistics available in 2004 (out of a total population of 110 million people):

	Members	Congregations/Clergy
JELC	22,000	130/119
NRK	2,800	38/49
KELC	2,700	30/33
WELC	3,700	43/49
Reformed	195,000	1,500/ 2,100
Anglican	56,000	310/ 270
Protestants Total:	*612,000*	*8,300/ 9,900*
Roman Catholic	478,000	1,000/1,600
Christian Total:	***1,117,000***	***9,400/11,600***

It should be noted that there are two other very small church bodies who identify themselves as Lutheran, yet have very little contact with the other Lutheran church bodies; namely the Lutheran Brethren Church (1,200 members) and the Lutheran

Evangelical Christian Church (founded by the Lutheran Church-Wisconsin Synod, which has 450 members).

A noteworthy aspect of Christianity in Japan is that in addition to the one percent of Japanese people who are Christian, there are five to ten percent of the population who are not avowed Christians but nevertheless express sympathy for the Christian faith. All of these Christian denominations are now recognized and protected by national law and are free to practice their work and worship without state interference. Each denomination is also free to govern itself according to its own constitution and by-laws.

Mission and Evangelization

The missionary efforts of the so-called main-line churches have stagnated. However, the evangelical and charismatic denominations are showing remarkable activity. Whether these efforts will have a significant effect on the number of Japanese who convert to Christianity is not yet clear.

Lutheran Japanese pastors are actively sent out, both to serve in Japanese congregations in other parts of the world and also as missionaries. Since the 1960s, the Japan Evangelical Lutheran Church has sent missionaries to Brazil, who work in cooperation with the Lutheran church there, especially in Sao Paulo, where there is a Japanese Lutheran congregation there. For Japanese expatriates living on the west coast of the United States, the church sends pastors to two congregations of the Evangelical Lutheran Church in America. Further, through an official exchange program, a Japanese pastor is sent to the town of Helmstedt (Braunschweig), Germany. Still, Japanese Lutherans are engaged in traditional missionary work. The KELC has focused its missionary activity on Thailand. It currently has a pastor serving there. The WELC, for its part, has sent missionaries to Indonesia, either to serve in a congregation or as a dialogue partner in theological education.

Growth and Retraction

The development of congregations in Japan confronts the same challenges met by most urban congregations in the industrialized world. Due to the shortage of clergy, church officials have been discussing the value of retaining the current system, which stipulates that a congregation with an average membership of thirty should provide for the pastor's salary and expenses of the congregation themselves. Given the responsibility of such an arrangement, many congregations are searching for ways to merge with neighboring congregations into larger communities. The difficultly therein lies, however, in question of whether labeling most congregations "missionary parishes" (who must share a pastor) will make them more able and stronger for the mission of the Church or if it is simply a shortsighted stop-gap method to protect personnel and finances.

Worship, Hymnody, Liturgy

The Lutheran churches in Japan are strongly influenced by the model provided by the Lutheran churches in United States, which is itself a model of Luther's own *formula missae*. Every time the Lutheran churches in the United States revised their liturgy and hymnbooks, the Japanese Lutheran churches sought to simply translate these revisions into their own context. Only in the author's generation, after their own liturgical and theological reflections, have Japanese Lutherans sought to develop their own liturgy, though still based on the traditional model. Liturgical music usually borrows from either the Gregorian, or the Anglican, or the particular Japanese model.

In a spirit of both necessity and ecumenism, for many years Japanese Lutherans used the hymnbook of the United Church of Christ in Japan. Efforts to establish a common hymnbook failed, and since 1975 Lutherans have used their own hymnal, arranged according to the traditional liturgical year and highly influenced by German chorales and Scandinavian songs. Sadly, out of five hundred hymns, only twenty five are from Japanese hands, though there is hope that the future will provide for more.

Relation to the Culture

After the Second World War, German Christians – particularly Lutherans – had to re-examine the role that "A Mighty Fortress Is Our God" (*Ein Feste Burg*) was to play, and even whether it should be included in the new hymnbook. The hymn is deeply ingrained in German culture and consciousness, certainly given its use in the immediate past. The result was that the song was both an integral part of the German Church, but also a new inhibition given its recent abuse. A similar parallel is to be found when one considers the relationship of Christians and the Christian churches to Japanese culture. For the Japanese, Christianity is first and foremost something foreign, a religion of the West. During the industrial revolution and modernization of Japan in the late nineteenth and early twentieth century, the oft-repeated motto was "western technology but nonetheless with a Japanese spirit." The Christian churches tended to offer not only a religious but also a cultural criticism and engagement, especially since Japanese culture was so deeply and thoroughly influenced by Shintoism and Tennoism. Little theological compromise could be found. For Christians, anything that might endanger the doctrine of the divine Trinity (such as recognizing the Emperor as deity) was deemed unacceptable.

Nonetheless, that is exactly the compromise that many Japanese Christians made for the benefit of their survival. This is exactly the crisis and the guilt of which many Japanese Christians are aware of today: their failure to speak out against the atrocities of the Emperor during the Second World War. As a result, the crisis continues today. Many Japanese Christians wish to integrate their faith into the larger context of Japanese society; yet they are simultaneously aware of the failures of the past and worry about how far such efforts can be taken without doing harm to both faith and society. In particular, Japanese Lutherans are aware of Luther's insight that the Gospel always comes from outside of ourselves (*extra nos*); though we are responsible for bringing the Gospel into the world, it can also come in spite of our efforts and even contrary to them.

Still, Japanese Lutherans are committed to bringing the Gospel of Jesus Christ deep into the heart of every Japanese person. Each

Christian is responsible for proclaiming the Gospel, to make its joyous message something decisively meaningful to each Japanese heart and captivating to each Japanese mind. For centuries, Christianity has been able to address itself to ever new situations, cultures, and mindsets. Japanese Christians are called – and are thereby given hope – to continue these efforts to their own history and in their own culture.

Relationship to Society (Politics, Ethics, War, and Peace)

When one is aware of the sins of the past, not only as a church but as an individual, one is sometimes obliged to stand in opposition to the ruling government. Through conjunction with the National Christians Council of Japan (NCCJ), the Christian churches are often critical of the government and political parties. Here, concerning issue of human rights and concerns for political and religious freedoms throughout the world the Christian churches express their opinions freely, often finding echoes in non-Christians voices. Christians and non-Christians often work cooperatively to address these issues which are of concern to every human person.

The Ecumenical Situation

From its inception, the JELC has had an ecumenical focus. It is, however, reluctant to form union or full-communion arrangements with other denominations since it affirms that such actions must be based on a common, explicit formulation of faith. In 1941, under pressure from the military government, the various churches of Reformed, Methodist, Congregationalists, Baptists, Lutheran and some Anglican backgrounds joined to form the United Church of Christ in Japan, but with reluctance and resistance. As a result, after 1948, the Anglican, Lutheran, and Reformed (Presbyterian) churches respectively separated from the United Church and formed their own denominations in Japan again.

Since that time, the JELC has remained committed to ecumenical dialogue and charitable cooperation with other denominations. The JELC is an active and prominent member of the NCCJ. In fact, members of the JELC have served as president of the NCCJ, the contributor of this article himself from 1995 to 2000. Beyond Japan, the JELC is also a member of the Christian Churches of Asia (CCA). The activities of the JELC stand in contrast to the three other Lutheran churches of Japan, which are neither members of the NCCJ nor the CCA. On the international level, the JELC and the KELC are both members of the Lutheran World Federation; and the NRK is an associate member of this organization. The JELC also has members working in the Lutheran World Federation, either in Geneva or on any one of its various commissions and committees (The contributor served as member of the Lutheran-Roman Catholic dialogue of the world level from 1995 to 2006).

Beginning in the late 1980s, the JELC has continued a most fruitful dialogue with the Roman Catholic Church in Japan. These dialogues have produced two books. One is a review of the results of the ecumenical dialogue between these two churches, *Catholic and Evangelical: What We Share and Do Not Share in Common.* This book has been widely read (over 15,000 copies) and has generated much discussion. The other book is a joint translation and brief commentary of the *Joint Declaration on the Doctrine of Justification,* signed by the Vatican and the Lutheran World Federation in 1999. The JELC has also sought ecumenical dialogue with the Anglican Church in Japan. The two churches have sought ways to bring the results of their international dialogue to fruitful discussions on the local level. Both churches have recognized the validity of each other's baptism and, though in a limited fashion, showed hospitality to invite both members to the Holy Communion and readiness to extend their pastoral care.

Korea, Hong Kong, and Taiwan

The Lutherans most involved in Asia are the Americans. Most Lutheran churches in Asia are founded by and affiliated with either the Evangelical Lutheran Church in America (ELCA) or the Lutheran Church-Missouri Synod (LC-MS).

In Korea, only one church has its origins in the LC-MS, which was founded in the 1950s and established a College and Seminary in the suburbs of Seoul. Although small in a Korean context, the church is very influential in the field of lay education in Korea through its biblical studies course, the Bethel Method.

Two churches of ELCA and LC-MS backgrounds are established in Hong Kong and operate separate schools and educational programs. There they are joined by another church, of German origin, called the *Tun Tsing Mission* which also runs a school.

These parallels are also found in Taiwan, where the ELCA and LC-MS have founded churches. Yet here, there is a theological seminary in which members of both cooperate to run the school. They are joined by the work of the Finnish Lutheran church in the southern half of the island.

In the Chinese-speaking regions, one also finds a Lutheran church affiliated with the ELCA which calls itself in the Chinese language *Shin-I-hoe* (the Church of Justification through Faith). The LC-MS affiliated church calls itself simply *Luther-hoe* (the Luther Church).

Luther Reception in Asia

In the space remaining, I wish to say a few words about the phenomenal growth in recent years concerning the reception of Luther studies in Asia.

1. Translations of Luther into Asian languages

In many of the Asian countries, such as India and other areas, where English is at least one of the common languages, they use the American Edition of *Luther's Works*. They do not think it therefore necessary to translate Luther into their own language. The author knows of no Indian or Indonesian translation. The situation in the Far East Asia, however, is somewhat different. In Japan, Korea, and China, efforts have been made to create translations.

a. Japan

One of the earliest translations of Luther into Japanese (from the English) was "On the Christian Freedom," made in the mid of

1910s. Later, Shigehiko Sato and Ken Ishiwara followed with their own translations of the same work, this time from the Weimar Edition. Without the aid of basic translation tools, such as a Grimm or Truebner in those days, it was difficult for them to create an authentic translation. In1933, they engaged in a harsh debate concerning the translation of many central terms, especially concerning "fromm"(not "pious" but "just"). Nevertheless, other translators tried their Luther translation on the basis of the modern German translations. From these early days, much progress has been made. Today, the library of Japan Lutheran Theological Seminary is equipped with the Weimar Edition and also with a good library for Luther research in general. It offers the best library for the study of Luther and the Reformation in whole Asia.

The plan to publish Luther's writings in Japanese translation (Luther's Works, Japanese Edition in thirty-six volumes) based on the Weimar Edition was started in early 1960s. The project is divided into three series: Luther's occasional writings in twelve volumes; biblical exegesis in twelve volumes; and sermons, letters and tables talks in twelve volumes. The first volume (volume two of series one) appeared in 1963 and includes Luther's writings from 1520. So far, ten volumes from series one and six volumes of series two have appeared, the most recent being Luther's "Lectures on Romans." The contributor has served as Editor-in-Chief and as one of the main translators for the series.

b. Korea

In the1970s, a Korean edition of Luther's Works in twelve volumes was begun. Under the leadership of Dr. Won Yong Ji of St. Louis, the project, based on the American Edition, made remarkable progress and is now completed.

c. China

In 1970s and early 1980s, when the author had several occasions to stay as visiting professor in Taiwan and as a guest lecturer at Lutheran seminaries in Hong Kong, some Luther translations in the Chinese language as pamphlets and monographs were found. In 2001, when the Lutheran Theological Seminary in Hong Kong celebrated its acquisition of the whole Weimar Edition, the plan to

257

produce a Chinese translation of Luther's Works was announced. The project is undertaken as a cooperative between theologians in Hong Kong and historians throughout mainland China. It will consist of fifteen volumes, using the American Edition as basic texts. It is not clear, however, how the project has progress since its inception.

2. Luther Studies Symposia from 1980 to 1990

In early 1970s, a circle of people around the LWF discussed the possibility of establishing an Asian Center of Advanced Studies (ACAS) of the LWF as a Lutheran Graduate School of Theology in Asia. Within the ecumenical circle of Asian churches, this idea was debated and attacked as a project which would hinder the ecumenical atmosphere in Asia. Given these concerns, the plan was changed to create a program, instead of a center, as the *Asian Program for Advanced Studies* (APAS). The Program would seek affiliation with certain graduate schools in other parts of the world. Many leaders of the Lutheran churches in Asia have affirmed that such a program should serve not only clergy and theologians but also the lay leaders.

a. The APATS of the LWF

Based on this proposal, work began to establish such a program in 1975. After much discussion (in which the contributor was involved) we came to the conclusion to make a proposal to the leaders of Lutheran churches, to set up the *Asian Program for Advancement of Training and Studies* (APATS). On the one hand, the common program of training and studies for the whole of Asia could be planned by the committee for lay leaders and theologians in Asia in cooperation with the Asia Secretary of the LWF. At the same time, each area and country has the freedom and flexibility to have its own program of training and studies. In Japan, visiting and exchange program of seminary students with Thailand, Indonesia, and Hong Kong was planned and practiced. Programs especially for women have successfully continued, not only among Lutherans inside Japan but also exchange with the women of the Korean Lutheran Church.

b. Luther Studies Symposia

The preparatory committee of APATS then became responsible for a common program. Near the anniversary year of the Augsburg Confession (1980), the committee decided to start the *Luther Studies Symposia in Asia*, with the following purposes:

1) to interpret and understand Luther and the Lutheran Theology on Asian soil

2) to make ecumenical contributions in Asia, based on the above effort

3) to make contributions to the mission and evangelism in Asia

4) to foster the understanding of Luther among laypeople on grass-root level

5) to equip congregations and laypeople for mission and ecumenism

6) to share the results with the Lutheran churches of other parts of the world

To achieve these ends, six symposia were held between 1980 and 1990:

a) "The Augsburg Confession in Asia Today" (April 1980, Hong Kong)

b) "Nature and the Natural in Luther's Thought" (December 1982, Bangkok)

c) The Holy Spirit and Christian Witness in Asia" (December 1984, Manila)

d) "Theology in Dialogue" (December 1986, Seoul)

e) "Responsibility for the World – Luther's Intention and its Effects" (March 1988, Hong Kong)

f) "Christian Spirituality in Asia" (November 1990, Madras)

Papers presented at these symposia were later published from the desk of Asia Secretary, LWF and circulated among Lutheran churches and theological institutions not only in Asia but also throughout the world. To the regret of many participants there has been little international feedback from our sister churches.

As indicated above, each symposium examined one of six topics related to the theme "Luther in Asia." At each symposium, Asian theologians gave presentations, and responses were made by both Asian and non-Asian scholars from around the world. Participants from other continents were asked to follow and understand discussions in Asia, to engage the Asian mentality, to understand and interpret Luther and Lutheran tradition with the Asian mentality (considering both its unity and diversity among those from Near East to Far East), and to give their reactions. Said another way, while western theologians were welcome, they were first asked to be active observers rather than speakers and commentators. In this way, the symposia became forums of cultural and theological exchange and encounter between theologians from different parts of the world on Asian soil. Therefore, theologians from Latin America and Africa were also invited. These guests offered their own contributions following our orientation.

Lutheranism in Asia: Challenges and Contributions

We Asians ourselves are discovering again our Asian diversity. This brings with it many themes related to our "challenges and contributions." Indian theologians have engaged in profound and meaningful dialogues within their own multi-religious context. Japanese scholars are concentrating themselves (though perhaps often too much so), in the historical and traditional texts of the Lutheran tradition. We Japanese must be careful not to close our eyes to our own situation. Theologians of Chinese background are often much too Confucian in their outlook. Palestinian Lutherans are much too burdened by their own destiny and struggle in the Holy Land to discuss Luther. Our Indonesian colleagues from the Batak Church are several steps ahead with their proud "Batak Confessions," celebrating their freedom from the "western captivity" of tradition. Nationalism plays a certain role in some parts of Asia, but on the whole such impulses are subdued, especially in Japan.

When interpreting Luther, we Japanese tend towards the nominalist, existential understanding. This can make it difficult to dialogue with other Lutheran theologians from India and China, whose own milieu leads them to prefer a Thomistic, ontological way of thinking. This might cause difficulties in reaching a common understanding of Luther and his theological tradition; yet, it might also open new possibilities and new venues for dialogue, not only among Lutherans but with other Christians and even people of different faiths. We need to read and understand texts of Luther and Lutheran tradition, but at the same time to interpret them in our own present day contexts to proclaim the Gospel to our people. *(Trans. H. Ashley Hall)*

Bibliography

Huddle, B. P., *History of Japan Evangelical Lutheran Church*, 1954

Vikner, D., "LCA in World Mission 1842-1982," *Called to Global Mission, Division for World Mission*, LCA, 1982

Tokuzen, Y., *Japan Evangelical Lutheran Church in Mission*, JELC, 1993

Nature and the natural in Luther's Thought, East Asia Journal of Theology,

I/1, 1983

Luther Studies Symposia 1980-1990, DWM, LWF, 1991

The Lutheran Church in Latin America and the Caribbean: An Overview

Martin N. Dreher, Universidade do Vale do Rio dos Sinos, Brazil

1. Historical Development and Legal Status

At the outset of the sixteenth century European expansion to the Americas, the Portuguese and Spanish possessions remained off-limits for Lutheranism. There were, to be sure, a few isolated episodes during the colonial period in which Lutheran Christians took part. Thus, for instance, in 1528, in the period when the Spanish Kingdom and the Holy Roman Empire were ruled by the same monarch, under the titles of Charles I and Charles V, respectively, Welser came to Venezuela and a handful of Lutherans participated in the exploration of that territory. Whether they bore witness to their faith is unknown. The same might be said of Ulrich Schmiedl from Straubing and Hans Staden from Hessen. The former took part in the foundation of Buenos Aires; the latter stayed on after being stranded on Brazilian shores. Although the first Lutheran congregation in the region was founded in 1666 on the Danish Virgin Island of St. Thomas, and the second followed in 1743 in present-day Suriname (also a Dutch colony at that time), we can only speak of a Lutheran history in Latin America and the Caribbean from the nineteenth century onward. Only after the independence movements of that period did significant Lutheran influx into Latin America take place. Whatever their origins, whether immigrants, merchants, craftsmen, refugees or missionaries, the different strands of Lutheran influx also explain the variety of influences found within Latin American Lutheranism.

1.1. Immigrant Lutheranism

In 1824, only a few weeks apart, the first Lutheran congregations were founded in Brazil, one in Nova Friburgo, near Rio de Janeiro, the other in São Leopoldo, in southern Brazil. Further South, German immigrants likewise founded congregations in Buenos Aires (1843), Montevideo (1857) and Asunción (1893). Since 1870 a number of congregations were formed in the provinces of Misiones and Entre Rios, in Argentina. In 1890 the Evangelical Synod of the River Plate was established. Finally, around Lake Llanquihue in southern Chile, Lutheran congregations were set up in Osorno (1863) and Puerto Montt, again by German immigrants. The Evangelical Synod of Chile was established in 1903.

1.2. Merchant and Craftsmen Congregations

In northern Latin America, merchants and craftsmen founded congregations in Mexico (1861), Caracas (1894), Lima (1899), La Paz (1923) and Guatemala (1929). Though the congregations of Rio de Janeiro and São Paulo in Brazil were originally merchant and craftsmen congregations as well.

1.3 Lutheran Missions

The evangelical missionary societies established primarily during the nineteenth century never really viewed Latin America as a missionary field. Strange as it may seem, this observation expresses a characteristic attitude of Lutheranism vis-à-vis the Roman Catholic church. Lutherans always viewed Roman Catholics as Christians, therefore not objects of mission work, let alone of rebaptism. This attitude did not change even when it became clear that the Roman Catholic Church was not in a position to evangelize even half the population to which it was entitled under the old rights of patronage. Such was also the conduct of Lutheran immigrant congregations and synods. This posture is often wrongfully claimed to have had racial or ethnic origins. Instead, it was grounded on theological order. Quite a different stance was taken by churches from Reformed and Anglo-Saxon backgrounds, which actively carried out mission work among Catholics from the mid-nineteenth century onward, and

263

adopted rebaptism as a rule, on the grounds that Roman Catholics were not Christian. North American Lutherans only later came to change this point of view, which can be traced back to the North American Evangelical movement and the Monroe Doctrine.

The East Pennsylvania Synod had been doing mission work in British Guiana since 1890. The same was true in Puerto Rico since 1898 by the United Lutheran Church, which in 1917 took over the Danish work on the Danish Virgin Island. In 1908 the same church was also involved in mission work in Argentina. This work originated the United Evangelical Lutheran Church of Argentina. The membership of this church was originally only Spanish-speaking; today it consists mostly of descendants of European immigrants. In 1901 the Lutheran Church – Missouri Synod started sending out missionaries to Brazil, followed in 1905 by missionaries to Argentina, whose activity was limited, a few exceptions notwithstanding, to descendants of German immigrants. Thus, all Lutheran churches in the southern cone of Latin America share the same ethnic background.

As is commonly known, the first Lutheran congregation in North America was founded in New York in 1649. The second was established in 1666 on St. Thomas, one of the Danish Virgin Islands. St. Thomas, St. John and St. Croix were known as "Lutheran pastor's graveyard" in the past. Of thirty pastors sent out in the first one hundred years of missionary activity a total of fifteen died of tropical diseases shortly upon arrival. Sermons were held in Danish or in German. Danes and Germans had immigrated as colonizers. Beginning in 1675, African slaves were brought to the island, transforming St. Thomas into the most important slave market in the world fifty years later. The Lutheran pastors, however, felt responsible for the white settlers alone. In fact, not until 1713 was the first African slave baptized. The situation only changed when Zinzendorf intervened. On the occasion of Christian IV's crowning ceremony, Zinzendorf made the acquaintance of a slave from St. Thomas and took him to Herrnhut. In 1732 the Brotherhood decided to send out the first missionaries to the Caribbean: Leonhard Dober and David Nitschmann. Thus came into being the first Lutheran congregations of African origin in the Caribbean. St. Thomas became the foothold for the Herrnhut work on Antigua (1756), Barbados (1765), St. Kitt (1777), Tobago (1786) and Trinidad (1885).

When in 1917 the Danish Virgin Islands were sold to the United States, the Evangelical Lutheran Church in America took over the work among Lutheran Christians. In 1951 this missionary field, together with the mission on Puerto Rico, formed the Caribbean Synod of the American Lutheran Church. The mission in Puerto Rico was initiated by theology student Gustav Sigfrid Swenson, who arrived on the island only two months after the armistice of the Spanish-American war. Deeply influenced by the revival movement, he held the opinion that the American protectorate over Puerto Rico had great missionary significance. His activity must be compared to what today would be called a "faith mission." Swensson's work was taken over by the General Council (later the Lutheran Church in America), in 1899. A further Lutheran activity in the Caribbean region that merits mention is the mission work initiated in Cuba in 1912 by the Lutheran Church-Missouri Synod. These congregations were left to their own devices after the North American pastors pulled out of Cuba in 1959, but since 1987 the Lutheran World Federation (LWF) has been sending pastors to Cuba again.

The oldest Lutheran congregation in South America was established on October 15, 1743 in Fort Nassau, then the Dutch Guiana. When Guiana became British in 1803, most Lutherans abandoned the territory. The missionary work entered a new stage with the arrival of missionaries from the Pennsylvania Synod. The highest percentage of Protestants within a Latin American country's population is found in Suriname. As early as 1665 the Lutheran missionary activity in that country was initiated by Baron Justinian von Welz. In 1735 the Herrnhut Brethren started their work among slaves and the native population. From a total of 800 brethren sent out to that country, 230 perished as a consequence of tropical diseases. This work gave rise to the *Evangelical Broedergemeente* in Suriname, which operates side by side with the Evangelisch-Lutherse Kerk in Suriname.

All Lutheran congregations in Central America basically hail from the activity of the Lutheran Church-Missouri Synod. German immigration to Guatemala goes back to 1908. Initially, German pastors were active in that country, but after the Second World War the work was taken up by Missouri Synod pastors. Guatemala became a base for further work in El Salvador (1952) and Costa Rica (1962). In Panama, the Lutheran presence started with the activity of a military chaplain (1942). When European refugees started coming to Central America, the LWF sent out itinerant ministers to the region, beginning in 1953. This led to the creation of congregations in San José (Costa Rica), Managua, Tegucigalpa and San Salvador. A characteristic trait of present-day Lutheran churches in Central America is the cooperation among congregations, in remarkable contrast to the past, when they often operated apart from one another, or even against each other.

Bolivia holds a particular position in South America. This is where the highest proportion of Lutherans among the indigenous population is found. A German-speaking congregation already existed in La Paz since 1923. Missionary activity got under way after the involvement of an organization created within the Lutheran Bible School in Minneapolis. This led to the South American Mission Prayer League in 1937, later renamed World Mission Prayer League. In 1938 the first two missionaries to Bolivia were sent out. Without any kind of institutional ties, they lived on donations from individual North American Lutherans. In this sense they belong to the group of so-called "Faith Missions." Missionary stations were set up, and in 1944 the Hacienda Coaba was purchased, which was used to house a home for orphaned children. A school and Bible school to promote the development of native workers soon followed, and the first home-grown missionaries were ordained in 1954. The Bolivian Evangelical Lutheran Church was established in 1957. However, following a ground swell of nationalism, local leaders assumed overall control of the church in 1967, at which point North American missionaries left the country.

The Lutheran church in Venezuela goes back to nineteenth-century German craftsmen. After the Second World War, the church was given a boost with the arrival of Latvian and Hungarian refugees. The gradual consolidation of these traditions resulted in present-day Evangelical Lutheran Church in Venezuela. Also active in the country since 1951, the Lutheran

Church – Missouri Synod gave rise to the Lutheran Church of Venezuela.

In Colombia we have a Lutheran church that looks back at a tale of woe. As was the case with other evangelical denominations, the Lutheran church faced persecution between the years 1948-1957. Historically, the church originated from immigration, Wisconsin Synod missionary efforts and a "faith mission" initiative. The beginnings in Ecuador were similar. Primarily at work there were immigrants, the World Mission Prayer League and the Santal Mission. The small number of Lutherans in Peru hails from German immigration, as well as the Sower Bible Mission and the Norwegian Mission.

1.4. Immigrant Churches

On the southern cone of South America, we find Lutheran churches almost exclusively made up of immigrant descendants. One exception would be the United Evangelical Lutheran Church in Argentina, and a small group of Lutheran congregations in Uruguay. However, even in those churches there is a mix of immigration and missionary backgrounds. This is also the area with the largest group of Lutherans in Latin America and the Caribbean.

In Argentina one must start with the United Evangelical Lutheran Church, which originated from a 1908 LCA mission initiative among Spanish-speaking Argentines. The picture changed after WWII and the heavy influx of European refugees. Besides Spanish, sermons now were held in Latvian, Estonian, Hungarian, Slovak and German. Church membership in 2005 is 7,000. The 30,000 member, Lutheran Church – Missouri Synod associated Evangelical Lutheran Church of Argentina is the second largest Lutheran church in that country. Its history goes back to 1905, when Missouri Synod pastors arrived to take care of German immigrants and their descendants. Most of the members have Russian-German background. The largest Lutheran World Federation member church in Argentina is the Evangelical Church of the River Plate, with 45,000 members, a "United" church, characterized by the fact that about half its members come from a Lutheran background, while the other half comes from the

Reformed Confession. The church was originally established in 1843. In 1899 the Evangelical Synod of the River Plate was founded, encompassing congregations in Argentina, Uruguay and Paraguay. Almost all members descend from German immigrants.

The history of the Lutheran Church in Chile started in 1849, when Germans and Swiss settled in the southern part of the country. The first congregation was founded in 1853, the Evangelical Synod in 1903. Having changed its name to German Evangelical Church in Chile in 1937, it was renamed Evangelical Lutheran Church in Chile in 1959. After the US-supported military coup d'état deposed President Salvador Allende and Augusto Pinochet seized power (September 11, 1973), there was a great deal of tension within the church, which eventually led to a split. The Lutheran Church in Chile was then established, which now has a membership of 11,800, while the Evangelical Lutheran Church in Chile numbers 3,000 members. At present both church bodies are entering into dialogue with a view to reunification. Some isolated congregations remain independent; one is linked to the Lutheran Church – Missouri Synod.

Lutheranism was introduced in Brazil in 1824, though accounts of sporadic previous Lutheran visitors to the country exist, as was mentioned earlier. Five synods were established that eventually formed the Evangelical Church of Lutheran Confession in Brazil (2005 membership: 710,000), as well as the Evangelical Lutheran Church of Brazil (223,588 members), formerly the Brazilian District of the Missouri Synod. An Association of Free Lutheran Congregations counts 1,050 members. Some additional free congregations also exist, most of which of Pomeranian immigration background, but their precise membership has not yet been clearly determined.

Lutheran congregational and church life in Latin America and the Caribbean will be illustrated below based on the example of the Evangelical Church of Lutheran Confession in Brazil. However, some overall characteristics of Lutheranism in this part of the world could be summarized at this point: (1) Lutheranism did not come to the area in the wake of the sixteenth century European expansion (2) Originally, it had traits of isolated European colonies, as seen on the Virgin Islands, Puerto Rico and

Suriname, but Lutheranism also came as a diaconal ministry to these islands (3), siding with suffering African slaves at an early stage, specifically in the case of the Herrnhut mission work. In contrast, (4) Lutheranism as an immigration church arrived to Brazil and Argentina as part of an official attempt to "whiten" countries with a high proportion of African slaves in its population (5) The multiplicity of theological tendencies nowadays has given rise to some division within the churches (6) Some congregations have been heavily influenced by Pentecostal movements, in some cases leading to outright Donatism with the practice of rebaptism (7) On the other hand, there are remarkable signs of cooperation between churches as well (8) Although Lutheran churches on the whole have maintained a strong ethnic profile, there has been a concerted effort to break through ethnic barriers, especially in greater cities (9) Lutheran churches have taken a strong stand on political and social issues (10) The main contributing factor for this socio-political awareness has been the independent theological reflection taking place throughout Latin America and the Caribbean.

2. The example of the Evangelical Church of Lutheran Confession in Brazil (ECLCB)

The history of ECLCB cannot be dissociated from the wretched living conditions a broad spectrum of the European population was exposed to during the nineteenth century. Rural exodus, industrialization, failed agrarian reforms, unbridled urban growth, and agricultural collapse due to cheaper imports from Argentina, Australia and the United States: all this led to a massive emigration from Europe, as hordes of laborers, peasants and indentured servants took every opportunity available to leave behind the torn social fabric and widespread economic crises of their homeland.

Germans, Swiss, Dutch, Danes, Norwegians, Swedes, Austrians, Italians, Poles, Russians, Spaniards, Portuguese and many other nationalities immigrated to Brazil. From among them came many Protestants: Lutherans, United, Reformed, Waldensians and Baptists. The congregations and synods of these immigrants would later form the ECLCB, which explains one of the main characteristics of this church: a great diversity of piety. This distinguishing trait grew out of concessions and discussions, as well as the ability on the part of its congregations to live together and grow together.

The arrival of the different groups of immigrants that later formed the ECLCB, as well as other mainstream Protestant denominations, was made possible by world events that gave rise to huge transformations in the former Portuguese colony. At the time of Brazilian independence (1822), the Portuguese Patronage system was preserved, but a special arrangement reached between the British and the Portuguese Crowns in 1808: people of other beliefs were allowed entry into Brazil, provided that their religious gatherings were held in houses that did not look like churches, and that the official religion be respected. This meant that there was no specific legislation concerning Protestant marriages and burials, and above all, that it was impossible to raise the children of mixed marriages in the Lutheran faith.

Such areas of ambiguity would later become a source of mounting tension, but in the meantime, economic and political motives spoke louder than religious considerations. Newly independent, Brazil needed an army. For security purposes the settlement of unpopulated areas was called for, especially in southern Brazil, threatened as it was by encroachment from the River Plate region. Roads had to be built. The military outposts to protect these roads needed provisions.

Finally, two further aspects, perhaps not overtly manifested, but nevertheless evident, justified the Brazilian interest for European immigrants. One was based on race, the other on economics. Ever since the 1804 rebellion in Haiti and the slaughter of its white minority, slave-holding oligarchies in Brazil had felt a growing sense of unease. The Brazilian population pyramid presented an overwhelming proportion of slaves and slave descendants. Slave rebellions in the state of Bahia in 1806, and the Portuguese royal family's transfer to Brazil in 1808 led to the conclusion that a "whitening" of the population was urgently needed. Such a "whitening" process, however, could only be reached by granting permission for large scale intake of European immigrants, including Protestants, and by the substitution of slave workers by white salaried workers. This led to the rise, on the one hand, of small rural properties, tilled by the peasant and his own family. On the other hand, it led to the gradual replacement of slaves by immigrants on large rural properties. In fact, when slavery was finally abolished in 1888, the black population, which had been responsible for the wealth of the nation up to that point, was pushed to the margins of the Brazilian production system and confined to the slums in the major cities.

On a larger economic scale, the influx of white immigrants and the establishment of small agricultural properties made it easier for the Brazilian economy to adapt to the international market. An intermediary social class was formed between large landowners and slaves, a Brazilian middle class as it were, a consuming class for the products available on the world market.

These aspects of demographics, economics and political history are highly significant to understand the history of ECLCB. First of all, despite having come to the country as "substitutes" for slaves, the descendants of Brazilian Lutherans have never showed any particular solidarity for the fate of the black population. For many years, in fact, belonging to ECLCB was synonymous with belonging to the middle class. Nowadays, however, due to long-standing economic difficulties in the country as a whole, this social group has dwindled sharply, which has undeniably had dramatic consequences on church membership. Second, for historical reasons, most church members to this day come from a rural background. In very large urban centers, by contrast, Lutherans belong to a minority. Congregations there have different characteristics: businessmen or employees of foreign companies who only stay in the country for a limited number of years. This explains why assimilation into the Brazilian context has been easier for rural congregations than for urban ones, where an openness to discuss national issues has only recently become commonly accepted.

In summary, Lutheranism did not come to Brazil as a result of the activity of mission societies, but as a consequence of immigration. Lutherans in Brazil descend mainly from the 300,000 German immigrants that came to the country, 60% of whom were Protestant.

2.1. The Beginnings

The beginnings were anything but easy. The immigrants were sent to the three southernmost provinces of the country, Rio Grande do Sul, Santa Catarina and Paraná, though there were some smaller groups that settled in São Paulo, Rio de Janeiro, Minas Gerais and Espírito Santo. As the first immigrant groups brought their own pastors along, the first congregations were established shortly upon their arrival to the new country: in Nova Friburgo (1824), São Leopoldo (1824), Três Forquilhas (1826). In the imperial capital Rio de Janeiro the first congregation was founded in 1827. Santa Catarina only started receiving immigrants at a later date, so the first congregations in that state were Blumenau (1850) and Dona Francisca (Joinville) (1851).

Lutheran congregations were basically on their own and could only express their faith within certain bounds. For instance, Protestant marriages were neither recognized nor legally valid until 1861/63, when the issue was finally given some attention. Mixed marriages could only be celebrated in Roman Catholic parishes, and the children of such marriages could only be raised in the Catholic faith. This situation changed only with the proclamation of the Republic in 1889.

The immigrants had to organize their church life themselves. The first worship services were held in palm-covered huts. Sometime later the first congregational building would be raised, with the dual purpose of school and church. Adjacent this building would be the Lutheran cemetery, since Protestants could not be buried along with Catholics. A building serving exclusively as a church would not be allowed until much later.

As the number of pastors was limited, the immigrants had to improvise, and choose ministers among the members. The theological principle of the *priesthood of all saints/believers* was turned into a practical reality within Brazilian congregations in the figure of the "Colonist-Pastor," This individual would work on his fields and take up some pastoral duties whenever needed. When, in later years, pastors with seminary education or academic studies were sent to Brazil, these colonist-pastors would be derided as "pseudo-pastors." As they often carried out the duties of school teacher and pastor, and as the school building often served as the place of worship, this gave rise to the dyad church-school, pastor-teacher, which became a distinguishing trait of ECLCB history. Through this intense collaboration on the part of teachers in congregational life the clericalization of the church could be averted for an extended period of time. In recent years, most teachers who perform catechetic duties in the church have been ordained, and the church is finding it difficult to clearly define the position and the role of the catechists in its midst, which has unfortunately led to growing clericalization within the church. However, we can still to this day observe the strong collective sense revealed in the language used by members of the congregation when referring to "our" cemetery, "our" school, "our" parsonage, "our" pastor. The ecclesiological shortcoming of such a communal church was that the concept "church" rarely went beyond the congregational or parish boundaries. The ecclesiological shortcoming of the present-day development is that the concept "church" becomes more and more centralized on the pastor alone.

2.2. Initial Church Structures

The dominance of Prussia and the emergence of Pan-Germanism led to the "rediscovery" of the immigrants that left for Brazil after the failure of the liberal revolution (1848). The *Oberkirchenrat* in Berlin, the Basel Mission Society and the Evangelical Society for Protestant Germans in America (Barmen) started sending out pastors with university education or graduates from mission houses to evangelical congregations in Brazil in 1837, 1861 and 1865, respectively. In 1897, the Lutheran organization *Gotteskasten* (God's Chest) started sending out pastors educated in Hermannsburg, Kropp and Neuendettelsau. The same institutions also sent out a number of teachers. This important aid was supplemented with the foundation of the *Diasporaseminar* in 1911, originally set up by the *Oberkirchenrat* Berlin in Soest/Westphalia, then in Ilsenburg/Harz. In this seminary pastors were educated exclusively for the South American Diaspora. While undeniably important for the church at the time, it also seems clear that this initiative from the Prussian *Landeskirche* had the effect of delaying considerably the implementation of pastoral education in Brazil.

The arrival of large numbers of pastors, especially after 1864, marks the beginning of a second stage in the history of the Evangelical Church of Lutheran Confession in Brazil: the first attempt undertaken to unite the different congregations into one body dates from 1868. Although that particular attempt failed, others followed and led to the formation of four regional churches: the Rio Grande Synod (1886), the Evangelical-Lutheran Synod of Santa Catarina, Paraná and other States of South America (1905), the Association of Evangelical Congregations of Santa Catarina and Paraná (1911) and the Central Brazil Synod (1912).

The activity of the pastors sent out from the United States by the Lutheran Church – Missouri Synod led to the foundation in 1900 of a fifth church organization, which, however, went its own way and eventually became the Evangelical Lutheran Church of Brazil (ELCB). In spite of differences in teaching, the members of both churches have the same immigration background, which often allows for a certain amount of flexibility in the allegiance of church members.

In the beginning the main task of the synods was to advance and defend the interests of the different congregations and their members in the face of state authorities. The distinctive presence of the laity in their governing bodies preserved the unity of the congregations. On the other hand, the emergence of synods also allowed for cooperation over the years in the field of church publications, pastoral care of internal migrants and new immigrants, youth groups and women's groups. Yet, very rarely did the synods use the opportunity to take a stand regarding issues of Brazilian life. Most importantly, the synods were a heterogeneous gathering place for religious, economic, political and ethnic groups that lived on the fringes of the Brazilian society. This marginalized existence was encouraged by the legislation during the Empire and by the predominance of Augusto Comte's Positivism during the first four decades of the Republic (since 1889). All this notwithstanding, the synods did make an important contribution to the community at large through their teachers: until the Second World War there was practically no illiteracy among Lutherans in Brazil.

2.3. Between the Gospel and Ideology

At the time of the Second Reich's expansionism, especially following the fall of Bismarck, the hardships faced by descendants of German immigrants in Brazil – and meanwhile also Swiss, Scandinavian and Dutch – were relentlessly exposed by German diplomacy. By providing substantial aid for local German publications and schools, and by intensifying visits by German Navy vessels to countries with a significant German immigrant population, an outright attempt was made to secure markets for the German industry. Among the theorists of German colonialism there were some who went a step further, and worked out a plan that would create a "New Germany" in Southern Brazil. Chief among them was Friedrich Fabri, the mission inspector of the Rheinische Mission Society. German diplomacy aimed to attain its objective mainly by preserving the German character of German immigrants overseas. This explains why, in 1900, a church law was passed that allowed the inclusion of German congregations within the Berlin *Oberkirchenrat*, which would provide them with personnel and material support. Undoubtedly, this assistance from church entities must also be understood as Christian charity. Nevertheless, it contributed little to the autonomy of the Brazilian Lutheran church, which to this day still struggles with an identity that owes more to *Deutschtum* than to Lutheranism.

When the *Deutsche Evangelische Kirchenbund* allowed the inclusion of Lutheran Synods in Brazil in 1924, the life of the Lutheran church in Brazil became even more dependent on Germany. Furthermore, all internal discussions within the German church were thereby transposed to Brazil as well, with the establishment of organizations such as "German Christians in Brazil," "National Socialist Ministry in Brazil," and "Working Group of the Confessing Church in Brazil."

The congregations suffered the most during the two world wars. Financial difficulties intensified; pastors were interned in prisoner camps; the German language was outlawed in school and church. Despite such tribulations, the war years did have a salutary effect, for they allowed the strengthening of the synods, which had lost sight of their self-reliance due to their dependence on German church institutions. They were suddenly forced to lead the life of the Lutheran church in Brazil themselves. The education of teachers already had a long tradition, the first teacher seminary having been founded in 1899. In terms of pastoral education, however, little had been done. The noticeable shortage of pastors led to the opening of the Evangelical Pre-Seminary in Cachoeira do Sul by Pastor Hermann G. Dohms in 1921. The *Proseminar* was later moved to São Leopoldo and served as the foundation for the *Spiegelberg* educational complex, where in 1946 the Theological School was established which now, as the Higher School of Theology, is responsible for the whole theological training program of the ECLCB.

A diaconal mother house has also existed on the *Spiegelberg* since 1939. Collaboration among women was a feature of immigrant life ever since the first settlements were founded. Used to helping each other in daily life, women in congregations soon started working together, using the proceeds from their handicrafts to provide for their needs, be it the care of newborns and their mothers, or new church towers and bells. This later gave rise to the Evangelical Women's Association, the *Frauenhilfe*, which was initially supported by deaconesses from Wittenberg or Kaiserswerth. Evangelical women promoted the education of local deaconesses and the establishment of a Brazilian Diaconal Mother House and were in fact able to fulfill this dream even before the church leaders could carry out the plan of educating local pastors. Female deacon work has been a hallmark of autonomous local church work in the Lutheran church in Brazil ever since.

2.4. A New Beginning

The end of the Second World War marked the beginning of a third stage in the history of ECLCB. While some presaged the end of the Lutheran church in Brazil along with the decline of its ethnic foundation, others viewed the moment as a sign for reorientation. Seeking collaboration among the sister synods, they founded the Sinodal Federation in 1949. At its first General Council in 1950 in São Leopoldo, the Federation, shortly thereafter renamed Evangelical Church of Lutheran Confession in Brazil, gave expression to its identity and program by declaring itself a Church of Jesus Christ in Brazil, bound by the *Augsburg Confession* and *Luther's Small Catechism*, and open to the worldwide Church as a member of the World Council of Churches (WCC) and of the Lutheran World Federation (LWF).

This programmatic statement has since guided the service of ECLCB in Brazil and within the ecumenical community. Whereas in the past the synods were more strongly oriented toward Europe than Brazil, it is now emphasized that the future of this church lies in the Latin American continent. The commitment to the Gospel has consequences for the political, cultural and economic life for Brazil and for Brazilians. In addition, the confessional commitment has been highlighted. In the past, only one of the synods had a clearly confessional foundation, acknowledging the Book of Concord as its Confession of Faith. Over the years, however, the other three synods adopted the Small Catechism and the Augsburg Confession as their Confession.

The years between 1949 and 1968 were devoted to structural issues and adjustments, and to the quest to implement responsible stewardship of property, time and gifts.

2.5. In the Eye of the Storm

During the years that followed the Second World War, Brazil had to deal with all the problems associated with the quick transition from an agrarian to an industrial society. The political, social and economic turmoil that rocked the country did not leave the church unaffected. After a military coup in 1964, the country lived under a dictatorship for over twenty years. Growing political unrest, both in the countryside and in the large cities, led to increased repression on the part of the government. At the same time ECLCB was preparing the Fifth General Assembly of the Lutheran World Federation, to be held in Porto Alegre in 1970, following the refusal by German Democratic Republic authorities to hold it in their country. However, the assembly was transferred to Evian at short notice due to protests over the abuse of human rights in Brazil, and in hindsight, because of lacking missionary vision on the part of global Lutheranism.

This was a hard blow to ECLCB, for at the same time the decision was taken to move the Assembly to Evian, the document that would later be called the "Curitiba Document," as it was made public in that city in October 1970 at the General Council of the

277

Church, was ready for publication. In it, ECLCB announced the abandonment of its self-centered perspective in favor of an attitude of responsibility for the country as a whole. By stressing that the church "must turn itself to human beings as a whole, not just to their souls," the document maintained that this view had "consequences for all aspects of life, including physical, cultural, social, economic and political, for all issues connected to public welfare." The document made it clear that ECLCB had been given a prophetic task toward Church and Society. Citing Ezekiel 33:7 it asserted that the church had "to carry out a critical function – not a controlling function, but that of watchman and conscience to the nation. In certain situations the church, in an unbiased manner and always with the intention of finding a just and appropriate solution, will seek to call the attention of authorities and remind them of their responsibilities."

The objection to the demands placed by the State on its citizens in the name of the doctrine of national security is clear from the following quote: "The fatherland will be honored and loved, its symbols will be respected and displayed with civic dignity. However, a Christian may not speak of the fatherland in deifying categories."

What caused such a change of course? The guidelines from the 1950s? No doubt. The shock from the relocation of the Fifth General Assembly? Perhaps. The main reason, however, might be found in everyday life in Brazil, which became unbearable for small landowners and rural workers in the 1970s. This affected ECLCB in a number of ways. While historically its members had been concentrated primarily in the southern states of Brazil, the church of immigrants started undergoing a demographic transition: pushed out of their land, a growing share of church members was gradually joining the shantytown populations on the outskirts of large cities. Others sought new frontiers to settle, with the consequence that more and more Lutherans settled in remote colonization areas deep in the tropical forests of Mato Grosso, Rondônia and Goiás.

The following years saw wave upon wave of change. The political and social situation in the country led one wing of the church to engage in intense collaboration with the theological current known as Liberation Theology. Here the rediscovery of Luther's *Theologia Crucis* was particularly important. Church declarations were regularly made on a number of issues: appeals for amnesty, protests against the suffering of small landowners displaced by dam constructions, disputes with the National Foundation for Indians (FUNAI), demands for land rights and agrarian reform. These activities were also responsible for continuous growth in the ecumenical collaboration of ECLCB.

In a parallel development, another wing of the church became strongly involved in the evangelical piety movement introduced to ECLCB by pastors from the World Mission Prayer League. To begin with, there was a sharp cleavage between these seemingly irreconcilable camps. Lately, however, mutual appreciation has gained the upper hand, giving rise to a new awareness of the richness of diversity, which has resulted in broad efforts to renew the worship services, hymns and liturgy in order to include and reconcile these previously opposing views.

Bibliography

BACHMANN, Theodor. Lutherische Kirchen in der Welt 1977. In: Lutherische Rundschau. Zeitschrift des Lutherischen Weltbundes. 27 Jg. Heft 2/3. 1977.

BACHMANN, E. Theodore. Lutheran Churches in the World. A Handbook. Minneapolis: Augsburg Publishing House, 1977.

BASTIAN. Jean-Pierre. Historia Del Protestantismo em América Latina. México: CUPSA, 1990.

DREHER, Martin N. Igreja e Germanidade. Estudo crítico da História da Igreja Evangélica de Confissão Luterana no Brasil. 2ªed. São Leopoldo: Sinodal, 2003.

DREHER, Martin N. A Igreja Latino-Americana no Contexto Mundial. São Leopoldo: Sinodal. 2ªed. 2005.

HENNIG, Martin. Sie gingen übers Meer. Die evangelischen Kirchen deutscher Herkunft in Übersee, ihre Eigenart, ihre Probleme und ihre Arbeit. Hamburg: Agentur des Rauhen Hauses, o.J. 1960(?)

HERMANN, Stewart. Die Reformation in Latein-Amerika. In: BRUNOTTE, Heinz und RUPPEL, Erich. Gott ist am Werk. Festschrift für Landesbischof D. Hanns Lilje zum sechzigsten Geburtstag am 10. August 1959. Hamburg: Furche-Verlag, 1959, 126-134.

LAMPE, Armando. Mission or Submission. Moravian and Catholic Missionaries in the Dutch Caribbean During the 19th Century. Göttingen: Vandenhoeck & Ruprecht, 2001.

LESKÓ, Béla. Die Entdeckung der Identität in einer neuen Kultur und Gesellschaft in Südamerika. In: VAJTA, Vilmos (ed.). Die Evangelich-Lutherische Kirche. Vergangenheit und Gegenwart. Stuttgart: Evangelisches Verlagswerk, 1977, 341-357.

PFEIFFER, Johannes. Auf Luthers Spuren in Lateinamerika. Erlangen: Verlag der Ev.-Luth. Mission, 1969.

PRIEN, Hans-Jürgen. Die Geschichte des Christentums in Lateinamerika. Göttingen: Vandenhoeck & Ruprecht, 1978.

Lutheranism in North America

Maria Erling, *Lutheran Theological Seminary at Gettysburg*

Lutheranism in North America encompasses many peoples and traditions spanning several centuries. Separate waves of migration brought people with distinctive traditions and practices. The tradition of "Eastern Lutheranism" denotes those Lutheran churches that were founded by German settlers in the seventeenth and eighteenth century who came to Pennsylvania, New Jersey, New York, Georgia, and the Carolinas. The largest "Lutheran migration" occurred during the late nineteenth century, bringing peoples from Germany, Norway, Finland, Estonia, Lithuania, Latvia, Slovakia, Sweden, Denmark, and Iceland. Lutheranism in North America has not been limited to the heritage of Northern Europeans. A Lutheran community in the Danish Virgin Islands developed through the slave trade that encompassed both African slaves and their Danish owners. The long American history for Lutheran church bodies has also been one of expansion beyond ethnic borders. Mission work among Native American Indians began as early as John Campanius translated Luther's Catechism to the Lenni Lenape language in 1638. Lutheran urban ministry efforts from the middle of the twentieth century strove to break down the fortress mentality of churches in changing neighborhoods so that they might become more hospitable. At the break of the twenty-first century, Lutheranism in North America is becoming more diverse through new migrations of African, Latin American, and Asian Lutherans. These new arrivals continue the process of transplanting the church that began with the first settlements in the sixteenth century.

The task of characterizing American Lutheranism as it relates to Lutheranism around the world is made more manageable if the many theological and confessional disputes that raged among

American Lutherans are bracketed, at least initially. This makes it possible to provide a clearer view of the programmatic and organizational style that most American Lutheran groups had in common. Of course the theological and confessional foundations of Lutheranism are hard to ignore, even in America, and even temporarily. In the course of developing an activist and pragmatic Lutheranism in America, for instance, theological disputes often threatened to derail an emerging unity even as the train headed out of the station, but in the end there were always more trains, more stations, and more rails heading somewhere. I hope that the reader will recognize the pragmatic leanings of even the most diehard confessional protagonist if they are shown how the proponents of an "American" Lutheranism argued consistently for a Lutheranism that uses or attempts to use its considerable theological and confessional heritage to do something rather than to rest content and just be Lutheran.

After a brief sketch outlining the diverse origins of the various Lutheran churches in North America, this chapter will describe how various Lutherans came into their own as fully developed denominations with full-time chief executives and programmatic organizational structures during the massive Protestant missionary movement nineteenth and twentieth centuries. The missionary movement that swept through American Protestant churches influenced the development of Lutheran churches at a critical juncture. The effort to amass resources to support missionary work became an important dimension of the Americanization process for ethnic Lutherans, and provided the rationale and mode for Lutherans to move out of European patterns of thought and piety into a particular American and activist Lutheran identity.

When the Rev. Rasmus Jensen died along the Hudson River on Christmas Day in 1621, he left behind no Lutheran church; only a record of having been the first Lutheran pastor in the new world. Further south along the Delaware River, a few hundred colonists from Sweden and Finland founded their short lived Delaware colony in 1638, but the more substantial presence of Lutherans in North America occurred in Pennsylvania in the 1690's. German settlers responded to William Penn's invitation and arrived in numbers in the early 1700's. Migration peaked between 1745 and 1755. All through the middle colonies of New

York, New Jersey, Pennsylvania, Maryland and Virginia, there were scattered settlements of Germans; but a united Lutheran church took some time to develop. Lay initiative and worry prompted by the organizing activity of the Moravian pietist Count Nicholas Ludwig Zinzendorf finally prodded a missionary-minded organization in Germany, the Francke Institute in Halle, to send Henry Melchior Muhlenberg to Pennsylvania in 1743. The German settlers he encountered had come to America on their own without official pastoral leadership. Muhlenberg cultivated lay acceptance of his ministerial authority but also organized the "United Pastors," a ministerium organized to train and ordain pastors and provide oversight for congregations.

The missionary-oriented Halle Institution that sent Muhlenberg to Pennsylvania put a pietistic stamp on American Lutheranism, but the encounter with other confessional groups from Germany - Reformed, Moravian, and Anabaptist - pushed Lutherans to emphasize their own confessional heritage as well. America's religious diversity did not lead to homogenization, but instead worked to accentuate distinctive religious convictions. German immigrants continued to emphasize their respective Lutheran and Reformed identities, even while they accommodated economic necessity and created Union congregations in rural communities throughout the Middle colonies.[1] An intensification of religious particularism affected all groups as they defined themselves against a confusing and often contentious religious backdrop. The focus on what made each group distinct, however, was not conducive to the development of an outgoing and expansive Lutheran church. Lutherans entered the national period after the Revolutionary war with strong congregational traditions, but without strong common institutions to address the expanding ministry needs of a growing nation. The debates that attended the organization of the first General Synod for Lutherans in America in 1820 testify to the strains that accompanied national expansion. Lutherans in Ohio wanted assurances that Lutherans in Pennsylvania would not dictate how and in what language they would worship.

---

[1] E. Clifford Nelson, ed., *Lutherans in North America* (Fortress Press: Philadelphia, 1980), 61.

The first General Synod, however, provided the organizational means for Lutherans to cooperate and develop common educational institutions. Hartwick Seminary, founded in 1819, was soon followed by Gettysburg Seminary, founded in 1826, and the Theological Seminary in Columbus, Ohio, and Southern Seminary in Columbia, South Carolina, both founded in 1830.[2] Each of these schools served both local and regional needs and trained ministers to plant churches on the rapidly expanding frontier. The "home mission" efforts of the Eastern Lutheran churches may have seemed straight forward enough, but the ambassadors for an unreflective American Lutheranism soon met up with determined Lutherans of another stripe. Hoping to simplify matters for frontier ministers, a group of anonymous Lutheran leaders drafted the *Definite Synodical Platform* in 1855. Never officially adopted by the General Synod, it was widely distributed and the authors eventually identified themselves. The chief writer, the Rev. Samuel S. Schmucker of Gettysburg Seminary, sought therein to clarify the position of American Lutheranism for the churches in Indiana and other places that had been thrown into confusion by confessional arguments of other Lutheran ministers in their territory. By 1855 there was a growing conservative faction within the General Synod led by Charles Porterfield Krauth of Philadelphia, who became the standard bearer for a confessional resurgence among Eastern Lutherans.

Eastern Lutheran debates were fought on the pages of church newspapers, a technological innovation that accompanied the vast migrations of settlers to the mid-continent. Aided by the decision of the national post office (that postage for newspapers be the same whether it was to be sent to the next town or to the next state), Lutheran newspapers gained national readership. The theological controversies that might have been contained within the annual meeting were now conducted in public. The launch of a new paper, a frequent event during the 1850's and 1860's, provided the occasion for the editor to state his approach to the great issues of the day. Charles Porterfield Krauth's inaugural editorial for the *Lutheran and Missionary* showed the self-

---

[2] More on the various tendencies of the several schools, see Nelson, *Lutherans in North America,* 128-9.

consciousness of the confessional movement in the context of the exacting scrutiny American Lutherans had received on the frontier. "We are not 'old Lutherans.' If there be a Lutheranism which is exclusive, harsh, and repellant . . . that is not our Lutheranism. The Lutheranism we have learned to love is moderate in its tone, free from the spirit of false exclusiveness, and makes no pretensions which have any show of extravagance."[3] The title of the newspaper signals the importance of missionary ideals within this emerging confessional movement. If any labels were used among Lutherans, a "missionary friend" could be counted on to appeal to a popular audience.

Lutheran particularism intensified during the migrations of the mid nineteenth century. American Lutherans acknowledged their heritage in the German Reformation in the sixteenth century, but even this common theological and historical did not unite Lutherans on the North American continent. German migrations to the Midwest occurred in the context of the cultural and political revolutions in the 1840's and leaders who had forged their views in the context of political and social turmoil shared very little with the long settled German American communities on the East coast. Even the travel routes of the new settlers kept them separate, as nineteenth-century Germans entered into the North America States via the Gulf of Mexico and settled in the Ohio and Mississippi River valleys. While "Missouri" Lutherans colonized the area around St. Louis, great waves of Scandinavian Lutherans flowed into the land around the Great Lakes of the upper Midwest and in the central plains in Canada. Slovak and Finnish Lutherans arrived at the end of the nineteenth century and found work in mining and forestry. Separated by language, history, and custom, ethnic groups poured their energy and resources into constructing schools, training pastors, and establishing themselves as independent denominations. New leaders – all immigrants themselves – such as T. N. Hasselquist, E. Carlsson and E. Norelius for the Augustana Synod, J. A. A. Grabau for the Buffalo Synod, H. A. Preus and U. V. Koren for the Norwegian Synod, A. Weenas, S. Oftedal and G. Sverdrup for the Augsburg Norwe-

---

[3] Quoted in Adolph Spaeth, *Charles Porterfield Krauth*, vol.II, (New York: The Christian Literatures Company, 1898), 36.

gians, C. F. W. Walther for the Missouri Synod, the Fritschels for the Iowa Synod, G. Christensen and P. S. Vig for the Inner Mission Danes, J. K. Nikander for the Finnish church, J. Bjarnason for the Icelanders, provided theological and cultural direction for new arrivals in the Midwest and in Central Canada.

Given the fact that the mid-nineteenth century was a time of enormous geographic expansion in America, it might seem that all the resources of the various Lutheran church groups would be tied up in starting churches, educating pastors, and supporting the needs of local congregations. These home mission efforts did demand the larger portion of the free will offerings given by Lutheran church members. New settlements needed pastors, and seminary students were sent out as fast as they could be trained to meet the minimum qualifications. The early Lutheran efforts and the confused diversity in Indiana were described by home missioner Abraham Reck:

> The name of a Lutheran was hardly known there. Then its population was three thousand, and mixed with a number of tolerably intelligent Yankees, one of whom asked me one day, 'What new sect are you bringing in here? What do you believe, &c?' Why sir, replied I, the Bible is our creed-book; but if you come to the court-house at such a day and hour, you can hear and judge for yourself.' I and my whole family took chills and fever in the very worst type, notwithstanding, in less than six years, I organized nine congregations.[4]

Reck had been ordained in 1812, before there were any Lutheran theological seminaries in America. He was trained by a village pastor, and had a very modest education. It suited him for the groundbreaking work of home mission among frontier settlers. Once theological seminaries were established, students began to get their education for ministry there. The crying need for home mission work had overstrained the more informal apprenticeship system that had so far supplied the needs of settled communities in the eastern states.

---

[4] Abraham Reck's memoirs are recorded in John G. Morris, *Fifty Years in the Lutheran Ministry* (Baltimore, 1878),167.

At Gettysburg Seminary (founded in 1826), the focus on home mission needs was supplemented by specific attention to foreign mission. Students were required to join the Society for Inquiry on Mission, a society formed in 1824 by Samuel S. Schmucker. The society continued at the seminary in Gettsyburg and served to orient the study of the students toward the advancement of the foreign missionary cause. Student recitations for the society meetings cover the gamut of missionary efforts, from work among Native Americans and Greenlanders to the missionary exploits of Halle missionaries in India during the 1750's.[5] The regular focus on foreign mission did not result in many Lutheran missionaries, however. Instead, the cultivation of a devotion to mission was directed toward the strong demand on the American frontier.

Newly arrived immigrants were also interested in missionary work. The pioneer Swedish pastor, Lars Paul Esbjorn had been a supporter of missionary work in Sweden, and when he came to America in 1849, he brought that interest to his ministry among immigrants. The first newspaper published for Swedish American church people, *Hemlandet*, began in 1855 with both a practical and a religious focus. The paper included missionary work from the beginning, and in 1863 the focus was made explicit with the words *Missionary Leaf* included on the masthead. Readers could follow developments in Europe, where missionary societies linked mission work to the emerging confessionalism in the theological faculties. While Swedish Americans had strong ties to the Swedish Evangelical Mission, founded in 1836 on more evangelical principles, they began to support the Hermannsburg Mission Society, founded in 1850, as they developed a higher confessional consciousness.[6] Similarly, Norwegian Americans had their pick of several missionary societies in Norway, and chose the Norwegian Missionary Society founded in 1842, a society determined to apply strictly Lutheran principles to missionary work. The connection of immigrant church bodies with missionary societies established on strictly Lutheran foundations indicates that American Lutherans

---

[5] *Society for Inquiry on Mission* records are housed at the Lutheran Theological Seminary archives in Gettysburg, Pa.

[6] George Hall, *The Missionary Spirit in the Augustana Church* (Rock Island: Augustana Historical Society, 1984), 2.

kept abreast of theological and ecclesiological debates in the Lutheran Churches in Europe. Their choices provide indirect evidence of the kinds of theological movements and networks Scandinavian Lutherans in America felt comfortable supporting.

Lutherans belonging to the General Synod were pioneers in sending their own missionary abroad. As early as 1842 Frederick Heyer had begun work in the Guntur mission field in India. The Rev. Walter Gunn joined him four years later, but soon succumbed to tropical disease and died. "Father" Heyer outlived several younger associates and survived on a very meager salary. An early review of his work attributed his success to his decision to live in the manner of the native peoples. Heyer believed "it was most probable that, in the long run, the natives of any country would adopt habits of life most conducive to their preservation . . . . because a certain manner of living may be well adapted to the climate of America, it does not necessarily follow that every conceited peculiarity must be observed in a tropical residence ten thousand miles away."[7] Heyer's practical accommodation to the cultural and social conditions in India provided an important model for American Lutheran missionaries who followed.

American Lutheran interest in the missionary movement grew when women became involved. The first student to train specifically for missionary service at the Lutheran Theological Seminary in Gettysburg, Walter Gunn, got his support from a women's society of the Hartwick Synod, who had prayed in earnest for a way to advance the missionary call. They found Walter, a poor student who had undergone a conversion in 1837 during the evangelical revivals of the second Great Awakening and after they convinced their husbands to support him, he went for a year of study to the seminary in Gettysburg. In taking this abbreviated course he was typical of many of his fellow students, since a full course was rarely completed until the end of the nineteenth century. For Gunn the missionary call took precedence, and for others the needs of congregations took precedence over an extended theological education.[8] Walter served a short term in

---

[7] Morris, *Fifty Years*, 215.

[8] A.R. Wentz, *History of Gettysburg Seminary.* Similarly, the Augustana Seminary in Rock Island, Illinois, did not demand the BD degree of its

India - he died of tuberculosis in 1851 - but his limited term on the field turned his wife into an extremely able promoter of the mission. Mrs. Walter [Lorena] Gunn moved to Ohio after her husband's death. In the Springfield community associated with the Wittenburg College and the seminary, she devoted herself to generating support for the missionary task of the church. Professor John H. W. Stuckenberg and his wife Mary Gingrich Stuckenberg expanded the local work of the Springfield women and advocated women's missionary society work among Lutherans on a national basis. Mary solicited materials from the societies of other denominations. In 1879 her efforts paid off and the General Synod meeting in Canton, Ohio called the women of the church to form local auxiliaries of the Synods Women's Missionary Society.

John H. Stuckenberg was a well-known Lutheran liberal during this time of organizing in the General Synod. He taught during a time of ongoing theological debate in that body over liturgical and confessional issues. Stuckenberg defended the historic progressive tradition of that synod against efforts within the body to introduce a more rigid confessional subscription. In order to promote a more inclusive, less rigid Lutheranism, and to attempt to overcome the stagnation that resulted from ongoing doctrinal controversy, a number of leaders began to plan for a newspaper, *Lutheran Evangelist,* which would attempt to engage the church in more active work. In a letter to his wife in 1875 Stuckenberg laid out what some of those plans might mean for her. "I hope that you will be able to contribute to its columns in some way or other. The ladies of our church must be brought out more. They are not prominent enough in the great movement of the Church. Can you not do something in the matter?" After the newspaper was started, Stuckenberg devoted several of his own editorials to women's missionary society work. This corresponded with the design of the newspaper, that it would devote itself to two

---

candidates for ordination until 1900. Until that time students could be ordained after completing an abbreviated course. Conrad Bergendoff, *The Augustana Ministerium: A Study of the Careers of the 2,504 Pastors of the Augustana Evangelical Lutheran Synod/Church 1850-1962* (Rock Island: Augustana Historical Society, 1980), 2.

aims: promoting peace within the General Synod, and inciting women to their share in the denominational work. [9]

If getting doctrinal disputes off the pages of the newspaper was the primary aim of the *Lutheran Evangelist*, getting women's work onto the page seemed to them to be the way to do it. The promoters of a more open and evangelical Lutheranism in the General Synod became pioneers in organizing the women of the church. In response to her husband's request, Mary Stuckenberg began to gather information from the women in other Protestant churches in order to provide models for the organizing of a Lutheran Women's Missionary Society. This early women's work was built on a practical foundation and demonstrated one way to overcome the preoccupation of Lutherans with the defense of their doctrinal positions. During the last decades of the nineteenth century, young people's societies also began to become a part of local parish activities. Both the youth and women's societies used their meetings for devotional and social fellowship, but they also directed their energies to advancing the interests of their church, particularly its missionary task. In taking part in the missionary movement, Lutheran women joined the largest women's movement of their day. Twice as many American women associated with missionary societies as with of any kind of women's rights organization.[10] Women's Missionary Society work gave American women educational opportunities, leadership roles, publishing outlets, and a stake in the wider work of the church in the world.

After Eastern Lutherans in the General Synod organized their synodical society, the South Carolina Synod organized one in 1885. Lutheran women in the Midwest organized local societies and became models for women who belonged to the immigrant churches. The Swedish Lutheran Augustana Synod became the first of the Scandinavian Lutheran churches to organize a Women's Missionary Society in 1892. Their leader, Emmy Carlsson Ewald, had been a pioneer in organizing a young

---

[9] John O. Evjen, *Life of J H W Stuckenberg* (Minneapolis: The Lutheran Free Church Publishing Co., 1938), 233.

[10] Patricia Hill, *The World Their Household* (Ann Arbor: University of Michigan Press, 1984), 4.

people's society in Andover, Illinois in 1880. When she became a pastor's wife in Chicago, she organized a sewing society and raised money for an orphanage and hospital. With the founding of the Women's Missionary Society, the Augustana Synod stepped out of an ethnic isolation and into an engagement with the popular movements of other American churches. The up and coming pastors and leaders of the synod had missionary interests at the heart of their program, as well. The men were encouraged by an energetic proponent of "inner mission" and the diaconate in America, William A. Passavant. In spite of the appeal of the European model to the pastors, the larger significance of the women's missionary societies for American Lutheranism was evident in the fact that the deaconess movement really never took hold among American Lutheran women, while membership in a local mission society was very popular.[11]

Women supported the missionary efforts of their denominations. Other Lutheran church bodies began to see the advantage of organizing their women, if only to shore up their mission budgets. The United Norwegian Lutheran Church, facing a deficit in 1903, realized that they had fewer missionaries in the field. They resolved to organize their work at home, and part of that effort involved organizing their women's societies. By 1911 they had organized a Women's Missionary Federation, which succeeded in helping the church increase donations to mission from $18,000 to $153,000.[12]

Throughout the early twentieth century, various Lutheran churches began to see the wisdom of organizing their women. In 1913, at the Men's Missionary Conference in Sandusky, Ohio, the men there resolved: "That the women of our Synod be encouraged to form a Conference of their own." After a year of formal organizing, the women had their own conference. The women and men who organized missionary society work operated along the lines typical of the democratic polity of the churches. At the

---

[11] Many contemporaries of Passavant wondered why the deaconess movement did not take hold in America. See George H. Gerberding, *Life and Letters of Passavant* (Greenville, Pa: Young Lutheran Co., 1906).

[12] *Our Church Abroad* (United Lutheran Publishing House: Philadelphia, 1926),137.

organizing convention a new constitution was adopted, elections of officers took place, and the plans for the next meeting were announced.[13]

The feverish organizing activity of these American Lutherans reflected the similar managerial revolutions that were going on within the American denominations as they developed structures to support social ministry, education, and foreign mission. At the fifth convention of the Ohio Synod's Women's Missionary Conference, the women of the conference were encouraged to raise money for a dormitory to be used by female students at Capitol University. The next year they zeroed in on something that would become "their very own" project: a hospital in India. The extensive organizational, advocacy and fundraising efforts that women engaged in gave them visibility and respect within their own denominations. There were women's missionary societies in nearly all of the Lutheran Churches in North America by the early 1930's. The Lutheran Church - Missouri Synod continued to debate the wisdom of organizing the women of their church, but finally sanctioned the creation of the Lutheran Women's Missionary League in 1942.[14]

The attractiveness of the missionary movement induced the Lutheran churches to create organizations for their women, who learned through this activity how to lead and finance large enterprises. Emmy Ewald's superb organizing efforts among the women in the Augustana Synod were a large factor in the positive development of that church. In 1910 the women surpassed their goal of giving $10,000 to retire the Home Mission debt of the church and gave the church $12,000. In the same year they also had completed and dedicated a hospital in Rajamundry, India. The large gift "inspired" the male leaders of regional conferences in the synod to go home and "do something" in their respective conferences. For these second-generation Swedish American Lutherans, "It was an awakening and realization of the power in

---

[13] A Brief History of the Women's Missionary Conference, Ohio Synod, 1929, 2-3.

[14] Mary Todd, *Authority Vested* (Eerdmanns: Grand Rapids, Michigan, 2000),126.

organization."[15] Missionary Society women learned what it was to serve on a board of directors, to draft and amend a constitution and its bylaws; they produced and published newspapers, and mastered the ins and outs of financing for construction and maintenance of hospitals, schools, and residence halls. The women who led these efforts were college educated, and they shared their organizational talents with women in congregations throughout North America. The effect was a broadly educated and tightly managed corps of women in congregations. The women, along with the men and children in their families, were well informed about missionary work and what it took to equip the church to support it. The church newspapers reflect this interest and focus within their pages throughout the middle part of the twentieth century. An interest in mission was evident in every weekly issue of the Augustana Synod's *Lutheran Companion,* the United Lutheran Church's *Lutheran,* the American Lutheran Church's *Lutheran Standard,* and the Evangelical Lutheran Church's *Lutheran Herald.*

The English language newspapers listed above replaced the foreign language papers that had informed an earlier generation of Lutherans. These new American Lutheran papers steadily took over the work of communicating with the lay people of the churches. With the transition in language also came a transition in style. The devotional language of the older Scandinavian piety was replaced with the purposeful language of the American businessman. With the coming of the world war in 1914, extreme anti-German feeling forced Lutherans to reexamine and define their relationship with their European heritage. Due to the pressure of popular sentiment during World War I, Lutheran pastor Carl Tappert was forced to leave his successful ministry in Winnipeg, Canada and take a call in a much smaller parish in a city much safer for German speakers, Philadelphia. In Canada, pro-British sentiment was so strong that a mob of young men beat the pastor and demanded that he conduct his confirmation service in English, rather than German.[16] The extensive plans made for a celebration

---

[15] Peter Peterson, *These Fifty Years: 1892-1942* (Woman's Missionary Society of Augustana Synod: Chicago, 1942),31.

[16] Carl Reinhold Tappert, *Reminiscences of an Octogenerian* (Philadelphia, 1946), 26.

of the 400th anniversary of the Reformation in 1917 resulted in more muted affairs as the United States entered the war, even while mergers uniting Norwegian and Eastern Lutherans were accomplished.

When wartime demands presented themselves to American Lutheran churches the need for inter-Lutheran cooperation forced the churches to design some way to provide for the needs first of soldiers and the families of military personnel. Calamity seemed to be the mechanism that worked to get Lutherans to recognize each other, so that they were able to provide chaplaincy services and basic pastoral care for families that had been displaced. This minimal level of cooperation, however, presented church leaders with a dilemma. Some of the American Lutheran Church bodies were unwilling to work with other Lutherans.

The decades of the 1920's and 30's involved many attempts to define principles that would allow Lutheran churches across the North American continent to recognize each other as fully Lutheran churches. The churches of the Lutheran Church - Missouri Synod led Synodical Conference would not enter into any fellowship with other churches except on the basis of their judgment concerning the doctrinal purity of the other. Their confessional scruples were so pronounced that they had undertaken mission work in Germany. In addition, a 1932 statement on scripture specifically articulated an acceptance of the inerrancy of scripture, in all its parts, as an additional criterion for fellowship.[17] The Neo-Scholastic approach to the confessional tradition outlined by the Missouri theologian Franz Pieper protected that synod against any taint of Modernism. In their exclusive stance toward American theological movements, the Missourians had plenty of company. Throughout the efforts to forge a broad Lutheran unity in America three camps developed. Directly opposite the Missourian camp, Charles Jacobs and Frederick Knubel of the United Lutheran Church promoted a

---

[17] The Evangelical Lutheran Wisconsin Synod and the Evangelical Lutheran Synod [Norwegian] were aligned with Missouri but split from the Synodical Conference in the mid-1960's as a protest to the involvement of the LC-MS in conversations leading to their brief altar and pulpit fellowship with the American Lutheran Church.

broad Lutheran catholicity, and the principle that Lutheran churches should recognize other Lutheran churches as Lutheran without demanding additional tests of their purity beyond their own self-avowed subscription to the confessional statements. In the middle ground a group Lutheran churches attempted to provide a conservative basis for unity. They were not pure enough for Missouri, but the leaders of the American Lutheran Conference, and especially H. A. Stub of the Evangelical Lutheran Church were unwilling to make any move that would possibly alienate the Missouri camp. So the American Lutheran Conference, formed in 1930 by the American Lutheran Church, the Swedish Augustana Synod, the United Evangelical Lutheran Church [Danish], and the Norwegian Evangelical Lutheran Church remained suspicious and wary of the larger United Lutheran Church. A stalemate over scriptural interpretation, ecumenical openness, and social policy lingered within Lutheranism in America and kept the churches tending to their own schools, young people, mission efforts, and social ministries.[18]

During both world wars, difficulties in gaining recognition and respect from each other kept Lutheran church leaders busy writing theses and drafting statements defining their doctrinal positions. This did not unite American Lutherans. The churches for the most part were young, products of recent mergers, and their theological leaders were also grappling with the difficulty of articulating their theology and church practice in English, as opposed to German, Norwegian, or Swedish. Even with the need for a more rigorous theological voice from the churches, seminary course offerings reflected the call from the pews and introduced practical courses. Bertha Paulssen, a trained sociologist who had escaped from Nazi Germany, the first woman professor at the Lutheran Theological Seminary in Gettysburg, pioneered training in social ministry. Her practical, sociologically-based courses corresponded to a deepening organizational competence among the lay people of the American churches.

Broad expertise was also needed in order for the churches to recognize and respond to the needs overseas. Mission fields of

---

[18] Nelson, *Lutheranism in North America, 1914-1970,* Augsburg Publishing House, Minneapolis, 1972, chapter 3.

German societies needed personnel and support. American Lutherans stepped into rescue "orphaned" mission sites in India, Tanganyika, Namibia, and Southeast Asia during and after both world wars. In responding to the recovery needs of European and mission churches after the war, North American Lutherans discovered how American they were. The differences between American and Continental approaches to world mission had surfaced in the early missionary conferences, especially at the 1900 New York meeting of the Ecumenical Mission Conference. The great German mission theorist, Gustav Warneck in Halle refused to attend a conference dominated by activists. He sent words, including: "Christ bids us 'go' into the world, not 'fly' and that our Lord did not command us to 'Go ye and teach English to all nations.'"[19] When American Lutherans took up the task of providing for the orphaned German Lutheran missions in Tanganyika during the Second World War, their confessional association with German Lutheranism looked suspicious to colonial British authorities, but the Augustana missionaries became known as Americans, and were trusted with the enormous responsibility of managing schools, hospitals, and mission stations throughout the colony.[20] British authorities made one stipulation that assistance to the mission be handled through a national organization in America and not in Europe. Any missionaries recruited to assist in the mission work, whether from Rhodesia, Sweden, or Canada, would have to travel to the offices of the National Lutheran Council in New York before making their way to Tanganyika.

After the war, American Lutherans realized that they had assumed a new responsibility as Americans in the negotiations that formed the World Council of Churches and the Lutheran World Federation. Their experience in America with pan Protestant agencies made them aware of the importance of confessional representation in the proposed World Council. In ways that the territorially defined European state churches did not recognize, a

---

[19] Gustav Warneck, quoted in William R. Hutchison, *Errand to the World* (University of Chicago Press, 1987), 134-5.

[20] Gustaf Bernander, *Wartime Assistance in Tanganyika* (Studia Uppsaliensa Missionalia, Uppsala, 1964), passim.

geographical principle of organization for the World Council could lead to the eventual domination of that body by ecumenical experts and spokesmen for national interests that would undermine its promise as a council of the churches. American Lutherans, led by Abdel Ross Wentz, argued for representation along confessional lines, and urged that a frank facing of doctrinal differences in an environment of mutual respect fit the character of a world council of churches better than the preliminary proposals of geographic representation allowed.[21]

At the first meeting of the Lutheran World Federation in Lund, Sweden, in the summer of 1947, American Lutherans were active participants, and their exposure to European ways made them even more self-conscious of what they felt to be their American advantage. The president of the Augustana Synod, P.O. Bersell described what it felt like to witness the reunion of Lutherans after the scourge of the war, "All were gripped by the consciousness of the fact that this was a unique and epochal reunion of Lutherans, a union of hearts and a meeting of minds in a new consecration to the great mission of the Lutheran Church throughout the world." The week-long meeting involved several study sessions that taxed the energy of the Americans. Bersell was especially impatient with the time it took to read papers in smaller sections and again in plenary gatherings, "This made for much tiring repetition and waste of time in academic, dogmatic, and platitudinous discussions and left little time for discussion of practical problems and matters of policy and immediate action." He especially took aim at the theologians, "It took several days to overcome the theological ponderousity and academic exactitude of the German delegation of 35." The Americans had another approach. He wrote how they "spoke with conviction and with typical drive, urging action." He may have missed what must have been extraordinary patience on the part of the Europeans for the typical American rush to accomplish things.

---

[21] Dorris Flesner, "Frederick H Kunbel: Pioneer in American Lutheran Participation in the Modern Ecumenical Movement," *The Maturing of American Lutheranism* (Augsburg Publishing House, Minneapolis, 1968), 178-180.

Bersell had reorganized the Augustana Synod's boards and programs in the preceding decade. He knew how to run a convention, too, and gave his frank assessment of the way that the Lutheran World Federation meeting had gone. "The Americans who had not had previous acquaintance with European traditions were surprised at the ineptitude of the Europeans in the matter of parliamentary procedures and general convention management," he wrote. The several decades of organizational development that had been so important for the development of different branches of activity in home missions, youth work, and missionary efforts had created American Lutheran church members who were adept at parliamentary procedure and quick to grasp how to use the language of collective action in order to direct their churches. In spite of the difficulty in assembling so many different churches, he felt that the "ground work was laid for Lutheran unity of action." Other messages of the convention from the Norwegian American church leader Gullixson stressed the unity that was felt at the meeting that strengthened the potential for united action: "A bond is here, so strong that even the terrible centrifugal forces within the mad whirl of revolution and war cannot rend it asunder."

The first president of the Lutheran World Federation, Anders Nygren, a Swedish bishop and theologian sought to lay deep foundations for this unity by calling the Lutheran churches around the world to go "forward to Luther." American interest in Luther research was strengthened considerably by an extensive translation effort that produced *Luther's Works* during the 1950's and 1960's. The series of over fifty volumes of Luther's writings were translated by a team of scholars from across the spectrum of American Lutheranism and published jointly by Concordia Publishing House and Fortress Press. Similar joint efforts to cooperate in translating the *Book of Concord* into English has made it possible for discussions of the confessions among Lutherans in North America to relate to the same text and language.

North American Lutherans hosted the 1957 meeting of the Lutheran World Federation in the heartland of Lutheranism, Minneapolis, Minnesota. The city gave free rein to the arriving Lutherans, closing the main avenue for a Lutheran parade and clearing the lawn of the capitol so that seats could be set up for the closing session. In 1963 the assembly met in Helsinki, Finland, with Franklin Clark Fry as the presiding officer. Fry's facility with parliamentary procedure had always intimidated the ordinary American Lutheran, and at Helsinki his dismissive handling of a delegate was one of the reasons that the assembly meeting failed to achieve its major goal of passing a common statement on the fourth article of the Augsburg Confession, justification by faith. In Helsinki, delegates realized the difficulty of capturing the essence of theological principles in language to be accepted by resolution and voting. As Lutheran churches headed into the years of protest during the latter 60's and 70's, the problem of capturing the essence of the faith in language suited for political assemblies intensified. Parliamentary language fosters a culture of action and common resolve, but does not easily lend itself to nuance or depth.

Theological revolutions among North American Lutherans happen on convention floors. When the Lutheran Council in the USA study on the ordination of women reported in 1969 that "there are no conclusive grounds for forbidding the ordination of women and no definitive ones for demanding it,"[22] the three major Lutheran Church bodies in North America were free to make up their own minds about this significant issue. The Lutheran Church in America [formed in 1962] and the American Lutheran Church [1960] decided to ordain the women who had been studying at their seminaries. By the mid 1970's this new development threatened the developing relationship between the American Lutheran Church and the Missouri Synod. Conservative forces in the Missouri Synod took over the board of the seminary. The forced resignation of seminary president John Tietjen, and the exodus of faculty and students shoved moderate and liberal members out the door or into a quiet corner of the church. Those who left the Lutheran Church - Missouri Synod became catalysts for a wider merger of Lutherans in North America in the 1980's. During the merger discussions in the United States, Canadian Lutherans formed the Evangelical Lutheran Church in Canada [ELCIC] in 1986.

---

[22] "The Ordination of Women: A Study Conducted Under the Auspices of the Division of Theological Studies, Lutheran Council in the USA, 1968-1970."

The theological work of North American Lutherans during the decades at the end of the twentieth century focused largely on the ecumenical movement. Throughout the mergers that united Lutherans in North America during the twentieth century, the ecumenical stances of the churches have been decisive in defining the nature of Lutheranism. When Eric Gritsch and Robert Jenson wrote their book on the Lutheran Confessions in 1976, the ecumenical character of Lutheranism was being explored and promoted by the many dialogue teams, international and national, that brought American Lutherans into a common effort to overcome doctrinal disagreement with other confessional traditions. The success of the dialogue teams in rendering Lutheranism in an ecumenical mode to their dialogue partners resulted in ecumenical agreements with Roman Catholics, Reformed Churches, and Episcopalians. But translating the success of the dialogues into language that Lutheran lay delegates would understand was more difficult. The ecumenical decisions of the Evangelical Lutheran Church in America, especially related to the agreement on full communion with the Episcopal Church in the United States, caused significant political turmoil, especially in the Upper Midwest. After an initial defeat in Philadelphia in 1997, a new drafting team of Michael Root, Martin Marty, and Todd Nichol set about to write an agreement that would attempt to bridge the differences between the ecumenists who were enthusiastic about ecumenical advances, and a party who defended historic Lutheran distinctiveness in a key they called "Word Alone." The language of mission was again employed to salvage the ecumenical agreement and the new document "Called to Common Mission" gained a slim margin over the two-thirds majority they needed at the ELCA assembly in 1999.

American visitors to the first meeting of the Lutheran World Federation in Lund in 1947 had grown tired of the long-winded theological discussions; at the Helsinki meeting of 1963, Franklin Clark Fry used his podium effectively – perhaps too much so. American Lutherans are dogged by the trouble of connecting theological insights with their preferred language of action. They are impatient with any inefficiency in church structures and bored with traditions. In 1976 Eric Gritsch reminded his readers that the efforts of ecumenical dialogue teams in the twentieth century had some precedent in the sixteenth century. They were also "forced to make an attempt to cast Luther's burning faith into statues of doctrine submissible to political assemblies."[23] The task of conveying the burning faith of Luther in a language that modern people will understand and accept is ongoing. The communication department of the ELCA is currently undergoing a transition as they seek ways to get the church's message across. The magazine of the Missouri Synod, *The Lutheran Witness,* reveals self-consciousness about image and language in a review of the recent film, *The Lion, the Witch, and the Wardrobe,* when the author cautions that "we should not be too aggressive" in responding to the interest in the film. A quiet stance will "just let the story unfold for itself." [24]

The confident activism expressed by American Lutherans who attended the organizing convention of the Lutheran World Federation in the middle of the twentieth century has also subsided. The Evangelical Lutheran Church in America is still creating its own history. The missionaries who were so prominent a part of Lutheran identity have become a much smaller corps of workers. National churches of the former mission fields have come into their own. American Lutherans function as partners and companion churches for churches throughout the world, and the language of leadership has been changed to articulate themes of partnership and sharing. At a missionary retreat in Arusha, Tanzania in October, 2005, the missionaries listened to a report from their field director who told them that the older paradigm, where the missionaries were told to work themselves out of a job, and to go home, was not the paradigm the church was working with any longer. "We'll be here for the long haul," he said, not to be in charge, certainly, but to be part of a church that was not bound to nation, or culture, or style. Americans have many things to say, and also many things to hear.

---

[23] Eric W. Gritsch and Robert W. Jenson, *Lutheranism: The Theological Movement and Its Confessional Writings* (Fortress Press: Philadelphia, 1976), 33.

[24] Steven P. Mueller, "The Lion, the Witch, and the Savior," *The Lutheran Witness* (December, 2005), 8.

Quo vadis Ecclesia? Theses for the Direction of the Lutheran Church into the Third Millennium

Markus Wriedt, *Goethe University, Frankfurt am Main, Germany*

1. What is Protestantism?[1]

The term "Protestant" was not originally a self-designation of "evangelical"[2] Christianity. The term goes back to the political conflict situation at the second imperial Diet of Speyer in 1529. Since the resolutions of this, as well as earlier, imperial diets endangered the progress of the Reformation, some princes and cities which, though in the minority, had joined the reform movement, submitted a "Protest" (*protestatio*), provided for such expected occasions by imperial *law*. Thereafter, they were called "Protestants" --- the historical origin of the word with a legal designation coined by the opposing side.[3] Only after about 1700 did Lutheran Christianity adopt the name for itself. The term, the complete history of which has yet to be written,[4] developed as a

---

[1] See "Protestantismus" in *Theologische Realenzyklopädie*, 31 vols.Ed. G. Krause and G. Müller (Berlin: de Gruyter, 19777-2005), 27, 542-51.

[2] From the Greek *euangelion*, "gospel," the enduring legal term for "Lutheran" in Europe. "Lutheran" needs to be distinguished from "evangelical," a designation for conservative American Protestants.

[3] It soon had a controversial, theological meaning. Already in 1564, the Catholic theologian Georg Cassander (1513-1566) published an "opinion" (*Gutachten*), titled "Consultation About Articles Between Catholics and Protestants (*Consultatio de articulis inter Protestantes et Catholicis*).

[4] See the preliminary work in Conrad L. Maurer, *Die Prinzipien des Protestantismus und die unirte Kirche der Pfalz* (Kaiserslautern, 1863); Kurt Leese, *Der Protestantismus im Wandel der neueren Zeit* (Stuttgart: Kröner 1941); Gottfried Hornig, „Protestantismus" in *Historisches*

result of two contrary tendencies, which were decisive for the beginning of the Reformation: critical demarcation and constructive formation. Luther's criticism of the abuses of the late medieval church aimed at a renewal of the church but always had the unity of the church and never its division as a goal. Luther did not want to establish a new church. That could not be avoided in the course of further historical development. Originally, the critical protest was to serve positive-formative reforms. This double element is noticeable in the protestation at Speyer in 1529. It was not directed primarily against the teachings of the Catholic Church but instead legally and politically against the suspension of the resolution passed at the first imperial diet at Speyer in 1526. The acceptance of the continued use of the term "Protestants" as self-designation only was possible because the term had a positive meaning from the very beginning besides the critical- polemical one.

Since about the middle of the eighteenth century, the expressions "Protestants" and (later) "Protestantism" were claimed as a programmatic self-understanding of Lutheran Christianity which not only expressed Luther's declaration at Worms (1521) and the protestation at Speyer (1529) against the teaching and practices of the Roman Catholic Church but also against the danger of an ecclesiastical and theological narrowing in Protestantism. The term connotes the sense of a Lutheran return to God's self-revelation in Scripture.

Originating in a historically contingent conflict-situation, Protestantism was first defined from outside: whether it was a term coined by opposing representatives from the traditional, i.e. Roman Church, or as a protest directed against a certain political or ecclesiastical form of occidental Christianity, Protestantism was at first anti-Catholic, in fact: anti-Papal and anti-Imperial, and formed by the crystallizing principal of a criticism of the papacy and its close linkage to political power. To the degree that ecclesiological and structures of popular piety of the discarded confessional Catholicism became visible in Protestantism, the principal criticism turns inward. Only after the Enlightenment did

---

Wörterbuch der Philosophie, 12 vols, ed. Joachim Ritter and others (Basel: Schwabe Verlag, 2005), 7, 1529-36.

a qualitatively new direction of Protestantism emerge. It was associated with names like Friedrich Schleiermacher, Christian Baur, Richard Rothe, Ernst Troltsch, and Paul Tillich, among many others. The mere confrontation with confessional Catholicism becomes a new definition of the essence of Lutheran Christianity. Schleiermacher emphasized, above all, the ethical quality of the individual who, as a result of justification, lets the relationship with God become the principle of relationships with others and with the church. Baur accentuates more strongly the ethical autonomy of the human person as a result of the freedom discovered by Luther. The basic dependence of people upon God becomes a possibility for individual freedom on the basis of which Protestantism is understood as a constantly changing system for the individual realization of human freedom. Therefore, its form cannot be identical with the original situation and form of the sixteenth century. This axiom, on the one hand, removes the need for an on-going definition of what is essential and, on the other hand, calls for a constant scholarly self-reflection of Protestant Christianity. Richard Rothe accentuates strongly the moral quality of Protestantism and emphasizes the necessity of dissolution of the church in favor of the autonomous individual state. Ernst Troltsch explains Protestantism as an independent and continually developing spiritual principle. Against this background, he differentiated between Old Protestantism as a two-century –old flowering of the Middle Ages and a New Protestantism, in which the subjectivity of Christianity became a formative principle and abandoned the notions of unity held by earlier epochs. Finally, Paul Tillich transforms the Protestant principle in its modern appearance into an independent religion with a singular significance.

2. Luther and Protestantism

As a result of such a self-definition, the ecumenical dialogue becomes a farce. Historical hindsight also becomes increasingly obsolete because it cannot be much more than a more or less burdened retrospective of stages of tradition which have long been overcome and no longer have any relationship to a religious

Protestant reality. The term Protestantism itself becomes so radically new that it is no longer bound to the historical past.

And what has become of Luther? Eric Gritsch recalls in his history of Lutheranism the speech of Anders Nygren given at the foundation of the Lutheran World Federation in Lund, reminding the delegates that Luther had rediscovered the gospel as a power to lead Christians through the perils of the world to the joyful, never-ending union with Christ. Nygren contended that this eschatological kernel of Luther's thought had been neglected in Lutheranism during decades of secularization, tyranny, and war. "Our purpose is not to reiterate what the Reformers said, but to re-think our Gospel, the one and only Gospel, the whole Gospel, to study it anew, possibly from a new point of approach and to express [it] in terms of today. . . . This, therefore, must be our watchword: Always forward to Luther."[4] Fifty years later, the German church historian Bernhard Lohse explained the motives for his work on the theology of Luther with the bon mot, "I want to put Luther back into the sixteenth century – and leave him there."[5] Lohse did not diminish Luther's significance but saw the anachronism of his work, namely to make the heir of the late Middle Ages fruitful for the present. This is the task of systematic theology rather than a genuinely historical enterprise.

The historical interpretation of Luther and systematic appropriation of Luther are two different tasks which can only be achieved in mutual tension One of the few who could combine historical knowledge with systematic competence in a congenial way was Gerhard Ebeling. His interpretation of Luther will guide us on the way to an answer.

---

[4] Eric W. Gritsch, *A History of Lutheranism* (Minneapolis: Fortress Press, 2006), 257.

[5] The work is *Martin Luther's Theology. Its Historical and Systematic Development*, tr. and ed. Roy A Harrisville (Minneapolis: Fortress, 1999). The bon mot is in Bernhard Lohse, *Eine neue Darstellung derTheologie Luthers* (Hamburg: Katholische Akademie Hamburg 1996) p. 23

LUTHERANISM: LEGACY AND FUTURE: *Essays in Honor of Eric W. Gritsch*

2.1. Gerhard Ebeling and the Lutheran Interpretation of Luther

In a brief introduction to Martin Luther's thought, [6] Ebeling, the hermeneutical theologian with an existential-philosophical base,[7] traces Luther's theology in its rational tension of opposite pairs of thought. According to Ebeling, Luther is not a systematic theologian who creates a concise system in the sense of establishing concrete formulas. Instead, Luther's theology is the announcement of Christ's message of salvation in the tension from within and from without (*extra nos*), the perspective before God (*coram Deo*) and before humanity (*coram homanibus*), the righteous and sinners, theology and philosophy, letter and spirit, law and gospel, person and work, belief and love, the kingdom of God and the kingdom of the world, resulting in citizenship, freedom and slavery, the hidden and revealed God.[8]

2.1.1. Philosophy and Theology

"Indeed I for my part believe that I owe to the Lord this duty of speaking out against philosophy and of persuading me to heed Holy Scripture. For perhaps if another man who has not seen these things, did this, he might be afraid or he might not be believed. But I have been worn out by these studies for many years now, and having experienced and heard many things over and over again, I have come to see that it is the study of vanity and perdition. Therefore I warn you all as earnestly as I can that you finish these studies quickly and let it be your only concern not to establish and defend them but treat them as we do when we learn worthless skills to destroy them and study errors to refute them. Thus, we study also these things to get rid of them, or at least, just to learn the method of speaking of those people with whom we

---

[6] *Luther. An Introduction to His Thought.* Tr. R. A Wilson (Philadelphia: Fortress, 1970).

[7] For more information see Albecht Beutel: Gerhard Ebeling. Eine Biographie (Tübingen: Siebeck Mohr 2012) and Ingolf U. Dalferth, Radikale Theologie.Leipzig: Evangelische Verlagsanstalt 2010 – soon to be translated into English under a similiar title.)

[8] Cf. also Oswald Bayer, Martin Luther's Theology transl. by Thomas H. Trapp (Grand Rapids MI: Eerdmans 2008

must carry on some discourse. For it is high time that we undertake new studies and learn Jesus Christ, "and Him crucified" (1 Cor.2:2). [9]

It is not difficult to find other quotations similar to this one. Luther battled for theology against philosophy, not in the sense of opposites or as an exclusive alternative. [10] Luther sees the value of philosophy naturally as a manner of speech for the explanation of connections and insights which do not belong to the genuine interest of theology. Philosophy cultivates for theology an inadequate way of speaking. Theology opens up a genuine understanding of Holy Scripture as the will of God in his own genuine Word. Philosophical thinking dominated mostly by Aristotelian terminology and method misplaces this insight. Luther was not interested in abolishing philosophy, but in the right balance between philosophical epistemology and theological awareness of revealed truth. Luther's battle against Aristotle is a battle for proper theological thinking --- and speaking! That

---

[9]"Lectures on Romans" [8:19], 1515. *D. Martin Luthers Werke*. Kritische Gesamtausgabe [Schriften] (Weimar: Böhlau, 1883-). Hereafter cited WA. 56, 371, 17-27, („Ich jedenfalls glaube dem Herrn diesen Gehorsam zu schulden, gegen die Philosophie anzubellen und zur Heiligen Schrift zuzureden. Denn wenn es vielleicht ein anderer täte, der es nicht aus eigener Anschauung kennengelernt hat, hätte er nicht den Mut dazu oder wäre nicht glaubwürdig. Ich aber habe mich daran schon viele Jahre lang aufgerieben und habe es ebenso aus Erfahrung und aus Gesprächen mit vielen vor Augen, dass es ein eitles und verderbliches Studium ist. Deshalb ermahne ich euch alle, so viel ich nur kann, dass ihr dieser Art Studien schnell erledigt und darauf allein aus seid, diese Dinge nicht etwa in Kraft zu setzen und zu verteidigen, vielmehr so, wie wir üble Fertigkeiten erlernen, um sie unschädlich zu machen, und Irrtümer zur Kenntnis nehmen, um sie zu überwinden. So auch dies, um es zu verwerfen, oder allenfalls um die Redeweise derer uns anzueignen, mit denen wir Umgang haben müssen. Denn es ist Zeit, dass wir uns andern Studien hingeben und Jesus Christus lernen, und diesen als Gekreuzigten.") *Luther's Works*, ed. Jaroslav Pelikan and Helmut Lehmann, 55 vols. Philadelphia: Fortress; St. Louis: Concordia, 1955-1986. 25, 361. Hereafter cited LW.

[10] See now Jennifer Hockenbery Dragseth (ed.), *The Devil's Whore: Reason and Philosophy in the Lutheran Tradition*, (Minneapolis MN: Fortress Press, 2011)

Luther did not want to abandon philosophy becomes clear when one pursues further the tension between theology and philosophy. Luther's criticism of Scholasticism presents theology with new tasks the accomplishment of which closely connects with philosophy. For Luther's relevance in the present, the ecclesiastical and theological proclamation must reflect about language, metaphysics and the choice of topics and statements. Luther's relevance cannot be dictated by Zeitgeist, topics, and terminology, or by a desired isolation of the self and lose sight of others who need to hear the gospel of salvation.

2.1.2. *Law and Gospel*

"All of Scripture and theology centers in the right knowledge of law and gospel." [11] Whoever knows the proper distinction of law and gospel should thank God and may know that he is a theologian." [12] "Everything depends on this distinction...Do not mix it up! If that happens, one or the other is lost, or both. Under the papacy, no one knew this distinction because they had a faith related only to the law." [13] This distinction is, according to Luther, no mere encyclopedic mathematical ordering. Christian proclamation must at all times concern itself with the distinction between Law and Gospel. What is at the bottom of it? Luther describes a hermeneutical task: law in the Bible uncovers human sin and condemns it. The Gospel, however, means all consoling and saving words of divine grace. The gospel can neither be limited to the literary body of the New Testament, nor is every biblical text as such gospel and law. Their respective function occurs in the personal situation of the hearer or reader within the divine plan of salvation as a whole. A literal application of Old Testament mandates converts Christian freedom into a law, for example, pictures and altars in a church so that the law has an enduring task of punishment, directing believers again and again to confront sin and promising the judgment of God.

---

[11] "Sermon on Matt. 11," 1521. WA 7, 502:34-5.

[12] "Lectures on Galatians," 1531. WA 40/1, 207:17-18.

[13] "Sermon on the Day of Circumcision," 1532. WA 36, 6-8; 10:2-5.

The distinction between Law and Gospel allows a proper interpretation of Scripture, without falling prey to a superficial tendency: mere punishment and atonement, or harmony of an all-forgiving kingdom of Christ. Regarding the actuality of Luther in the present, this means: the Church has full authority and responsibility to point out the abuses in our society. But the church's responsibility is indeed not limited to the role of vigilance and warning. The Church can also intervene as a mediator of reconciliation, empowered by the gospel which promises the reconciling and healing presence of God in the crises of our times. The Church can lay open and denounce sins, but it also has the authority to forgive these same sins and call people to a blessed future in and with Christ.

2.1.3. The Kingdom of Christ and the Kingdom of the World

The Augustinian distinction between the "kingdom of God" (*civitas* Dei) and the "earthly kingdom" (*civitas terrena*) was received by Luther from its medieval connection with the two regiments, and formed into his "two regiments doctrine." Ever since Karl Barth's designation "two kingdoms doctrine" its reception in the context of Lutheran political ethics has been exposed to various distortions and errors. It should now have become sufficiently clear that here, too, it is not a question of a static differentiation of being or condition, as it were, but precisely the description of the tension a Christian encounters on the basis of various loyalties. To blame Luther for a retreat into inwardness or mere subjectivity need not be discussed. Rather it is a question of the relations in which the Christian faith has to prove itself. "I must always again and again drive home this difference between these two kingdoms, so often with word and pen that it becomes annoying. For the miserable devil does not stop to cook and to brew these two kingdoms together. The worldly rulers always want to teach and to command Christ in the devil's name how he should conduct his church and the spiritual regiment. The false priests and evil hordes also want to have their way how to organize the worldly regiment not in the name of God. So the devil is intemperate and very busy on both sides. May God restrain him. Amen, if we are worth it." [14] In his basic design for a political ethics oriented by Paul, Luther separates the spheres of influence: "Here we must divide the children of Abraham and all mankind into two classes, the first belonging to the kingdom of God, the second to the kingdom of the world. Those who belong to the kingdom of God are all true believers who are in Christ and under Christ, for Christ is King and Lord in the kingdom of God...He also calls the gospel a gospel of the kingdom of God because it teaches, governs, and upholds God's kingdom." [15] On the other hand, all those who are not Christians belong to the worldly kingdom or are under the law. [16] Since Christians do not need an enforcement of God's orders because they have them internalized, sword and power are given to government in order to enforce these orders where they are not self-evident. "There are few true believers, and still fewer who live a Christian life, who do not resist evil and indeed themselves do evil. For this reason God has provided for them a different government beyond the Christian estate and kingdom of God. He has subjected them to the sword so that, even though they would like to, they are unable to practice their wickedness, and if they do practice it they cannot do so without fear or with success and impunity. For this reason God has ordained two governments: the spiritual, by which the Holy Spirit produces Christians and righteous people under Christ; and the temporal which restrains the un-Christian and wicked so that --- no thanks to them --- they are obliged to keep still and maintain an outward peace."[17] So the regiments do not indicate two ways of being but two ways how God meets creation: on the one hand, with the gospel which gives the Holy Spirit; on the other hand, with the law which outwardly curbs the consequences of sin. As long as Christians live in this world, they are simultaneously righteous and sinners, and, therefore, basically in need of both regiments.. The two regiments describe, therefore, not two ways of being, but two directions of how God encounters His creation: on

---

[14] "Exposition of Psalm 101, 1534/35. WA 51, 239:22-30.

[15] "Temporal Authority: To What Extent It Should Be Obeyed," 1523. WA 11, 249:24-27, 33-35. LW 45, 88.

[16] WA 51, 251:1-2.

[17] Ibid. 251:2-18. LW 45 90, 91.

the one side is the Gospel, which is given by the Holy Spirit, on the other side is the Law, which outwardly stems the succession of sins. The Christian is, as long as he lives in this world, simultaneously justified and sinful and therefore in need of both regiments.

Luther's entire theology is carried by the distinction of the two kingdoms. First of all, it is to be noted that both kingdoms are related to each other and belong to each other. God is Lord in both. For, "the worldly regiment may also be called the kingdom of God, since God wills that it should remain and make us obedient in it. But it is only the kingdom of the left hand. God's true kingdom, where God alone rules, has not father and mother, emperor and king, hangman and bailiff. But God is there, preaching the gospel to the poor."[18]. Consequently, both kingdoms are not distinguished like competing and conflicting laws but in such a way that they are constituted by the distinction of law and gospel. Here is a perspective that should be mentioned in passing: A person is seen in varying perspectives although he remains one and the same person: *coram deo* and *coram mundo*. Both ways of being do not count like optional alternative possibilities, or as divided realities, but in a strict simultaneity of an interrelation. Whoever reflects on being before God does not stop existing in the world. The totality of the person remains. But, indeed, being this person is constituted through the affection by the Word of God which judges and liberates.--- in the tension between law and gospel. But being a person in the world is constituted by being carried and commissioned by the Word of God which commissions to service through works. Luther demonstrates this in an example, an exposition of the Sermon on the Mount, Matt. 5:5: "Blessed are the meek, for they will inherit the earth." From the outset here you must realize that Christ is not speaking at all about the government... He is only talking about how individuals are to live in relation to others, apart from official position and authority --- how father and mother are to live, not in relation to their children nor in their official capacity, but in relation to those for whom they are not father and mother, like neighbors and other people. I have often said that we must sharply distinguish between

---

[18] "Sermon on the Third Sunday in Advent,: 1544. WA 52, 21-27.

311

these two, the office and the person who is called Hans or Martin is a man quite different from the one who is called elector or doctor or preacher. Here we have two different persons in one man. The one is that in which we are created and born, according to which we are all alike --- man or woman or child, young and old. But once we are born, God adorns and dresses you up as another person. He makes you a child and me a father, one a master and another a servant, one a prince and another a citizen. Then this one is called a divine person, one who holds a divine office and goes about clothed in its dignity --- not simply Hans or Nick, but the Prince of Saxony, father and master. He is merely about talking about how each individual, natural person is to behave in relation to others." [19]

Luther's enduring actuality is the notion that existing social structures are no longer seen and judged from the perspective *coram mundo* but again in the light of the gospel, *coram Deo*. The burning questions of the present, such as the aggravating consequences of gene-technology and it's unfortunate consequences for the formation of human life, life-and-death decisions, questions of people living together, or the need for demarcations and measures for orders --- all of that is no longer the subject of human considerations but is to be seen and judged in the light of the gospel from the perspective of God.

We could continue in this way for ages. Yet, limits are set on our reflection. The design of a theology of Luther as a structure for relations, rich with tensions, allows us to hold on systematically to the current relevance of Reformation theology, although important historical reasons speak against an anachronistic use of Luther for the present. I want to demonstrate this by looking at a topic in the teaching of the church, not frequently treated in the past but increasingly of interest because of the ecumenical dialogue: the doctrine of the church.

---

[19] "The Sermon on the Mount," 1530/32. WA 32, 316:6-7, 10-29. LW 21, 23.

3. Luther's Message for the Church Today

In his rejoinder to his church's reproaches, which accused him of a false understanding of the church and of contradicting the Bible, Luther writes in 1520: "Scripture speaks about Christendom very simply and in only one way... that Christendom means an assembly of all people on earth who believe in Christ, as we pray in the Creed, 'I believe in the Holy Spirit, the communion of saints.' This community essence, life, and nature of Christendom is not physical assembly, but an assembly of hearts in one faith." [20]

Ecclesia --- the spiritual community of those called by God who live in faith, love, and hope. This basically says already everything about the essence and the commission of the church. All people, who have heard the Word of salvation and experienced it as orientation for life, are assembled in the Community of Called, the original meaning of ecclesia in Greek..

On the one hand, this really says everything. On the other hand, the problems begin here, not just with Luther, but already since the first days of the Church: according to which rules is the visible Church constituted? Who has the authority in it? Are there authorities, hierarchies, offices? What are the roles, if there are to be any, of hierarchies and offices? Who belongs to it? How does the Church deal with those who break the rules (questions of order and discipline)?

I believe that these questions cannot be answered generally for all times, cultures, and people. Historical periods change too fast, and with them the demands of individual Christians and Christian communities for a universal formation of the congregation. Nevertheless, the Reformers have rediscovered an important principle of the early church: that of the local congregation, the community of Christians on the spot, here and now. Each congregation must find for itself the structure and constitution that correspond to their respective faith and the practice resulting from it. It is, of course, important that every congregation remains conscious of its individual singularity and particularity. Only the spiritual community of all Christians establishes the church. The

---

[20] "On the Papacy in Rome, Against the Most Celebrated Romanist in Leipzig," 1520. WA 6, 292:35-293:4. LW 39, 65..

respective, visible local congregations are part of that church, its fore-runners, as it were, and they reflect elements of Christendom (as Luther would say).

However, one can list a few elements which should become visible in every congregation, pointing to the community of all Christians. This list is neither complete, nor to be understood as criteria which distinguish a good, true church from a false, not genuine church. It is not that simple.

The following these are postulated in a certain theoretical abstraction. I intentionally do without actual problems in the church today: on the one hand, not to let my view into a church of the future is disarranged by mini-offenses and personal offenses. On the other hand, not to be guided by formal questions of the organization of worship, pastoral care, or the role, of the church in the media, etc., but by the starting point of the history of the church, lasting now almost two millennia: The promise of God that all people who believe in His Son are saved and reconciled to Him. It should also determine our criticism and intensify our ability to be self-critical. Finally, I am concerned that the afore-mentioned elements of individuality and peculiarity of cultural, historical, social, or any other origin are not thrust aside. They must have their place in congregational life. Otherwise, the community pursues a bloodless and estranged, ultimately incomprehensible rite.

I see the challenges and chances of Lutheran Protestantism in the western world, above all, in three respects. Emancipated western thought, indebted to Luther and to Protestantism, first of all, made its unique contribution through the emphasis on the pious individual. This emphasis expanded to the discovery of the autonomously acting subject in the theology after the Enlighten-ment. It is difficult to reconcile this stance with Luther. It moves historically with a growing particularism that manifests itself in a territorially established Lutheranism and later in an even stronger differentiated Protestantism. Modernity and the subsequent period, which today is anachronistically, called Post-Modernity, exhibit individuality and particularism as those centrifugal forces which should be opposed by a centripetal potential of energy in the sense of an ecumenical, ecclesiology. An incalculable loss of identity is connected with individuality and particularity. Neither church nor office, or the individual features of the Lutheran faith can be clearly determined and identified in the cacophony of modern or post-modern societies.

Here, Luther's legacy can become a comforting corrective of a reformation within the Lutheran church. His reformation, always blamed for innovation also in the sixteenth century, aimed at the preservation of the true church, as it was modeled in his naïve, uncritical view, above all, in Christian antiquity and in the first five centuries. A reform, based on a revival of the original situation of the Lutheran, would only, like Luther's concern for reform, implicate the anachronistic repristination of conditions long past. Reclaiming what is originally "reformed" in Luther's theology means more than an innovative happening in view of the Reformation based on the testimony of the living Word of God; this Reformation was already in its original situation estranged and changed by various other influences. It is not a question of transferring Luther straight into the present but of making his hermeneutical insights fruitful for the present in order to do justice to the original concern of the Reformation: to let the authority of the Word of God be the only authority --- *sola scriptura.* Beyond all required historical criticism, Lutheran Christianity in the West has only a chance if it vigorously and with concentration returns to what is essential in the theological declarations, in the sense of the Ninety-Five Theses and the theses against scholastic theology. The question of authority must not only be raised but answered. I will do this with regard to three main chances and challenges of Lutheranism in the West.

3. 1. Against Protestant Particularism --- On the Way to Unity According to the Gospel

The one truth about salvation through Jesus Christ is experienced by every human being anew in his/her situation and applied to life. This leads naturally to a very manifold feature of the message of the gospel in the church. Aware of the limitation of human insight and the borders of communication between people, there can hardly be a community that exclusively controls the message and the promise of salvation, as well as those to whom it is proclaimed. That is why one must carefully distinguish between

315

the church of Jesus Christ and the churches of the world. While the former claims to anticipate the heavenly community of the end-time, the latter emphasizes the community of sinners and righteous ones whose separation is reserved for the judgment of God.

Contrary to this insight, the ecumenical reality of recent years is marked by an increasing confessionalism that runs counter to the biblical witness and the commission of the church. It begins, to be sure, not only where other communities of faith are excluded but is already there where a relatively greater part of truth is claimed, before the background of existing or aspired unity of churches. No matter how important the engagement for the truth is, also for individual identity, it should not result in the destruction of the unity of the church established by Christ. I imagine the Church of the third millennium as a diverse community of believers who have not divested themselves of their pious identity but profit from the dialogue and common life with other believers.

Along with that, a further perspective comes into view: the church --- the churches --- are not the only institutionalized administrative units and its representatives --- from the pope and bishop to High Consistories and church presidents. The church is, first of all, the believers assembled in it. You and I...Thus, the church is always as good, beautiful, trustworthy, energetic, etc. as we ourselves are, or prepared to be. No finger-pointing at others and demanding from them to be active but to see what you are able to do with your own ability granted from God.

Those who criticize the church, are dissatisfied with it, are obliged also to ask themselves what they have contributed to this reason for criticism, dissatisfaction, and to remove abuses.

3.2. Identity --- Church Must Again Become Clear and Mediate Identity

What every political party, every sports team, indeed, even every club with an uppermost differing community goal achieves seems to have been lost in the church in recent years: the mediation of identity. Christians are less and less able to identify with their church. Here the research of the reasons remains to be seen. The fact remains that numerous, quite pious Christians, living in their faith, find no room for their form of piety in the church, or cannot reconcile their own piety, grounded in Scripture, with the piety demanded and lived by the church. While one large group of critics blames the church for dealing too little, or not taking seriously, the existential questions and needs of the people entrusted to it; another group criticizes the church for defining itself too much by daily politics and social action, thus betraying its message, or way of proclamation, by the effort of appearing to be timely.

The tight-rope walk between both justified demands and critical points regarding the present image of the church can only be overcome when one strives for the highest singleness of meaning in the proclamation. I want to discuss this effort in terms of three wishes and to discuss this in the following way based on the three problems.

3.2.1. Clarity in Administration --- Against the Church of Clerics, Concentrated in Pastors

Large organizations, like those of the current churches, require administrative structure. But this is often precisely the subject of justified criticism: inflexibility, isolation, bureaucracy, self-serving legalism, and whatever all the blames are called. A clear administration must, first of all, be concerned about an understanding of an office as service to the community of members. No church administration exists just for its own sake! This common situation is justifiably criticized: inflexibility, being withdrawn from the daily realities of life, bureaucracy, autonomy, and like all the other reproaches sound.

Conversely, ecclesiastical offices are clearly necessary; not only their validity but also their coordination --- to avoid, for once the charm word of the ecclesiastical hierarchy. On the other hand, the necessity of church offices is clear; naturally, its justification but also its place — in order to avoid the irritating word of the church's hierarchy.

I have said earlier that the church consists not only of administrators but, in the first place of believers. The office of preacher and priest presuppose, of course, a certain education and can, therefore, not be undertaken by everyone. The office, of course, does not imply an extraordinary style of life or special character traits (solid faith, etc.). The priestly office bearer is different from other services of believers in the church through special privileges: the exercise of this office is exempt of other duties. Thus it is unjust when individual bearers of the office expand their powers and wrongly concentrate in themselves power that does not belong to them. In fact, the priest or pastor has the task to preach, administer the sacraments, and do pastoral care. He/she is educated and set aside for this in order to devote his/her time to do these tasks, undivided and unencumbered by the care for daily necessities. Here, it is self-evident that parts of this office can also be used at any time by other fellow Christians. The unpleasant question arises less with respect to do priestly duties than, above all, under the aspect that the multiple gifts of the believers in the church are not used, or even forced out by an improper understanding of the priestly office.

3.2.2. The Clarity of Proclamation --- For a Trustworthy Teaching Office of the Church

The conflict about the interpretation of Scripture and its practical consequences for life presuppose a common foundation of the truths of faith. The church must, for the sake of the clarity of its proclamation, set itself clearly apart from all those groups that deny the fundamental truths of faith and thus radically jeopardize the gospel. The basic consent of the truth must be re-examined again and again and reformulated for the respective time. This is one of the main tasks of scientific theology which, of course, can only be fruitfully mastered in the close exchange with ecclesiastical reality. The discursive character of theological research is good for the teaching office of the church. Minds need not take offense at the institution of the teaching office as long as it again and again reformulates the basic consent of the faithful according to their understanding of it. But then the clarity of the teaching office can, in turn, only exist by being fed from the faith of the church members and not by seeking to control it. The principal tasks of the teaching office is to formulate the consent of faithful in such a way that the majority, in favorable circumstances even all Christians, can identify themselves with these formulations.

The conflict about the interpretation of the gospel regarding these questions and problems must surely be conducted with total engagement --- albeit always before the background of knowing of the acceptance of all humankind through Christ. To put it somewhat trivially: I can, indeed, I must come to terms with my fellow Christians about the proclamation and its practical consequences for life. But the conflict and the separation may never go so far as to make the common attendance at the Eucharist afterwards impossible. We live by the forgiveness through Jesus Christ and are able to follow him only by handing on his gift of grace given to us gratis. That we are forgiven is nowhere more persuasively documented than where we practice forgiveness, and meet the neighbor in the love of Christ.

3.2.3. Clarity of Pastoral Care --- For the Agreement of Life and Doctrine

The demand for clarity in pastoral care can only be achieved when life and doctrine, that is, the action of the pastor resulting from it, agree. The criticism of numerous believers regarding ethical or moral declarations of ecclesiastical office-bearers ignites, as a rule, where life and doctrine – and that means, of course, also circumstances of life which are, in part, not even a personal responsibility --- and the demand of the church go different ways. Without going into details, some examples are chosen: the equality of women, the ethics of marriage and family planning, and the political engagement of Christians. [21]

For many people, these are the so-called practical questions of conduct which are answered on the basis of reflection and experience. Reason and experience, as authorities for finding a decision, or as standard for finding a judgment, take the place of Scripture. The argument from Scripture as well as other considerations, which do not necessarily appeal to experience or to realistic, pragmatic interpretations of the world, are sidelined with such nasty designations as "theoretical," "academic," "intellec-

---

[21] See Christian Möller, *Auf dem Weg zu einer seelsorgerlichen Kirche* (Göttingen: Vandenhoeck & Ruprecht, 2000).

tual." "I am taking this under consideration and take up a popular catchword forgetting theology." (Theologievergessenheit)

3.3. Against the Dictatorship of Experience in Scientific Theology --- For a Discursive Discovery of Truth

"Theology is a positive science insofar as it is needed to solve a practical task." [22] To put it inversely: the quality of a theological statement is measured by the question whether and how a practical task can be accomplished. Modern critics of the church seem to argue the same way when they blame the loss of theology in the churches on their increasing loss of social significance, attractiveness, and future ability. The point of this argument, with its criticism of the church, can hardly be underestimated.---- since we also judge the quality of our pastors, by their sermons,

And yet, I assert that this argument leads astray: If Jesus were judged by his capacity for a social-reformatory criticism of his time, his disciples by their power to succeed, or the quality of their respective assemblies, nothing else could be ascertained but the failure of his mission.

But the witness of the resurrection turns exactly this standard on its head. It is not a question of success, measured in quantity and quality. It is not a question of numbers, successes, stamina, strategies, etc. It is a question about something else.

It is a question of how life becomes new, the radical and complete reorientation of all previous values and norms. They cannot be verified by experience nor proven by logic and theory. The contrast theory-praxis is here completely out of place.

The core of the biblical message is the First Commandment, "I am the Lord your God. You shall have no other gods but me alone." But what are our gods if we acknowledge reason, experience, and the relevance of praxis in all our considerations ---

---

[22] Daniel Friedrich Ernst Schleiermacher, *Kurze Darstellung des theologischen Studiums zum Behuf einleitender Vorlesungen*, critical ed Heinrich Scholz (Darmstadt: Wissenschaftliche Buchgesellschaft, 1977), 1.

also about the future and the church --- as the final authorities of our conversations and discussions?

But this commandment is not the end. Jesus supplements it with the well-known Double Commandment of Love (Matt. 23: 37-39). The basis of the relationship between God and humanity is love, as it is also between human beings. This is precisely not just a purpose-bound, pragmatic, realistic, cost-oriented assessment, or whatever other unsavory, degrading relations between people can be described. But it is an emotional relation from the bottom of one's heart, soul, and mind. In love, two give themselves to each other, and separate only to leave behind something essential of one. Where love becomes the fundamental model relations between people the world changes. This is true also in the church.

4. Prospective

The Church is created through the Word of God. People gather around Scripture: listen to it, live it, give thanks for it, sing it, pray it. The church is one way, possibly even the way in which the Word of God comes to us. "Where two or three are gathered in my name, I am there among them" (Matt.18:20). What is promised here, goes. This promise is true. This is the question – whatever the criticism.

That is why a treatise on the church must always have only recourse to the Scripture --- to be sure, not just as one, more or less, optional opinion, authorized by myself or by theological examinations, but as exposition of Holy Scripture. My opinion is not the issue. The theme of scriptural exposition, today or on any other day, is what God has to say to us, generally, and specifically, in the sermon. Such exposition has nothing at all to do with a point of view. It is the task to which God calls.

The temptation is great to misuse the pulpit and to degrade the congregation to a mere claque of vain self-description. The office of preaching is pledged to evoke the Word of God in law and gospel, especially also when it is perceived as untimely, uncomfortable, not very appropriate, and disturbing. Not for anything, intense discussions and, at times, even personal quarrels, ignite through the sermon. There is a need for a Lutheran homiletics with an ecclesiological dimension. [23] This cannot be elaborated here. But it becomes the crucial test for the survival of Lutheran Protestantism in view of the demands of post-modernity in a globalized world with corresponding offers for a new orientation that transcends geographical, cultural, and mental limits. Luther did not encounter nor see these dangerous dimensions --- *Anfechtung* in his terminology. But his heirs were not and are nor spared from them. They stood against them, not where Luther or Lutheranism were the focus of their efforts, but the living Word of God. Thus the chance and the limitation of Western Lutheranism rests, wholly in the sense of the Wittenberg theologian, in the provocative slogan of the Berlin celebrations of the 500th birthday: "Forget Luther" --- and preserve the gospel.

---

[23] See Christian Möller, *Seelsorgerlich Predigen*, 3rd ed. (Waltrop: Spenner, 2003).

PART IV

The Ecumenical Commitment
of Lutheranism

The Recovery of the Unity of World Lutheranism And of its Ecumenical Commitment

Günther Gassmann

I. Preface and Dedication

Professor Eric Gritsch has presented in two of his many publications a highly instructive historical and theological description and interpretation of the origins, historical developments, and specific characteristics of world Lutheranism.[1] And, in fact, he himself has been a living symbol of the breadth of Lutheranism by having his roots and memories in European Lutheran past and present and having become a leading representative of the North American member of the Lutheran family. Eric Gritsch, furthermore, has actively and efficiently promoted awareness and knowledge of the world-wide Lutheran communion among lay-people, generations of theological students, pastors, and church leaders – also beyond his Lutheran tribe.[2] Through his participation in the work of the Lutheran World Federation, in Lutheran-Roman Catholic dialogue, and through his innumerable lectures in congregations and theological institutions (not exclusively Lutheran), he has been and fortunately still is a living example of being at the same time both a loyal locally-rooted Lutheran and an ecumenically committed Lutheran. Thus, my contribution honours, celebrates, and affirms the Lutheran life and work of Eric Gritsch by dealing with two

---

[1] Eric W. Gritsch, *Fortress Introduction to Lutheranism*, Minneapolis: Fortress Press, 1994; Eric W. Gritsch, *A History of Lutheranism*, Minneapolis: Fortress Press, 2002.

[2] One example is the book put together for a Catholic audience: *Martin Luther. Faith in Christ and the Gospel*, introduced and edited by Eric W. Gritsch, Hyde Park/NY: New City Press, 1996.

specific elements of world Lutheranism, the framework of his thinking and doing.

II. The Basis: the Reformation Affirmation of Unity

The word "recovery" in the title of this paper presupposes a prior and given reality that may have been lost or forgotten and, consequently, is to be recovered. But in order that such recovery might be achieved, a process of rediscovering has to precede the recovery and becomes part of it. Recovery – or re-appropriation – is, however, not simply repetition, a re-pristination of something past. Rather, it involves new interpretation and reformulation in changed historical and cultural circumstances. This paper will outline this process from a given reality, its loss, and its rediscovery, and ultimately, leading to its renewed appropriation. Accordingly, we will start with the basic reality of the Lutheran reformers' affirmation of unity and ecumenical commitment.

Already at the beginning of the Lutheran reformation movement in the sixteenth century we find, together with the call for reform and renewal, the theological conviction of and emphasis on the given and present reality of the one, universal, catholic Church. Thus, Martin Luther consistently uses the term and concept of the universal Church, the *ecclesia universalis* (e.g. WA 2,279; WA 6,287/LW 39,58; WA 54,213/LW 41,271), even in the midst of heated controversies with a papalist, juridical, and institutional concept of the Church on the right and a picture of the church reduced to the assembly of the small band of pure believers on the left. This universal Church is an object of faith, but it is also visible and present in the different churches of all places and in all times wherever a church clearly has its center in Jesus Christ, where his word is alive, his sacraments are celebrated, and the confession of Jesus Christ continues (WA 26,147&506; WA 40/I,69; WA 43,597; LW 40,231; LW 37,367; LW 26,24). We find this trans-provincial and trans-confessional ecclesiological horizon also with Luther's co-reformer Philipp Melanchthon. In his *Apology of the Augsburg Confession* (Apol VII.10), one of the Lutheran Confessions, he affirms that the *ecclesia catholica* "consists of people scattered throughout the entire world who agree on the gospel and have the same Christ, the same Holy

Spirit, and the same sacraments, whether or not they have the same human traditions."[3] In Article VII of the *Augsburg Confession* (AC), also written (with the help of some earlier texts) by Melanchthon, we encounter again this comprehensive perspective of the universal, catholic Church in a concentrated formulation. The constitutive elements of the Church, the pure proclamation or teaching of the Gospel and the right administration of the sacraments according to the Gospel are at the same time defined as the constitutive and necessary elements of ecclesial unity in so far as one agrees on these elements (*consentire de doctrina evangelii et de administratione sacramentorum*) (*The Book of Concord*, 43).

Accordingly, what makes a church a manifestation of the Church is also indispensable for its unity. Article VII of the AC is not limited to the later Lutheran church, but refers to the Church of Jesus Christ, the community of believers and saints assembled by the Holy Spirit through word and sacrament served by a called and ordained ministry. This looks to a reality beyond the late medieval church in which the reformers still lived and which they sought to reform. In their vision of reform, they desired to preserve the unity of the Church, for example by the intention and content of their *Augsburg Confession* as well as by conducting several colloquies with Reformed and Roman Catholic theologians. They pursued this goal despite the controversies and conflicts that resulted from their reforming activities and from the negative reaction of the Roman authorities.

However, the Lutheran reformers ideal of simultaneously implementing reforms and maintaining visibility was not successful. The division of western Christianity became inevitable. To the confessional divisions were added the fracturing of the Lutheran movement into numerous, unrelated territorial churches in Europe. This diversification of Lutheran churches even increased after the eighteenth century with the establishment of Lutheran migrant churches in North and South America and Australia, and the Lutheran mission churches in Africa and Asia,

---

[3] *The Book of Concord. The Confessions of the Evangelical Lutheran Church*, ed. by Robert Kolb and Timothy J. Wengert, Minneapolis: Fortress Press, 2000, 175.

the children of intensive mission efforts in the nineteenth and early twentieth centuries. The contradiction between the Reformers' confession of the one Church of Jesus Christ and the unrelated diversity even within their own confessional family (quite apart from the deep, bitter and sometimes bloody confessional divisions within Christianity over the centuries) was felt by some individuals. But it was only in the second half of the nineteenth century that we encounter first efforts towards closer inner-Lutheran relations and cooperation.[4] These efforts led in the twentieth century to institutionalized forms of Lutheran unity. The slow rediscovery of forms of Lutheran unity during the late nineteenth and early twentieth centuries was followed by and partly coincided with the rediscovery of the Lutheran ecumenical commitment as part of its heritage and the beginning of Lutheran participation in the ecumenical movement.

III. The Recovery of Inner-Lutheran Unity

It is a remarkable and surprising fact that Lutheranism awoke relatively late in history to the call to overcome its internal territorial separations and lack of closer relationships. While other worldwide communions already in the late nineteenth century created institutional forms of cooperation – for example the Lambeth Conferences of all Anglican bishops since 1867, the Reformed/Presbyterian World Alliance 1875, the Methodist World Council 1881 – world Lutheranism was a late-comer with its first Lutheran World Convention in 1923. One reason for the late appearance of organized Lutheranism on the international scene may have been that the overwhelming presence of Lutheranism was found in the large European state and folk churches which for a long time did not see the necessity of a worldwide fellowship; while on the other side of the ocean North American Lutheranism

---

[4] See e.g. Bengt Wadensjö, *Toward a World Lutheran Communion. Developments in Lutheran Cooperation up to 1929*, Uppsala: Verbum, 1070; E. Clifford Nelson, *The Rise of World Lutheranism. An American Perspective*, Philadelphia: Fortress Press, 1982; Eugene L. Brand, *Toward a Lutheran Communion: Pulpit and Altar Fellowship*, LWF Report 26, Geneva: Lutheran World Federation, 1988 – a most helpful survey up to 1987.

was preoccupied with overcoming its own internal divisions. The first impulses, however, to transcend the national Lutheran boundaries came from the *General Evangelical Lutheran Conference* (founded at Hannover in 1868) and especially from the international involvement of the *National Lutheran Council* that was founded in the United States in 1918. There were also calls for more cooperation from the mission field, especially after the experience of the care for "orphaned missions" during World War I.

These earlier calls for Lutheran unity were forcefully expressed and highlighted by the *First Lutheran World Convention* (LWC) at Eisenach in 1923, the first large international Lutheran gathering since the Reformation.[5] Quite naturally the primary interest of the participants was to initiate steps towards forms of Lutheran cooperation, joint consultation and theological reflection, and inner-Lutheran unity. "It is necessary," it was said, "that we as Lutherans from all parts of the world recognize our unity as really present" and that we should further its main convictions and practical realizations (Nelson, 154). But this was not so easy given the various theological convictions and ecclesial developments among the different Lutheran churches, their diverse social-political and cultural contexts, especially given the impact of the post-war situation in Europe. An ecclesiological awareness of being members of the one Lutheran church was alive only among some participants. One sign of this situation was the fact that a joint communion service was not yet possible at Eisenach. Nevertheless, "a genuine spirit of unity and a remarkable longing for continuing fellowship grew and prevailed at Eisenach" (Nelson, 173). The rediscovery and recovery of Lutheran unity had begun, and the appointment and work of an Executive Committee of the LWC was an indication that the LWC was to be consigned to a single event, limited to one occasion. The proposal to establish a central bureau for the LWC, however, was for some time resisted by the Americans and most Scandinavians for fear of "centralization" over against a free international association of Lutherans (Nelson, 188-196).

---

[5] For the main issues in Eisenach 1923 see E. Clifford Nelson, 167-175.

The next two Lutheran World Conventions in Copenhagen (1929) and in Paris (1935) had as their positive background the experience of growing contacts, increased information – e.g. in the form of a first edition of a handbook on global Lutheranism,[6] - and beginning cooperation – e.g. by helping Lutherans in the Soviet Union. Considerations on Lutheran unity were, as was the case already in Eisenach, usually connected with reflection on Lutheran identity as the fundamental presupposition of unity. One year after the World Convention in Paris the Executive Committee of the LWC issued a statement on Lutheran participation in the ecumenical movement[7] that, significantly, began with two recommendations to the LWC on inner-Lutheran identity and unity: furtherance of Lutheran self-consciousness in the individual churches with the help of the LWC; and furtherance of worldwide fellowship and cooperation of Lutheran churches with the condition that thereby relations with other churches and "ecumenical movements and organizations" must not endanger the existing unity of ecumenical Lutheranism. This qualification shows that at that time the recovery of Lutheran unity was still underway and, consequently, for many had priority over against broader ecumenical involvement.

The Second World War and the post-war sufferings of people in Europe had dramatically changed the historical and ecumenical context of the efforts towards inner-Lutheran unity. Now unity and fellowship were concretely experienced through the material help and the spiritual, theological assistance for Lutherans – and not only for them – in Europe. Things began to move faster than before. The creation of the Lutheran World Federation (LWF) at its *First Assembly* in Lund, Sweden (1947) was a natural outcome of the new situation and spirit. The "Doctrinal Basis" of the first Constitution of the LWF[8] referred to the elements that constitute

---

[6] *The Lutheran Churches of the World*, Minneapolis: Augsburg Publishing House, 1929.

[7] In *The Lutheran World Almanac and Encyclopedia 1934-1937*, New York: The National Lutheran Council, 1937, 36-38.

[8] Reprinted in *From Federation to Communion. The History of the Lutheran World Federation*, ed. by Jens Holger Schjørring, Prasanna Kumari, Norman A. Hjelm, Minneapolis: Fortress Press, 1997, 527.

the basis of Lutheran unity: The LWF acknowledges the Holy Scriptures "as the only source and the infallible norm of all church doctrine and practice, and sees in the Confessions of the Lutheran Church, especially in the Unaltered Augsburg Confession and Luther's Catechism, a pure exposition of the Word of God" (II). But a certain hesitation and reluctance – for the traditional fear of "centralization" as well as for leaving the door open for the membership of the conservative Lutheran Church-Missouri Synod - is still clearly noticeable in the definition of the nature of the new LWF which "shall be a free association of Lutheran churches. It shall have no power to legislate for the churches belonging to it or to interfere with their complete autonomy ..." Still, it is conceded that the LWF may act on behalf of member churches "in such matters as one or more of them may commit to it" (III). These two statements surround a list of purposes that reflect the still necessary task of further solidifying inner-Lutheran fellowship by (1) cultivating unity of faith and confession among the Lutheran churches of the world; (2) promoting fellowship and cooperation in study among Lutherans; (3) developing a united Lutheran approach to responsibilities in missions and education; (4) and supporting Lutheran groups in need of spiritual or material aid (III).

After this new theological, organizational, and operational basis of world Lutheranism had been laid at Lund, the following years were marked by an intensive recovery and implementation of inner-Lutheran unity with the help of the many activities of the LWF, the largest confessional organization, while at the same time the ecumenical commitment of Lutheranism was further clarified and formulated (see next chapter). It was only at the *Fourth Assembly of the LWF* at Helsinki (1963) that the issue and understanding of global Lutheran unity returned to the stage of an LWF Assembly.[9] The debate was prepared and oriented by Peter Brunner's programmatic article "The Lutheran World Federation as Ecclesiological Problem"[10] and by the LWF Commission on

---

[9] *Offizieller Bericht der Vierten Vollversammlung des Lutherischen Weltbundes, Helsinki, 30. Juli-11. August 1963*, Berlin & Hamburg: Lutherisches Verlagshaus, 1965, 302-324, 402f., and 530-539.

[10] In *Lutheran World*, 7/3, 1960, 237-256.

Theology's preparatory booklet for Helsinki *The Nature of the Lutheran World Federation*.[11] The main thesis in these texts and then at Helsinki in the main paper by E. Clifford Nelson on "The One Church and the Lutheran Churches" was that fellowship of confession (i.e. a relationship marked by the common acceptance of the same Confessions), signifies and justifies according to Article VII of the *Augsburg Confession* an ecclesial fellowship which should find its expression in pulpit and altar fellowship. Accordingly, the discussion in Helsinki circled around the question whether the acceptance of the doctrinal basis of the LWF by the member churches justifies, even calls for, the declaration that the member churches consider themselves to be in a relationship of pulpit and altar fellowship. But there were still many who did not dare to take this step, also because of the reawakened hope that "Missouri" might now be ready to join the LWF. Thus a further step in the recovery of inner-Lutheran unity had to be postponed once again.

More than twenty years later, but also after twenty years of growing contacts, cooperation, theological exchange, and common ecumenical involvement, the theme of Lutheran unity was forcefully brought back to the *Seventh Assembly of the LWF* at Budapest (1984). Two developments added further urgency to this issue again. The new international bilateral dialogues between Christian World Communions in which the LWF became one of the most active participants, raised the question: who do the representatives of the LWF represent – a communion of churches or a free association of individual churches?

The same question was raised in view of the action of the LWF at its preceding *Sixth Assembly* at Dar-es-Salaam (1977), which appealed to "our white member churches in southern Africa to recognize that the situation in southern Africa constitutes a *status confessionis,*" a situation in which churches should "publicly and unequivocally reject the existing apartheid system."[12] What kind of body issued this judgment and call in

---

[11] *Helsinki Preparatory Document 4*, Geneva: LWF, 1963.

[12] *In Christ – A New Community. The Proceedings of the Sixth Assembly of the Lutheran World Federation, Dar-es-Salaam, Tanzania, June 13-25, 1977*, Geneva: Lutheran World Federation, 1977, 180.

1977? Budapest 1984 responded with its "Statement on the Self-Understanding and Task of the Lutheran World Federation."[13] Its central affirmation is that the communion (the new key term!) "in which the Lutheran churches of the whole world are bound together" is rooted in and based on "the unity of the apostolic faith as given in the Holy Scripture and witnessed by the ecumenical creeds and the Lutheran confessions. ... And it is based on agreement in the proclamation of the gospel and celebration of the sacraments (AC VII). This Lutheran communion of churches finds its visible expression in pulpit and altar fellowship, in common witness and service, in the joint fulfilment of the missionary task, and in openness to ecumenical cooperation, dialog, and community. The Lutheran churches of the world consider their communion as an expression of the one, holy, catholic, and apostolic church." This is, together with its additional sentences, perhaps the most theologically concise statement on the foundation, nature, and calling of the Lutheran communion of churches. No wonder that it helped to move the Assembly in Budapest to, finally, adopt the crucial step to add Article III.1 to the LWF Constitution: "The member churches of the Lutheran World Federation understand themselves to be in pulpit and altar fellowship with each other." In other words: The member churches do not enter into such fellowship or create it but they *are* in this fellowship as a consequence of their common confession.

In Budapest the hopes of Helsinki had been fulfilled – but not yet completely. The original formulation in the Constitution that the LWF is "a free association of Lutheran churches" was still there. Therefore, the next *Assembly* at Curitiba (1990) brought consistency into the Constitution by formulating a new Article III on the nature of the LWF: "The Lutheran World Federation is a communion of churches which confess the triune God, agree in the proclamation of the Word of God and are united in pulpit and altar fellowship."[14] The *Augsburg Confession* is no longer mentioned only in the "Doctrinal Basis" but the content of its Article VII is

---

[13] *In Christ – Hope for the World. Official Proceedings of the Seventh Assembly of the Lutheran World Federation, Budapest, Hungary, July 22-August 5, 1984*, Geneva: Lutheran World Federation, 1984, 176f.

[14] *From Federation to Communion*, 530.

now also incorporated into the Constitution. A rather extensive theological commentary on the new formulation of the Constitution and its implication was elaborated and presented by a theological working group of the LWF under the title *The Church as Communion.*[15]

The *Tenth Assembly* at Winnipeg (2003) simply underlined what had been achieved on the way to the recovery of inner-Lutheran unity on the basis of an ecclesiology of communion applied to the members of the LWF. The Assembly accepted an expansion of the name of the LWF – where the use of the longer name is appropriate – to "The Lutheran World Federation – A Communion of Churches."[16] The same Assembly returned to a problem that since 1947 limits the fullness, at least quantitatively, of the recovery of Lutheran unity because of the non-membership of the Lutheran Church – Missouri Synod and some smaller churches associated with it. In this perspective and perhaps stronger than before the Winnipeg Message expresses the commitment "to give priority to the regular meetings with the International Lutheran Council (ILC), and support member churches of the ILC and the LWF to develop and further their relationships locally" (53).

Beginning with first efforts in the second part of the nineteenth century the rediscovery and the recovery of inner-Lutheran unity has been achieved, to a large degree, in the form of a worldwide Lutheran communion, constitutionally affirmed in the Constitution of 1990 and practised in the work of the LWF and the many relations between Lutheran churches. This gift of the Holy Spirit and of faithful obedience is now here to be nourished, experienced, and further extended.

---

[15] Geneva: Lutheran World Federation, 1997, the statement is on pp. 13-29.

[16] *For the Healing of the World. Official Report, LWF Tenth Assembly, Winnipeg, Canada, 21-31 July 2003*, Geneva: Lutheran World Federation, 2004, 70.

IV. The Recovery of Lutheran Ecumenical Commitment

The inability and unwillingness of the late medieval church to respond positively to the Reformation call to reform the church while at the same time preserve its unity led to the parting of the ways in the second half of the sixteenth century. The division between emerging Lutheranism and what then became the *Roman* Catholic Church was institutionalized by the Religious Peace of Augsburg in 1555 and theologically undergirded by the Council of Trent (1545-1563) on the one hand and the Lutheran *Formula of Concord* of 1577 that was added to the collection of Lutheran Confessions in the *Book of Concord* of 1580. Both the Formula of Concord and the Book of Concord also sealed at the same time the separation between Calvinistic/Zwinglian and Lutheran Reformation movements (I believe it is more appropriate to speak about "Reformation movements" than of "Reformations"). The age of mounting confessional conflicts and enmities (e.g., Counter-Reformation) as well as doctrinal controversies had begun. These conflicts had a deep and broad impact on European social, political and cultural history, and its heritage of shaping mentalities is still felt today (e.g., in the opposition to the Lutheran-Catholic *Joint Declaration on the Doctrine of Justification* of 1999).

It is against this dark background that the rediscovery of the original Lutheran commitment to Christian unity captured anew the hearts and minds of many of the same people who were also beginning to work for inner-Lutheran unity. Like many religious or theological developments this was influenced also by contextual factors, in this case by the beginning of the modern ecumenical movement in the first decades of the twentieth century. Thus, it is remarkable that at the *First Lutheran World Convention* at Eisenach (1923) the quest for *Christian* unity appeared on the agenda together with the reflections on *Lutheran* unity. At that time the first *Universal Christian Conference for Life and Work* at Stockholm (1925) and the *First World Conference on Faith and Order* at Lausanne (1927) were prepared. This new church historical overture was felt also in Eisenach. Even though the Convention did not issue a statement on Christian unity, the issue was present in several main papers and here both in the affirmation – typical for many voices at that time – of an already existing spiritual and invisible unity of faith among Christians of different churches and a marked reluctance to consider external and visible forms and structures of unity and their implementation.

The rediscovery of the Lutheran ecumenical commitment continued one year after the *Third Lutheran World Convention* at Paris (1935) when its Executive Committee issued the first representative statement on Lutheran participation in the ecumenical movement.[17] This was, of course, not the first Lutheran expression of ecumenical commitment: For example, in the 1930s, Swedish Lutheran Archbishop Nathan Söderblom had already become a leader in both the Life and Work and Faith and Order movements; and the outstanding confessional Lutheran Hermann Sasse had edited the large German report of the First World Conference on Faith and Order at Lausanne in 1927. The statement of the LWC Executive Committee addressed recommendations to the Convention that had as their first priority, representative of Lutheran ecumenical thinking at that time, the fostering of Lutheran self-consciousness and worldwide Lutheran fellowship and cooperation. Relations to other churches and ecumenical movements and organizations should not endanger the existing unity of ecumenical Lutheranism. Lutheran churches should approach relations with ecumenical movements and organizations with an open spirit and should be ready for service and cooperation in the work of Christian love, and they should approach such relations in a "united front." The conditions for their ecumenical participation were that the respective movements and organizations pursue goals that belong to the proper tasks of the church, that they acknowledge a series of convictions and principles of faith that are fundamental for the Christian message, and that they guarantee the participating churches a free witness to their convictions of faith and their rejection of errors. The judgement of Siegfried Grundmann that this statement of 1936 is the most comprehensive document of world Lutheranism on the ecumenical question,[18] (to which Kurt Schmidt-Clausen adds that

---

[17] The Lutheran World Almanac and Encyclopedia, 36-38.

[18] Siegfried Grundmann, *Der Lutherische Weltbund. Grundlagen - Herkunft – Aufbau*, Köln/Graz: Böhlau, 1957, 360.

content-wise it is also the most significant document[19]) seems to be overly enthusiastic in light of this rather cautious text with its carefully guarded conditions.

After the Second World War and under the impact of the new ecumenical relations in the post-war period the common Lutheran ecumenical position became much more open. Only now a true recovery – in the sense of a re-reception and new interpretation – of the original ecumenical spirit and commitment began. A sentence in the draft of the Constitution for the Lutheran World Federation (LWF) in 1946 was taken over from the 1936 LWC text. As a result, the affirmation that a common Lutheran position should be developed in view of ecumenical Christian movements and organizations was replaced at the founding *First Assembly of the LWF* (1947) by the much more positive formulation: "to foster Lutheran participation in ecumenical movements" (III.2,d). It was also an expression of support for the World Council of Churches (WCC) "in process of formation" that the Executive Committee of the LWC in 1946 proposed that the future WCC should be structured confessionally and not geographically;[20] a proposal that was, unfortunately, only partially taken up.

The first important common Lutheran statement on Christian unity, formulated during the early history of the LWF, was the statement *Christ Liberates and Unites* prepared by the Theological Commission of the LWF for the *Third Assembly* at Minneapolis (1957).[21] Central to the carefully developed theological document is the unrestricted affirmation of the Lutheran participation in the endeavours for the unity of the Church. Other important characteristics of the document include: a Christological basis characteristic of Lutheran thinking (18f.), the rejection of human construction of unity or its mere outward justification, the necessity of making visible "the unity always already given in Christ and through Christ" (28-30), the foundation of such unity on agreement in the means of grace, the realization of unity (when

---

[19]   Kurt Sachmidt-Clausen, *Vom Lutherischen Weltkonvent zum Lutherischen Weltbund*, Gütersloh 1976, 227.

[20] Grundmann, 228f.; Nelson, 381-384.

[21]   *Die theologische Arbeit in Minneapolis*, Berlin: Lutherisches Verlagshaus, 1958, 16-52.

the necessary consensus has been achieved, in the form of a church fellowship – a concept that later became so important), a fellowship of proclamation, sacramental life, and confession (AC VII) but not necessarily in the form of organic union. Fellowship in the Lord's Supper is conceived as the expression of church fellowship and not as a means of reaching it. The particular ecumenical contribution of the Lutheran Church would be the struggle for theological-confessional consensus. Where such a consensus has been given, church fellowship should be practiced (30-33). In this description a particular Lutheran concept of ecclesial unity was brought forward that is continuous with the Lutheran confessional tradition, but is also critical of certain aspects of ecumenical discussions at that time (e.g. concerning the concept of organic unity/union and the view of intercommunion as a means towards unity).

A significant step in the recovery of its ecumenical commitment was taken at the *Fourth Assembly of the LWF* at Helsinki (1963).[22] The Assembly created the "Lutheran Foundation for Interconfessional Research" (433-439), placed in the "Institute for Ecumenical Research" at Strasbourg, France (Eric Gritsch served on its Board for several years). The LWF gave itself a precious ecumenical instrument that has in remarkable ways contributed "to the fulfilment by the Lutheran churches of their ecumenical responsibility in the area of theology" (Constitution of the Foundation, III). Its work consisted initially in the interpretation of the process and results of Vatican II and then was broadened to include: the responsible participation in bilateral conversations of the LWF until today, to the involvement in the theological work of the LWF, and to the communication of ecumenical reflection and developments through seminars, consultations, and publications. The creation of the Strasbourg Institute was surrounded by energetic calls at Helsinki for inter-confessional dialogues with other major Christian communions, especially those historically close to the Lutheran tradition: Roman Catholic, Anglican, and Reformed (e.g. 168f.; 171f.; 322-324; 433). Soon after Helsinki the dialogues with these three partners began: with the Reformed

---

[22] *Offizieller Bericht der Vierten Vollversammlung des Lutherischen Weltbundes*

and United Churches in Europe 1963-1973 (*Leuenberg Concord*); in the "Joint Working Group" of the Vatican Secretariat for Promoting Christian Unity and the LWF in 1965 and 1966 that prepared the still on-going international Lutheran-Roman Catholic bilateral dialogue, the first dialogue of this kind; and in the Anglican-Lutheran International Conversations (1970-1972). These dialogues initiated, together with other dialogues, a new phase in the ecumenical movement. At the same time they signified a further step in the recovery of the ecumenical commitment of Lutheranism by moving beyond theoretical considerations to ecumenical theological practice in the form of church to church conversations.

The recovery of Lutheran ecumenical commitment was further developed at the *Fifth Assembly of the LWF* at Evian, France (1970). Again the Commission on Theology of the LWF had prepared a substantial document.[23] Its title *More than Unity of the Church* already indicates a new concern for the interconnection between the search for Christian unity and a united witness and service for reconciliation in a divided world. Other interconnections mentioned were between unity in the agreement on the Gospel mediated by word and sacrament and legitimate diversity in secondary issues; interpretation of the fundamental agreement in word and sacrament in the perspective of the doctrine of justification; bilateral inter-confessional doctrinal conversations preparing of a binding consensus as condition of unity; possible steps towards closer church relations and fellowship. The ecumenical section in the Report of the Evian Assembly, significantly entitled "Ecumenical Commitment,"[24] draws on the work of the Theological Commission. It reflects the new emphasis, according to the general spirit of that period, on the connection between the search for Christian unity and the ecumenical commitment to common witness and service. At the same time continuity with the Lutheran faith tradition is obvious when it is affirmed: "that which is necessary for the unity of the

---

[23] Printed in Lutheran World XVII, No.1, 1970.

[24] Sent Into the World. The Proceedings of the Fifth Assembly of the Lutheran Worldd Federation, Evian, France, *July 14-24, 1970,* Minneapolis: Augsburg, 1971, 71-83.

church is identical to that which constitutes the church: Jesus Christ, present in the gospel, proclaimed through word and sacrament, and received by faith," so that people are justified through grace alone. Wherever this proclamation takes place we have "the prerequisite for church fellowship is already present" (72).

Still existing differences in the interpretation and application of the Gospel are not valid reasons for continuing division, nor should there be in the search for Christian unity an insistence on uniformity in theological formulation and in practice (72f &75). The particular responsibility of Lutheran churches in meeting with other churches is to affirm the role of justification both for the interpretation of Holy Scripture and as a source from which right action proceeds (75). Evian welcomed the on-going dialogues with the Roman Catholic Church and the European Reformed and United Churches and proposed the continuation and extension of these theological dialogues that were regarded as a method congenial to Lutheranism (74-83). The historical significance of the new Lutheran-Roman Catholic dialogue and relationship was underlined by the impressive address of Cardinal Willebrands in Evian (54-65&156f) – a sign that a new epoch of relations between past "arch enemies" had begun.

The next *Assembly of the LWF* at Dar-es-Salaam (1977) took another step in furthering the recovery of Lutheran ecumenical commitment. Representatives of World Confessional Families (as they were called then) adopted in 1974 a "Discussion Paper" on *The Ecumenical Role of World Confessional Families in the Ecumenical Movement.*[25] Over against the concept of organic church unity/union still prominent in ecumenical (WCC) statements (e.g., New Delhi 1961, Nairobi 1975) the 1974 LWF paper claims that the unity of the Church can be realized in its full sense also where confessional traditions and identities can be preserved in a process of reconciliation and renewal that leads to full church unity "in reconciled diversity" (8 & 9, 27-32). The

---

[25] Cf. Günther Gassmann/Harding Meyer, *The Unity of the Church. Requirements and Structure*, LWF Report 15, 1983, Geneva/Stuttgart: LWF, 1983, 27-32.

statement of Dar-es-Salaam on *Models of Unity*[26] proceeds from the 1974 discussion paper and receives the concept of unity in reconciled diversity, understood as a reference to the "abiding value of confessional forms of Christian faith in all their variety" that "can be reconciled into a binding ecumenical fellowship in which even the confessional elements have an essential role to play." This is regarded as "a way to unity which does not automatically entail the surrender of confessional traditions and confessional identities. This way to unity is a way of living encounter, spiritual experience together, theological dialogue and mutual correction ..." It is a way in which differences are not simply preserved – a reaction against the charge that this concept preserves the *status quo* – but are transformed, renewed, reconciled and thus lose their divisive character (174). The new bilateral dialogues are an obvious instrument of the move towards consensus in faith and thereby to church fellowship in reconciled diversity. Accordingly the Assembly resolved "to give high priority to the continuation and extension of bilateral dialogues with other Christian traditions ..." (202).

We have seen how step by step the recovery and new conception of Lutheran ecumenical commitment has been developed since Eisenach 1923, how it has been anchored in the Constitution of the LWF, how it has been put into practical realization in the bilateral dialogues, and how it has been oriented toward a preliminary goal in the form of church fellowship envisaged as a unity in reconciled diversity. This development is received and authoritatively formulated in the statement on *The Unity we Seek* of the *Seventh Assembly of the LWF* at Budapest (1984).[27] Similar to the Statement of this Assembly on the *Self-Understanding and Task of the LWF* (see above the end of part III) this one page statement is of outstanding significance because it harvests and formulates in a comprehensive and precise text the clarifications and insights so far achieved in the reflection on the unity of the church. The Statement opens with a Trinitarian affirmation that connects at the same time with AC VII: "The true unity of the church, which is the unity of the body of Christ and participates in

---

[26] *In Christ – A New Community*, 173-175.

[27] *In Christ – Hope for the World*, 175.

the unity of the Father, Son, and Holy Spirit, is given in and through proclamation of the gospel in word and sacrament. This unity is expressed as a communion in the common and, at the same time, multiform confession of one and the same apostolic faith. It is a communion in holy baptism and in the Eucharistic meal, a communion in which the ministries exercised are recognized by all as expressions of the ministry instituted by Christ in his church. It is a communion where diversities contribute to fullness and are no longer barriers to unity. It is a committed fellowship, able to make common decisions and to act in common." The new term "communion" becomes now the key designation in this vision of unity. The Dar-es-Salaam expression "reconciled diversity" is not mentioned but clearly included when the document states that, in the process toward unity, "traditions are changed, antagonisms overcome, and mutual condemnations lifted. The diversities are reconciled and transformed into a legitimate and indispensable multiformity within the one body of Christ" (175). The enumeration of constitutive conditions and elements of church unity in this statement resembles the corresponding "lists" of the statements on unity of the WCC in New-Delhi (1961) and Nairobi (1975) and later also in Canberra (1991).

The Budapest statement (and the following two paragraphs not quoted here) can be considered the most important short text or formula of the LWF's understanding of Christian unity so far. In addition to this text the Assembly adopted a whole series of resolutions on ecumenical matters, for example on the importance and study of the multilateral ecumenical dialogue in Faith and Order and its convergence text on *Baptism, Eucharist and Ministry* (Lima, 1982), the significance of the interrelation and extension of the range of bilateral dialogues, the necessity of interpreting and communicating their results, the study and initiation of processes of reception of dialogue results in the churches, the possibility of further extending bilateral dialogues (211-220). The concept of "reception" that appeared here for the first time, was prepared by a LWF study on *Ecumenical Methodology* (1972-1976)[28] that

---

[28] *Ecumenical Methodology: Documentation and Report*, ed. by Peder Højen, Geneva: LWF, 1978, 3-30.

described the way from doctrinal consensus through its official and implicit reception in and by the churches to lived communion between churches.

The recovery of the ecumenical commitment of world Lutheranism was, so to speak, "completed" at the *Eighth Assembly of the LWF* at Curitiba (1990) when the ecumenical commitment of the LWF has been integrated directly into the definition of the nature of the LWF: "The Lutheran World Federation confesses the one, holy, catholic, and apostolic Church and is resolved to serve Christian unity throughout the world." [29] What followed since then were affirmations and implementations. Affirmations were expressed at the *Ninth Assembly of the LWF* at Hong Kong (1977) [30] which highlighted and celebrated in particular the Lutheran-Roman Catholic *Joint Declaration on the Doctrine of Justification* (1999) (62) that, indeed, expresses for the first time a "differentiated consensus" between the Roman Catholic Church and a Reformation Church. During the years before Hong Kong a theological working group of the LWF addressed the theme of *The Church as Communion* (mentioned above at the end of part III). In its statement on *Toward a Lutheran Understanding of Communion*[31] the insights on Christian unity are situated within a comprehensive description of the biblical, confessional, and spiritual foundations and forms of expression of communion. The assertions about *koinonia* (communion) of the Lutheran churches and of the goal of church unity were integrated into a wider ecclesiological, Trinitarian, and salvation-historical picture in which the work for church unity that already now is furthered and deepened through bilateral dialogues, cooperation in witness and service, common prayer, and in solidarity finds a prominent place (24-27). The most recent Assembly, the *Tenth Assembly of the LWF* at Winnipeg in (2003),[32] explicitly underlined "the conviction that ecumenical commitment is integral to Lutheran

---

[29] *From Federation to Communion*, 530.

[30] *In Christ – Called to Witness. Official Report of the Ninth Assembly of the Lutheran World Federation, Hong Kong, 8-16 July 1997*, Geneva: Lutheran World Federation, 1997, 45-48 & 62f.

[31] *The Church as Communion*, 13-29.

[32] *For the Healing of the World, 52-54.*

confessional identity" (53) – a conviction that has been recovered and clarified, as we have seen, over eight decades. Winnipeg further emphasized the importance and, consequently, continuation of bilateral dialogues and the improvement of reception of dialogue results in member churches, and it welcomed the "agreements with churches of the Anglican, Methodist, Moravian and Reformed traditions that member churches have entered into since the last Assembly" (53f.).

The reference to these agreements brings us to the process of implementation. I have argued above that the transition from theoretical reflection on ecumenical commitment to practical steps of such commitment came with the Lutheran participation, and it is indeed a prominent one, in bilateral theological conversations with other Christian World Communions. But even here the dialogues would remain on a theoretical level – and therefore not affect the course of church history – should there fail to be a reception of their results and their translation into changed church relationships. And this translation has happened: On the basis of the Leuenberg Concord of 1973 church fellowship has been declared between by now over 100 Lutheran, Reformed, and United Churches in Europe and Argentina; a similar agreement was concluded in 1997 between the Evangelical Lutheran Church in America (ELCA) and three Reformed/Presbyterian churches in the USA. Beyond this new fellowship between Reformation relatives, a remarkable achievement – remarkable because it included agreement on the episcopate in apostolic succession –was the declaration in 1995 of full communion between all four Anglican and, so far, six Lutheran churches in Northern Europe on the basis of the *Porvoo Common Statement* of 1992, soon followed in 2003 by a similar declaration between the ELCA and the Episcopal Church, USA and between the Anglican Church of Canada and the Evangelical Lutheran Church in Canada. In 1999 the ELCA and the Moravian Church in the United States celebrated their full communion, too. These declarations of full communion and other agreements on the way to this goal are, indeed, a test of the seriousness of the ecumenical commitment of the Lutheran communion and individual members of it. Lutherans might still do better ecumenically, but they are doing better than several others.

V. Conclusion

I have surveyed a rediscovery and recovery that has stirred up, moved forward, and changed our Lutheran family of churches during the last 100 years. It is a remarkable history that has led Lutheranism back to its origins and forward to a renewed ecclesiological and ecclesial self-understanding as a communion of churches that affirms and practices its ecumenical commitment in many ways. Lutheran and ecumenical veterans such as Eric Gritsch and myself have experienced and participated in this process of growing inner-Lutheran unity and Lutheran ecumenical involvement during the last 50 years. This has been and is an encouraging and transforming blessing of the One who accompanies, judges, justifies, and saves Lutherans and other Christians, too.

The Future of Lutheran-Roman Catholic Relations

John Reumann, *Lutheran Theological Seminary at Philadelphia*

Lutheran-Roman Catholic relations are broader than Lutheran-Roman Catholic dialogue. But given the doctrinal, confessional commitments of Lutherans and Catholics, relations depend to a considerable extent on dialogue results; these pave the way for all sorts of relationships. Because of the structure of the Roman Catholic Church, dialogue results must apply worldwide. But the relations will vary, from region to region, from country to country, especially within a large country like the United States.

To date, dialogue has been carried out internationally,[1] in the United States and Germany, though there are contributions from Scandinavia, Africa, Asia, and elsewhere. International statements have the advantage - but also the difficulty - of involving people from all over the world. Climactic to date has been the *Joint Declaration on the Doctrine of Justification* in 1999 (hereafter the "JD") by the Lutheran World Federation and Roman Catholic Church.[2] The ten volumes from the US dialogue, 1965-2005, have

---

[1] Reports include "The Gospel and the Church" (1972) from the Joint Lutheran-Roman Catholic Study Commission ("Malta Report"); "The Eucharist" (1978); "Ways to Community" (1980); "All Under the One Christ" (1980, 450th anniversary of the Augsburg Confession); "The Ministry of the Church" (1981), all reprinted in *Growth in Agreement*, Ecumenical Documents II, ed. Harding Meyer and Lukas Vischer (New York/ Ramsey: Paulist, Geneva: World Council of Churches, 1984) 167-275; "Martin Luther, Witness to Jesus Christ" (1983, 500th anniversary of Luther's birth); "Facing Unity" (1984); *Church and Justification: Understanding the Church in the Light of the Doctrine of Justification* (Geneva: Lutheran World Federation, 1994).

[2] German 1999; Eng. translation, Grand Rapids: Eerdmans, 2000.

usually included supporting essays.[3] Round XI began in 2005 on "The Hope of Eternal Life." The German Catholic, Lutheran, Reformed, and United Churches Working Group provided detailed studies on the anathemas of the Reformation Era.[4] The Bilateral Working Group of the German National Bishops' Conference and the Church Leadership of the United Evangelical Lutheran Church of Germany (to give the full but awkward title of instrument created by German Catholic Bishops and the (ELKD) has produced two studies: *Kirchengemeinschaft im Wort und*

---

[3] Lutherans and Catholics in Dialogue: I. The Status of the Nicene Creed as Dogma of the Church (1965); II. One Baptism for the Remission of Sins (1966); III. The Eucharist as Sacrifice (1967); IV.Eucharist and Ministry (1970); V. Papal Primacy and the Universal Church (1974); VI. Teaching Authority and Infallibility in the Church (1980); VII. Justification by Faith (1985); VIII. The One Mediator, the Saints, and Mary (1992); IX. Scripture and Tradition (1995); X. The Church as Koinonia of Salvation: Its Structures and Ministries (2005). Vols. I-IV were published by the Bishops' Committee for Ecumenical and Interreligious Affairs, Washington, D.C., and the U.S.A. National Committee of the Lutheran World Federation, New York. Vols. V-IX were published by Augsburg Fortress, Minneapolis. Vols. I-III have been reprinted together in one volume by Augsburg Fortress (no date), as has vol. IV in 1979. Vol. X was published by the United States Conference of Catholic Bishops. For recent assessments, see Ecumenical Trends 34,8 (Sept. 2005), 1-11/113-23, George H. Tavard, "Reflections on the Lutheran/Catholic Dialogue," and J. Reumann, "The Development of the Ecumenical Vision of Vatican II: A Lutheran's Reflections on the First 40 Years of Lutheran-Catholic Dialogue USA." Dr. Eric Gritsch took part in rounds V through IX and often served on the drafting committee for the Common Statement.

[4] German, *Lehrverurteilungen--- kirchentrennend?* ed. Karl Lehmann and Wolfhart Pannenberg (Freiburg im Breisgau: Herder, Göttingen: Vandenhoeck & Ruprecht): I. *Rechtfertigung, Sakramente und Amt im Zeitalter der Reformation und heute*, Dialog der Kirchen 4 (1986); *Materialien zu den Lehrverurteilung und zur Theologie der Rechtfertigung*, Dialog der Kirchen 5 (1989); *Materialien zur Lehre von den Sakramenten und vom kirchlichen Amt*, Dialog der Kirchen 6 (1990). Translation (partial) by Margaret Kohl, *The Condemnations of the Reformation Era. Do They Still Divide?* (Minneapolis: Fortress, 1990).

Sakrament (1984) and *Communio Sanctorum* (2000).[5] These volumes document what progress has been made in dialogue as the basis for better and fuller relationships in the future between Catholics and Lutherans.

How one assesses results and project expectations on future relations vary with one's vantage point. Some in official ecumenical positions tend to be optimistic. Others see little that is hopeful. What will happen in the future is difficult to predict. One could hardly have guessed in 1965 or 1985 what happened in 1999. The decades since the Second Vatican Council have been filled with both pleasant surprises and delays and disappointments. We have passed through periods of high hopes (in the late 1960's and early 1970's) and "a wintertime for ecumenism." It is worth sketching both a scenario of great optimism on what might occur and a worst-case scenario. The truth may prove to lie between these possibilities.

On the one hand, the JD may serve as a platform of agreement to which others besides Lutherans and Catholics can sign on. The two worldwide communities achieved, in 1999, and articulated "Common Understanding of Justification," as the heart of the gospel and so a "consensus in basic truths," a norm that also serves as criterion for all church life, and agreement on what we confess together in seven related areas, in the spectrum of Catholic and Lutheran views on each item. In the future, they (and other Christians) may build on this foundation to achieve new agreements in ecclesiology, ministry, authority, unity, and other topics. By 2017 (the 500th anniversary of Luther's posting the 95 Theses) the goal beckons of a joint declaration on the Eucharist.[6]

---

[5] Both published in German by Bonifactius Verlag, Paderborn. The 2000 volume was translated by Mark W. Jeske, Michael Root, and Daniel R. Smith as *Communio Sanctorum: The Church as Communion of Saints*, Unitas Books (Collegeville, Minn.: Liturgical Press, 2004).

[6] Proposed by ELCA Bishop Mark S. Hanson; deemed "very worthy of consideration" by Bishop Stephen Blaire (Stockton, Cal.), Chair of the Committee for Ecumenical and Interreligious Affairs, U. S. Conference of Catholic Bishops, in addressing the ELCA Churchwide Assembly, Aug.12, 2005 (ELCA News Service CWA 36-05-TW).

On the other hand, each church may react, in view of pressing concerns internally and with the world and by reconsiderations of the JD, so as to question some of the achievements claimed for the 1999 benchmark. Catholics may press for several criteria, not just Justification by Faith. The impossibility or at least the remoteness of "full communion" will become apparent; interchange of ministers will prove impossible. Eucharistic sharing will remain a chimera. The commitment ecumenically of Lutherans and Catholics will find more likely outcomes than deeper relations with each other. The 450th anniversary of the Book of Concord (1580-2030) may find us more in the spirit of Martin Chemnitz's critical *Examination of the Council of Trent* (1565-73) and Robert Bellarmine's *Disputationes* on controversies over the Christian faith with heretics of the time (1586-93).

Between these contrasting possibilities, which depend in part on what happens within each of the two churches, including commitment to ecumenism (and what kind of ecumenism), several landmarks point the way toward the future.

The JD of 1999 will continue as foundation, touchstone, and target for testing.[7] It has already been examined in the US dialogue with regard to Mary and the saints. The original intention of Round VIII was to test what had been said in the dialogue on justification in relation to Marian dogmas and piety. It soon became apparent, however, that a more important point of division in the sixteenth century and subsequently was "the saints" (definition of "holy ones"; their intercession for us, especially after their death; our invoking them for aid, in contrast to trust in Christ alone). The issues were resolved as not "church-dividing," the

---

[7] Joseph Ratzinger, "The Augsburg Concord on Justification: How Far Does it Take Us?" *International Journal for the Study of the Christian Church*, 2 (2002) 5-20. While the JD puts "new heart into people," it deals with a theme absent from contemporary consciousness, where the experience of sin is also missing. Four important points in the "justification debate" call for further consideration: the *simul justus et peccator* (JD 4.4; Annex to the JD 2.A); "cooperation" (4.7; Annex 2.D); "criterion" (JD #18; Annex 3, justification or Trinitarian *regula fidei*?); and authority to declare a "great consensus" with ecclesial standing (cf. Annex 4).

consequences sketched as "church-uniting." The German volume *Communio Sanctorum* tackled some of the same issues.

US Round X built on the JD in a different way. Its implications provided "fresh impetus and encouragement" to examine again ministries and church structures. That meant revisiting the work of US Round IV, *Eucharist and Ministry*, on the parish presbyter/priest/pastor (where the work in 1970 stood up rather well), but also with awareness of the recommendations in US Round VI on *Papal Primacy*. As a new lens on old problems, Round X employed koinonia, a term not prominent on either side in sixteenth-century controversy, though increasingly recognized as a theme in Vatican II and prominent in recent LWF self-understanding (as a "communion of communions"). Koinonia was employed to look at the "local church" (for Lutherans the parish, where the word is preached and the sacraments administered; for Catholics, the diocese) and at the ministry of presbyter and bishops (for Lutherans, following Jerome, the presbyter-bishop). While reactions are only beginning to be heard, it has been hailed[8] as an application of "differentiated consensus" in a move from salvation to koinonia, and "normative complementarity" in aspects of the local church. Praxis is given theological weight. Not unrelated, the International Lutheran/Roman Catholic dialogue has completed its treatment on The Apostolicity of the Church (2005).

US Round XI may seem simply to treat old divisions over Purgatory, Limbo,[9] and Indulgences (an issue raised afresh by the Jubilee Year in Rome in 2000), but behind these specifics loom basic themes in the Christian faith such as anthropology (the human condition and destiny), eschatology, resurrection, hope, and life.

---

[8] Minna Hietamäki, "Merely Partners in the Fishing Business? Theological Issues in *The Church as Koinonia of Salvation: Its Structures and Ministries*," *Ecumenical Trends* 35.1 (January, 2006) 1-7.

[9] The "abode of the fathers" (Old Testament saints, Socrates, Plato,) and "of the babies" (unbaptized), excluded from supernatural beatitude but also from suffering (Pius X, 1905, "they do not enjoy God, but they do not suffer either"). A theological conference at the Vatican, in December 2005, moved in the direction of dooming Limbo (New York *Times*, Dec. 27, 2005, p. A-1).

It remains to be seen whether the US dialogue will get to "decision-making in the church," a subject on the cutting edge that some favored for Round XI, or in the dwindling number of years between, say, 2010 and work needed for a new JD in 2017, must other tasks be tackled? Perhaps we will discuss the Eucharist again? Will international or German or other dialogues and studies take up still other topics?

Such steps through dialogue can lay a sound foundation for improved Roman Catholic/Lutheran relations. But even with good will, success in dialogue, and advances in cooperation, Lutherans and Catholics will not in the foreseeable future be anywhere near "full communion." In terms of the stages outlined in the ELCA Vision statement on ecumenism, we might be by 2017, at stage two or three of the five steps toward full communion.[10]

As noted in the "pessimistic scenario" above, Lutherans and Catholics are a long way from sharing in common ministries and interchange (within rules on each side) of ordained ministers for short or longer periods of service in parishes or agencies of the other church. In Lutheran-Episcopal relations the very name of the 1998 proposal, *Called to Common Mission*, was an attraction, far more than *Concordat of Agreement* in 1996.[11] In many quarters, "mission" (like "evangelization") has been an almost magical word to attract support. While the picture differs in different parts of the United States, there are probably far more joint projects involving Lutherans and Episcopalians or Lutherans and the United Church of Christ (fewer with Presbyterian and Reformed churches) than with Roman Catholics. It is hard to think of

---

[10] *Ecumenism: The Vision of the ELCA* (Minneapolis: Augsburg, 1994); in the stages that lead to full communion (pp. 27-28), already traversed by the ELCA with several dialogue partner churches, Lutherans and Catholics are well into stage two (bilateral dialogues), plus 3a on a worldwide level (agreement on doctrine, justification), but not "partial, mutual recognition of church and sacraments" (or does this exist for baptism, in part for the Lord's Supper? the ecclesial issue remains more complicated). Hardly as yet 3b, mutual "recognition of ordained ministers."

[11] Chicago: ELCA, A Lutheran Proposal for a Revision of the Concordat of Agreement, which was published in Ecumenical Proposals (1997).

examples where a Lutheran congregation and a Roman Catholic parish have teamed together for much beyond soup kitchens, building houses for the poor, or other projects for those in need, certainly none for regular worship or even education. Events during the Octave of Christian Unity may be an exception, but one hears less of these nowadays than ten to twenty years ago, in my experience. As both bodies painfully close parishes (and schools) in urban areas, there is little likelihood that dwindling congregations, either Lutheran or Catholic, will make common cause to survive. In the suburbs, where there is growth in membership, each aims at creating new, strong parishes, not cooperative ministries.

All this is in contrast to cases where for Lutherans interchange of pastors with partner churches in full communion is creating new patterns.[12] Pennsylvania is dotted with UCC and ELCA churches where the Lutheran minister may be rostered also in the United Church of Christ. A UCC pastor may, in a former "union church,"[13] cover for the Lutheran congregation at times. Anywhere in the country a new mission may be started by Lutherans and Episcopalians together, initially with one pastor, perhaps Episcopal, for the Lutheran group. Lutheran-Catholic examples of such shared ministries are years distant. Even if dialogue results now in print were fully accepted, the practical details and differences in clergy culture (Denk- and Praxis-strukturen?) would be enormous, quite apart from the question of married pastors on the Lutheran side and ordained women from 1970 on, for every form of ministry, including bishop. There are noteworthy examples of agreement between Catholic and Lutheran parishes, like the local version of the JD for two mega-churches in

---

[12] Cf. in this volume, for a fuller reading of the situation, Michael Root, "The Future of Lutheran Relations with the Protestant Traditions." The few examples here are needed to point up differences from the situation with Catholics.

[13] Stemming from colonial times, such congregations housed a Lutheran and an Evangelical Reformed congregation in the same building, served by the Lutheran pastor one week, the Reformed pastor the next Sunday. While for much of the twentieth century the strategy was to have one group move out and the other keep the old site, there is now much more a tendency to share ministries because the groups are in full communion.

Lansdale, Pa., Trinity Lutheran and St. Stanislaus, but nothing approaching what Lutherans know from full communion with some other mainline Protestant churches.

It may be asked what effect such mission and worship patterns and clergy interchange as are emerging under full communion will have on Lutheran identity in the ELCA, by the time steps toward full communion are possible with Catholics. One may think of the ELCA as a strategically placed "bridge church," bringing together a spectrum of kindred communions, or, perhaps, as finally having achieved acceptance by the old-line Protestant establishment that once dominated ecumenism and much of US life. Will Lutherans in these linkages be more influenced by "liberal Protestantism" more than by catholic orthodoxy?

Once, one could also have listed deaconesses or sisters as significant in ministry for Catholics and Lutherans. They still are in some parts of the world. But in the US, diminished numbers, with disproportionate percentages of older, retired persons, makes this once glorious area an unlikely place for ecumenical advance.

Most US churches, in recent years, have been caught up in financial, sexual, and other scandals. While each church realizes there is a beam in its own eye and that it ill behooves anyone to cast the first stone (even at tarnished Conservative Evangelical televangelists), the effect on Lutheran-Catholic relations may be especially deleterious. One wishes in the partner church for a bright and shining counterpart, the Catholic church with its pre-1960 strengths and Vatican II reforms, a sort of ecclesiastical Camelot, but reports of abuse, dioceses in bankruptcy, dissident voices in the church with whom so much has been invested in dialogue make the partner less attractive to many for closer relationships. Lutherans too fall short of being a shining city set on a hill. Opposition to the JD by theologians in Germany and America, in the replies of some LWF member churches during the "consensus project," and officially by bodies like the Lutheran Church-Missouri Synod raise questions about "unanimity."[14] More recently, especially in reaction to the ELCA "sexuality study," even with the compromises achieved at the 2005 Churchwide

---

[14] Cf. J. Ratzinger (note 7, above) p. 19.

Assembly, several large congregations in Pennsylvania have left the ELCA, in opposition. One whole synod (Metropolitan New York) has threatened to go its own way in support of gay/lesbian ordinations and relationships. Those leaving the ELCA may well agree with Roman Catholics on lesbian/gay issues, but their outlook will not move them toward Rome (as can happen with individuals) but to what they see as biblical, confessional Lutheranism.

If prospects are remote for relations between Lutheran and Catholic parishes akin to those with other churches where the ELCA has full communion, what about other types of ministry, often quite specialized and similarly developed in each of our churches?

One example of great potential exists in social ministry organizations. As is well-known, Lutherans and Catholics in the United States have the two largest networks of hospitals, health-care facilities, homes for the elderly and disadvantaged youth, retirement communities, etc. They share common problems and often common support from government programs. US dialogues have sometimes lifted up such institutions as part of our ecumenical potential.[15] But these agencies, affiliated with the church to varying degrees, also face difficulties in that church teaching differs in matters like birth control, abortion, and physician-assisted suicide.[16] In some of these matters, "feminist" positions are a fixed factor among Lutherans (the sanctity of the Supreme Court decision on Roe vs. Wade); the denomination is not likely to move closer to classic and current Catholic positions (though, it may be added, some Catholics find the ELCA, mainline Protestant views here attractive).

---

[15] E.g., *The Church as Koinonia of Salvation* (note 3, above) p. 55, #122, point 4.

[16] The Pew Research Center for the People and the Press reported in November 2005, "By two to one (61 percent to 30 percent), white evangelical Protestants opposed physician-assisted suicide laws; by nearly identical margins, white mainline Protestants and seculars approve such laws. Catholics, on balance, oppose such laws (by 50 percent to 40 percent)" (New York *Times*, Feb. 11, 2006, p. A-12).

Campus ministries in colleges and universities of two churches that prize education, military and hospital chaplaincies, and disaster relief are areas where some evidence exists of Catholic-Lutheran cooperation, but chiefly anecdotal and not always formalized. What about involvement of a representative or observer from the other church in studies being undertaken by a church? The ELCA had Catholic input in its Study of Ministry (1988-93), but not in treating sexuality (2001-2005, with more to come). But the sheer number of ecumenical partners now available, whether at the full-communion stage or with whom a church is in dialogue, can be overwhelming; costs and logistics are against such serious counsel and admonition as a reality, though ecumenism in principle favors it. Could completed statements be shared with the other church(es) for reaction, or does this impinge in the integrity and independence of the church making the study? Or are studies under the World Council of Churches, Faith and Order, or National Council of Churches any better?

A special area of study deserving comment has to do with biblical scholarship, where Lutheran-Catholic work together has often been basic in the progress of dialogues. It has been sparked by the commonality of approach under historical/literary criticism (for Catholics, since *Divino Afflante Spiritu*, the encyclical of Pius XII in 1943). But it is widely apparent that exegetical methods and hermeneutics are today, among many in academia, fluid or in chaos. So there have been efforts to retreat in a "post-modern age" to pre-critical, often patristic treatment. A particular aspect, not yet much reflected in ecumenism, is the onslaught against "the 'Lutheran' Paul." (Actually, Reformed, Anglican, and Roman Catholic scholars often hold the same views attributed to a Lutheran hijacking of the apostle.) Since the attack may be said to have started with E. P. Sanders' effort to redress caricatures of Judaism in the 19th century,[17] Luther was the obvious poster boy

---

[17] *Paul and Palestinian Judaism* (Philadelphia: Fortress, 1977) 1-11, 33-59, 434-42, cf. 523-42, on the history of scholarship. The Law (Torah) is often the focus. In many scholars, Sanders sees as "the real grounds for the evaluation of Judaism" that "it is not Lutheranism" (53). Cf. for reflection in papers in the US dialogue, Round VII, J. Reumann, with responses by J. A. Fitzmyer and J.D. Quinn, *"Righteousness" in the New Testament: "Justification" in the United States Lutheran-Roman*

and target, given his unfortunate anti-Semitic statements late in his career. The "new look" in Pauline studies that resulted is often a repudiation of Reformation (and other classical) theological understandings of Paul.[18] In some quarters, even to mention "justification," let alone champion it, is regarded as an outmoded prejudice. Neither Lutherans nor Catholics in the US have been much involved in these battles over Pauline theology,[19] but they have genuine interests in some of the issues at stake.[20] Left to the trends in academia, foundational materials worked out in our dialogues could go by the board.

For 2017 hope has been expressed for a JD on the Eucharist, with the goal of shared fellowship at celebrations at the Lord's Supper. For many, this has been the goal of dialogue and in ecclesial relations. It reflects a view that eating and drinking the Body and Blood together is the end result of ecumenism, rather than a means to achieve that end.[21] Joseph Cardinal Ratzinger

---

Catholic Dialogue Philadelphia: Fortress and New Y/Ramsey: Paulist, 1982) 217-223, 408. Cf. JD 4.5 "Law and Gospel."

[18] Stressed by, among others, J.D.G. Dunn in *Romans 1-8* Word Biblical Commentary 38A (Dallas, Texas: Word, 1988) "The New Perspective on Paul," "lxiii-lxxii. Dunn's results may be seen in more popular terms in his book with Alan M. Suggate, *The Justice of God: A Fresh Look at the Old Doctrine of Justification* (Grand Rapids: Eerdmanns,1994)

[19] The best account arguing that Luther and the Reformation may not have been entirely wrong is Stephen Westerholm *Perspectives Old and New on Paul: The 'Lutheran' Paul and His Critics* (Grand Rapids: Eerdmans, 2004). The most detailed work in English on Sanders' proposal about "covenantal nomism" comes in the two volumes edited by D.A. Carson, Peter T. O'Brien, and Mark A. Seifrid (Tubingen: Mohr Siebeck, Grand Rapids: Baker Academic), *Justification and Variegated Nomism,* Vol. 1, *The Complexities of Second Temple Judaism* (2001), and Vol. 2, *The Paradoxes of Paul* (2004).

[20] A subset in the debate is the proposal by many (Richard Hays, Morna Hooker, among others) always to render *pistis Christou* as "Christ's faith" rather than "faith in Christ" (so now NRSV margin at Gal 2: 16 b; Rom. 3:22, 26). Here Dunn has resolutely battled for the traditional objective genitive, faith in Christ. Cf. JD 4.3.

[21] Such was the traditional position of Lutherans. A shift came in the US Lutheran-Episcopal Dialogue, Round 1, with the position that where agreement in the Gospel exists, that is enough to begin Eucharistic

spoke of such "longing for fellowship with respect to the sacramental center of church life" as "in itself a good thing."[22] But he went on, "It should, however, give us grounds for concern if it appears to reduce our entire consciousness of the faith to the celebration of communion," the Eucharist "atrophied into a kind of communal act of socialization" or "ritual representation of unity." Far better might be, he said, the task of "translating the past"--- like Justification by Faith--- "into modern language so as to make it intelligible to us once again" (p. 7). In a more recent response to the LWF-Catholic dialogue,[23] Benedict XVI expressed the hope that "issues will not only be placed in the context of 'institutional' questions, but will take into account the true source of all ministry in the Church," for "the mission of the Church is to witness to the truth of Jesus Christ." "Word and witness go together."

One way to mark 2017 might be joint Lutheran-Catholic studies on what theologically and biblically they hold in common, done even in popular terms for a wide audience, at times in the face of prevailing cultures. For example, with regard to "The Hope of Eternal Life," assertions on eschatology might be made in opposition to pervasive chiliasm in American religion, the Rapture, and phenomena like the "Left Behind" novels. Or on death and resurrection, our hope in Christ, in contrast with New Age and other alternatives like reincarnation or hopelessness.

All this would accord with the key adjective in a famous proposal and definition of Lutheranism as "a theological movement within the church catholic."[24] "Theological" involves

---

sharing, which becomes a means to further agreement. See *Lutheran-Episcopal Dialogue: A Progress Report* (Cincinnati: Forward Movement Publications, An FM Maxi Book, 1973), especially the essay by Robert W. Jenson, originally "Dann Dies is Gnug."

[22] Ratzinger (note 7, above)

[23] Pope's Address to President of Lutheran World Federation, "We Are All Aware That Our Fraternal Dialogue Is Challenged," Nov. 7, 2005 (ZEO5110703).

[24] Eric W. Gritsch and Robert W. Jenson. *Lutheranism: The Theological Movement and Its Confessional Writings* (Philadelphia: Fortress, 1976) 207, cf. vii "we try to explicate the one article of faith in the promoting of

what we believe and how we live. "Movement" was an attractive, even dynamic term, for placing Lutherans within the catholic church, though it probably had the effect of discounting ecclesiology. The Augsburg Confession was already using the formula, "The churches among us teach..." (Article I.1). "Movement" abetted the notion that Lutherans have no ecclesiology except for the local Gemeinde. The whole phrase might today be expanded: a theological church for reform and unity within all Christendom, catholic, evangelical (including Conservative Evangelicals), and pentecoastal, thus reflecting today's situation where, in terms of growth and where power often is, far more than even Roman Catholicism and mainline Protestantism needs to be involved.

---

which the Lutheran movement exists: justification by faith apart from the works of law."

The Future of Lutheran Relations with the Protestant Traditions

Michael Root, *Lutheran Theological Southern Seminary, Columbia, SC*

The last fifty years have seen a marked change in the relation of the Lutheran churches to the range of Protestant traditions. In 1956, few Lutheran churches were in altar and pulpit fellowship, as the term would have been then, with any non-Lutheran church. Whether many Lutheran churches were even in fellowship with each other was an open question.[1] Today, most Lutheran churches in Europe and North America are in varying degrees of communion with a range of Protestant churches with roots in the magisterial Reformation: Reformed, Anglican, Methodist.[2] This change came about with far less internal controversy than might have been expected. While just what the future holds in store for the complex network of ecumenical relations that has ensued cannot be predicted, the trends in the present situation and the challenges these trends will create for the future can be described

---

[1] On the history of the discussion of altar and fellowship within the Lutheran World Federation, see Michael Root, "Affirming the Communion: Ecclesiological Reflection in the LWF," in *From Federation to Communion: The History of the Lutheran World Federation*, ed. J. H. Schjørring, Prasanna Kumari, and Norman A. Hjelm (Minneapolis: Fortress Press, 1997), 216-47.

[2] The focus of this essay will be on Lutheran relations with these churches whose history is much like that of Lutheranism. How best to label them (mainstream, mainline, old-line) can be a touchy question. They will here simply be called Protestant. In this essay, the Anglican churches will be treated for the most part as Protestant. Some Anglicans insist that they are not Protestant, while others insist with equal vehemence that they are.

and analyzed. Unfortunately, the two trends that will be discussed here present Lutherans with a complex situation, in which we seem to be pulled in differing directions.

I. The Ecumenism of Denominational Communion

The changes of the last fifty years were not simply the creation of doctrinal dialogue, but were rooted in deep changes in the social dynamics of Protestantism. As Robert Wuthnow has demonstrated, during the decades following World War II the boundaries between American Protestant denominations became increasingly porous. While in 1955 only 1 in 25 Americans had switched denominations, in 1985 that figure was 1 in 3. Surveys show that denominational identity is of small importance to most American Protestants and few American Protestants have strongly negative feelings about other Protestant denominations. Higher levels of education (and thus, probably, greater social influence) correlate with a greater tendency to switch denominations.[3] Studies in Germany have shown that Protestant parishioners identify with the local parish and with the national Evangelical Church in Germany much more than with the confessionally specific regional *Landeskirche.*[4] The greater mobility of post-war Germany led to "moving-van ecumenism." If one moved from Lutheran Hamburg to Bremen, where the regional Protestant church was United with a strong Reformed background, one shifted confessional allegiance simply by registering one's address and writing the generic *evangelisch* on the line for religion. The situation among Protestant traditions today can be described as one of friendly division with permeable borders.[5]

Official changes in the relations among Protestant churches were a part of this total process, both cause and effect. Barriers to intercommunion or, in contemporary terms, Eucharistic hospitality

---

[3] The data in this and the preceding sentences all comes from Robert Wuthnow, *The Restructuring of American Religion: Society and Faith Since World War II* (Princeton: Princeton University Press, 1988), 88-91.

[4]. Wolfgang Huber, *Kirche*, 2nd ed. (Munich: Chr. Kaiser, 1988), 25.

[5] Michael Root, "The Unity of the Church and the Reality of the Denominations," Modern Theology 9 (1993): 385-401.

(i.e., inviting communicants of another church to receive the Eucharist in celebrations within one's own church), have been removed in most Protestant churches.[6] Many of the traditional doctrinal barriers that separated various Protestant traditions came to seem less significant not only to the laity, but also clergy and theologians. Dialogue after dialogue demonstrated that, with the exception of the question of episcopacy, no church-dividing doctrinal differences exist among the Lutheran, Reformed, Anglican, and Methodist churches. Among these churches, we have reached the "end of the dialogue."[7] Further ecumenical dialogue is pointless, since the issues have been resolved.

In the 1950s and 1960s, one could easily imagine that in the US and other countries with a similar diversity of denominations these changes would have led to corporate merger, the creation of a single, very large mainstream Protestant body. The Church of South India, inaugurated in 1948, was for many the great model to be emulated. The Consultation on Church Union, begun in the US in 1962 with the participation of Episcopal, Methodist, Presbyterian, and United churches, had such a merger as its initial goal and in 1970 it presented a bold plan for the creation of a Church of Christ Uniting. Like many other similar proposals for Protestant merger across the lines of differing traditions, however, this proposal failed. While theological issues (especially episcopacy) played a role in such failure, the lack of enthusiasm for the creation of a large denominational body also was evident. What has come to pass instead of corporate merger is a loosely organized system of denominational communion, in which the

---

[6] For a good example of the debate over intercommunion in one church (the Church of England), see Archbishops' Commission on Intercommunion, *Intercommunion Today* (London: Church Information Office, 1968).

[7] Harding Meyer, "To Serve Christian Unity: Ecumenical Commitment in the LWF," in *From Federation to Communion: The History of the Lutheran World Federation*, ed. Jens Holger Schjørring, Norman A. Hjelm, and Prasanna Kumari (Minneapolis: Fortress Press, 1997), 278.

churches remain fully autonomous while practicing varying degrees of fellowship with other Protestant bodies.[8]

Lutherans, with a heritage of ecumenical reticence and of insistence on detailed doctrinal agreement as a precondition for fellowship, could not participate in this movement toward denominational communion without settling the traditional dogmatic issues and developing a theological model of church fellowship. In both respects, the 1973 Leuenberg Agreement among Lutheran, Reformed, and United churches on the European continent was decisive.[9] On the one hand, on the basis of extensive theological work on the question of Christ's presence in the Lord's Supper, the Agreement adopted much of the solution already present in the Wittenberg Concord of 1536 that brought Strasbourg and other Upper German cities into the Lutheran fold by affirming the reception of Christ's body and blood "with" the bread and wine by all recipients, worthy and unworthy alike (paras. 15, 18). On the other hand, the signatory churches stated that "agreement in the right teaching of the gospel and in the right administration of the sacraments is the necessary and sufficient prerequisite for the true unity of the Church" (para. 2). This agreement "leaves intact the binding force of the confessions within the participating churches. It is not to be regarded as a new confession of faith" (para. 37). The specific Lutheran, Reformed, and United doctrines and identities of the churches are thus not touched (although the mutual doctrinal condemnations found in the respective confessions are declared non-applicable to the present churches; para. 32). No immediate organizational consequences follow from the agreement (the section on "organizational consequences, paras. 42-45, focuses on what does not need to happen as a result of the Agreement). The churches do commit themselves to "realizing church fellowship" in common

---

[8] Michael Root, "A Striking Convergence in American Ecumenism," *Origins* 26 (1996): 60-64.

[9] An official English translation of the text can be found in *Agreement Between Reformation Churches in Europe (Leuenberg Agreement). Trilingual Edition with an Introduction* (Frankfurt a.M.: Verlag Otto Lembeck, 1993). References are included above by paragraph number.

witness and service (paras. 35-36), but no structure of common governance is created.

The Leuenberg approach was taken up by the Lutheran World Federation under the slogan "unity in reconciled diversity."[10] Significant variations exist, however, in how this approach is elaborated. At its 1984 Assembly in Budapest, the LWF adopted "The Unity We Seek," a statement of the ecumenical goal as the LWF understands it. In many ways, what it describes resembles the sort of fellowship achieved by the Leuenberg Agreement, but it adds as a characteristic of such fellowship: "It is a committed fellowship, able to make common decisions and to act in common."[11] While the Leuenberg Agreement called for common witness and service, it created no structure for common decision-making and action. A position somewhere between Leuenberg and the LWF Budapest statement was sketched by the international Lutheran-Anglican Joint Working Group, meeting in Cold Ash, England, in 1983. It described the goal of Anglican-Lutheran dialogue as full communion, which is defined in ways that closely resemble the fellowship achieved by the Leuenberg Agreement. "By full communion we here understand a relationship between two distinct churches or communions. Each maintains its own autonomy and recognizes the catholicity and apostolicity of the other." They are to be "interdependent while remaining autonomous." It adds, however: "It is also a necessary addition and complement that there should be recognized organs of regular consultation and communication, including episcopal collegiality, to express and strengthen the fellowship and enable common witness, life and service" On the one hand, it speaks only of organs of consultation, not of any capacity for common decision-making, even though this consultation should lead to "an exchange and a commitment to one another in respect of major decisions on

---

[10] On this development, see especially Meyer, "To Serve Christian Unity: Ecumenical Commitment in the LWF".

[11] Lutheran World Federation, Seventh Assembly, "The Unity We Seek," Assembly Statement in *Budapest 1984: In Christ--Hope for the World*, Proceedings of the Seventh Assembly, Lutheran World Federation, LWF Report, no. 19 (Geneva, 1985), 175.

questions of faith, order, and morals."[12] On the other hand, it introduces, without defining, the phrase "episcopal collegiality." What does this imply about commonly exercised governance?

The variations in the Budapest and Cold Ash statements point to a significant ambiguity in Lutheran ecumenical theology. Is communion adequately realized in an unstructured fellowship, without any forms of common decision-making, not to mention common governance, or is some sort of structure of consultation and joint decision-making on matters of common importance essential to "committed fellowship" in the present historical situation?[13] Lutheran theologians and churches differ on this question. The Church Council of the United Evangelical-Lutheran Church in Germany adopted in 2003 a statement on "Ecumenism According to the Evangelical-Lutheran Understanding," in which the essential unity of the church is defined as strictly invisible. Between churches which share this invisible unity, there exist "possibilities of cooperation, structural commonality [*strukturellen Gemeinsamkeit*], and common fulfillment of the church's mission" which should be taken up wherever strong grounds do not exist not to do so.[14] Common decision-making seems strictly optional. The Evangelical Lutheran Church in America, however, in its policy statement "Ecumenism: The Vision of the Evangelical Lutheran Church in America," explicitly lists "a means of common decision making on critical common issues of faith and

---

[12] All quotations from Cold Ash can be found in Sven Oppegaard and Gregory Cameron, eds., *Anglican-Lutheran Agreements: Regional and International Agreements 1972-2002*, LWF Documentation, 49 (Geneva: Lutheran World Federation, 2004), 76-77.

[13] I have discussed this ambiguity in the model of "unity as reconciled diversity" in Michael Root, "'Reconciled Diversity' and the Visible Unity of the Church," in *Community-Unity-Communion: Essays in Honour of Mary Tanner*, ed. Colin Podmore (London: Church House Publishing, 1998), 237-51, and Michael Root, "Once More on the Unity We Seek: Testing Ecumenical Models," in *The Unity We Have and the Unity We Seek: Ecumenical Prospects for the Third Millennium* (London: T & T Clark, 2003), 167-77.

[14] Kirchenleitung der VELKD, *Ökumene nach evangelisch-lutherischen Verständnis*, Texte aus der VELKD (123) (Hanover: Lutherisches Kirchenamt der VELKD, 2004), 10.

life" as one of the characteristics of the full communion it seeks with other churches.[15]

These theological differences, however, are for the most part theoretical. None of the various communion agreements the Lutheran churches have entered into, full and otherwise, actually includes effective structures of common decision making. Various sorts of "joint commissions" are created by such agreements to facilitate the new relation,[16] but such commissions have led to little that might be called joint decision making or indeed to a common life that touches more than the margins of the church's existence. The obvious example of a matter of importance faced together by the various churches is the debate over sexuality. The question of blessing same-sex unions and permitting partnered homosexual persons to serve in ordained ministry is the same in the various Protestant churches. And yet, each church carries on its own debate and decision making in isolation from the others. When a matter is truly important, autonomy trumps ecumenical relations. (To speak from personal experience, as a member of the Board for the Division for Ministry of the ELCA, I complained repeatedly that the ELCA's Task Force for Studies of Sexuality had no ecumenical participation; this complaint had no effect.) Cooperation between churches in communion does occur, but it tends to occur at points where no church has the resources to go it alone. Separation remains the dominant fact; the hard core of division is not touched.

If the unfriendly division of the past expressed itself in polemics, the friendly separation of the present is expressed in concerns for denominational identity. It is perhaps not accidental that, following the ecumenical actions taken at the end of the 1990s (the various full communion agreements, the *Joint Declaration on the Doctrine of Justification*), American Lutheranism has seen an at least small swing toward a renewed emphasis on Lutheran

---

[15] *Ecumenism: The Vision of the ELCA*, English text with Spanish, German, and French translations (Minneapolis: Augsburg, 1994), 29.

[16] See, e.g., Evangelical Lutheran Church in America, *Called to Common Mission: A Lutheran Proposal for a Revision of the Concordat of Agreement* (Chicago: Evangelical Lutheran Church in America, 1999), para. 23.

identity. The publishing house of the church began a series of books entitled "Lutheran Voices" with a volume entitled "Reclaiming the 'L' Word: Renewing the Church from its Lutheran Core." Effective mission requires knowing who we are and that means knowing who we are as Lutherans.[17] With surprising speed, one is back in the context in which only Lutherans rightly grasp the meaning of grace.[18] In a situation of friendly division, the market pressures toward finding one's niche without overly narrowing one's appeal make identity an attractive concern.

Only if one has the sort of exceedingly reduced ecumenical expectation embodied in the German Lutheran statement on "Ecumenism according to the Evangelical-Lutheran Understanding" referred to above (and perhaps not even then) could one see these communion agreements, with their marginal impact on the lives of the churches, as the embodiment of the ecumenical goal. They are more describable as forms of status-quo-ecumenism, a redescription of friendly division as a form of unity.[19] An underlying difficulty is that the obvious alternative to denominational communion is corporate merger. The corporate mergers that occurred in the US within the various traditions over the last fifty years (to form the United Methodist Church, the Presbyterian Church USA, the ELCA) all proved in their varying ways difficult and did not lead to any manifest surge in mission. A major challenge for Lutheran ecumenism in its relations with Protestant churches over the next decades will be how to live into the truly common life to which these agreements should lead, but have not. The challenge is both to mind and to will. We need a better

---

[17] Kelly A. Fryer, *Reclaiming the 'L' Word: Renewing the Church from Its Lutheran Core* (Minneapolis: Augsburg Fortress, 2003), 25.

[18] See the "five principles" that come together to constitute the uniquely Lutheran, Fryer, *Reclaiming the 'L' Word*, 35.

[19] See the sharp critique of Lukas Vischer, "Is This Really 'The Unity We Seek?': Comments on the Statement on 'The Unity of the Church as Koinonia: Gift and Calling' Adopted by the WCC Assembly in Canberra," *Ecumenical Review* 44 (1992): 467-78 and Carl E. Braaten and Robert W. Jenson, eds., *In One Body Through the Cross: The Princeton Proposal for Christian Unity* (Grand Rapids: Eerdmans, 2003).

theological model of what we are trying achieve ecumenically, but also the sheer will to risk our denominational traditions.

II. Protestantism and Catholic Traditions

When Lutheran churches have entered into dialogue with mainstream Protestant churches on the classical issues of Reformation theology - justification and sanctification, the Lord's Supper, predestination and election - these differences have almost always proven surmountable. The sharp Lutheran-Reformed debates over these topics have become matters of the past. Continuing Lutheran-Reformed differences reappear when the discussion widens to include Catholics (or the more Catholic elements of the Anglican tradition). The difference was visible in the contrasting reactions to the Vatican declaration of an indulgence for the millennial jubilee in 2000. One might have thought that Lutheran reaction would have been more pointed, since the Lutheran churches had just signed with the Vatican the *Joint Declaration on the Doctrine of Justification* and the Lutheran Reformation began as a protest against an indulgence campaign. Nevertheless, while Lutheran bodies endured the indulgence proclamation as a minor event, Reformed reactions were quite sharp. The Reformed representative on the commission set up by the Vatican to make the Jubilee a more ecumenical event was finally withdrawn over this concern. That the indulgence was proclaimed and expounded in strikingly evangelical ways was simply ignored by the Reformed.[20]

Similarly, the World Alliance of Reformed Churches showed little interest in participating in the process that led to the *Joint Declaration on the Doctrine of Justification*. Following the signing of the JDDJ, a consultation was held in Columbus, Ohio, in November, 2001, among representatives of the Vatican, the LWF, the World Alliance of Reformed Churches, and the World Methodist Council on whether the Methodist or Reformed bodies would be interested in pursuing the possibility of some form of

---

[20] On the varying reactions to the Jubilee indulgence, see Michael Root, "The Indulgence Controversy, Again," *First Things* no. 118 (December 2001): 24-26.

affirmation of the JDDJ. While the Methodists were interested and have now officially endorsed the JDDJ, the Reformed were decidedly cool.[21]

Similarly, Reformed reactions to the ecumenical encyclical of John Paul II, *Ut unum sint,* were on the whole far less welcoming than those from Lutheran corners.[22]

Lukas Vischer, for many years director of the Faith and Order Commission of the World Council of Churches and a leading Reformed ecumenist, has complained about the "priority" given to the dialogue with the Roman Catholic Church by Lutherans.[23] The differing attitudes toward the JDDJ show that there is certainly a difference in the ecumenical priority the two traditions give to Catholic relations. This difference is not accidental, but rooted in much deeper differences in attitudes toward the Reformation and the pre-Reformation heritage of Western Christianity. Already in the Reformation period, Reformed leaders complained about the Lutheran insistence that the differences between them were church-dividing. The Reformed advocated a common Reformation heritage, which the Lutherans doubted. While the Reformed could appear irenical, the Lutherans were put in the position of stubborn spoilers.[24] The present ecumenical situation can appear similar,

---

[21] See the communique from the 2001 consultation in Joint Working Group between the Lutheran World Federation and the World Alliance of Reformed Churches, *Called to Communion and Common Witness (Report: 1999-2001)* (Geneva: Lutheran World Federation, 2002), 45-48.

[22] See the discussion of Lutheran and Reformed responses in Edward Idris Cardinal Cassidy, *"Ut Unum Sint* in Ecumenical Perspective," in *Church Unity and the Papal Office: An Ecumenical Dialogue on John Paul II's Encyclical Ut Unum Sint (That All May Be One),* ed. Carl E. Braaten and Robert W. Jenson (Grand Rapids, MI: Eerdmans, 2001), 19-24.

[23] Lukas Vischer, "A History of the [Leuenberg] Agreement," in *Rowing in One Boat: A Common Reflection on Lutheran-Reformed Relations Worldwide,* ed. Lukas Vischer (Geneva: Centre International Réformé, 1999), 20.

[24] Wilhelm Kahle, "Fragen lutherischer Einheit von der Reformation bis zum Ende des 18. Jahrhunderts," in *Wege zur Einheit der Kirche im Luthertum,* Die Lutherische Kirche, Geschichte und Gestalten, vol. 1 (Gütersloh: Gerd Mohn, 1976), 17-18.

with the Reformed wishing a common, lower priority (and more negative) approach to Catholicism, with the Lutherans more interested in their own specific, higher priority (and more positive) approach. While generalizations are hazardous, it would appear that the Reformed tradition has tended to see the break with Rome and with the medieval past as more decisive, more irreparable, and as less tragic than does much of the Lutheran tradition.

Since communion with the Catholic Church for both Lutherans and Reformed is, as "real, but imperfect," quite limited, this difference often remains implicit. It becomes more open in relations with Anglicans. The single issue in this relation, episcopacy, is also an issue in relations with Catholics and Orthodox, which gives relations with Anglicans a greater weight than they might have on their own. During the 1990s, Lutheran churches in the US, Canada, the Nordic countries (with the exception of Denmark), and the Baltic countries (with the exception of Latvia) all entered into full communion agreements with Anglican churches that involved the Lutheran church adopting as one element of communion the interconsecration of bishops (i.e., a shared laying-on-of-hands on bishops) and the acceptance of a succession of episcopal consecrations as one sign of the continuity of the church in apostolic ministry.[25] As was often argued at the time, these proposals realized a preference for "the traditional polity" stated in the Lutheran Confessions, but historically rarely fulfilled outside the Nordic countries. The proposals were not ecumenically isolated, but fit into a wider pattern exemplified by the Ministry section of *Baptism, Eucharist and Ministry*.

Reformed churches have been hesitant to join in any such move and have on occasion been critical of their Lutheran colleagues for having made them.[26] The rejection of episcopacy is

---

[25] These agreements are surveyed in Michael Root, "Porvoo in the Context of the Worldwide Anglican-Lutheran Dialogue," in *Apostolicity and Unity: Essays on the Porvoo Common Statement*, ed. Ola Tjørhom (Grand Rapids: Eerdmans, 2002), 15-33.

[26] In an official publication of the World Alliance of Reformed Churches, Irish Reformed theologian and WARC staff member Páraic Réamonn reprimands the Lutherans who produced the report of the Anglican-

much more deeply ingrained in Reformed theology and culture.[27] Issues of ministry and polity were decisive in the failure of the Reformation in the British Isles to achieve unity, as can be seen in the names of the churches that came out of that Reformation: Episcopal, Presbyterian, Congregational. These identities were exported to the lands of the British Empire, including the United States. While Reformed churches on the Indian subcontinent have entered episcopally structured United churches and the United Reformed Church in the United Kingdom was willing to accept episcopacy within the Covenanting for Unity proposals (rejected by the General Synod of the Church of England in 1982),[28] Reformed churches have often balked at church unity proposals that included the office of bishop. Decades of work within the Consultation on Church Union (COCU) within the United States ultimately proved incapable of surmounting the differences over ministry between the Presbyterian and Episcopal churches.[29]

This difference over ministry and especially episcopacy has created the complex series of partially overlapping agreements of communion in contemporary Europe and America. The ELCA is in full communion with the Episcopal Church, three Reformed churches, and the Moravian Church, but the Episcopal and Reformed churches are only in limited communion through Churches Uniting in Christ, the successor organization to COCU.

Lutheran International Working Group report for violating "the Lutheran and Reformed understanding" of unity. Páraic Réamonn, "Whose Visible Unity?" *WARC Update* 13 (May 2003), Http://www.warc.ch/update/up132/ 06.html.

[27] David Ferguson describes the interweaving of Presbyterianism and Scottish national identity, David Ferguson, "Porvoo and the Church of Scotland," in *Leuenberg, Meissen, and Porvoo: Consultation Between the Churches of the Leuenberg Church Fellowship and the Churches Involved in the Meissen Agreement and the Porvoo Agreement*, ed. Wilhelm Hüffmeier and Colin Podmore, Leuenberger Texte, 4 (Frankfurt: Verlag Lembeck, 1996), 172-77.

[28] Churches' Council for Covenanting, *Towards Visible Unity: Proposals for a Covenant* (London: Churches' Council for Covenanting, 1980).

[29] This history is recounted in Daniell C. Hamby, "The Murmur of a Dove's Song: A Brief History of the Consultation on Church Union," *Mid-Stream* 37 (1998): 387-406.

In Europe, the Norwegian, Estonian, and Lithuanian Lutheran churches are in full communion both with the Anglican churches of the British Isles through the Porvoo Common Statement and with the Reformed, United, and Methodist churches of Europe through Leuenberg. The other Nordic Lutherans churches are in communion with the Anglicans, but have not entered the Leuenberg Church Fellowship. Almost all continental Lutheran churches are in Leuenberg, but only the French and German Lutherans have a less-than-full communion agreement with the Anglicans.

This situation is an anomaly, as has been widely noted.[30] Communion should be a transitive relation: if church A is in communion with church B and if church B is in communion with church C, then churches A and C should also be in communion. Something is amiss when such relations do not hold. At most, such intransitivity can be a passing anomaly which we bear temporarily for the sake of a larger unity to come.[31]

The source of this anomaly should be clearly noted, however. Many Lutheran churches share in a common Reformation heritage that allows them to enter into full communion with Reformed, Methodist, and other Protestant churches. At the same time, these Lutheran churches are, for the sake of unity, interested in and open to Catholic elements (both theoretically, e.g., in a greater willingness to discuss what an acceptable papacy might look like, and practically, in a greater willingness to adopt a succession of episcopal consecrations as a sign of unity) than are, in particular, most Reformed churches. The Lutheran churches are thus capable of playing a unique ecumenical role: defined by the Reformation emphasis on justification by grace through faith for the sake of Jesus Christ in a way not typical of Anglicans or Methodists, but open to the Catholic and pre-Reformation tradition in ways not typical of the Reformed or other Protestant traditions. Ecumenical-

---

[30] For example, see Lambeth Conference, *The Official Report of the Lambeth Conference 1998: Transformation and Renewal, July 18–August 9 1998, Lambeth Palace; Canterbury, England* (Harrisburg: Morehouse Publishing, 1998), 221.

[31] For the language of transitivity and bearable anomalies, see Oppegaard and Cameron, *Anglican-Lutheran Agreements*, 310-11, 315-18.

ly, the presence of a church to play such a role must be seen as positive.

III. The Specific Ecumenical Role of Lutheranism

The two previous sections of this essay embody an ecumenical quandary for Lutherans. The present system of denominational communion is radically inadequate as a form of church unity. It cannot represent the ecumenical goal. But would the pursuit of a closer communion with other Protestant churches undercut the specific ecumenical role that Lutheranism has played with the more "catholic" Anglican and Roman traditions? How do we pursue greater unity where unity is possible (which, for the moment, is with other Protestant churches), while not forming a "Protestant bloc" that would make future unity with Catholics and Orthodox more difficult?

The recent ecumenical actions and outlook of the German Lutherans, still the largest national body of Lutherans in the world, intensify these concerns. The Lutheran *Landeskirchen* in Germany are not only within the Leuenberg Church Fellowship, but also within the much closer fellowship of the Evangelical Church in Germany, which defines itself as a church which is a fellowship or communion [*Gemeinschaft*] of Lutheran, United, and Reformed churches.[32] While the authority to make decisions about ecumenical relations resides with the *Landeskirchen*, ecumenical discussions with Anglicans are carried out by the EKD as a whole. Unlike the discussions of the 1990s in Northern Europe, Canada, and the US, the German discussions were not able to resolve differences over episcopacy and thus led in the Meissen Agreement only to a limited communion, closely resembling the 1982 interim fellowship between the Episcopal Church USA and the predecessor bodies of the ELCA.[33] Similarly, the French Lutheran churches also exist in close fellowship with their

---

[32] Constitution of the EKD, Article 1.1. http://www.ekd.de/EKD-Texte/grundordnung_1948_verfassung1.html.

[33] *The Meissen Agreement: Texts*, Council for Christian Unity Occasional Paper, no. 2 (London: Council for Christian Unity, General Synod, Church of England, 1992).

Reformed sisters and brothers and have pursued their discussions with Anglicans together with the Reformed. Again, episcopacy proved a stumbling block and only limited communion was achieved.[34]

The question cannot be avoided whether a Lutheran-Anglican agreement within Europe was blocked by conducting the dialogues as a Lutheran-Reformed group. If the Lutherans had done so, however, and an agreement on episcopacy similar to that embodied in the other Anglican-Lutheran statements had been reached, would the fellowship between Lutheran and Reformed in Europe have been harmed or even destroyed?

George Lindbeck has expressed the additional concern that closer Lutheran-Reformed union at the present historical moment could further erode the biblical and doctrinal density of both churches, hastening the development in both of a hollow, lowest-common-denominator Protestantism.[35] Especially in a situation in which doctrinal commitment has become thin, would ecumenical action be motivated by what is most clearly shared, viz., difference from Rome?[36]

The challenge is clear: how do the Lutheran churches enter into a fuller communion with Protestant churches with which they

---

[34]. *Called to Witness and Service: Conversations Between the British and Irish Anglican Churches and the French Lutheran and Reformed Churches. The Reuilly Common Statement with Essays on Church, Eucharist and Ministry* (London: Church House Publishing, 1999).

[35] George A. Lindbeck, "The Reformation Heritage and Christian Unity," *Lutheran Quarterly* 2 (1988): 496f.

[36] This worry increases when one reads an excellent scholarly contribution to the German-British ecumenical discussions from the Reformed theologian Jan Rohls, which begins however with the sentence: "The commonality of the Lutheran and Reformed traditions with regard to the questions of apostolicity, *episkope*, and succession results from demarcation over and against the Roman position." Jan Rohls, "Apostolicity, *Episkope* and Succession: The Lutheran, Reformed and United Tradition," in *Visible Unity and the Ministry of Oversight:The Second Theological Conference Held Under the Meissen Agreement Between the Church of England and the Evangelical Church in Germany* (London: Church House Publishing, 1997), 93.

share all the essentials of the faith, while also remaining open to possibilities of catholic fellowship about which other Protestants are skeptical? A more penetrating form of common life within the existing agreements of full communion is possible without endangering those possibilities. Serious thought must be given, however, to the limitations of pan-Protestant ecumenism if the better is not to prove an enemy of the best. Individual ecumenical steps need to be judged in terms of their contribution to the larger ecumenical goal. For example, if Episcopal and Reformed representatives had been invited to participate in a greater way in the ELCA Sexuality Study, should Catholic representatives have been invited also, even though we are not yet in full communion with the Catholic Church? Such proactive inclusion of Catholics (and Orthodox), where possible, in the new arrangements among Protestants might avoid the "ecumenically justified immobility," the Lutheran limitation of relations with other Protestants out of fear it would harm possible relations with Rome or the Orthodox, about which Lukas Vischer has complained.[37] *Full* communion agreements among *parts* of the church are always, in a sense, less than full. They are full only proleptically, as they are open to the greater unity for which we pray and work.

---

[37] Vischer, "History of the Agreement," 20.

The Lutheran-Orthodox Relationships and the Future of Ecumenism

Risto Saarinen, *University of Helsinki*

Over the past decade (1995-2005) many Orthodox churches have been very critical of the ecumenical movement. Some of them, e.g. the Orthodox churches of Georgia and Bulgaria, have withdrawn from membership in the World Council of Churches (WCC) and others have seriously considered whether they wish to continue their ecumenical work in the WCC in future. The causes of this development are diverse. Some observers believe that the criticism relates to the social situation in the post-Communist states. Such explanations assume that it is mainly non-theological factors which form an obstacle to the ecumenical work of Orthodoxy world-wide at the present time.

In relation to the WCC, however, the Orthodox themselves emphasize that their criticism mainly concerns the theological development of ecumenism. Many Protestant churches have taken theological decisions which diverge considerably from Orthodox practice, e.g. in connection with the role of women in the church. These decisions are described as obstacles to ecumenical cooperation. At the same time, however, a number of bilateral theological dialogues with the Orthodox churches have continued in good spirits. These facts invite us to examine the nuances of the Orthodox criticism.

In what follows, we shall examine the complicated developments of the past ten years by referring to the example of certain theological dialogues and renewal processes. First, we shall describe the progress in regional Lutheran-Orthodox dialogues from1995 to 2005. Then, we shall report on the development of the discussion on Orthodox participation in the WCC up to the Porto Alegre assembly in February 2006. Next, we shall analyze the new ecumenical guidelines of the Russian Orthodox Church. Finally, on the basis of these examples, we shall attempt an ecumenical diagnosis.

I have recently described the developments of global Lutheran-Orthodox dialogue elsewhere. In the following, I will concentrate on regional dialogues.[1] The attempted diagnosis will underline the theological factors and to some extent leave the political, national and social background aside. The non-theological background is naturally also important and is also a specific topic of discussion in the ecumenical context.[2]

In connection with the dialogue reports it must be emphasized that the Lutheran-Orthodox dialogues represent only one part of the dialogues of Orthodoxy world-wide. Significant progress has also been made in other fields.[3] The Lutheran-Orthodox conversations offer an interesting parallel and a contrast to the discussions within the WCC, which describes itself in its basis as a fellowship of churches and whose members are Protestant and Orthodox churches. It is important to remember that these dialogues have quite a long history which has been relatively independent of political events. Four subjects will be selected from the wealth of material: soteriology, ecclesiology, baptism and Trinitarian theology.

---

[1] Risto Saarinen, "The Lutheran-Orthodox Joint Commission: Our Work 1994-2003", in: *Cracks in the Walls, Festschrift for Anna Marie Aagaard*, ed. E.M. Wiberg Pedersen & J. Nissen, Frankfurt: Peter Lang 2005, 121-130. That piece and the present article update my earlier book *Faith and Holiness: Lutheran - Orthodox Dialogue 1959-1994*, Göttingen: Vandenhoeck & Ruprecht 1997. A regular update of all Lutheran-Orthodox dialogues is attempted at my website <www.helsinki.fi/~risaarin>. Note that the following list includes the most recent round (2004) of the global dialogue.

[2] For a particularly insightful new study of German - Russian dialogues and their non-theological factors, see Heiko Overmeyer, *Frieden im Spannungsfeld zwischen Theologie und Politik*, Frankfurt: Lembeck 2005.

[3] See *Orthodoxie im Dialog. Bilaterale Dialoge der orthodoxen und der orientalisch-orthodoxen Kirchen 1945-1997. Eine Dokumentensammlung*, ed. T. Bremer et al., Trier: Paulinus 1999.

1. The Lutheran-Orthodox Dialogues

In this overview, the following dialogues are surveyed and their texts are referred to in the footnotes. Printed books are quoted according to each title, other texts according to the dialogue in question.

Evangelische Kirche in Deutschland (EKD) - Romanian Orthodox Church:

7th conversation: "Gemeinschaft der Heiligen – Berufung unserer Kirchen und ihre Erfüllung in der säkularisierten Welt, Nov 27 – Dec 5, 1995 at Selbitz, Bavaria.

8th conversation: "Dienen und Versöhnen. Europäische Integration als Herausforderung an unsere Kirchen", Oct 3-8, 1998 in Bucharest.

9th conversation: "Die Kirche und ihre politisch-gesellschaftliche Verantwortung heute", Oct 7-12, 2000 at Herrnhut.

10th conversation: "Das Wesen und die Einheit der Kirche Christi - die Verschiedenheit der Kirchen in der Geschichte", Nov 14-20, 2002 at Cluj-Napoca.

Texts:

- Gemeinschaft der Heiligen/Dienen und Versöhnen, ed. R.Koppe, Hermannsburg: Missionshandlung 1999.

- Die Kirche - ihre Verantwortung und ihre Einheit. Das neunte und das zehnte Gespräch im bilateralen theologischen Dialog zwischen der Rumänischen Orthodoxen Kirche und der Evangelischen Kirche in Deutschland. Hg D. Heller und R. Koppe. Beiheft 75 zur Ökumenischen Rundschau. Frankfurt: Lembeck 2005.

EKD–Moscow Patriarchate:

2nd conversation: "Die Kirche, das Volk und der Staat in Europa" (The Church, People and the State in Europe), May 23-27, 1998 at Minsk.

3rd conversation: "Religiöse Bildung und Erziehung; Zwischenkirchliche Beziehungen: Situation und aktuelle Dokumente" (Religious Education and Instruction; Inter-church Relationships: Contemporary Situation and Texts), June 1-7, 2002 at Mülheim an der Ruhr.

Texts:

- Hinhören und Hinsehen. Beziehungen zwischen der Russischen Orthodoxen Kirche und der Evangelischen Kirche in Deutschland, Hg. vom Kirchenamt der EKD in Hannover und dem Kirchlichen Außenamt des Moskauer Patriarchats, Leipzig: Ev. Verlag 2003.

- Bilateraler Theologischer Dialog Evangelische Kirche in Deutschland/ Russische Orthodoxe Kirche 1998 und 2002 (Bad Urach II & III, Minsk 1998, Mülheim 2002, Studienheft 28), hg. R. Koppe. Hermannsburg: Missionshandlung 2005.

EKD–Patriarchate of Constantinople:

11th conversation: "Der Kosmos als Schöpfung Gottes. Die Kirche vor dem ökologischen Problem", Oct 21-27, 1997 in Rhodos.

12th conversation: "Die Kirchen im zusammenwachsenden Europa", Jun 30 - Jul 6, 2001 in Brandenburg/ Havel

13th conversation: "Die Gnade Gottes und das Heil der Welt", Sep 16-22, 2004 in Phanar.

Texts:

- Das Handeln der Kirche in Zeugnis und Dienst. [EKD - Constatinople Texts 1994-2001]. Studienheft 27, Hg. von Rolf Koppe, Hermannsburg : Missionshandlung 2003.

- Die Gnade Gottes und das Heil der Welt. Kommunique der 13. Begegnung im bilateralen theologischen Dialog zwischen dem Ökumenischen Patriarchat von Konstantinopel und der Evangelischen Kirche in Deutschland. www.ekd.de/orthodoxie/

Evangelical Lutheran Church of Finland-Moscow Patriarchate:

10th conversation: "The Mission of the Church; Peace Work of the Church and Nationalism", Aug 27 - Sept 5, 1995 in Kiev.

11th conversation: "Freedom of a Christian, Freedom of the Church and Religious Freedom", Oct 12-19, 1998 in Lappeenranta.

12th conversation: "Evaluation of the Dialogue 1970-1998", Sep 27 - Oct 5, 2002 in Moscow.

13th conversation: "Christian View of Human Person in Today's Europe; Salvation, Faith and Modern Society". Sep 20 to 25, 2005 in Turku.

Texts:

- Kiev 1995. The Tenth Theological Discussions between the Evangelical Lutheran Church of Finland and the Russian Orthodox Church. Documents of the Evangelical Lutheran Church of Finland 8. Helsinki: Kirkkohallitus 1996.

- Lappeenranta, Moscow and Turku Communiqués in Finnish. www.evl.fi/kkh/kuo/kk.htm.

Lutheran and Orthodox churches in America:

"Trinitarian Theology", 1994-1998. (A Lutheran-Orthodox Common Statement on Faith in the Holy Trinity, 1998.

Text:
www.elca.org/ecumenical/ecumenicaldialogue/orthodox/index.html

Lutheran - Orthodox Joint Commission:

12th conversation: "The Mystery of the Church: C. Baptism and Chrismation as Sacraments of Initiation into the Church", Oct 6-15, 2004, Durau, Romania.

Text: www.helsinki.fi/~risaarin/lutortjointtext.html

1.1. Soteriology

Between 1959 and 1994 the churches' understanding of salvation had already been discussed in most of the regional Lutheran-Orthodox dialogues. The Orthodox view of salvation as "deification" (*theosis*) proved to be a difficult problem because Protestant theology saw it as comprising the danger of a false apotheosis of human beings. However, in Finland, the USA and Germany joint statements were drawn up on the relation between justification and *theosis*.[4]

In the final document of the dialogue between the Evangelische Kirche in Deutschland (EKD) and the Romanian Orthodox Church of 1998, the EKD affirmed the idea of *theosis* in principle for the first time and thus accepted the insight which the Finnish Evangelical Lutheran Church had maintained in its dialogue with the Russian Orthodox Church since 1977. In this view, the Lutheran conception of the Christ who is present in faith as the effective aspect of the doctrine of justification constitutes a parallel to the Orthodox doctrine of deification or *theosis*.[5]

A "Joint Report to the leaders of the Romanian Orthodox Church and the EKD on the state of the bilateral theological dialogue" (1998) states that the main concern of the dialogue has been the issue of "Salvation in Jesus Christ." The report says that, despite different traditions on this question, a consensus can be "appropriately described." When the term "justification" comprises the whole path of human beings to salvation, it corresponds "in a broader sense" to the Orthodox understanding of the *theosis* of human beings. In addition, it is jointly observed: "In the specific sense of the final perfection of human communion with God, *theosis* means what is described in the Protestant tradition as the 'sanctification' of human beings. The essential difference between Creator and creature is thus in no way called into question. With regard to the problem of *synergeia*, it was observed that in the Orthodox tradition it in no sense implies an autonomous human contribution to their own salvation but rather

---

4 Risto Saarinen, "Salvation in Lutheran-Orthodox Dialogue", *Pro ecclesia* 1996, 202-213.

5 Cf. Saarinen 1997, 38-53, 147-155.

the work of love of which the baptized are made capable by the Holy Spirit who also makes them "God's servants, working together" (1 Cor 3:9)."[6]

Responding to this report on January 29, 1999, the Council of the EKD stated, among other things, that it saw this as "an appropriate expression for the right teaching about the Lord Jesus Christ."[7] This observation is important for three reasons. First, it confirms the results of the dialogue. Second, it should be remembered that at the same time in Germany the debate over the Lutheran-Roman Catholic "Joint Declaration on the Doctrine of Justification" had particularly emphasized the Protestant interpretation of the doctrine of justification where an approval of Orthodox soteriology cannot be taken for granted. Third, the German-Romanian dialogue has been criticized precisely because of problems related to *theosis* and *synergeia*.[8] Nevertheless, the Council of the EKD saw the right doctrine reflected in this dialogue.

For the history of the Protestant-Orthodox dialogue it is also significant that, with this official response, the EKD received the Orthodox conception of *theosis* and synergy maybe even more strongly as true teaching than the Finnish Evangelical Lutheran Church had done. In 1977 in the dialogue with Moscow the Finnish Church had noted a parallel between justification and *theosis*. Over the period 1988-1989 in their regional dialogues the German and the American Lutheran churches had taken a similar decision.[9] The Finnish-Russian dialogue returned to the treatment of salvific co-operation in its most recent document of 2005. The joint text says that "the grace of God in Christ liberates the human person from the servitude of law and sin. The Holy Spirit wakes the person to will and to do good (John 8:32, Rom 6:18 and 8:2, Gal 5:1). The freedom which is a gift of God comprises as its first

---

[6] Gemeinschaft, 145.

[7] Gemeinschaft, 149.

[8] Reinhard Flogaus, "Einig in Sachen Theosis und Synergie?" *Kerygma und Dogma* 42, 1996, 225-243. Cf. my response to Flogaus in Saarinen 1997, 244-248.

[9] Saarinen 1996.

fruit an experience of the integrity for which the human person is created and which is entirely accomplished only in the future (Rom 8:23)."[10]

1.2. Ecclesiology

In bilateral dialogues it is normal, after dealing with soteriology, to discuss the understanding of the Church. Many regional dialogues reached this stage between 1995 and 2000. The German-Romanian dialogue discussed the Communion of Saints in 1995. In their joint theses, the partners state that the Church "is not the work of human beings but exclusively God's work." The Eucharistic gathering is of fundamental importance for the Church; it is there that the church is constituted as the *communio sanctorum*. The common sharing in Christ who gives himself in the Eucharist is "the living source of divine life and the foundation for any communion of saints." Other theses describe the holiness of the church, the service of the saints and the veneration of saints.[11]

This 1995 document is one of the first joint ecclesiological documents in the Lutheran-Orthodox dialogue. The theses follow on from the fundamental soteriological insight formulated earlier about participating in Christ as the source of divine life; moreover, the Orthodox church affirms some important aspects of the western *communio sanctorum*. For its part, the Protestant side is able to identify with the Eucharistic ecclesiology influenced by Orthodoxy.

At Herrnhut in 2000, the German-Romanian dialogue continued the discussion of ecclesiology in the context of the overall theme: "The Church and its political, social responsibility today." In this conversation, ecclesiology was discussed in reference to society. The presentations analyze church-state relations and the ecclesiological grounds for action in society.[12] In the Herrnhut theses the partners in dialogue agree that the social responsibility of the church is an aspect of the "relational nature" of the church

---

[10] Finnish-Russian 2005, I,10 (my translation).

[11] Gemeinschaft, 13.

[12] Die Kirche 2005, 15-24.

which starts from the Eucharist and is related to the whole of creation. As a "living and loving community of the triune God," the church is a historical reality composed of the divine and the human and living in solidarity with the world.[13] These statements are also without precedent in the Lutheran-Orthodox dialogue. The basis for solidarity with the world is found in the concept of *communio* and in Eucharistic ecclesiology. A similar approach can be found, for example, in the documents of the fifth Conference on Faith and Order at Santiago de Compostela in 1993.

In 1995 the Finnish-Russian dialogue discussed "Church and Nationalism" and in 1998 "Freedom of the Church." The joint theses of 1995 emphasize the identity of the Church as the people of God consisting of many nations, "Christianity has crossed, and still crosses, ethnic, cultural and politico-social boundaries. Therefore, it is not in the nature of the Church to support hostility or patriotism of any kind." The Church of Jesus Christ is described as the "community of the believers," the members of which belong to different nations.[14] This term refers back to the *congregatio fidelium* of the Lutheran Confessions and interestingly enough the Russian Church is able to employ it here.

The conversations of 1998 also produced some significant common theses. The statements on freedom start by presenting the spiritual freedom of the Christian in terms similar to Luther's explanation in *De libertate christiana*. Freedom in the Church is described in the following way: "Since the Church is one with the heavenly, free Jerusalem, on earth it forms the inexhaustible source of the spiritual freedom of Christians (Gal 4:26, Heb 12:22-24, Isa 54). The Church is a divine-human reality: on the one hand, it is the communion of the Holy Spirit in the Christians who obey the commandments of Christ in their lives. As such, the Church is not subject to any human limitations. On the other hand, the Church is a human community marked by the unity of faith, the sacraments and spiritual life. As such the Church is subject to all human limitations."[15]

---

[13] Die Kirche 2005, 17-24.

[14] Kiev 1995, 15-16.

[15] Finnish-Russian 1998, n.p.

Luther's language has helped to formulate this joint statement. The Orthodox also speak of the theandric reality of the church in the EKD-Romanian and the global dialogue, but the link with Luther is unique at this point. Moreover, the equation of the church with the "free Jerusalem" of Gal 4:26 is an original idea which, to my knowledge, has not been used anywhere else in an ecumenical context. The basis for the church being a source is not clear because the biblical references quoted only describe Jerusalem "the mother." The joint text continues with stating that even in a situation of outward persecution the church is supported by an inner, invisible freedom.

1.3. Baptism

Some Lutheran-Orthodox dialogues have returned to the treatment of baptism. The reasons for this move are not obvious, but it is possible that the dialogues want to achieve concrete and binding results. Since these are not possible with regard to ecclesiology and other sacraments, baptism offers at least a point of departure. Many, if not most, Orthodox churches have in practice affirmed the Trinitarian baptisms of other traditional churches as valid, even if they lack some aspects of canonical fullness.

The dialogue between the EKD and the Ecumenical Patriarchate unequivocally affirms the mutual validity of baptism in their document of 2004. Although this affirmation is not theologically explained any further and although it more or less re-establishes good ecumenical practice, it is nevertheless significant that both sides clearly affirm this to be the case. Both sides explicitly condemn the practice of "new baptism" in the case of conversion.[16]

The global Lutheran-Orthodox Joint Commission also discusses baptism in its text of 2004. This text understands the Christian initiation as threefold reality, consisting of "death with Christ, resurrection with Christ, and the sealing with the Holy Spirit."

---

[16] EKD-Constantinople 2004, n.p.: "Obwohl zwischen unseren Kirchen noch keine Kirchengemeinschaft besteht, betrachten wir unsere Gemeindeglieder gegenseitig als getauft und lehnen es ab, im Falle eines Konfessionswechsels eine neue Taufe vorzunehmen."

Using Lutheran and Orthodox liturgical texts, the Joint Commission argues that water baptism in both churches comprises the two first elements. Whereas the Orthodox identify the event of chrismation in the immediate context of baptism as the third element of initiation, Lutherans say that in baptismal rite "the gift of the Spirit is connected with the laying on of hands and either a post-baptismal blessing or a prayer for the Spirit." Lutherans thus continue the Western tradition but do not omit the third element, the sealing with the Holy Spirit, in their rite of baptism.[17]

The presence of this threefold structure in both churches allows the Joint Commission to say together that "the three components of Christian initiation are to a large extent included in each other's rites."[18] This argumentation may become ecumenically fruitful in the future. Whereas many Orthodox churches traditionally hold that their approval of the validity of Western baptisms is only an "economical" emergency solution, the two texts of 2004 clearly move beyond this position and state a theological convergence with regard to baptism.

1.4. Trinitarian theology

In their global dialogues with the Roman Catholic Church on the one hand, and with the World Alliance of Reformed Churches on the other, the Orthodox have touched on the doctrine of the Trinity, but not in the global Lutheran-Orthodox dialogue. There are many reasons for this. First, the Lutheran churches have also not dealt with the Trinity as a separate issue in their other dialogues. Second, it is improbable that a bilateral dialogue would be able to say anything new concerning on the old dispute about the western addition to the Nicene Creed (*filioque*). It should be noted, however, that Trinitarian theology is being much discussed in western theology and therefore there certainly is interest in this issue among theologians.

The American dialogue group discussed Trinitarian theology from 1994 to 1998 and adopted a relatively general document, "A Lutheran-Orthodox Common Statement on Faith in the Holy

---

[17] Joint Commission 2004, § 2, 8.
[18] Joint Commission 2004, § 11.

Trinity." The document signed in November1998 by the chairmen, Bishop Donald J. McCoid and Metropolitan Maximos of Aenos, spells out three fundamental theological criteria for the right doctrine of the Trinity: i.) the monarchy of the Father, ii.) the existence of the divine essence only in three distinct, equal and undivided persons, iii.) the intimate relation of Son and Spirit in the economy of salvation.[19]

The Lutheran group recommended the use of the original version of the Nicene Creed in ecumenical services. At the same time, the Lutherans emphasized that, in their view, the Spirit also proceeds from the Son. The Orthodox found this view unacceptable but said at the same time that they could accept the idea of the "double procession" in the patristic sense, i.e. that the Father sends the Spirit through the Son. For the Orthodox, the relation between the Son and the Spirit in the economy of salvation was not identical with the relationship within the Trinity.[20]

The American document of 1998 is the first thorough statement on Trinitarian theology in the Lutheran-Orthodox dialogue as a whole. One point of comparison is the document from the Orthodox-Reformed dialogue in 1992, "Agreed Statement on the Holy Trinity."[21] This document places more emphasis on the doctrine of relationships and states that the divine monarchy that it "is not limited to one person." Nevertheless it is an important fact that the Orthodox were prepared in the 1990s to draw up detailed statements on Trinitarian theology with the Protestants. For example, the Finnish-Russian dialogue in 1995 also formulated a Trinitarian basis for missionary work. In this statement, mission is based on the love within the Trinity: "The source and motivation of mission is the love of the Triune God. Love prevails between

---

[19] USA, Statement 1998, § 12.

[20] USA, Statement, § 11: "...Orthodox may accept the teaching of the 'double procession' of the Spirit from the Father and the Son in the patristic sense that the Spirit is sent from the Father through/and the Son in the mystery of our salvation in Christ. The relation of the Son to the Spirit in the context of salvation (oikonomia) is not the same with their relation in the eternal Trinity (theologia)."

[21] *Growth in Agreement 2*, ed. J. Gros et alii, Geneva: WCC 2000, 282-283.

the Father, the Son and the Holy Spirit. The Triune God loved the world when he created and redeemed it, and he continues to love the world in sanctifying it."[22]

To summarize, it can be stated that the dialogue results outlined above (1.1.-1.4.) provide evidence of the intensive ecumenical activity of the Orthodox churches. Although binding agreements must still be awaited, the results of the dialogues justify the claim that the Orthodox continue to devote a lot of attention to theological work in the ecumenical movement.

2. The Renewal of the World Council of Churches

In recent years, the World Council of Churches (WCC) has been particularly subject to criticism from the Orthodox churches. The criticism of ecumenism at the world level is related to a concern about the inner coherence and credibility of the local churches. However, the successful continuation of many bilateral relations leads one to assume that the criticism is not directed against ecumenism in general but that the WCC has given special cause for concern among the Orthodox.

At the Bishops' Council of the Russian Orthodox Church in 1997, a motion was introduced to leave the WCC. The motion was only narrowly defeated. Shortly afterwards, the Orthodox churches of Georgia and Bulgaria did indeed leave the WCC. The Orthodox churches met in April-May 1998 at Thessaloniki and published a short statement saying that they considered their participation in the assembly of the WCC at Harare in 1998 possible only on certain conditions. The WCC needed to be re-structured in order to take sufficient account of the Orthodox concerns. In the Thessaloniki statement mention is made of women's ordination and the rights of sexual minorities as issues which the Orthodox had found particularly problematic in the WCC.[23]

---

[22] Kiev 1995, 12.

[23] Special Commission on Orthodox Participation in the WCC, Background Materials, November 1999, Geneva: WCC 1999, 26: Thessaloniki, §9.

The major patriarchates were satisfied with the proposals from Thessaloniki and so the WCC assembly at Harare in December 1998 took place relatively peacefully. In accordance with the proposals, the assembly set up a "Special Commission on Orthodox Participation in the WCC." At the first meeting of the Commission in December 1999 at Morges, Switzerland, the work was distributed among four sub-committees: Orthodox participation in the present organization; Style and ethos of the WCC; Theological convergences and differences in the WCC; Proposals for a new structure.[24]

The Russian Church had already prepared a suggestion for a new structure in 1999. According to that proposal, the WCC should consist of two chambers; in addition to the traditional "council," a "forum" would deal with the question of church unity. The forum would take no votes but always work on a consensus basis. The churches would be divided into four "families" in the forum: Orthodox, Catholic, Reformation and Free churches. The forum would not use quotas (women, youth, etc.) and the churches would be represented by their real leaders. Even the Orthodox churches which had withdrawn from cooperation in the WCC could be represented in the forum.[25]

All four sub-groups met in the course of 2000 and drew up reports. The Russian proposal was discussed at length. At the same time other forum proposals were being discussed in the WCC which would, for instance, make it possible for non-member churches to participate in the WCC. Because of the large number of suggestions, the Russian model was found difficult to be spelled out in administrative terms. In addition, the Protestant churches wanted to be represented directly and not by "families." It also seemed clear that the two-chamber model, in which every church would have veto power because of the principle of consensus,

---

[24] Background Materials 1999, 60: Harare Report of Policy and Reference Committee I,V.

[25] Kirill, "A Possible Structure of the WCC", *The Ecumenical Review* 51, 1999, 351-354.

would result in a very loose structure, resulting only in a loss of significance for the WCC as a whole.[26]

The second plenary meeting of the Special Commission took place during October 2000 in Cairo. Although it was generally felt in Cairo that the various two chamber and forum models could not be implemented, the demand for consensus in the decision-making process continued to be an Orthodox concern. Theological discussion of common prayer, ecclesiology and social ethics took place in Cairo. The Thessaloniki document had prohibited Orthodox participation in common prayer at Harare. In fact, at ecumenical conferences there is diversity in the worship practice, but in the light of the results of Cairo the Thessaloniki document has lasting validity for the Orthodox churches.[27]

Concrete proposals on important issues were further discussed at Cairo and drawn up for the Central Committee of the WCC. The interim report thus compiled puts forward the introduction of the consensus principle as a possible solution for most WCC decisions. The interim report adopted at Cairo was made public at the meeting of the Central Committee in January 2001.[28] The work of the Special Commission, together with the proposed practical amendments to the structure of the WCC and for the future participation of the Orthodox churches, was more or less completed at its last plenary meeting in Järvenpää near Helsinki in May 2002. The Central Committee received the recommendations of the Special Commission in September 2002. In February 2005, new procedures of decision-making were adopted in the WCC.

The new ecumenical rules which include consensus in the decision-making process as well as moderation in the joint worship life have continued to be debated. The German Lutheran Bishop of Hanover, Margot Kässmann, was so critical of this

---

[26] Special Commission on Orthodox Participation in the WCC, Reports of the Sub-Committees, Geneva: WCC 2000.

[27] I follow here Bishop Voitto Huotari's (Finnish Participant of Special Commission) written report for the Finnish church.

[28] Interim Report of the Special Commission on Orthodox Participation in the WCC, Cairo, 25 October 2000. Central Committee Meeting Agenda 2001, Geneva: WCC.

compromise that she resigned from her post in the Central Committee. It is still too early to see whether the Special Commission has been successful, but at least it has integrated many Orthodox churches to the daily work of the WCC. First attempts of consensual decision-making at the Porto Alegre assembly of the WCC in February 2006 were encouraging.[29]

3. The New Ecumenical Guidelines of the Russian Orthodox Church

The Bishops' Synod of the Russian church, meeting in August 2000, adopted some basic theological documents. They are of great significance for Orthodoxy world-wide because the Orthodox churches have so far rarely made normative statements on modern issues. For example, the very extensive document on the foundations of social doctrine will certainly be much discussed in the coming years. In addition, the new documents from Moscow have been very thoroughly prepared and presented in detail. Here we shall proceed briefly to discuss the ecumenical document on guidelines for the attitude of the Russian Orthodox Church in its encounter with other Christian confessions.[30]

According to the document, the Russian church can take part in the work of inter-church organizations if the following criteria are met. i.) The organization does not violate the doctrines of the church, ii.) The Orthodox church can bear a genuine witness, iii.) The decision making processes of the organization respect the particularity of the church, iv.) Majority decisions are not binding on the individual members (para. 5.2.). The Russian proposal for a

---

[29] The WCC website <www.wcc-coe.org> offers plenty of relevant material, as do the documents of Porto Alegre assembly 2006.

[30] For the background see also Pauliina Arola - Risto Saarinen, "In Search of Sobornost and New Symphony: The Social Doctrine of the Russian Orthodox Church", *The Ecumenical Review* 54, 2002, 130-141 and the thematic issue of *Ökumenische Rundschau* 2/2001. I have used the English translation available at the website of the Moscow Patriarchate. Over the years, various translation amendments have been made and my quotes may therefore not have the most recent wording.

renewal of the WCC described above clearly follows these guidelines.

The document on ecumenism uses the word "Church" only for the Orthodox church which "is the true Church in which the Holy Tradition and the fullness of God's saving grace are preserved intact" (1.18.). Orthodoxy is not a national or cultural attribute of the Eastern Church. On the contrary, "Orthodoxy is an inner quality of the Church" (1.19.). Since unity belongs to the essence of Christianity, the goal of ecumenical conversations must be the restoration of this unity. Unity is "a task of the highest priority for the Orthodox Church at every level of her life. Indifference to this task or its rejection is a sin against God's commandment of unity" (2.1.-2.2.). Thus decisive importance is attributed to ecumenical work.

The document contains an extremely interesting evaluation of the various models of unity in the ecumenical movement. For example, it rejects: i.) the conception of the church as a tree with many branches, ii.) the view of the unity of the invisible church, iii.) the idea of the fundamental equality of all denominations, and iv.) the conception that what lies behind the differences is a lack of love. Similarly, v.) the differences "cannot all be reduced to various non-theological factors" (2.8.).

Genuine unity can be found only "in the bosom of the One, Holy, Catholic and Apostolic Church" (2.3.). The restoration of unity in faith and love can come only "from above as a gift of Almighty God"; God is "the source of unity" (2.13.). The ecumenical dialogue of the Russian Church is primarily of a theological nature. The aim of the theological dialogue is to present the ecclesial consciousness of the Orthodox Church (4.2.). The necessity of the theological dialogue is emphasized throughout. Other forms of cooperation, such as *diakonia*, social service and peacemaking, are important as a witness to the secular world (5.5.), but dogmatic theological dialogue is the only really relevant means for re-establishing unity.

On the "canonical territory" of the Russian Orthodox Church, the non-Orthodox Christian communities should be treated in the same spirit of fraternal cooperation as in the global ecumenical context. However, proselytism is firmly rejected. A clear distinction is made between non-Orthodox Christians, who affirm the Trinity and the doctrine of the two natures and the sects, who reject these fundamental Christian doctrines. Whereas Christians in Russia enjoy the protection of religious liberty, the Church rejects the activity of sects (6.1.-6.3.).

A western theologian reading these guidelines wants to see how they fit into philosophical history and to understand the terms used in the criteria in a historical way. In my book I have made a distinction between two fundamental types of contemporary Orthodox theology, namely "school theology" on the one hand, and "mystical theology" on the other. Whereas neo-Palamism and many trends in modern academic Orthodox theology belong to the mystical type, the theology of the Russian Church can be summarized as belonging to a type of school theology. School theology emphasizes the canonical rules and the power of the bishops in their canonical territory. It makes little reference to Palamism and Eucharistic ecclesiology. Instead, it uses terms which are historically related to the language of Roman Catholicism.[31]

In line with the criteria for these types, the new guidelines very clearly constitute "school theology." Scholastic expressions such as "Orthodoxy is not ... attribute ... [but] quality" (1.19.), "necessary truths ... formal unity ... essential conditions" (2.10.-11.) are typical of school theology. The terminological similarity to the documents of the Vatican is striking in the Moscow guidelines. The one Church is defined mainly in terms of the *notae* "One, Holy, Catholic, Apostolic" and here the sacraments (not mysteries!) serve an ecclesiology which is defined legally. Thus, although the Eucharist "guarantees" the unity of the Church, it is not described as constituting the Church (1.8., 2.12.). The formal canonical conditions for membership of the church are characteristic of the presentation of the various "rites of reception," namely Baptism, Chrismation and Repentance (1.10.-20.).[32] The

---

[31] Cf. Saarinen 1997, 217-223.

[32] Para. 1.17. speaks of "various rites of reception (through Baptism, through Chrismation, through Repentance)". This passage is similar to the "rites of initiation" in the new Roman Catholic catechism, especially because traditionally the Orthodox have not made much distinction

universality of the Church is emphasized. In relation to this universality, the local churches have only a secondary role. There is no discussion of the principle of autocephaly (1.7). Spirituality and liturgy also only have significance subordinate to the legal provisions and are hardly mentioned as issues relevant for ecumenism. In general, there is scarcely any link between Orthodox dogma and liturgy.

The wording of the document follows Roman Catholic terminology not only in regard to canon law and the doctrine of the sacraments but also, for example, in the doctrine of grace. The Church is presented as the guardian of the gifts of grace (3.1). Violations of canon law affect the Christian's state of grace (1.10). Non-Orthodox Christians have been able to retain a kind of grace (1.14) but the purity and fullness of grace belong to the Orthodox church (1.18). A western reader gets the impression that the liturgical and mystical elements of Orthodoxy are scarcely represented because canonical and Roman Catholic terminology plays such a dominant part.

4. Attempt at a Diagnosis

Deliberate emphasis has been given above to the positive developments in the bilateral dialogues (Section 1) and to the sometimes very critical discussion in the World Council of Churches (Section 2) against the background of the dialogues. This presentation underlines the fact that, at the same time as the Orthodox churches were questioning their future in the World Council of Churches, their ecumenical work proceeded at the bilateral and regional level in part better than ever before.

First, one can observe different and in part contradictory developments in the ecumenical activity of Orthodoxy. Second, there is no doubt that in any case the Orthodox churches wish to and can take an active part in ecumenical work. Even though the new ecumenical guidelines from Moscow (Section 3) represent the usually critical position of Orthodoxy today, they also give high

---

between stages of initiation but rather propagated an "integrated initiation" (baptism and chrismation).

priority to genuine ecumenical theology. Third, it can be said that the discussion in the World Council of Churches is to some extent a discussion *sui generis*. The Orthodox churches in the WCC feel threatened in a way which is not visible in bilateral relationships. In Protestantism, the situation is not infrequently the reverse: whereas the WCC is considered either inclusive enough or at least relatively harmless because it is not a church fellowship in the true sense of the term, bilateral and binding theological agreements are often fiercely debated and sometimes rejected completely by the critics.

In my earlier study I speak of counter-productive ecumenism, where the good will of the one partner is interpreted by the other as obtrusive or "colonizing the other."[33] Perhaps the language of the WCC is in some way obtrusive and counter-productive. The Thessaloniki statement lists five signs to which the Orthodox object: i.) inter-communion being practiced already, ii.) inclusive language, iii.) women's ordination, iv.) sexual minorities and v.) syncretism.[34] They are obtrusive when they are signs of the church. A Protestant observer sees them all not as signs of the church but as products of modern times and perhaps therefore finds it easier to deal with them. The bilateral dialogues have avoided these signs or issues and have been able to make progress.

Moreover, these "signs" relate not so much to dogmatic theology as to church practice. This observation gives grounds for a fundamental question to the Orthodox position: to what extent can ecumenism really progress by means of dogmatic principles – as recommended by the Moscow guidelines – if the major problems for the Orthodox are found in the area of forms of Christian living or in church practice? The results of the doctrinal conversations can only be of concrete significance when a precise definition of the relation between dogmatic theology and church practice has been achieved by both sides.

The question of the relation between doctrine and practice also arises for the Lutheran and other Protestant churches. Since the doctrine of justification constitutes the core of the Protestant faith,

---

[33] Saarinen 1997, 268-269.
[34] Background Material 1999, 26.

the truth of which takes precedence over all practice and which can serve as a criterion for other doctrines and for practical decisions, there is a danger that this core teaching may be understood as a limited group of theoretical theses. But many theories of doctrine emphasize that doctrine is inevitably related to practice. A doctrinal approach in which doctrines can be formulated as mere theses would be inadequate.[35]

If doctrines are discussed repeatedly as if they were mere propositions unrelated to practice, the ecumenical dialogue will soon become perpetual motion, producing more and more documents but never coming to any conclusive agreements and never changing church practice. This danger is obvious in the bilateral Lutheran-Orthodox dialogues, even though the conversations are still able to reveal interesting points of theological convergence. It is also possible that the crisis in the WCC will compel the churches seriously to evaluate their different practical ways of acting so that church practice again becomes a central issue for ecumenism. If this happens, the crisis may prove beneficial for the future of the doctrinal conversations as well.

---

[35] See e.g. Kevin Vanhoozer, *The Drama of Doctrine*, Louisville: WJK 2005.

PART V

Ministry and Publications of Eric W. Gritsch

The Ministry of Eric W. Gritsch

Personal Life

Born on April 19, 1931 in Neuhaus, Austria in a Lutheran parsonage.

BAPTIZED on May 3, 1931.

CONFIRMED on September 26, 1945.

Experienced the reign of Adolf Hitler in the "Hitler Youth" (1941-45) and Russian military occupation as part of the political decisions of the Allies (Russian, French, British and American "zones"(1945-55).

Married to Ruth C. Sandman (1955-94). Bonnie A. Brobst (1995-).

Father of four Foster Daughters.

1962 Naturalized American citizen

Residence in Baltimore, MD.

Education

Elementary School in Bernstein (1937-41).

"Gymnasium" in Oberschützen (1941-50), a combination of High School and College. "Matura" Degree (equiv to BA)., 1950.

Protestant Theological Faculty of Vienna University (1950-51). "Cand.Theol." Degree, equiv. M. Div. (1956).

Zurich University (1952), Switzerland.

Basel University (1952-53), Switzerland.

Fulbright Scholar at Yale Divinity School. "Sacred Master of Theology" (STM) Degree (1955)

Yale University, MA Degree (1958), Ph.D in Church History (1960).

Career

1956-57 Commissioned "Vicar" of the Evangelical Lutheran Church of Austria, serving its parish in Bruck an der Mur.

1959-61 Instructor, Department of Religion at Wellesley College, Wellesley, MA.

1961-94. Professor of Church History at the Lutheran Theological Seminary in Gettysburg, PA

1962 June 2, ORDAINED by the Central Pennsylvania Synod of the United Lutheran Church in America to serve as a member of the Seminary Faculty.

Special Tasks

1964-2011 Member of the International Congress for Luther Research.

Principal Lecturer in Lund, Sweden (1977), Oslo, Norway (1988), Seminar Leader in Heidelberg, Germany (1997).

1970-94. Director of the Institute for Luther Studies, Gettysburg Seminary.

1970-94 Member of the Lutheran-Roman Catholic Dialogue in North America.

1971-90 Part-time teaching at the "Washington Theological Consortium," an exchange program involving Episcopalian, Lutheran, Methodist, Roman Catholic Seminaries and the Catholic University of America.

1975 Conference on the "charismatic movement," Minnesota Synod of the Lutheran Church in America.

1983 Lecturer (with Marc H.Tanenbaum) on Lutheran-Jewish Relations, Lutheran Council USA, New York.

1984 Lecturer at the Anniversary of the "Barmen Declaration" of 1934 against the regime of Adolf Hitler, Berea College, Kentucky.

1986-98 Member of the Bishop Ordass Foundation in Oslo and Budapest.

1987 Nominated for the Office of Bishop of the Lower Susquehanna Synod, ELCA

1988 First Bainton Lecturer at Yale Divinity School.

1989-92 Three annual conferences of American Reformation scholars and historians of the Academy of Sciences of Communist East Germany, in Berlin.

1992-2004 Member of the Board of Directors, Ecumenical Institute of the Lutheran World Federation, Strasbourg, France.

1994 One of two theologians appointed to serve on the ELCA Task Force on Human Sexuality.

1995 Lecturer at Southern Lutheran Seminary, Columbia, SC.

Teaching at the Melanchthon Institute, Houston, TX.

Lecturer (with Avery Dulles) on the Lutheran-Catholic Dialogue, St. Thomas College. Houston, TX.

First of four annual meetings on "Lutheran-Cherokee Relations" in Cherokee, NC.

Director, Forum for German Culture, Zion Lutheran Church, Baltimore, MD.

1996 Lecturer at the Lutheran Theological Faculty in Budapest, Hungary.

1996-2005 Adjunct Faculty Member at the Ecumenical Institute of St. Mary's Seminary and University, Baltimore, MD. Board Member, 2006-09.

1996 Lecturer at the Joint Meeting of the ELCA Conference of Bishops and the Episcopal Church-USA (ECUSA), White Haven, PA.

1997 Distinguished Lecturer at The Catholic University of America, Washington, DC.

1998 Guest Professor, Belgum Chair, California Lutheran University. Thousand Oaks, CA.

2000 Lecturer at the North American Meeting of the Lutheran World Federation in Columbia, SC.

2001 Participant in the National Catholic Workshop on Christians and Jews, Houston, TX.

2001 Lecturer at the Interdenominational Conference on "Christian Unity and Peace-Making." Notre Dame University, Indiana.

2001 Lecturer at the Conference of the German "Luther Covenant" (*Lutherbund*), Gallneukirchen, Austria.

2002 Teacher in the "German Travel Seminar," a 12-day bus tour to locations of the 16th century Reformation in Germany.

2004 Lecturer at a Conference on the Future of Lutheran Theology, Aarhus, Denmark.

2010 Lecturer and Theologian in Residence, Lenoir-Rhyne University, Hickory, NC.

2011-12 Sojourner Connect Retreat, Mar-Lu-Ridge, Jefferson, MD for ELCA Pastors, one day every month on catechetical formation in the parish.

2012 Preacher and Lecturer at the Methodist Haefner Preaching Mission, Lincolnton, NC.

Parish Work

1961-70. Member of Christ Lutheran Church, Gettysburg, PA. Adult education Teacher.

1967-94. About 100 week-ends of teaching and preaching in parishes across the US, staffed by former students.

1970-89.Member, Christ Lutheran Church, York, PA. Adult Education teacher and one-term member of the Council.

1990-94. Member of St. John's Lutheran Church, Fairfield, PA. Annual Adult Forum Facilitator.

1990-91 Spent Sabbatical leave to serve as Interim Pastor at John's Church.

1995 Worshipped at Christ the King Lutheran Church, Houston, TX. Adult Education Teacher.

1995- Member of Zion Church of the City of Baltimore, MD. Director of the Forum for German Culture. Lecturer at annual "Lutherfest," celebrating Martin Luther's birthday (November 10).

1998-99. Interim Worship Pastor at Zion Church, conducting English and German language services each week. Chair of the "Call Committee."

Publications of Eric W. Gritsch

Books

Authored

Reformer Without a Church. The Life and Thought of Thomas Müntzer (1488?-1525). Philadelphia: Fortress Press, 1967.

The Continuing Reformation. Lutheran Church in America. Adult Education Series. Ed. Frank W. Klos. Philadelphia: Lutheran Church Press, 1971.

(With Robert W. Jenson). *Lutheranism. The Theological Movement and Its Confessional Writings.* Philadelphia: Fortress Press, 1976.

Born Againism. Perspectives on a Movement. Philadelphia: Fortress Press, 1982. 2d. Edition, 2007.

Martin---God's Court Jester: Luther in Retrospect. Philadelphia: Fortress Press, 1983. Hungarian Edition, 2006. Reprint. Eugene, OR; Wipf & Stock, 2009.

Thomas Müntzer. A Tragedy of Errors. Minneapolis: Fortress Press: 1989. 2d. Edition 2006.

Fortress Introduction to Lutheranism. Minneapolis: Fortress Pres: 1994. Hungarian Edition, 2000.

A History of Lutheranism. Minneapolis: Fortress Press, 2002. 2nd Edition rev., 2010.

A Handbook for Christian Life in the 21st Century. Dehli, NY: American Lutheran Publicity Bureau, 2005.

The Wit of Martin Luther. Facet Book. Minneapolis: Fortress Press, 2006.

The Boy from the Burgenland. From Hitler Youth to Seminary Professor. I: A Memoir. II: Literary Legacy. West Conshohocken, PA: Infinity Publishing Company, 2006.

'Professor Heussi? I Thought You Were a Book!' A Memoir of Memorable Theological Educators (1950-2010). Eugene, OR: Wipf & Stock, 2009.

Toxic Spirituality: Four Enduring Temptations of Christian Faith. Minneapolis: Fortress Press, 2009.

Martin Luther's Anti-Semitism --- Against His Better Judgment. Grand Rapids, MI. Cambridge, UK: Wm B. Eerdmans Publishing Co., 2012.

Edited

(and translated with Ruth Gritsch). Vol. 41 of *Luther's Works: Church and Ministry III.* American Edition. Philadelphia: Fortress Press, St. Louis: Concordia Publishing House, 1966.

(and translated with Ruth Gritsch). Vol. 39 of *Luther's Works: Church and Ministry I.* American Edition. Philadelphia: Fortress Press, St. Louis: Concordia Publishing House, 1970.

(with Roland H. Bainton). *Bibliography of the Continental Reformation. Materials Available in English.* Hamden, CT: The Shoe String Press, Archon Books, 1972.

Gert Haendler, *Luther on Ministerial Office and Congregational Function.* Translated by Ruth Gritsch. Philadelphia: Fortress Press, 1981.

4 Volumes of *Encounters with Luther.* Lectures, Discussions and Sermons at the "Martin Luther Colloquia" of The Institute for Luther Studies. Gettysburg: Lutheran Theological Seminary. I, 1980. II, 1982. III, 1986. IV, 1990.

Martin Luther---Faith in Christ and the Gospel. Selected Writings. Hyde Park, NY: New City Press, 1996.

Translated

(with Ruth Gritsch). Wilhelm Dantine, *The Justification of the Ungodly*. St. Louis: Concordia Publishing House, 1968.

(with Ruth Gritsch), Heinrich Bornkamm. *Luther and the Old Testament*. Philadelphia: Fortress Press, 1969.

(with Ruth Gritsch). Karl Rahner and Heinrich Fries. *The Unity of the Churches. An Actual Possibility*. Philadelphia: Fortress Press, 1984.

Laszlo G. Terray. *He Could Not Do Otherwise. Lajos Ordass, 1901-1978*. Grand Rapids, MI and Cambridge, UK: Wm. B. Eerdmans Publishing Co., 1997.

The Augsburg Confession (1530). In *The Book of Concord. The Confessions of the Evangelical Lutheran Church*. Edited by Robert Kolb and Timothy J. Wengert. Minneapolis: Fortress Press, 2000.

Thomas Bremer. Cross and Kremlin. A Brief History of the Russian Orthodox Church. Grand Rapids, MI and Cambridge, UK: Wm. B. Eerdmans: Publishing Co., 2012

Chapters and Contributions in Books and Encyclopedias

"The Lordship of Christ in History." In *Christian Hope and the Lordship of Christ,* ed. Martin Heinecken. Minneapolis: Augsburg Publishing House, 1969. Pp. 33-46. Reprinted in Bulletin 49/2, Gettysburg Lutheran Seminary, 1969. Pp. 27-37.

"The Ministry in Luther's Theological Perspective." In *Encounters With Luther* 1. ed. Eric W. Gritsch. Gettysburg: Institute for Luther Studies, Lutheran Theological Seminary,1980. Pp. 180-94.

"Lutheran Teaching Authority: Past and Present." In *Teaching Authority and Infallibility in the Church. Lutherans and Catholics in Dialogue* 6, ed. Paul C. Empie, T. Austin Murphy and Joseph A. Burgess. Minneapolis: Augsburg Publishing House, 1976. Pp. 138-48. Nn 318-23.

"Nine and One Half Theses on Luther's Success and Failure as a Reformer of the Church. A Disputation With Albert Brandenburg at the Fifth International Congress for Luther Research." In *Luther und die Theologie der Gegenwart*. Referate und Berichte des 5. internationalen Kongresses für Lutherforschung, Lund, Sweden, August 14ß20, 1977, ed. Leif Grane and Bernhard Lohse. Göttingen: Vandenhoeck & Ruprecht, 1980. Pp. 97-111.

"Martin Luther and the Revolutionary Tradition of the West." In *Encounters With Luther* 1, ed. Eric W. Gritsch. Gettysburg: Institute for Luther Studies, Lutheran Theological Seminary, 1980. Pp. 7-23.

"Luther's View of Mary: Embodiment of Unmerited Grace." In *Mary's Place in Christian Dialogue*. Occasional Papers of the Ecumenical Society of the Blessed Virgin Mary, ed. Alberic Stackpole. Middle Green Slaugh, UK: Paul Publications, 1982. Pp. 133-41.

"Sharing of Teaching Authority: An Offering of Unity." In Testimonia *Oecumenica. In Honorem Oscar Cullmann Octogenarii Die xx Februarii A.D. MCMLXXXII*, ed. Karlfried Froelich. Tübingen: Hans Vogler, 1982. Pp. 114-15.

"Luther's Catechisms of 1529: Whetstones of the Church." In *Encounters With Luther* 2, ed. Eric W. Gritsch. Gettysburg: Institute for Luther Studies, Lutheran Theological Seminary, 1982. Pp. 198-237.

"Birth of the Baptist Movement: A Historical Introduction." In Will D. Campbell, *Caecilia's Sin. A Novella*. Macon, GA: Mercer University Press, 1983. Pp. 1-14.

"Lutheranism." In *Encyclopedia of the South*, ed. Samuel S. Hill. Macon, GA: Mercer University Press, 1984. Pp. 430-33.

"The Origins of the Lutheran Doctrine on Justification." In *Justification by Faith. Lutherans and Catholics in Dialogue* 7, ed. H. George Anderson, T. Austin Murphy and Joseph A. Burgess. Minneapolis: Augsburg Publishing House, 1985. Pp. 162-71, Nn, 350-53.

"Luther and the State: Post-Reformation Ramifications." In *Luther and the Modern State in Germany*. Sixteenth Century Essays and Studies 7, ed. James D. Tracy. Kirksville, Missouri: Sixteenth Century Journal Publishers, Inc., 1986. Pp. 45-59.

"The Orthodoxy of Conflict: Luther's Ecumenism." In *Encounters With Luther* 3, ed. Eric W. Gritsch. Gettysburg: Institute for Luther Studies, Lutheran Theological Seminary, 1986. Pp. 115-28.

"Luther and Schwenckfeld: Reconciliation by Hindsight." In *Schwenckfeld and Early Schwenckfeldianism*: Papers Presented at the Colloquium on Schwenckfeld and the Schwenckfelders, September 17-24, 1984, ed. Peter C. Erb. Pennsburg, PA: Schweckfelder Library, 1986. Pp. 401-14.

"Lutheranism." In *The Encyclopedia of Religion* 9, ed. Mircea Eliade. New York: Macmillan Publishing Company, 1987. Pp. 61-4.

"Müntzer, Thomas. In *The Encyclopedia of Religion* 10, ed. Mircea Eliade. New York: Macmillan Publishing Company, 1987. Pp. 156-7.

"Thomas Müntzer and Luther: A Tragedy of Errors." In *Radical Tendencies in the Reformation. Divergent Perspectives*. Sixteenth Century Essays and Studies 9, ed. Hans J. Hillerbrand. Kirksville, Missouri: Sixteenth Century Journal Publishers, 1988. Pp. 56-83.

"Thomas Müntzers Glaubensverständnis. In *Der Theologe Thomas Müntzer. Untersuchungen zu seiner Entwicklung und Lehre*, ed. Siegfried Bräuer and Helmar Junghans. Göttingen: Vandenhoeck & Ruprecht, Berlin: Evangelisches Verlagswerk, 1989. Pp. 157-73.

"Luther: From Rejection to Rehabilitation." in *Promoting Unity. Themes in Lutheran-Catholic Dialogue*. In Honor of Johannes Cardinal Willebrands, ed. H. George Anderson and James R. Crumley, Jr. Minneapolis: Augsburg Fortress Publishers, 1989. Pp. 38-45.

"Academia and Forum: Luther's Reformation in Wittenberg." In *Encounters With Martin Luther* 4, ed. Eric W. Gritsch. Gettysburg: Institute for Luther Studies, Lutheran Theological Seminary, 1990. Pp. 214-28.

"The Use and Abuse of Luther's Theological Advice." In *Luthers Theologie als Weltverantwortung: Absichten und Wirkungen*. Referate und Berichte des 7. internationalen Kongresses für

Lutherforschung, Oslo, August 14-20, 1988. In *Lutherjahrbuch* 57 (1990). Pp. 207-19.

"A Lutheran Response to Pierre Dupray's Fundamental Consensus and Church Fellowship: A Roman Catholic Perspective." In *In Search of Christian Unity. Basic Consensus/Basic Differences*, ed. Joseph A. Burgess. Minneapolis: Fortress Press, 1991. Pp. 148-51.

"Luther's Humor as a Tool for Interpreting Scripture." In *Biblical Hermeneutics in Historical Perspectives. Studies in Honor of Karlfried Froehlich on His Sixtieth Birthday*, ed. Mark E. Burrows and Paul Rorem. Grand Rapids, MI and Cambridge, UK: Wm. B. Eerdmans Publishing Company, 1991. Pp. 187-97

"The Views of Luther and Lutheranism on the Veneration of Mary." In *The Mediator, the Saints and Mary. Lutherans and Catholics in Dialogue* 8, ed. H. George Anderson, J. Francis Stafford, Joseph A. Burgess. Minneapolis: Augsburg Publishing House, 1992. Pp. 235-48, nn. 379-84.

"Preface." In *Daily Readings From Luther*, ed. Barbara Owen. Minneapolios: Augsburg Publishing House, 1993.

"Martin Luther's View of Tradition." In *The Quadrilog: Tradition and the Future of Ecumenism. Essays in Honor of George H. Tavard*, ed. Kenneth Hagen. Collegeville, MN: The Liturgical Press, 1994. Pp. 61-75.

"Luther and the Jews: Toward a Judgment of History." In *Stepping-Stones to Further Jewish-Lutheran Relations. Key Lutheran Statements*, ed. Harold H. Ditmanson. Minneapolis, MN: Augsburg Publishing House, 1994. Pp. 104-19.

"The Jews in Reformation Theology." In *Jewish-Christian Encounters Over the Centuries: Symbiosis, Prejudice, Holocaust, Dialogue*. American University Studies, Series 9, Vol. 136, ed. Marvin Perry and Frederick M. Schweitzer. New York, Berlin, Vienna, Paris: Peter Lang, 1994. Pp. 197-213.

"Commentary on Paragraphs 7-9." In *A Commentary on "Concordat of Agreement"* [between the Episcopal Church, USA and the Evangelical Lutheran Church in America], ed. James A Griffis amd Daniel F. Martensen. Minneapolis, MN: Augsburg

Publishing House. Cincinnati: Forward Movement Publications, 1994. Pp. 78-85.

"Luther, Martin." In *Concise Encyclopedia of Preaching*, ed. William H. Willimon and Richard Lischer. Louisville, KY, Westminster: John Knox Press, 1995. Pp. 313-316.

"Justification by Faith and Ecclesial Communion: Pointers From the Lutheran – Catholic Dialogue." In *Church and Theology. Essays in Memory of Carl J. Peter*, ed. Peter C. Phan. Washington, DC: The Catholic University of America Press, 1995. Pp. 161-81.

"Episcopacy: The Legacy of the Lutheran Confessions." In *Concordat of Agreement. Supporting Essays*, ed. Daniel F. Martensen. Minneapolis, MN: Augsburg Publishing House. Cincinnati: Forward Movement Publications, 1995. pp. 101-12.

"Asper, Hans." In *The Oxford Encyclopedia of the Reformation 1*, ed. Hans J. Hillerbrand. Oxford, New York: Oxford University Press, 1996. P. 84 "Vocation." 4. Pp. 245-6.

"Assemblies of the LWF: Minneapolis 1957." "Presidents of the LWF: Fredrick Schotz." "General Secretaries of the LWF: Carl Lund-Quist." In *From Federation to Communion. The History of the Lutheran World Federation*, ed. Jens Holger Schjorring, Norman A. Hjelm, Prasanna Kumari. Minneapolis: Fortress Press, 1997. Pp. 269-74, 445-49, 487-93.

"Christian Unity and Peacemaking: A Lutheran Perspective." In *The Fragmentation of the Church and Its Unity in Peacemaking.*," ed. Jeffry Gros and John D. Rempel. Grand Rapids, MI, Cambridge, UK: Wm. B. Eerdmans Publishing Company, 2001. Pp. 16-32.

"Der Schleier Gottes. Ein theologischer Rückblick auf Lajos Ordas." In *Lutherische Kirche in der Welt*. Jahrbuch des Matin-Luther-Bundes, Folge 49. Erlangen: Martin Luther Verlag, 2002. Pp. 17-27.

"Luther as Bible Translator." In *The Cambridge Companion to Martin Luther*, ed. Donald K. McKim. Cambridge, UK: Cambridge University Press, 2003. Pp. 62-72.

"Lutheran Theology and Everyday Life." In *The Gift of Grace. The Future of Lutheran Theology*, ed. Niels Henrik Gregerson, Bo

Holm, Ted Peters, Peter Widmann. Minneapolis, MN: Fortress Press, 2005. Pp. 264-76.'

"Confessionalization and Morality: Laying the Foundation for an 'Evangelical' Social Ethic." In *"Kein Anlass zur Verwerfung." Studien zur Hermeneutik des ökumenischen Gesprächs*. Festschrift für Otto Hermann Pesch, ed. Johannes Brosseder und Markus Wriedt. Frankfurt am Main: Otto Lembeck, 2007. Pp. 335-48.

"Faith Active in Love. The Development of Modern Lutheran Social Witness." In *Social Ministry in the Lutheran Tradition*, ed. Foster R. McCurley. Minneapolis, MN: Fortress Press, 2008. Pp. 69-83. Nn. 162-3.

"Luther on Humor." In *The Pastoral Luther. Essays on Luther's Practical Theology*, ed. Timothy J. Wengert. Lutheran Quarterly Books. Grand Rapids, MI: Wm B. Eerdmans Publishing Company, 2009. Pp. 85-99.

Essays in Journals

"Historical Reason and Theological Education." *Bulletin* 65/3 (Gettysburg Lutheran Seminary, 1962): 15-22.

"Wilhelm Dilthey and the Interpretation of History." *The Lutheran Quarterly* 15 (1963): 53-69.

"Thomas Müntzer and the Origins of Protestant Spiritualism." *The Mennonite Quarterly Review* 37 (1963):172-94.

"European and American Theological Education: Appraisal and Comparison." *The American Review* 3 (1984 The Johns Hopkins University Bologna Center, Italy): 44-55. Reprint in *Bulletin* 44 (1964 Gettsyburg Lutheran Seminary): 10-20.

"Martin Luther and Violence: A Reappraisal of a Neuralgic Theme." *The Sixteenth Century Journal* 3/1 (1972): 37-55.

"Lutheran Teaching Authority: Historical Dimensions and Ecumenical Implications." *The Lutheran Quarterly* 25/4 (1973): 381-94.

"Bold Sinning: The Lutheran Ethical Option." *Dialog* 14 (Winter 1975): 28-32.

"Concord 1977: Faith Seeking Understanding Through Controversy." *Dialog* 15 (Summer 1975): 170-75.

"Luther und die Schwärmer: Verworfene Anfechtung? Zum 50. Todesjahr

"Karl Holls." *Luther* 1976/3 (Zeitschrift der Luthergesellschaft): 105-21.

"The Glory of the 'Theology of the Cross'. A Review Essay of Walther von Loewenich's *Luther's Theology of the Cross.*" *The Cresset* 40 (February 1977): 16-19.

"An Ethical Critique of the U. S. Arms Policy." *Bulletin* 57, Gettysburg Lutheran Seminary (August 1977): 22-30.

"Infant Communion: What Shape Tradition?" *Academy* 36/3, The Lutheran Academy for Scholarship (October 1979): 85-108.

"The Church as Institution: From Doctrinal Pluriformity to Magisterial Mutuality." *Journal of Ecumenical Studies* 16/3 (1979): 448-56.

"The Function and Structure of Gospelling. An Essay on 'Ministry' According to *The Augsburg Confession,*" *The Sixteenth Century Journal* 11/3 (1980): 37-45.

"The Augsburg Confession: An Anniversary Assessment---1530-1980." *Central Penn Focus* in *The Lutheran.* Five-part series (February 6, April 16, June 3, September 17, November 19, 1980),

"The Cultural Context of Luther's Interpretation of the Bible." *Interpretation* 37/3 (1983): 256-76.

"Luther's Humor: Instrument of Witness." *Dialog* 22 (Summer 1983): 176-81.

"The Worldly Luther: Holistic Living." *Word and World* 3 (1983): 355-63.

"Lutheranism and Born Againism: Born again---Or Again and Again." *Academy* 40/1-2, The Lutheran Academy of Scholarship (1984): 17-37.

"Eucharist and Polity: What Kind of Relationship?" *Bulletin* 64, Gettysburg Lutheran Seminary (Fall 1984): 28-41.

"Life in Two Realms. Reflections of an Immigrant." *Katallegete* 9/1 (1984): 16- 20.

"Convergence and Conflict in Feminist and Lutheran Theologies." *Dialog* 23 (Winter 1995): 11-18.

"Thomas Müntzers Weg in die Apokalyptik." *Luther* 60/2 (1989): 53-65.

"Joseph Lortz's Luther: Appraisal and Critique." *Archiv für Reformationsgeschichte* 81 (1990): 32-49.

"The Wooing, Crucified God: An Exposition of Martin Luther's 'Theology of the Cross'." *The Lutheran*, October 17, November 7, November 28, December 19 (1990).

"Gospel and Stewardship: The Perspective of Martin Luther." *Bulletin* 70/4, Gettysburg Lutheran Seminary (1990): 32-45.

"Back to the Future: Manifest Destiny and Lutheran Identity." *Currents in Theology and Mission* 18/1 (1991): 17-24.

"The Radical Reformation in America: The Migration and Legacy of European Radicals." *Bulletin* 73/2, Gettysburg Lutheran Seminary (1993): 29-46.

"Der Humor bei Luther." *Lutherjahrbuch* 63 (1996): 19-38.

"Lutheran Identity: What is this Augsburg Confession?" *Sewannee Theological Review* 40/2 (1997): 146-57.

"Reflections on Melanchthon as a Theologian of the Augsburg Confession." *Lutheran Quarterly* 12/4 (1998): 445-52.

"From Servanthood to Serpenthood: Decision-Making in the Church." *Dialog* 37 (Summer 1998): 209-16.

"Response to Tuomo Mannermaa 'Faith, Culture and Community'." 9th International Congress for Luther Research, Heidelberg, Germany, August 17-23, 1997. *Lutherjahrbuch* 66, Sonderdruck (1999): 270-71.

"Luther's and Melanchthon's Concept of the Church." Summary of Seminar led at the International Congress for Luther Research, Heidelberg, Germany, August 17-23, 1997. *Lutherjahrbuch* 66, Sonderdruck (1999): 270-71.

"The Third Use [of the Law] for Doves and Serpents." *Lutheran Forum* 43/1 (Spring 2009): 54-6.

"Loving God and Country: Foundational Insights." *Lutheran Partners* 25/3 (May/June 2009): 18-21.

"Martin Luther's Humor." *Word and World* 32/2 (2012):132-140.

Editorials

"Third International Congress for Luther Research: A New Ecumenical Luther Image." *Una Sancta* 33/4 (1966): 85-7.

"Will the Real Müntzer Please Stand Up?" An Exchange With George W. Forell, *Dialog* 8 (Spring 1969): 139-40.

"A Critical Reaction to Bengt R. Hoffman's Installation Lecture." An Exchange on Kantian Intellectualism. *Bulletin* 50/1, Gettysburg Lutheran Seminary (1970): 27-8.

"Reformation Studies: Instrument for Modern Meaning." *Monthly Newsletter*, 37-38, Foundation for Reformation Research (1970).

"Ministry: Normed by Dualism of Word and Sacrament." *Dialog* 14 (Spring 1975): 86-87.

"Nine and One Half Theses on the Power and Efficacy of Lutheran Eucharistic Liturgiology." *Dialog* 16 (Winter 1977): 6-7.

"Defenders of Cruciformity---Detectors of Idolatry: The Case of Sixteenth Century Restitutionists." *Katallegete* 6/3 (1977): 10-14.

"Vatican Smoke Signals: Quo Vadis Papa?" *Dialog* 17 (Autumn 1978): 248-9.

"An Exchange of Letters on Communing Infants" (with Charles Anderson). *Lutheran Forum* 13/2 (1979): 8-10.

"Infant Communion: Old Bone in New Contention." *Lutheran Forum* 13/1 (1979): 6-7.

"First Communion: Birthright of the Baptized." *Lutheran Forum* 14/3 (1980): 25-28.

"Bilateral Dialogues: Discerning the Cruciform Church." *Ecumenical Trends 10/11*, Graymoor Ecumenical Institute (1981): 161-3.

"Whatever Happened to Ordination?" *Dialog* 21 (Spring 1982): 84-5.

"Martin Luther: God's Court Jester." *The Consortium Bulletin* 13/1, Washington Theological Consortium (1983): 10.

"The Power of Vocation." *Circle* 15/2, Campus Ministry Communications, National Lutheran Campus Ministry, Augsburg Publishing House (1983): Issue 2.

"Life in Two Realms: Reflections of an Immigrant." *Katallegete* 19/1 (1984): 16-20.

"An American Dilemma: God and the Constitution." *Report From the Capital* 41/7, Baptist Joint Committee on Public Affairs (1986): 4-5.

"Barth, Barmen and America: Lessons of Hindsight." *Katallegete* 10/1-3 (1987): 40-42.

"Mitres, Crosiers, Brooms? A Caveat on Episcopal Garb." *Dialog* 28 (1989):83-4.

"1517---Luther Posts the 95 Theses." "1521---The Diet of Worms." The Most Important Events in Church History. *Christian History* 9/4, Issue 28 (1990): 35-7.

"The Lutheran Parish: Marks and Mandates." *Challenges* 5/1, The Town and Country Institute, Gettysburg Lutheran Seminary (1992): 1-3.

"Guest Hosting or Guest Boasting? Focusing on Hospitality, Evangelism, and Church Growth." *Taking the Lead* 2, Rocky Mountain Continuing Education Center—ELCA (Fall 1992): Issue 1, 5-6, 14.

"Unstoppable" [Luther]. "The Unrefined Reformer." "Was Luther Anti-Semitic?"*Christian History* 12/3, Issue 39 (1993): 20-21, 35-39.

"The ELCA Dialogue with the Episcopal Church." *Lutheran Forum* 28/4 (1994): 29-31.

"Born Again and Again." *The Living Pulpit* (July to September, 1955): 5.

"Lutherisches Bekenntnis in ökumenischer Verpflichtung." Gesprächsbeitrag für Arbeitsgruppen. Arbeitsbuch mit Texten von der Generalsynode der VELKD in Lüneburg vom 19. bis 23. Oktober, 1996. Pp. 26-9.

"Die missionarische Dimension des Luthertums." *Kirchliches Monatsblatt* 55/1, Medicine Hat, Canada (1998): 9-12.

Sermons / Meditations

"Christ and the Cross-Eyed World." *Frontiers* 13/7, Lutheran Student Association of America (March 1962): 7-10.

"Advent." *Bulletin* 46, Gettysburg Lutheran Seminary (August 1966): 15-7.

"In Memoriam February 18, 1546. A Meditation on the Death of Martin Luther." *Bulletin* 49, Gettysburg Lutheran Seminary (November 1969): 44-5.

"Pentecost 1971." *Bulletin* 50, Gettysburg Lutheran Seminary (August 1970): 36-38.

"Reformation 1971." *Bulletin* 52, Gettysburg Lutheran Seminary (February 1972): 49-52.

"Two Dialogue Sermons" (with Herman G. Stuempfle). *Bulletin* 52, Gettysburg Lutheran Seminary (November 1972): 11-16.

"The Pressure of Grace." *Bulletin* 59, Gettysburg Lutheran Seminary (February 1979): 45-47.

"True Freedom." Luther Colloquy Sermon 2010. Gettysburg Lutheran Seminary (October 27, 2010). Seminary Ridge Review, 13/2, Spring 2011):56-59.

Audio/Visual Aids

"Luther and the Jews." A Video Dialogue with Rabbi Marc H. Tanenbaum, May 19, 1983, New York. Lutheran Council USA. Aired on October 16, 1983, Channel 4 of the National Broadcasting System, New York: "The First Estate---Religion in Review." Produced by Russel S. Barber, Religion Editor.

"The Question of Faith for Lutherans and Catholics." Audio Casset distributed by Augsburg Publishing House, Minneapolis, 1983 through *Resource,* Series 11, No. 2, October 1983. "The Wit and Humor of Martin Luther." Series 14, No. 14, October 1987.

"Luther at Gettysburg----A Birthday Party." Playlet (with Ruth Gritsch). *Bulletin* 64/1, Gettysburg Lutheran Seminary (1984): 46-55.

TV Presentations, Series "Faith Alive," York Council of Churches, Channel 4, York, PA: "Luther---Then and Now," March 16, 1989. "The Born-Again

Movement," September 14, 1989. "Theological Questions and Answers,"

September 14, 1989. "Civil Religion and Christianity in America,"

October 18, 1990. "Evangelism as Serpenthood," "Lent: History and Celebration," January 21, 1993. "The Legacy of Dietrich Bonhoeffer," October 21, 1993.

"Millennial Hope." 5 Video Lectures. *Select,* April 1997. Trinity Lutheran Seminary, Columbus, Ohio.

Book Reviews

102 reviews in various English and German journals (1960-2011).